Spreadsheet Toolbar

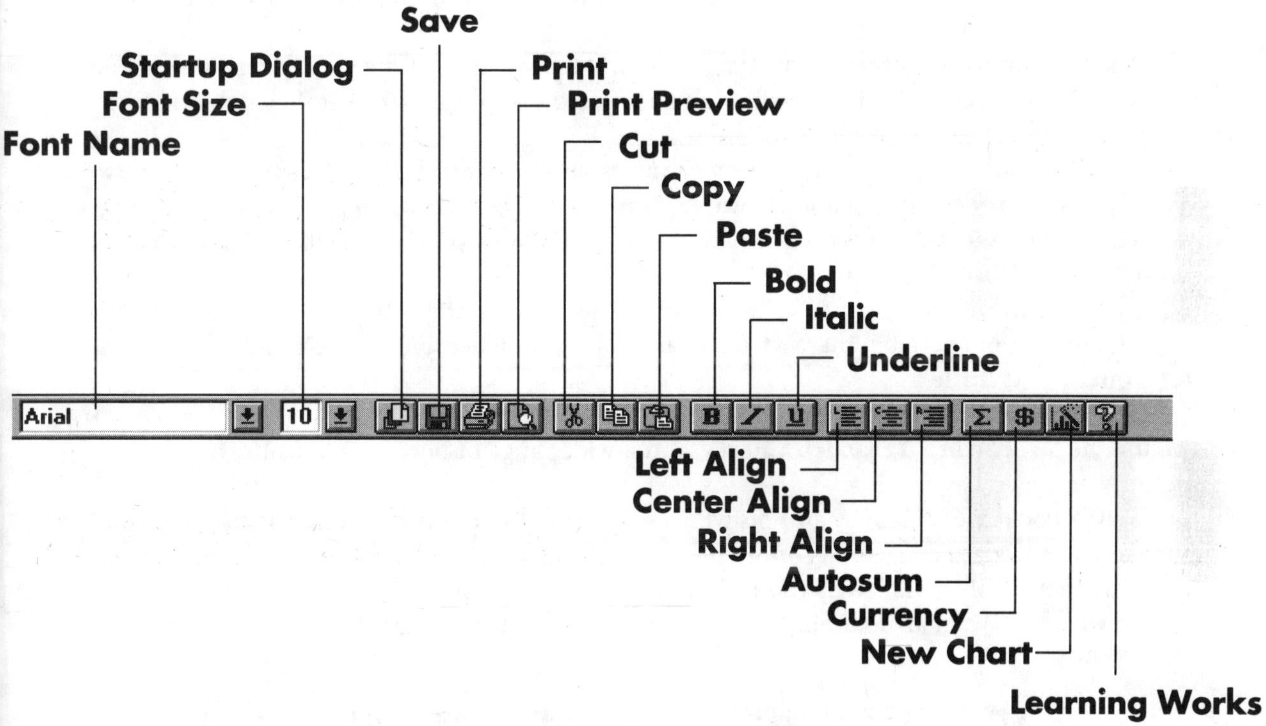

For every kind of computer user, there is a SYBEX book.

All computer users learn in their own way. Some need straightforward and methodical explanations. Others are just too busy for this approach. But no matter what camp you fall into, SYBEX has a book that can help you get the most out of your computer and computer software while learning at your own pace.

Beginners generally want to start at the beginning. The **ABC's** series, with its step-by-step lessons in plain language, helps you build basic skills quickly. Or you might try our **Quick & Easy** series, the friendly, full-color guide.

The **Mastering** and **Understanding** series will tell you everything you need to know about a subject. They're perfect for intermediate and advanced computer users, yet they don't make the mistake of leaving beginners behind.

If you're a busy person and are already comfortable with computers, you can choose from two SYBEX series—**Up & Running** and **Running Start**. The **Up & Running** series gets you started in just 20 lessons. Or you can get two books in one, a step-by-step tutorial and an alphabetical reference, with our **Running Start** series.

Everyone who uses computer software can also use a computer software reference. SYBEX offers the gamut—from portable **Instant References** to comprehensive **Encyclopedias**, **Desktop References**, and **Bibles**.

SYBEX even offers special titles on subjects that don't neatly fit a category—like **Tips & Tricks**, the **Shareware Treasure Chests**, and a wide range of books for Macintosh computers and software.

SYBEX books are written by authors who are expert in their subjects. In fact, many make their living as professionals, consultants or teachers in the field of computer software. And their manuscripts are thoroughly reviewed by our technical and editorial staff for accuracy and ease-of-use.

So when you want answers about computers or any popular software package, just help yourself to SYBEX.

For a complete catalog of our publications, please write:

SYBEX Inc.
2021 Challenger Drive
Alameda, CA 94501
Tel: (510) 523-8233/(800) 227-2346 Telex: 336311
Fax: (510) 523-2373

SYBEX is committed to using natural resources wisely to preserve and improve our environment. As a leader in the computer book publishing industry, we are aware that over 40% of America's solid waste is paper. This is why we have been printing the text of books like this one on recycled paper since 1982.

This year our use of recycled paper will result in the saving of more than 15,300 trees. We will lower air pollution effluents by 54,000 pounds, save 6,300,000 gallons of water, and reduce landfill by 2,700 cubic yards.

In choosing a SYBEX book you are not only making a choice for the best in skills and information, you are also choosing to enhance the quality of life for all of us.

This Book Is Only the Beginning.

Introducing the SYBEX Forum on CompuServe®.

Now, thanks to CompuServe, you can have online access to the authors and editors from SYBEX—publisher of the best computer books money can buy. From the privacy of your own home or office, you'll be able to establish a two-way dialog with SYBEX authors and editors.

Expert Advice at No Extra Charge.

It costs nothing to join the SYBEX Forum. All you have to do is access CompuServe and enter GO SYBEX. As a SYBEX Forum member, you'll have access to expert tips and hints about your computer and the most popular software programs.

What's more, you can download the source code from programs covered in SYBEX books, discover professional-quality shareware, share information with other SYBEX Forum users, and more—for no additional charge. All you pay for is your CompuServe membership and connect time charges.

Get a Free Serving of CompuServe.

If you're not already a CompuServe member, try it for free. Call, toll-free, 800•848•8199 and ask for representative #560. You'll get a personal ID number and password, one **FREE** month of basic service, a **FREE** subscription to *CompuServe Magazine,* and a $15 credit towards your CompuServe connect time charges. Once you're on CompuServe, simply enter GO SYBEX and start to explore the SYBEX Forum.

Tune In Today.

The SYBEX Forum can help make your computer an even more valuable tool. So turn on your computer, dial up CompuServe, and tune in to the SYBEX Forum. You'll be glad you did.

SYBEX. Help Yourself.

SYBEX

Mastering Microsoft® Works 3 for Windows™

Robert Cowart

SYBEX®

San Francisco
Paris
Düsseldorf
Soest

Acquisitions Editor: Dianne King
Developmental Editor: Sarah Wadsworth
Project Editor: Kristen Vanberg-Wolff
Editor: Peter Weverka
Technical Editor: Mac Dunn
Book Designer: Suzanne Albertson
Production Artist: Charlotte Carter
Screen Graphics: Cuong Le
Typesetter: Alissa Feinberg
Proofreader/Production Coordinator: Janet Boone
Indexer: Ted Laux
Cover Designer: DesignSite
Cover Illustrator/Photographer: Mark Johann

SYBEX is a registered trademark of SYBEX Inc.

TRADEMARKS: SYBEX has attempted throughout this book to distinguish proprietary trademarks from descriptive terms by following the capitalization style used by the manufacturer.

SYBEX is not affiliated with any manufacturer.

Every effort has been made to supply complete and accurate information. However, SYBEX assumes no responsibility for its use, nor for any infringement of the intellectual property rights of third parties which would result from such use.

Copyright ©1994 SYBEX Inc., 2021 Challenger Drive, Alameda, CA 94501. World rights reserved. No part of this publication may be stored in a retrieval system, transmitted, or reproduced in any way, including but not limited to photocopy, photograph, magnetic or other record, without the prior agreement and written permission of the publisher.

Library of Congress Card Number: 93-84303

ISBN: 0-7821-1081-9

Manufactured in the United States of America

10 9 8 7 6 5 4 3 2 1

To Geoffrey & Adele

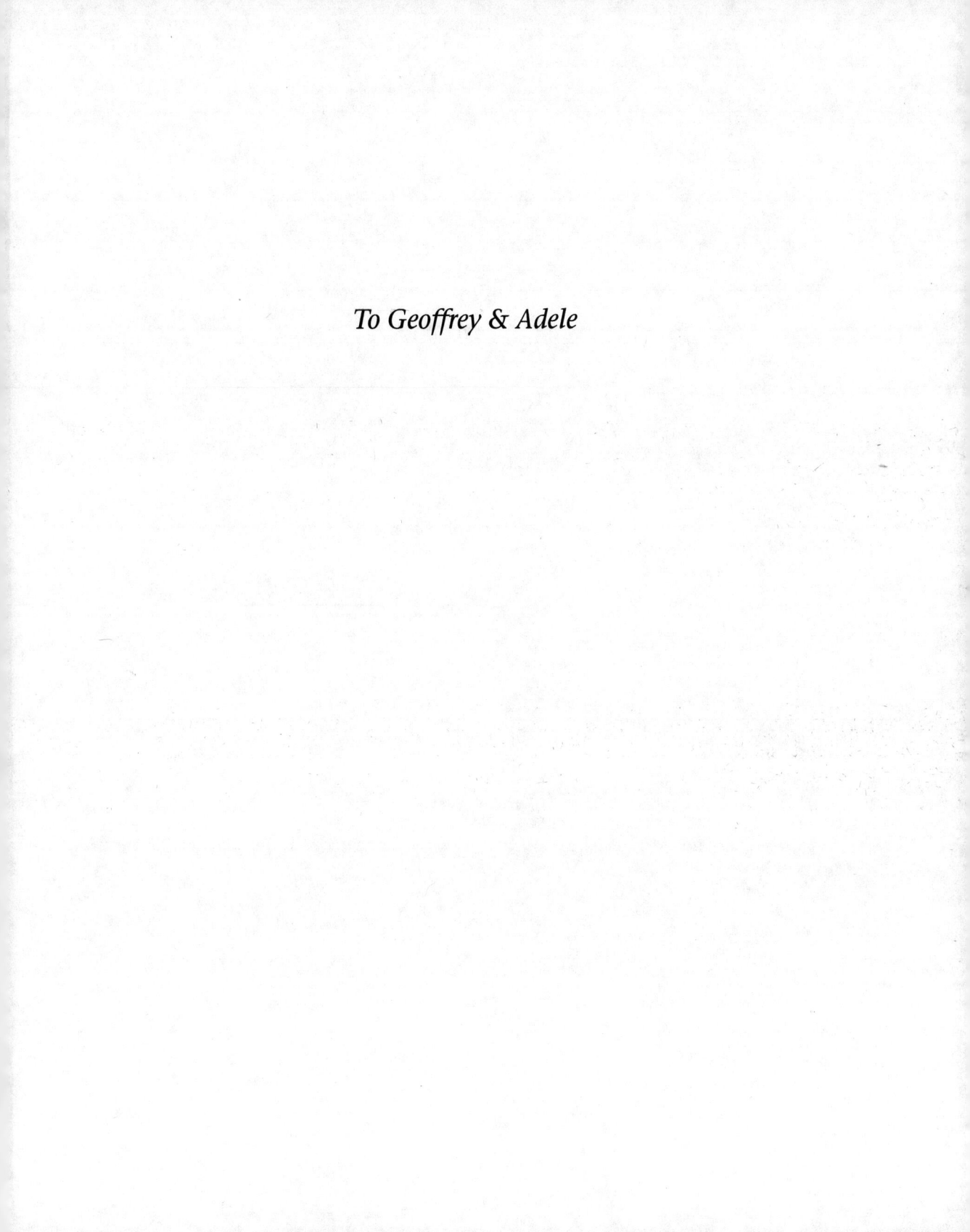

Acknowledgments

I want to extend my thanks to all those who participated in the creation of this book. Aside from the writing, the actual production of this book has been possible due, in large part, to the well-oiled machinery of the SYBEX editorial and production crew.

For this book, I would like to thank Christian Crumlish for revising the manuscript and writing the material having to do with the new release. Thanks as well to developmental editor Sarah Wadsworth, who gave me much needed advice for organizing the book, to Peter Weverka, who edited the manuscript and helped make it an excellent reference as well as a tutorial, and to Mac Dunn, who checked the manuscript for technical accuracy. Thanks as well to project editor Kris Vanberg-Wolff, proofreader Janet Boone, typesetter Alissa Feinberg, artist Charlotte Carter, and indexer Ted Laux.

I would also like to thank the SYBEX editors who worked on a previous version of this book: Kathleen Lattinville and David Peal.

Sincere thanks to my acquisitions editor, Dianne King, and to SYBEX's editor-in-chief, Dr. R.S. Langer, for their continued support over the years; and to my agent Bill Gladstone for his guidance, efficiency, and enthusiasm.

Contents at a Glance

Introduction		xxiii
PART ONE	**Introducing Microsoft Works**	**1**
1	What Is Microsoft Works?	3
2	Works for Windows Fundamentals	23
PART TWO	**Word Processing in Works**	**67**
3	Introducing the Word Processor	69
4	Advanced Word Processing Skills	105
PART THREE	**The Works Spreadsheet Tool**	**165**
5	Using the Spreadsheet	167
6	Advanced Spreadsheet Skills	203
7	Graphing and Charting	251

PART FOUR	**The Works Database Tool**	**301**
8	Using the Database	303
9	Advanced Database Skills	347
PART FIVE	**Harnessing the Power of Works**	**391**
10	Using the Communications Tool	393
11	Creating Documents Automatically	435
12	Putting It All Together	449
APPENDICES		**475**
A	Installing Works on Your Computer	477
B	Using Works with Other Programs	485
C	Quick Reference to Works Tools and Commands	503
	Index	517

Contents

	Introduction	xxiii
PART ONE	**Introducing Microsoft Works**	**1**
1	What Is Microsoft Works?	3
	The Advantages of an Integrated Program	6
	A Consistent User Interface	7
	Moving Data Made Easy	7
	The Four Productivity Tools	8
	Word Processing 101	9
	The Works Word Processor	11
	Spreadsheet Basics	13
	The Works Spreadsheet	16
	Introduction to Databases	18
	The Works Database	20
	What Is a Communications Program?	21
	The Works Communications Module	21
2	Works for Windows Fundamentals	23
	Keyboard Basics	27
	Up and Running with Works for Windows	32
	Opening the Works Program	32
	Opening a Works Tool	36
	A Works for Windows Primer	39
	The Parts of a Works Screen	39
	All about Menus	42

All about Dialog Boxes	45
Dialog Boxes for Working with Files	49
Working on Several Documents at Once	52
Managing Your Files	54
Saving a File for the First Time	55
Making Backup Copies of Files Automatically	56
Saving a File	57
Saving a File under a New Name	57
Opening a File	59
Getting Help When You Need It	59
Help Basics	60
The Help Buttons	62
Keeping Help Information On-Screen while You Work	64
Exiting Works	65

PART TWO Word Processing in Works — 67

3 Introducing the Word Processor — 69

Creating Your First Document	72
Finding Your Way around the Screen	74
Entering Text in a Document	76
Editing a Document	82
Moving around in the Text	82
Selecting Blocks of Text for Moving, Copying, or Deleting	87
Selecting and Replacing Words	91
Inserting Letters and Words in Documents	92
Moving and Copying Text Blocks in a Document	93
Moving Text with the Drag-and-Drop Method	97
Centering Titles and Other Text	97
Saving Your Work	99
Printing a Document	101

4 Advanced Word Processing Skills — 105

- The Importance of Paragraphs to Formatting — 108
- Changing Formats in a Document — 109
  - Finding Out What the Paragraph Format Is — 109
  - Aligning Text on the Margins — 111
  - Indenting Text — 112
  - Controlling the Space between Lines and Paragraphs — 116
  - Controlling How Paragraphs Break across Pages — 119
  - Using Works' Preset "Quick" Formats — 119
  - Invisible Characters for Seeing How a Page Is Formatted — 121
- Placing a Border around Text — 122
- Working with Type Sizes, Type Styles, and Fonts — 124
  - Changing Character Styles — 124
  - Changing Fonts and Type Sizes — 125
  - How You Can Tell What Character Formats You're Using — 128
- Reusing Paragraph and Character Formats in a Document — 130
- Working with Tabs — 132
  - The Different Types of Tabs — 133
  - Creating and Rearranging Tab Stops — 133
- Correcting Mistakes with the Undo Command — 137
- Finding and Replacing Text — 138
  - The Find Command for Locating a Word or Phrase — 139
  - Replacing Text with Find and Replace — 141
- Checking the Spelling in a Document — 142
- The Thesaurus for Improving Your Writing — 145
- Splitting the Window to View Different Parts of a Document — 147
- Creating Headers and Footers — 149
- Adding Illustrations to Documents — 151
  - Inserting Works Clip Art in Documents — 152
  - Making a Drawing of Your Own — 154
  - Placing Your Drawing in the Document — 161
  - Positioning the Picture in a Document — 163

PART THREE The Works Spreadsheet Tool   165

5 Using the Spreadsheet   167

Up and Running with the Spreadsheet Tool   171
- Why Planning the Layout of a Spreadsheet Is Important   172
- Starting a New Spreadsheet   172
- The Basic Elements of a Spreadsheet   174
- Moving around a Spreadsheet   177
- Entering Data in Cells   177

Example Exercise: Building an Invoice Spreadsheet   180
- Cutting and Pasting Spreadsheet Data   181
- Applying Boldface and Other Styles to Data   181
- Widening and Narrowing Spreadsheet Columns   183
- Formatting Cells for Currency   185
- Aligning Spreadsheet Cells in Columns   187
- Entering and Copying Formulas in Cells   189
- Using Cell Ranges in Formulas   194
- How Works Handles Dates in Spreadsheets   195

The F2 Key for Speeding Up Editing   197
Saving Spreadsheets on Disk   199
Creating a "Model" Spreadsheet You Can Use Over and Over   199
Printing a Spreadsheet   200

6 Advanced Spreadsheet Skills   203

Example Exercise: Building a Budget Spreadsheet   206
- Dividing the Spreadsheet into Assumption Data and Projected Data   207
- Formatting Cells before You Enter Data   209
- Entering the Data   211
- Inserting Rows in a Spreadsheet   219
- Splitting the Screen to See More of a Spreadsheet   222
- Absolute vs. Relative and Mixed Cell References   225
- "Freezing" Row and Column Names to Make Data Entry Easier   229
- Copying Several Formulas at Once   234

Tips and Tricks for Using Spreadsheets		236
Protecting Cell Contents from Being Erased		236
Viewing the Formulas in a Spreadsheet		238
Manual Calculation for Faster "What-If" Experiments		240
Inserting Page Breaks in a Spreadsheet		241
Sorting the Data in a Spreadsheet		242
Searching for Data in a Spreadsheet		245
Range Names to Make Entering Formulas Easier		247

7 Graphing and Charting 251

The Twelve Types of Charts You Can Create	255
Designing a Chart	258
Creating a Bar Chart	259
Adding Labels to the Chart	262
Naming and Saving a Chart	265
Deleting an Unwanted Chart	267
Copying Charts for Later Modification	267
Adding a Second Y-Series to a Bar Chart	269
Adding Legends to a Chart	271
Creating a Line Chart	273
Adding More Lines to the Chart	274
Adding Grid Lines to Make the Chart Easier to Read	274
Creating a Pie Chart	275
Adding Labels to a Pie Chart	277
"Exploding" Slices of a Pie Chart	279
Creating Different Chart Types	281
Making a 100% Bar Chart	281
Making a Stacked Bar Chart	283
Making a Stacked Line Chart	284
Making an Area Chart	285
Making a High-Lo-Close Chart	285

Making an X-Y Chart	288
Making a Radar Chart	291
Combining Lines and Bars on a Chart	291
Making a 3-D Chart	293
Fine-Tuning a Chart	294
Changing the Fonts in a Chart	294
Changing the Measurement Scale for Numbers on a Chart	295
Printing Charts	298
Getting Ready to Print	298
Printing the Chart	299
Printing to a Plotter	300

PART FOUR The Works Database Tool — 301

8 Using the Database — 303

Data Basics	307
List View and Form View for Working with Databases	307
Constructing a Database	308
Designing the Database Structure	309
Opening a New Database and Entering Data	310
Rearranging the Fields in a Record	313
Changing the Width of a Field	317
Adding More Records to a Database	319
Saving Your Work	323
Working with a Database in List View	324
Making Fields Wider in List View	325
Moving Around the List View Screen	326
Rearranging Fields in List View	326
Altering the Data in a Database	328
Editing Data in List View	328
Editing Data in Form View	330

Searching for Records and Fields in a Database	331
The Find Command for Locating a Record	332
Displaying All Records that Match the Find Criteria	333
Selecting Part of a Database to Search In	334
Sorting a Database	336
Sorting Terminology	336
Entering the Sort Criteria	337
An Introduction to Queries	339
Queries Involving Text	340
Queries Involving Numbers	342
Printing a Database	342

9   Advanced Database Skills   347

Making Data-Entry Forms Easier to Understand and Use	351
Placing Labels on a Form	352
Including Data-Entry Instructions	355
Inserting and Deleting Fields and Records	356
Inserting and Deleting Fields in Form View	356
Inserting and Deleting Fields in List View	357
Inserting and Deleting Records in Form View	360
Inserting and Deleting Records in List View	361
Hiding Records and Fields	363
Sample Exercise: Creating an Inventory Database	366
Formatting Fields for Alignment and Currency	367
Using Calculated Fields in Databases	368
Protecting Fields from Being Erased or Altered	371
Generating a Database Report	372
Works' Speed Reporting Feature	372
Creating Your Own Report with Statistical Totals	376
Sorting Records in Reports	379
Modifying a Report to Make It Easier to Understand	382
Opening a Report	389
Printing a Report	389

PART FIVE	**Harnessing the Power of Works**	**391**
10	Using the Communications Tool	393
	Setting Up Your Communications System	397
	About Modems	398
	Starting the Communications Program	399
	Setting the Phone Parameters	401
	Setting the Communication Parameters	403
	Setting the Terminal Parameters	407
	Setting the Transfer Parameters	409
	Saving Your Communications Settings	410
	Communicating with Other Computers by Modem	411
	Calling Up Another Computer	411
	Sending and Receiving Data Messages	415
	Sending and Receiving Data Files	418
	Ending a Communications Session	423
	Scripts for Automating Sign-On Procedures	424
	Computer-to-Computer Communications by Wire	426
	Setting Up a Direct Connection	426
	Linking Dissimilar Machines by Modem	428
	Troubleshooting the Communications Program	429
11	Creating Documents Automatically	435
	WorksWizards for Creating Complex Documents	438
	Creating a Form Letter	439
	Printing the Form Letter	443
	Templates for Using Complex Document Formats	443
	Creating a Sales Invoice	445
	Printing the Sales Invoice	447
12	Putting It All Together	449
	Including Material from the Other Tools in Word-Processed Documents	455
	Bringing In Files by Modem	455
	Spreadsheets, Databases, and the Word Processor	459

Inserting Charts in a Word-Processing Document	461
Inserting a Database Report in a Word-Processing Document	464
Creating Forms and Form Letters	464
Printing Mailing Labels	468
Printing Envelopes	471
Copying Data between a Spreadsheet and Database	472

APPENDICES 475

A Installing Works on Your Computer 477

System Requirements for Running Works	478
Running the Setup Program	479
What the Setup Program Does	479
Starting the Setup Program	480

B Using Works with Other Programs 485

Exchanging Word Processing Files	486
Letting Works Make the File Conversions	487
Converting Files to ASCII Text	489
Exchanging Spreadsheet and Database Files	492
Working With Lotus 1-2-3 Files	493
Working with dBASE Files	495
Using Databases and Spreadsheets as Text Files	495
Using the Clipboard to Move Data	499

C Quick Reference to Works Tools and Commands 503

Basic Works and Windows Information	504
Keys Used by All the Tools	505
Options That Affect Your Documents	506
Word Processor Information	508
Special Word Processing Keys	509
Special Find and Replace Characters	510

Spreadsheet Information	511
Special Function Keys	511
Entering Data into Cells	511
Database and Reporting Information	512
List and Screen Function Keys	512
Special Keys	513
Spreadsheet and Database Functions	513
Entering Dates and Times in Documents	515

Index   517

Introduction

Microsoft Works for Windows is a powerful, productive computer program designed for IBM PC and PC-compatible computers. It combines four of the most popular types of PC programs in one package—a word processor, a spreadsheet program, a database-management program, and a communications program. Actually, Works combines six programs if you count the spreadsheet's charting capability and the drawing program linked to the word processor.

With Works, you can quickly get up to speed and begin putting your PC to practical use, even if you are a newcomer to personal computing. You can do everything from writing letters to creating professional-looking business charts.

Who This Book Is For

This book is a direct, plain-English introduction to all the essentials of Microsoft Works for Windows. It was written for everyone who wants to learn Works quickly. The information is organized so you can find the information you need easily.

This book takes the computer novice from the first step of installing Works on a computer through creating and understanding complex word-processing, spreadsheet, and database documents, as well as charts and even drawings. For the experienced user, this book was designed so you could jump in and start working at the appropriate level. You will learn by creating real-world documents such as business letters, name and address lists, retail invoices, and company budgets. Then you will learn how to pull all these together into a single document, and to create form letters, mailing labels, and business charts from your data.

Introduction

Features of This Book

This book serves as both a tutorial and a reference. It is designed so you can find the information you need quickly. To help you learn Works and get the most out of the program, you'll find the following special features in this book.

Hands-on instructions Step-by-step exercises take you through procedures for completing important tasks. By doing the exercises, you'll get the experience you need to gain a solid understanding of how Works operates and the many options available to you.

Notes, Tips, Warnings Where applicable, this book provides special notes, tips, and warnings.

Notes define terminology, refer you to other parts of the book for further information, remind you how to complete an action, or tell you where something is located on the screen. Notes provide all-purpose information to help you become a better Works user.

Tips provide shortcuts or insights for using the program better.

Warnings, for example, let you know when completing an action is essential or when you are in danger of losing data. Pay close attention to warnings.

Features of This Book

Fast tracks At the start of every chapter you will find fast tracks. A *fast track* is a quick, concise explanation of how to do something in Works. Next to each fast track is a page number showing where to go in the chapter to find a complete explanation of the task.

Endpapers Inside the front and back cover of this book are charts showing the toolbars for each module. When this book refers to a tool and you're not sure what it looks like, look in the front and back inside covers of the book.

Pull-down menus Works, like most programs, has a pull-down menu structure. In other words, to complete a task with the menus, you start at the main menu, select an option, and from the next menu that appears you select another option. As a shorthand method of showing you how to use the pull-down menus, this book uses the ➤ symbol to show menu selections. For example, "Choose File ➤ Open" means "From the main menu, choose File, and then choose the Open option." You will find this shorthand method easy to follow.

Numbered lists For your convenience, step-by-step instructions are numbered. Simply follow the numbered steps to learn a new procedure.

Bulleted lists Sometimes, in step-by-step instructions, you will be given options for completing a task. These options are shown in bulleted lists, like so:

1. Choose the kind of chart you want to create:
    - A pie chart
    - A bar chart
    - A line chart

Boldface When you see boldface text in a step-by-step instruction list, it means to enter the text from your keyboard. For example, an instruction that says "Enter the file name **Letter1** in the dialog box" means to enter that very name.

Introduction

How This Book Is Organized

This book is divided into five parts, one for each of the Works modules—the word processor, spreadsheet, database, and communications tool—and one showing how to exchange files between modules and import files from other programs. The chapters are arranged as follows:

In Part One, "Introducing Microsoft Works":

- Chapter 1, "What Is Microsoft Works?," provides a short description of what Works is all about. Word processing, spreadsheets, and databases are explained—both in general terms and as they pertain to Works.

- Chapter 2, "Works for Windows Fundamentals," covers Windows basics—the things you need to know in order to use Works effectively in the Windows environment. You'll learn to use the mouse, make dialog box and menu choices, rearrange and move windows around on your screen, and more.

In Part Two, "Word Processing in Works":

- Chapter 3, "Introducing the Word Processor," shows how to create documents, edit and delete text, and do basic formatting.

- Chapter 4, "Advanced Word Processing Skills," explains how to work with type and type sizes, work with tabs, find and replace text, and use the spell checker and thesaurus.

In Part Three, "The Works Spreadsheet Tool":

- Chapter 5, "Using the Spreadsheet," introduces you to the Works spreadsheet, where you'll design a simple invoice for a retail store, fill it in, and watch as Works automatically performs mathematical calculations on the numbers.

- Chapter 6, "Advanced Spreadsheet Skills," covers all the essentials of spreadsheet design, including building formulas, using absolute and relative references, copying formulas, and data and label formatting.

- Chapter 7, "Graphing and Charting," covers something many people need to produce—charts. This chapter shows how to produce a variety of charts from numbers in a budget spreadsheet.

In Part Four, "The Works Database Tool":

◆ Chapter 8, "Using the Database," shows how to create a simple database—a telephone book/mailing list containing names, addresses, and phone numbers. You'll learn how to add and search for data, and sort and query a database.

◆ Chapter 9, "Advanced Database Skills," covers designing and printing database reports, something every small business needs to do from time to time.

In Part Five, "Harnessing the Power of Works":

◆ Chapter 10, "Using the Communications Tool," demonstrates how to connect to other computers and dial-up online services with Works and a modem.

◆ Chapter 11, "Creating Documents Automatically," looks at two of Works' special features for creating documents automatically: WorksWizards and templates.

◆ Chapter 12, "Putting It All Together," shows how to integrate documents from the four modules into single documents. You'll learn how to insert a chart in a business letter, print mailing labels and form letters, and exchange data with other programs.

The book includes three appendices:

◆ Appendix A, "Installing Works on Your Computer," shows how to install Works on your computer and lists the system requirements for running Works.

◆ Appendix B, "Using Works with Other Programs," explains how to export and import documents to and from other programs, including Lotus 1-2-3, dBASE, WordPerfect, and Microsoft Word.

◆ Appendix C, "Quick Reference to Works Tools and Commands," lists useful menu and keyboard commands pertinent to each of the Works tools.

PART one

Introducing Microsoft Works

1

What Is Microsoft Works?

2

Works for Windows Fundamentals

What Is Microsoft Works?

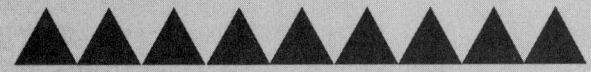

Fast Track

Works has four basic components, or modules.   6
>The four components are a word processor, spreadsheet program, database-management program, and communications program.

Works is an integrated program.   6
>"Integrated" means that the different modules of Works can interact with one another. Moving data between modules is easy, and the common user interface shared by all four modules makes learning Works easy as well.

Works' word processor has many features and capabilities.   11
>Like most word processors, Works' provides word-wrap, a find and replace feature, the ability to move and copy text to other parts of documents, a spell checker and thesaurus, and a host of formatting commands. Works also offers an Undo feature, margin notes, and WYSIWYG capabilities.

Works' spreadsheet is very useful.   16
>Like most spreadsheets on the market, it provides many editing and sorting capabilities. You can also scroll through the spreadsheet, view either numeric values or the formulas that produce them, and split the screen. You can create many kinds of charts with Works as well. By changing numbers on the spreadsheet, you can—for analysis purposes—quickly see the result of budget modifications.

The Works spreadsheet is compatible with Lotus 1-2-3.   17

You can transfer Works spreadsheets to and from Lotus 1-2-3 Versions 1.x or 2.0.

Works' database offers many of the capabilities of the popular database programs.   20

Like a telephone book, a database is a collection of related information. Unlike a spreadsheet, the information is often text-related rather than numerical, although numbers are often a part of a database. Using the information in a Works database, you can print form letters with people's names filled in, print mailing labels, keep track of inventory, and print fancy company reports.

A communications program is a program designed to work with a modem.   21

Works' communications program allows you to use a modem to connect your computer to another computer, bulletin board, communications service, or network so you can send and receive information and mail.

WORKS FOR WINDOWS COMBINES FOUR of the most popular types of PC programs in one package—a word processor, a spreadsheet program, a database-management program, and a communications program. This chapter looks briefly at the four chief components of Works. It explains how the four "programs within a program" work together and sets the stage for Chapter 2, which provides hands-on information about using Works.

If you haven't installed Works yet, see Appendix A for information about how to do so.

To run Works, your computer must have Microsoft Windows. Windows has to be installed and running properly before you can use Works.

The Advantages of an Integrated Program

In many respects, the four programs that make up Works perform as competently and as well as more expensive stand-alone word processors, database-management programs, spreadsheet programs, and communications programs (modems). But the chief advantage of Works is that it is an integrated program. *Integrated* means that the different modules of Works can interact with one another. In other words, you can move data from one component of the program to another quite easily. For example, you can move a copy of a graph, spreadsheet, or database into a word processing document. Or you can take a collection of data from a database table and drop it into a spreadsheet to perform some calculations or plot a chart with the information.

Being able to move data back and forth from spreadsheets to databases to word processors is nothing new. You can pass data back and forth among most Windows programs, including Lotus 1-2-3, Excel, Access, Word, and WordPerfect. But the cost of all those programs is far more than what you pay for Works. And moving data between different document types (say, a 1-2-3 spreadsheet and a Paradox for Windows table) can be tricky and doesn't always work out. Being able to transfer data easily from module to module, which you *can* do in Works, is what integrated software is all about.

Small businesses can use Works to do all their budgeting, calculating, graphing, correspondence, and electronic communication. Works will also take care of printing mailing labels, form letters, and envelopes, all for only a modest cash outlay.

A Consistent User Interface

Using an integrated program like Works has another advantage—the user interface is basically the same from module to module. The *user interface* is the term for the menus, toolbars, key presses, and screens with which you tell the computer program what to do. In Works, the commands, icons, and screen layouts are consistent from program to program. Once you know how to use one program in Works, learning the others is quite easy.

Moving Data Made Easy

In a good integrated program, facilities for "cutting and pasting" information—that is, moving data from one module to another—are usually right at your fingertips. Works, for example, allows you to keep several documents open at once in different windows, switch between them at will, and move information from one document to another quickly. Figure 1.1 shows the screen with several documents open. Moving data between these documents is easy.

CHAPTER 1 What Is Microsoft Works?

FIGURE 1.1
You can open several documents at once with Works and move data between documents.

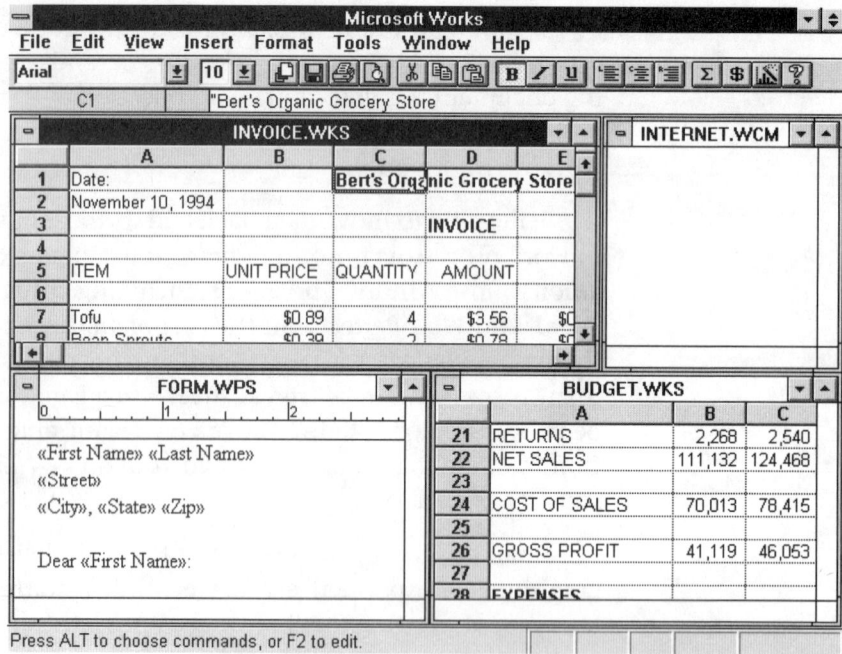

This type of convenience does come at a price. Powerful and comprehensive stand-alone programs such as Microsoft Word, dBASE IV, Crosstalk, and Paradox perform quickly and do the tasks they were designed to do quite well, whereas integrated packages such as Symphony and Jazz all trade some power for the convenience of data compatibility and a common user interface.

However, as computer technology matures, integrated packages are becoming as powerful as their stand-alone counterparts. Thanks to Windows, the modules that make up Microsoft Works are quite powerful in their own right. For many people the convenience of using Works will more than compensate for its shortcomings.

The Four Productivity Tools

Let's look at Works' four productivity tools to see what they are and what they can do for you. The details of how to use each tool will be

The Four Productivity Tools

discussed in upcoming chapters. This section explains the basics of word processing, spreadsheets, databases, and communications programs.

If you are already familiar with the four Works modules and how they work, consider going to the next chapter. The rest of this chapter explains basic computer terminology and describes what you can do with word processors, spreadsheets, databases, and communications programs.

Word Processing 101

A word processor is a clever typewriter that lets you fix mistakes and rearrange text before you print it. If you type a lot, a word processor alone can justify the expense of your entire computer system and software.

With a word processor you can write and edit business letters, form letters, lists, company reports, contracts, invoices, magazine articles, and books. The big advantage of a word processor is that you don't have to worry about making mistakes. You can throw away your eraser and forget about "white-out" forever because if you make a typing error on a word processor, you just back up and fix it.

> **Note** "The Works Word Processor," the next section in this chapter, looks at the specifics of the word processor that comes with Works. Part Two of this book explains in detail how to use the Works word processor.

Word-wrap As you type on the computer keyboard, the letters are displayed on-screen. When you reach the end of a line, the computer goes to the next line automatically and enters the text there for you. Word processors move to the next line automatically—it's called *word-wrap*. With a word processor you do not have to worry about typing too fast, because a computer can keep up with even the fastest typist.

RAM, or random access memory As you type, the letters are stored in the computer's memory. Specifically, the words are stored in the computer's *random access memory,* or RAM. As you move words around on-screen and

9

make revisions, the computer shifts the words around within RAM. When you are happy with the revisions, you can *save* your document, print it, and retrieve it later because it is stored in your computer's RAM.

Working with files Your work is not lost when you turn off the computer. Word processing programs, and other types of programs as well, store your work as *files* on disk. Each file is stored separately and can be reloaded, revised, and printed as many times as you wish. It can even be joined with other files to create new documents. You can cut and paste versions of, say, a contract for different clients without having to retype the contract again and again—you just have the computer change the names where necessary. This increases productivity and decreases typos at the same time.

Find and replace Most word processors have a *find and replace* feature. With find and replace, you can hunt down a particular word or phrase in a document and alter it automatically. For example, if you were writing a novel and you decided to change the heroine's name from Marna to Penelope, you could do it instantly with the find and replace feature. All text surrounding the name Penelope would be re-adjusted automatically to make room for the longer name.

Moving text in a document Using your word processor, you can move or copy blocks of text to other parts of a document. Obviously, this is a real time-saver. Usually, you have to mark the beginning and end of the text block you want to move, after which you simply insert the block where you want it to go with a Move or Copy command.

The spell checker and thesaurus Most word processors feature a built-in *spell checker* and a thesaurus. A spell checker proofreads documents, looking for mistakes in spelling. When it finds one, it gives you a chance to correct the error.

A built-in thesaurus can be very handy when you find yourself stuck for a word. Works for Windows has both a spell checker and a thesaurus. To find a *synonym*—a word with the same or a similar meaning—you simply place the cursor on the word you want a synonym for and click a button. A list of synonyms appears. Click another button and the new word drops into your document without your even having to type it.

Formatting commands Most modern word processors have formatting commands so you can determine exactly how your text will appear on the printed page. You can control how wide margins are, where headers and footers go, page numbering, bold and italic printing, and so forth. Moreover, some word processors show you what the final page will look like on your computer screen. Programs that display formatting effects on-screen are called *WYSIWYG* programs. WYSIWYG stands for "What You See Is What You Get." The document shown on-screen in Figure 1.2 will look exactly the same when it is printed.

FIGURE 1.2
Works has WYSIWYG capabilities. The document shown here will look like this when it is printed out.

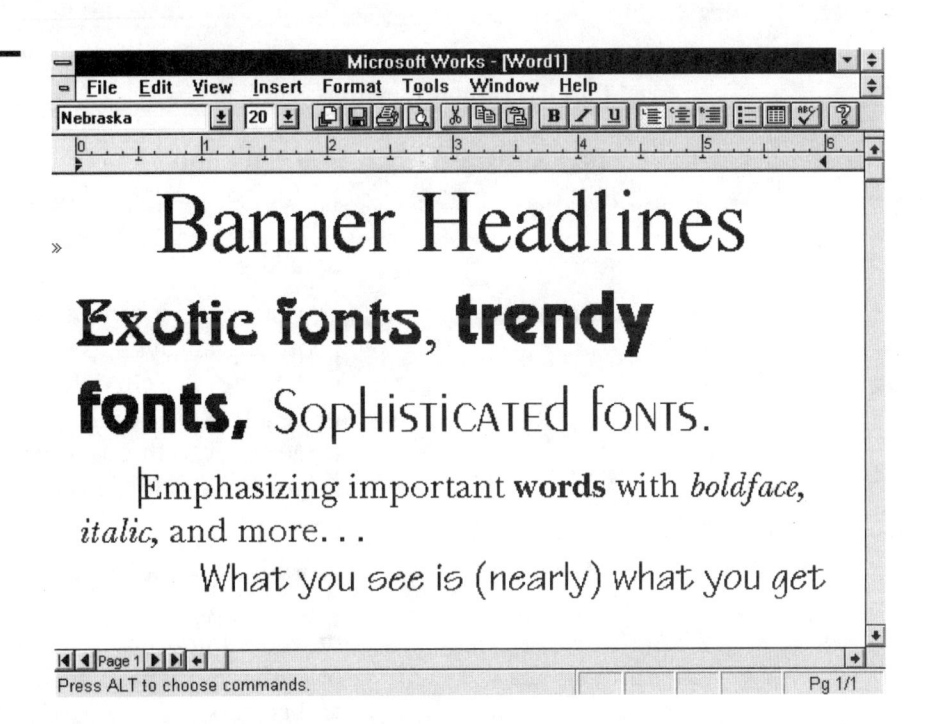

The Works Word Processor

Like all word processors, the Works word processor lets you create, edit, and print documents. Formatting is one of its strongest points. You can give individual characters, words, or paragraphs such attributes as boldface, underlining, and italics. You can establish your own tabs, paragraph indents, outdents, and margins. You can add headers and footers to documents. You can create formats for entire documents or create formats

CHAPTER 1 What Is Microsoft Works?

for individual paragraphs within a document. With Works, even complex documents such as a technical manuals, which usually have columns, indented quotations, and other difficult formats, are easy to create.

> **Note** Part Two of this book explains how to use the word processor.

Following is a description of some of Works' word processing capabilities. This list is by no means complete.

Importing text, data, and graphics
: You can import and print graphics such as line art, maps, and pictures from other programs. You can also import data from a database.

Footnotes
: You can place footnotes in documents. Footnotes always appear on the page on which they are cited. For example, if you place a footnote on page 2 but later add three pages to the start of the document, the footnote will move to page 5 along with its citation.

Margin notes
: Works has a special feature called *Note-It* that lets you enter notes about a document on what amounts to the electronic version of Post-It™ notes—a great feature for writers and editors.

The Four Productivity Tools

Editing multiple documents	You can open and view several documents at once, with each document appearing on-screen in its own window. You can copy, cut, and paste text from one window to another. This feature is particularly useful for piecing together form letters, contracts, press releases, and so forth from different documents. When you move blocks of text, insert text, or delete text, Works will repaginate your document for you.
Form letters and mailing labels	Works can print form letters and mailing labels using information from a Works database. Use this feature to "personalize" form letters by placing the recipients' names and addresses at the top of the letters and their names in the salutations and perhaps elsewhere.
WYSIWYG capabilities	The Works word processor is very WYSIWYG. The screen shows you exactly where each page begins and ends, which letters are bold or underlined, and what the fonts (the different typefaces) will look like in your document when it is printed. (Figure 1.2, shown earlier in the chapter, demonstrates Works' WYSIWYG capabilities.)

Spreadsheet Basics

Here's the scoop on what a spreadsheet is and what it can do for you. A *spreadsheet* is a table for forecasting, analysis, budgeting, planning, record keeping and other tasks related to finances. Spreadsheet tables are divided into columns and rows on which data and the formulas used to calculate the data are entered. Computerized spreadsheets are the electronic version of an accounting ledger. Of course, the computational capabilities of the computer add many powerful capabilities.

CHAPTER 1 — What Is Microsoft Works?

> **Note** If you already have a basic understanding of spreadsheets, skip to "The Works Spreadsheet," the next section in this chapter. Part Three of this book explains the spreadsheet in detail.

Most spreadsheets are used to store numbers, and those numbers are usually part of some overall mathematical formula. In a column of expenses, for example, the numbers are added together and a total appears at the bottom. To arrive at the total, a function is entered at the bottom which adds up all the numbers in the column. In a spreadsheet program, the computer performs all calculations. All you have to do is enter the numbers and formulas in all the right places.

Storing data in cells The place where a column and row intersect on a spreadsheet is called a *cell*. Cells are where you enter data or formulas. Each cell is referenced by its location on a spreadsheet. For example, the cell in the first row, first column is cell A1 (column A, row 1). The cell is the third row, seventh column is G3 (column G, row 3). Each cell can hold text, a number, or a formula.

Formulas in cells When a cell contains a formula, the formula is used to calculate the cell's numerical value. Usually a formula refers to other cells in the spreadsheet. For example, consider the cells in Figure 1.3. By using the formula entered in cell A6, the spreadsheet can easily calculate the total of cells A1 through A5. The result of the formulas is then placed into cell A6.

Formulas always refer to other cells by their location. Spreadsheet programs generally don't display the formula in the cell, but rather the result of the numerical calculation performed by the formula.

Built-in functions Beyond simple mathematical computations, the real power of electronic spreadsheets resides in their advanced built-in functions. *Functions* let you perform analytical, trigonometric, and statistical modeling computations on the numbers in a spreadsheet. Some functions perform date calculations as well.

FIGURE 1.3
Formulas refer to other cells on the spreadsheet and make calculations with those cells.

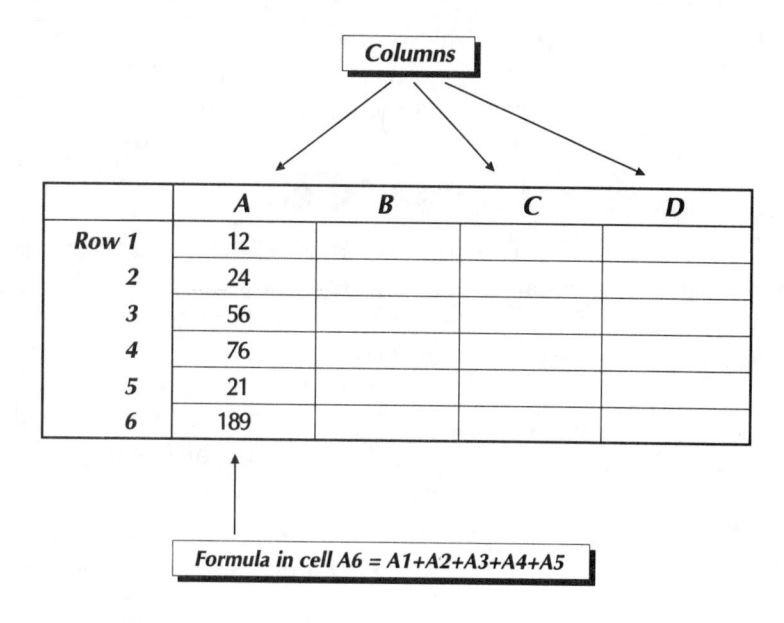

Columns

	A	B	C	D
Row 1	12			
2	24			
3	56			
4	76			
5	21			
6	189			

Formula in cell A6 = A1+A2+A3+A4+A5

By using functions, you can perform sophisticated "what-if" business analyses. As an example, if you changed the data in cell A1, 2, 3, 4, or 5 in Figure 1.3, the total in A6 would automatically change. In complex annual budget projections with many cells and formulas, you could quickly experiment with the bottom-line effect of altering key variables. What-if experiments of this kind are invaluable, whether you were budgeting for a large corporation or a small business. You can establish a bottom-line goal and alter the key variables, such as budget allocations, to see how the goal might be met. Experimenting this way is called *backsolving*.

Spreadsheet programs vary widely in the number and type of functions they offer. Some are designed for business and financial analyses, others for scientific and engineering problem solving. Some really expensive programs (often costing tens of thousands of dollars) let you hook up your PC to a mainframe computer and perform statistical analyses of very large databases.

Displaying the numbers Most spreadsheets will let you decide how you want the numbers in each cell to be displayed. For example, you could place a dollar sign next to dollar amounts or display numbers to a certain number of decimal places.

Labels Besides numbers, cells can also contain *labels,* the text information used to identify rows and columns. Without labels, it is easy to forget what each cell's contents represent.

The Works Spreadsheet

The Works spreadsheet includes a full range of editing commands similar to those in the word processor. It offers most of the basic functions found in all spreadsheets. Following is a look at some of the spreadsheet's most important features:

Editing	You can add or delete columns or rows, or change the size or position of rows inside the spreadsheet.
Size	Works spreadsheets can be quite large. The maximum size is 256 columns by 4096 rows.
Sorting	You can *sort* the data in the spreadsheet. Sorting means to rearrange the data according to a new scheme.
Viewing	You can scroll through large spreadsheets (all the data may not fit on the screen at one time). You can also "freeze" the column and row names so that, wherever you scroll in your spreadsheet, the column and row names will be visible and you will be able to identify the data you are working with. You can also choose between seeing the numeric values of formulas or the formulas themselves. Moreover, you can split the screen to display up to four sections of the same worksheet simultaneously.
Recalculation	You can have the spreadsheet automatically recalculate its formulas every time you alter a new cell value or you can wait until you have made all your changes before recalculating.
Charts	You can create various kinds of charts, including colored bar, line, pie, and scatter charts. You can create borders, legends, and labels for charts.

Printing   Works lets you print a wide variety of reports from your spreadsheets. You can print all or just a portion of the spreadsheet, include titles and descriptive phrases, and use various typefaces, font sizes, and styles. You can also print charts.

Tip Your Works spreadsheet can work with files created by Microsoft Excel.

Note See Part Three of this book for a detailed discussion of the Works spreadsheet.

Works and Lotus 1-2-3

As mentioned earlier, the Works spreadsheet can work with files created by Microsoft Excel. Works is also compatible with spreadsheet files created with or for Lotus 1-2-3 Versions 1.x or 2.0. The converse is also true: Works spreadsheets can be transferred to a 1-2-3-compatible Version 2.x format. However, Works cannot read in a 1-2-3 macro or PIC (graph) file, though Works does have its own internal charting to pick up the slack here.

The Works spreadsheet supports all the functions of 1-2-3 Version 1 and offers a few other functions as well. Other features, such as numeric alignment and the different fonts and styles, are also supported thanks to Windows.

Introduction to Databases

A *database* is really nothing more than a list of items you want to keep track of. In fact, most of us use databases everyday, but we just don't call them by that name. Encyclopedias, telephone books, and shopping lists are examples of databases.

The difference between a computer database and one on paper is just a matter of convenience. Rearranging the items in the database, sorting them, and searching for an item is done quickly and easily with a computer database. The computer is very fast at this kind of searching, even with a big database.

Computer databases are typically used in business to manage customer lists, inventory, transactions, and so forth. But there's no reason not to use a database for household chores such as organizing phone numbers or holiday card mailing lists.

> **Note** Part Four of this book explains the Works database program in detail.

Fields and Records

Information in a database is stored in columns and rows, in a layout similar to that of a spreadsheet. A database is sometimes called a *table*. The main difference between a spreadsheet and database is that, in a database table, the columns are called *fields* and the rows are called *records*.

♦ **Records.** A record comprises all the information pertaining to a single item or person in a database. Each row in a database makes one record. For example, consider the small database in Figure 1.4. This database provides the same information as that found in a telephone book. The second row is a single record. It comprises all information about somebody or other named J.S. Bach:

Bach, J.S.   618 St. Thomas   324-4665

◆ **Fields.** A field is one category of information. Fields are the equivalents of columns in a database. Usually there are several fields in each record. For example, in the database in Figure 1.4, three fields make up each record:

    Name   Address   Phone

Fields in databases are designed so you can find a particular piece of information quickly. If you needed to look up a particular phone number or see a list of everyone who lived in a certain city, a computerized database could quickly provide you with the information you needed. The fields in a database are simply pigeonholes for storing information—they are not used for performing calculations as the cells in a spreadsheet are. A database is similar to a filing cabinet, whereas a spreadsheet is more like a sophisticated calculator.

What Databases Can Do

Some database programs can handle enormous quantities of information; others have strict limitations. Moreover, the maximum size of each record and the size of each field varies from database to database program. Sophisticated database programs let you link or join different databases temporarily or permanently. In this way you can create larger databases or pull out only subsets of data from one database to create an entirely new one.

Any database program worth its salt allows you to print data in a variety of formats. For example, you should be able to print only certain records or fields. Some database programs let you perform calculations on the data as well.

FIGURE 1.4
Fields and records. You might think of each field as a category, and each record as a separate entry in the database list.

	Name	Address	Phone
Record 1	Bach, J. S.	618 St. Thomas	324-4665
Record 2	Beethoven, Ludwig	52 Operstrasse	492-1990
Record 3	Brahms, Johannes	10 Thornton Weg	449-2213

(Fields: Name, Address, Phone)

The Works Database

Following is a look at the most important feature of the Works database:

Records and fields	You can have up to 32,000 records and 256 fields in each document.
Viewing	Works gives you two ways of working with and viewing data in a table. In a *forms view,* you look at one record at a time in a layout of your own design. In *list view,* you see records and fields displayed in columns and rows, much like a spreadsheet. Custom layouts can be up to six screens long (two full printed pages). You can enter, edit, and view records in either view.
Calculations	You can set up some fields as calculated fields (just as you can in a spreadsheet cell). Calculated fields are the result of a mathematical calculation derived from data in other fields of the same record.
Sorting	You can sort data numerically or alphabetically.
Querying	You can search for specific records, which is known as *querying* the database. Querying means asking the database to search for certain records that meet specific criteria. For example, you could list all people in a database whose last names fall between the letters *C* and *M* who live in Sioux City. The records that fit the search criteria would then displayed, while the remainder of the records would be hidden from view. The Works database offers several powerful querying capabilities.

What Is a Communications Program?

A *communications program* is a program designed to work with a modem. With it, you can dial other computers, computer bulletin boards, or networks by modem and send information and mail. You also need a communications program to receive information and mail.

A *modem* (the word means modulator/demodulator) is a machine that converts data into sound pulses so they can be sent over telephone lines. On the other end, a second modem decodes the sound pulses it receives and reconverts them into data. A modem can be a separate box you plug into your computer or a "card" installed *inside* your computer. To send and receive data, the modem is connected to a telephone or jack.

To work properly, a communications program has to be given information about the modem it is working with. For sending data, it has to be given a telephone number to dial. Once you have connected to another computer, bulletin board, network, or communications service, the communications program acts as a window into the computer you are communicating with. Through this window, you communicate with other people and retrieve information.

The Works Communications Module

The communications module that comes with Works is a cut above the Terminal accessory that comes for free with Windows. The Works module takes better advantage of the Windows interface. Moreover, it offers some automated features to get you started. Ultimately, though, a communications program is just a window that lets you look into other computers. Once you're off and running, you won't think too often about the program you're using.

Most of what's really complicated about modems are things you don't actually need to understand. As long as you have the information written down somewhere, you're fine. And once you've got things working correctly, you can save your settings and phone numbers and then reuse them.

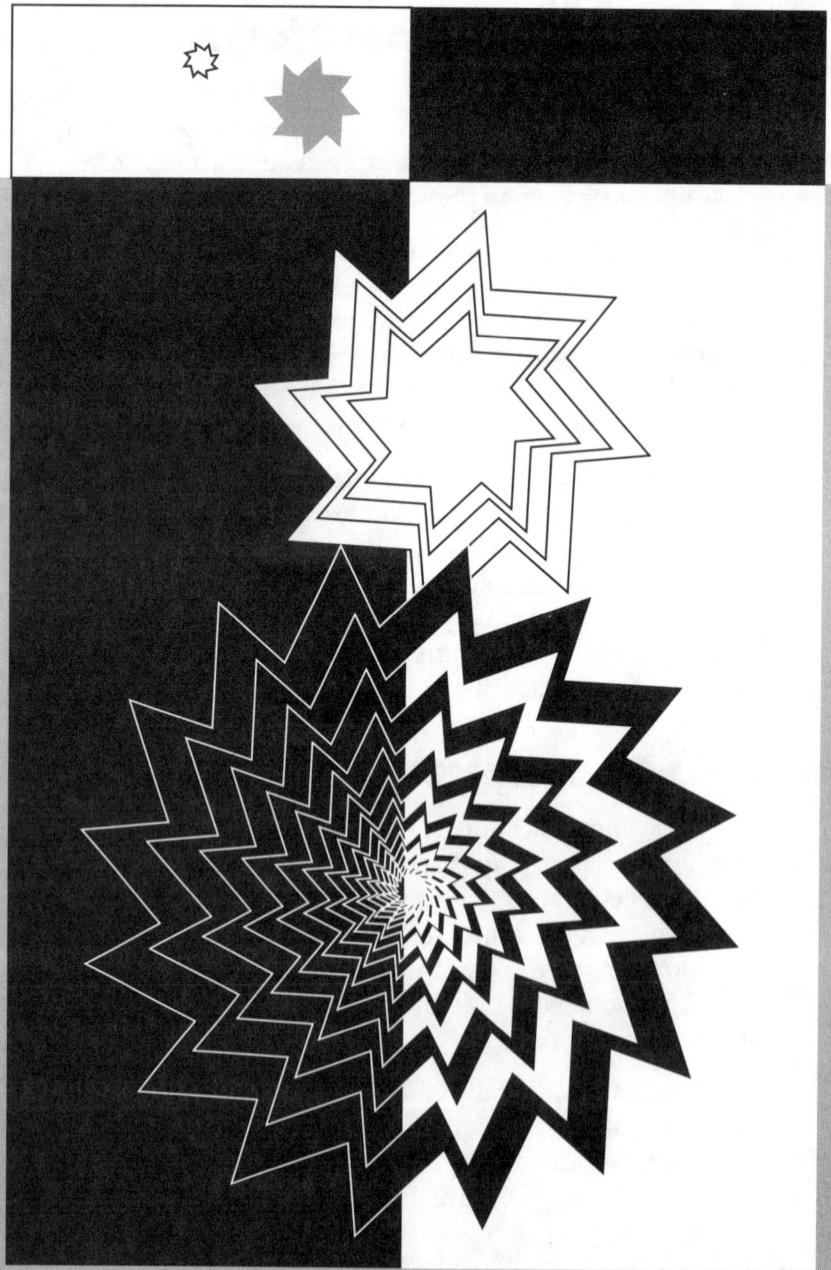

CHAPTER 2

Works for Windows Fundamentals

Fast Track

To bring up MS Works,   32

    turn your computer's power on and make sure Windows is loaded. In the Program Manager, double-click the Microsoft Works for Windows series group to open it, and then double-click the Microsoft Works icon.

To open one of Works' productivity tools,   36

    click on the tool you want if the Startup dialog box is visible, and if it's not visible, choose File ➤ Create New Document. From the dialog box, choose the type of document you want to create.

To change the size of a window,   41

    place the mouse pointer on a border or a corner. After the cursor changes to a two-headed arrow, click the left mouse button and hold it down, drag the window's border to a new position, and release the mouse button.

To open a menu and choose a command,   42

    either click on the menu or press Alt and the underlined letter in the menu. With the menu open, click on the command you want to use.

Works dialog boxes operate like all Windows dialog boxes.   45

Move between sections by pressing Tab or by clicking on the section you want. To activate a check box, click on it—a check mark in the box means the setting is on. To activate an option button, just click on it—the button with the solid center is the activated one. Click on the small ↓ at the right side of a drop-down list to activate it. To scroll through a list of items, click on the scroll bar or type the first letter of the item you want to jump to. You can back out of a box by choosing Cancel.

To switch between open documents,   52

click on the window you want if it's visible. If it isn't visible, open the Window menu and choose the document from the list.

You can make a copy of a file by saving it under a new name.   57

Select File ➤ Save As, enter the file's new name in the File Name text box, choose the file type (if you want to save it in a format usable by other programs), and click on OK.

To open a file,   59

choose File ➤ Open Existing File. In the Open dialog box, tell Works what type of files to list with the List Files of Type drop-down list box at the bottom. Select the file you want to open from the File Name list box and choose OK.

To quit Works,   65

choose File ➤ Exit Works and answer any questions about saving documents.

ALL FOUR OF WORKS' PRODUCTIVITY tools share a common *environment*—that is, the way information is displayed on the screen, and the way you interact with the program, giving it commands and typing in information, is the same from program to program. All four productivity tools make use of the Windows environment. Because Works' four tools have a common environment, you can pull together material that you created with different tools and produce a single finished document.

This chapter introduces Works and the Windows environment. Besides getting a basic feel for how the program works, this chapter explains how to

- ◆ Move from productivity tool to productivity tool
- ◆ Use the computer keyboard
- ◆ Get help when you need it
- ◆ Use menus and dialog boxes
- ◆ Work with and organize files on your floppy or hard disk

Once you have these fundamentals under your belt, you'll be ready to undertake useful projects with Works.

Note If you're already familiar with your PC and with the Windows environment, feel free to skim this chapter—or even skip it. It offers basic information about Windows.

Keyboard Basics

> 💣 **Warning**
>
> If you don't have a mouse, I strongly recommend getting one. Having a mouse makes moving the cursor and choosing menu items a lot easier. No matter if you're selecting and moving text around, editing a spreadsheet, or pasting a chart into a report, these tasks are simpler and quicker with a mouse.

Keyboard Basics

For the most part, Works follows well-established traditions for the PC when it comes to the keys you use to control the program. If you've used a PC at all and know your way around other Windows programs, you'll be able to learn Works quickly, especially if you take advantage of the on-screen help and built-in tutorials.

Figure 2.1 shows a computer keyboard. Yours should look like this, although the *function keys*—the keys labeled F1, F2, and so on—may be on the left instead of on the top row. This section describes the keys that are unique to the computer keyboard—the function and cursor keys, as well as the Control, Alt, Escape, Enter, PgUp, PgDn, Home, End, and Backspace keys.

FIGURE 2.1
A typical keyboard

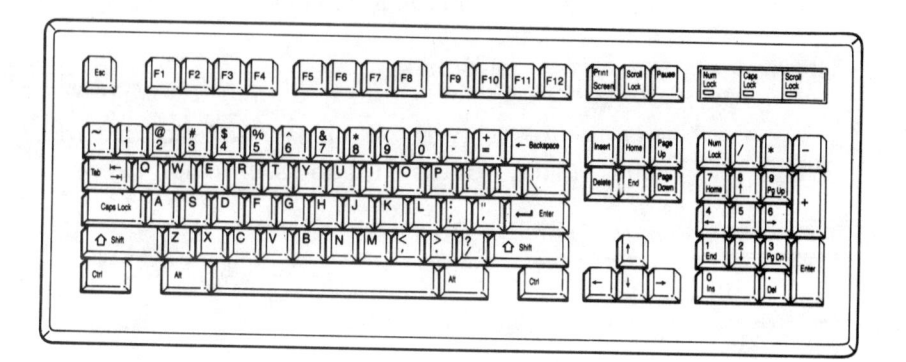

Function Keys

On the top or left side of the keyboard are the function keys labeled F1 to F10 (or F12 if the keys go across the top of your keyboard). The *F* stands for *function*. What happens when you press a function key depends on which tool you are using. However, some function keys work the same way from tool to tool:

KEY	USE
F1	The Help key. Displays the Help index. This index offers useful information about whatever it is you are currently undertaking. For example, if you are working with a particular dialog box, the Help index will provide information about it.
F2	The Edit key. Pressing this key allows you to make changes to database and spreadsheet data (this one doesn't apply to the word processor).

The Control Key

The Control key (labeled *Ctrl* on most keyboards) is located in the lower-left corner (or sometimes just left of the *A* key) of the keyboard. You always press the Control key along with another key, and sometimes with two other keys.

For example, to enter the current time into a cell with the spreadsheet tool you would do the following:

- Press Ctrl+Shift+;

In other words, you would press and hold the Ctrl key down, and meanwhile hold down the Shift and semi-colon keys.

Keyboard Basics

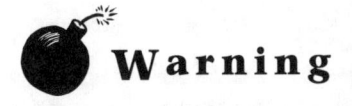

> **Warning** Be careful not to press Ctrl when you mean to press Shift to enter a capital letter. On some keyboards, Ctrl and Shift are close to each other, which makes it easy to press the wrong key accidentally.

The Alt Key

Also in the lower-left corner of the keyboard is the Alt, or "Alternative," key. Alt works just like Ctrl and Shift, in that it is used together with other keys.

The Alt key plays a central role in Windows and in Works—it produces a whole range of effects. If you aren't using a mouse or if you prefer using keyboard shortcuts to mouse actions, you'll press the Alt key often. In Windows, you can press Alt and a letter key to access menus. You can also press Alt and a letter key to make choices in dialog boxes.

> **Note** Menus and dialog boxes are explained later in this chapter.

The Escape Key

In the upper-left corner of the numeric keypad, or sometimes in the upper-left corner of the keyboard, is a key labeled *Esc*. This is the Escape key. In Works, pressing the Esc key lets you back out of—or escape from—a choice you made. When a menu or prompt is displayed, for example, pressing Escape returns you to the previous step. Think of the Escape key as the cancel, or backup, key.

CHAPTER 2 — Works for Windows Fundamentals

> **Tip** Often when running Windows programs, your computer can get "stuck." It's usually because you pressed Alt and accidentally activated the menu bar. Pressing Esc when nothing else seems to work will often bring your computer back to life.

The Enter Key

The Enter key is located three keys to the right of the *L* key. Represented in this book by the symbol ↵, this key has several effects, depending on what you are doing. In general, it tells the computer to accept what you just typed in. Think of it as the go-ahead key. Here are some examples showing how the ↵ key is used:

- When a menu is displayed, pressing ↵ selects the *highlighted* menu option (that is, the option that is chosen and lit up in bright letters).
- When you are done entering data in a spreadsheet cell or database field, press ↵ to finalize the entry.
- With the word processor, pressing ↵ ends a paragraph and moves the cursor down one line.

> **Note** The Enter key on your keyboard might be labeled "Enter," "Return," CR (for "Carriage Return" from the days of the typewriter), or ↵. It's all the same.

The Cursor Keys

To the right side of the keyboard is a block of four keys with arrows on them. These are called *cursor keys*. On some keyboards, these four keys can also be found or are only found on the 8, 6, 4, and 2 keys on the numeric keypad. Cursor keys control the movement of the cursor. You press ↑, ↓, ←, and → to move the cursor around the computer screen in order to highlight menu options, to type in commands, or to enter data. Think of the cursor keys as navigation keys. Often pressing a cursor key along with Shift or Ctrl sends the cursor long distances in one direction. I'll show you cursor-key shortcuts later in this book.

> **Tip** When using the cursor keys on the numeric keypad, make sure the Num Lock setting on your keyboard is turned off. Instead of moving the cursor, pressing a cursor key with Num Lock on enters a number. Most keyboards have a light indicating when Num Lock is on. To turn Num Lock on or off, find and press the Num Lock key.

The Home, End, PgUp, and PgDn Keys

Notice the block of keys labeled Home, End, PgUp (or Page Up), and PgDn (or Page Down). On some keyboards, these four keys can also be found or are only found on the 1, 3, 7, and 9 keys in the numeric keypad. These four keys move the cursor around in a document in larger jumps than the arrow keys do. For example, instead of moving one letter at a time, pressing one of these keys may move the cursor the length of an entire screen or from the beginning to the end of a line of text.

To give you an idea how these keys work, consider the following key presses used in the word processor:

KEY(S)	MOVES THE CURSOR
Home	To the beginning of a line
End	To the end of a line
Ctrl+Home	To the beginning of a document
Ctrl+End	To the end of a document
PgUp	Up the length of one screen
PgDn	Down the length of one screen

The Backspace Key

Not to be confused with the ← key is the Backspace key, which also has a ← arrow on it, but is located above the ↵ key. This key erases the letter to the left of the cursor. Holding the Backspace key down erases several characters. Be careful with the Backspace key. You can erase valuable information in your documents if you use it when you don't intend to.

Up and Running with Works for Windows

This part of the chapter explains how to

- Open Works
- Open one of the four productivity tools

Note Before you open Works, make sure you've loaded Works onto your computer. You should also have run the Setup program. Installing Works and running the Setup program are explained in Appendix A.

Opening the Works Program

To open Works:

1. Turn on your computer if you haven't already done so.
2. If Windows doesn't come up automatically, and you only see the DOS prompt (C:\>), type **win** and press ↵ to load Windows.

The Windows Program Manager appears, The *Program Manager* is for organizing your programs. Your screen should look something like Figure 2.2 (the arrangement of your windows will be different).

Up and Running with Works for Windows

> **Tip** If you don't see the Program Manager, press Ctrl+Esc to bring up Windows' *Task List*, press the arrow keys to highlight Program Manager, and press ↵ to display the Program Manager window.

FIGURE 2.2

The Program Manager with the Microsoft Works for Windows program group on top

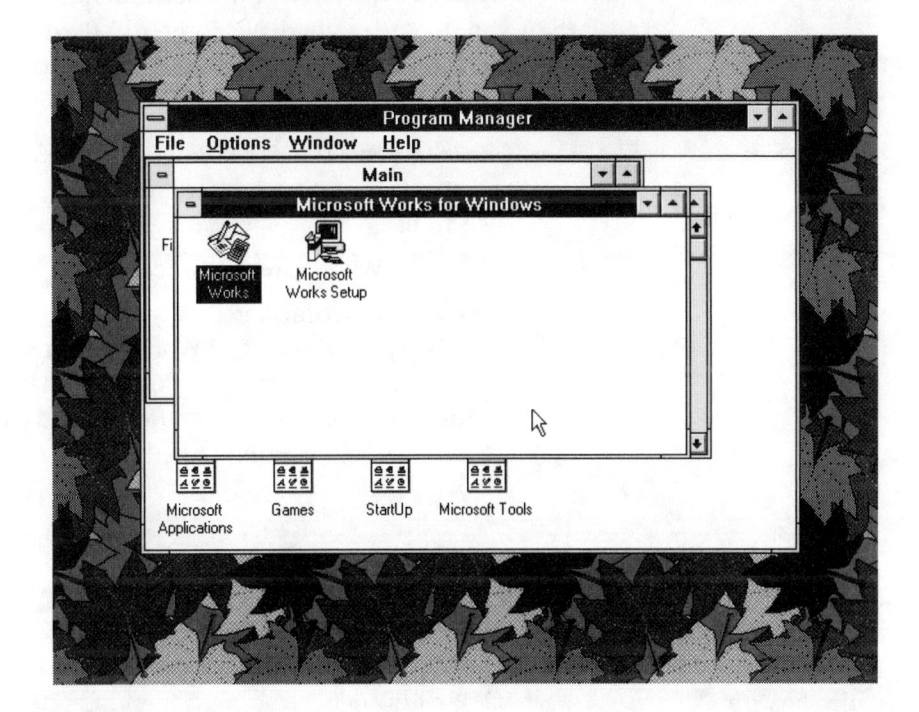

3. With the Program Manager on the screen, find the program group called Microsoft Works for Windows (or Microsoft SolutionSeries or Microsoft Applications). If this program group does not appear on your screen, see "If You Can't Find the MS Works Group..." below.

CHAPTER 2 **Works for Windows Fundamentals**

4. Double-click on the Microsoft Works icon.

The Works copyright information appears and disappears, and then a dialog box called Welcome to Microsoft Works appears, as in Figure 2.3. At the Welcome dialog box you have you have three options:

- Click Start the Tutorial if you want Works to take you through an interactive tutorial describing the basic skills you need for each tool.
- Click Start Works Now to proceed with Works.
- Click Skip Welcome Screen if you don't want to see these options every time you start Works. If you select this option, you'll go directly to the Startup dialog box whenever you double-click on the Microsoft Works icon (as you did in step 4 above). The Startup dialog box is explained shortly.

FIGURE 2.3
The Welcome to Microsoft Works dialog box. This box appears when you first start Works.

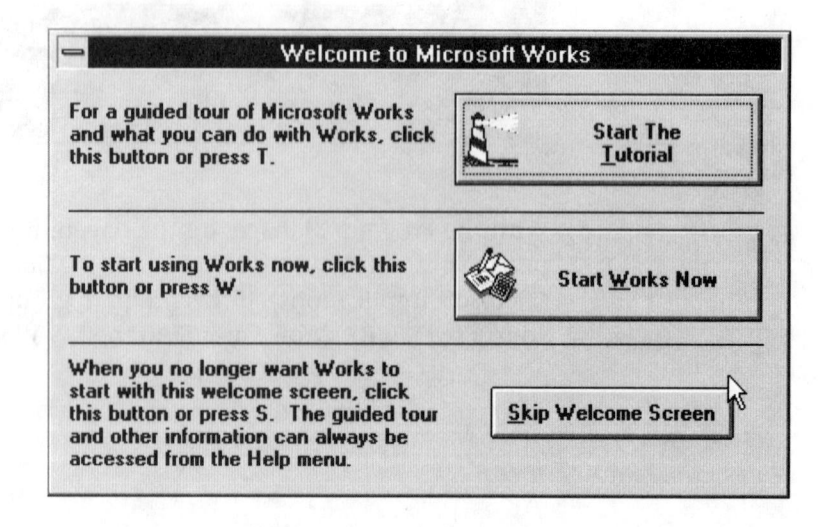

5. Click Start Works Now (or Skip Welcome Screen) to bring up the Startup dialog box.

Following is some advice about what to do if you couldn't find the Microsoft Works group to open the Works program in step 3 above. If you've successfully opened Works, skip ahead to the section following this one, "Opening a Works Tool."

If You Can't Find the MS Works Group...

If you can't find the Microsoft Works for Windows program group:

1. Press Alt+W in the Program Manager (see Figure 2.2) to open the Window menu. You should see the name Microsoft Works for Windows on the list of open windows. It should look something like this:

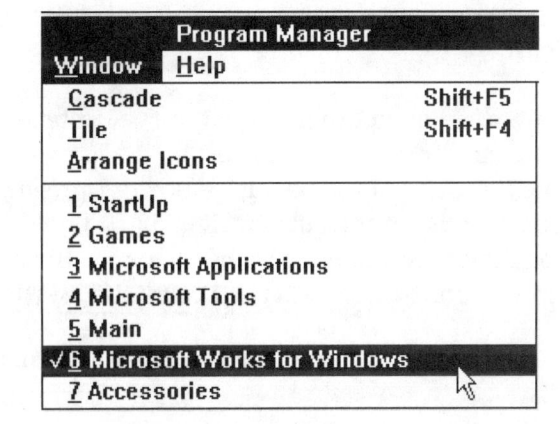

```
        Program Manager
 Window  Help
 Cascade                    Shift+F5
 Tile                       Shift+F4
 Arrange Icons
 
 1 StartUp
 2 Games
 3 Microsoft Applications
 4 Microsoft Tools
 5 Main
 √6 Microsoft Works for Windows
 7 Accessories
```

2. Click on the name Microsoft Works for Windows with the mouse or highlight it by pressing the ↓ key and then press ↵.

If MS Works doesn't appear in the list:

1. Choose More Windows at the bottom of the menu. This will show the complete list of program groups in your system:

   ```
   Select Window
   Microsoft Applications
   Microsoft Tools
   Main
   Microsoft Works for Windows
   Accessories
   Financial
   Paint Programs
   Fractals
   
   [OK]  [Cancel]
   ```

2. Use the mouse or ↓ key to highlight Microsoft Works for Windows on the list.

If there are more names than will fit in the list box, a scroll bar will appear along the right side. Scroll the list by dragging the little elevator button on the right side of the box up or down. *Dragging* means positioning the mouse pointer on the button, clicking and holding down the left mouse button, and then moving the mouse. Move the mouse toward you or away from you on the desk. This will cause the list to scroll up or down.

3. When Microsoft Word for Windows is highlighted, press ↵ or click on OK.

4. Follow steps 4 and 5 above under "Opening Works for Windows."

Opening a Works Tool

After you make a selection from the Welcome screen (see Figure 2.3), the Startup dialog box appears, as in Figure 2.4. This is where you start from each time you bring up the Works program for a session or when you want to open a new document. From this screen, you choose which of the four productivity tools you want to work with:

- Word processor
- Spreadsheet
- Database
- Communications

Notice the other options on the left side of the dialog box. With these options you can open a document you've worked with recently or create a new one, open any existing document, base a new file on a template, use the WorksWizards, or get instructions for using the four buttons.

> **Note** Wizards are covered in Chapter 12.

To choose a Works tool:

- Either click on a button or press Alt and an underlined letter.

FIGURE 2.4
The Startup dialog box. This is the starting point for running Works.

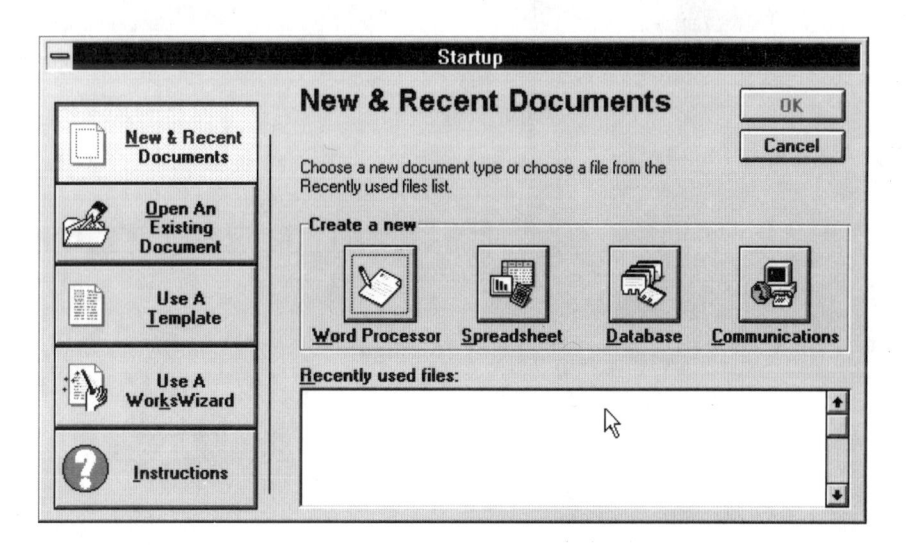

CHAPTER 2 Works for Windows Fundamentals

The Startup window will disappear and the tool you selected will appear on screen.

As an example, try opening the word processor tool:

◆ Click on the Word Processor button or press Alt+W.

A new, empty word processing document opens, as shown in Figure 2.5.

FIGURE 2.5
A blank word processing document showing the parts of a Works screen. You'll find these screen elements on all Works screens no matter which tool you're using.

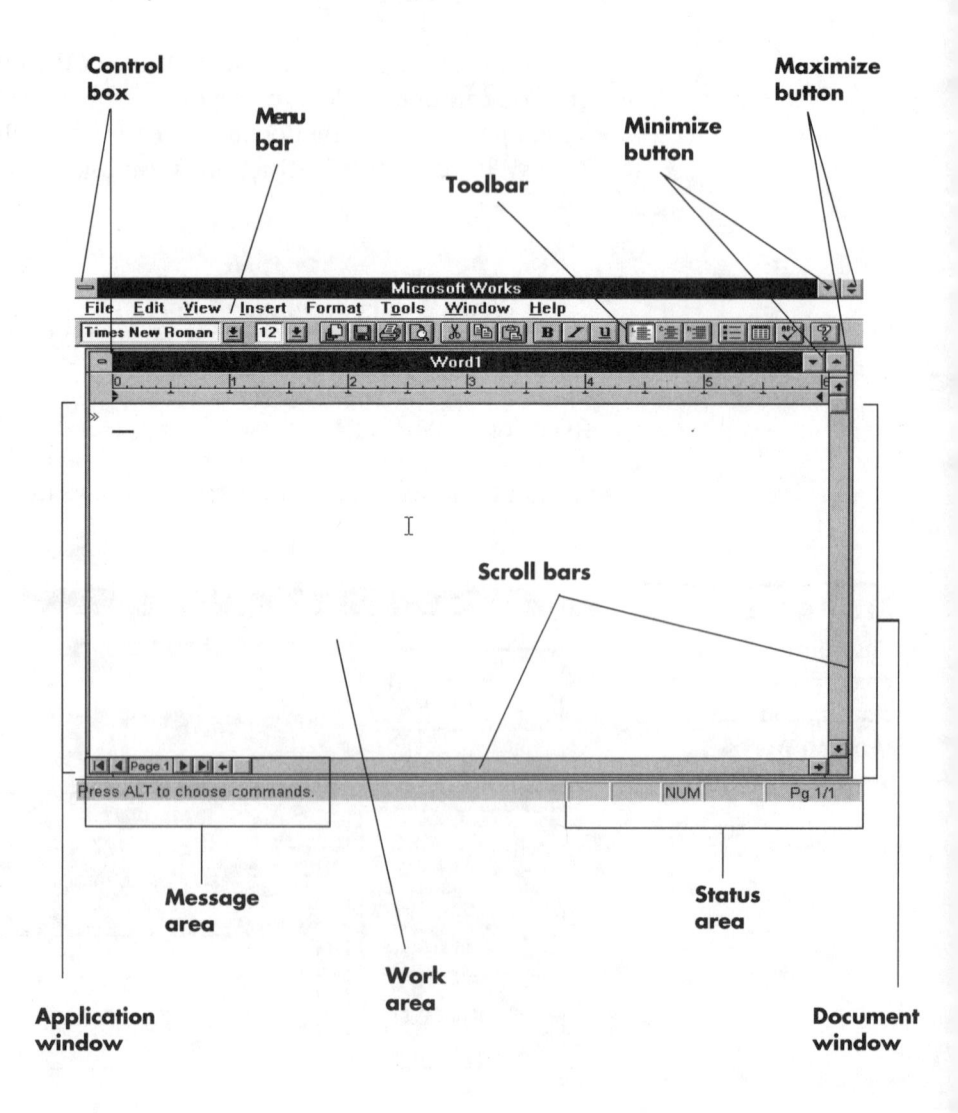

A Works for Windows Primer

No matter which tool you are using, many of the menu commands will be the same. Moreover, techniques for resizing windows, for scrolling through a document, for using dialog boxes, and for making menu selections are the same in all four productivity tools. This part of the chapter looks at the basic information you need for using all four tools.

The Parts of a Works Screen

Regardless of which tool you are using, the basic screen layout is the same. As shown in Figure 2.5, Works screens have the following primary elements:

menu bar — Clicking on or selecting a menu name on the menu bar opens up a *submenu*, a new menu from which you can choose more options.

work area — This is where you do most of your work, such as entering and editing text, creating spreadsheets, and so forth. Everything outside the work area is used for controlling or modifying data in the work area.

status area — The status area displays useful information about the settings of certain keys, such as the Num Lock key, and about which page of a document you're on.

message area — This provides helpful one-line messages about what commands you can use, and what steps to take next. The messages on this line change as you move around the screen.

> **Tip**
> The message area can be very helpful. It explains what the program is doing and what menu commands do.

CHAPTER 2 Works for Windows Fundamentals

Control box Clicking on a Control box opens a menu called a *Control menu* that lets you close the window or resize it. Double-clicking on a Control box closes a window. Double-clicking on a Control box in a document window (see description below) closes the document. Double-clicking on a Control box in an application window (see below) closes the Works application altogether.

scroll bars The scroll bars are located on the right and bottom sides of the work area. You use them to move up and down or side to side in a document.

application/ document windows All Windows programs have two possible types of windows, application and document. The application window is the one that the program, in this case Works, runs in. The document window is the one that contains the document that the application program is working on. Figure 2.5 shows a new word-processing document in the document window and the word processing application in the application window. Several document windows can be open at once in an application window.

Minimize button Clicking the Minimize button turns the Works window (the parent window) into an *icon,* a small representational picture, and places it at the bottom of the Windows Desktop. Clicking on the Minimize button in a document window turns the document into an icon and places it at the bottom of the Works window. Double-clicking an icon restores the window it represents to its previous size.

A Works for Windows Primer

> **Note** You can use the Minimize button to shrink a window just to get it out of the way so you can do other work.

Maximize button Click on a Maximize button to make a window fill the screen. (Maximize buttons are explained in detail below.)

toolbar A toolbar is a row of buttons, each representing a command. Click these buttons to underline words, check the spelling in a document, format spreadsheet cells, and do a host of other things. Toolbar buttons are shortcuts for executing the commands on the menus.

The Maximize Button for Resizing a Window

Unless the Works window is already *maximized* (is as large as possible), you will probably see a bit of the Program Manager or some other window behind the Works window. But you can make any window become as large as possible in order to see more of its contents. To do this, click on the Maximize button (see Figure 2.5).

Restore buttons After a window has been maximized, its Maximize button changes to a *Restore button*. Restore buttons have up/down arrows instead of an up arrow. Clicking on the Restore button returns the window to its previous size.

Manually Resizing a Window

You can also resize a window on your own by dragging one of its borders or corners:

1. Carefully place the cursor on any border or corner of the window that you want to resize. When you are in the right position, the cursor changes to a two-headed arrow.

2. Press and hold down the mouse button as you roll the mouse in the direction you want to move the window border. The window outline will move.

3. When the window border or corner is in the right position, release the mouse button.

All about Menus

Many of the things you do to manipulate a document involve using menus. This section explains

- Opening menus
- Making menu choices
- How to read menus and understand what options you have

Opening a Menu

To open a menu and use its commands, either click on the name of the menu or press Alt and the menu's underlined letter. Try it now with the word processor:

1. Either click on the File menu name or press Alt+F. The File menu opens to show the File commands arranged in a vertical list, as shown in Figure 2.6.

2. Press the → key to open the next menu over, the Edit menu.

3. Press → again to see what's on the next menu, the Insert menu.

4. Press → and view the options on all the menus.

Tip To go immediately to a new menu, you can always press Alt and the menu's underlined letter.

FIGURE 2.6

To open a menu, just click on its name or press Alt and its underlined letter.

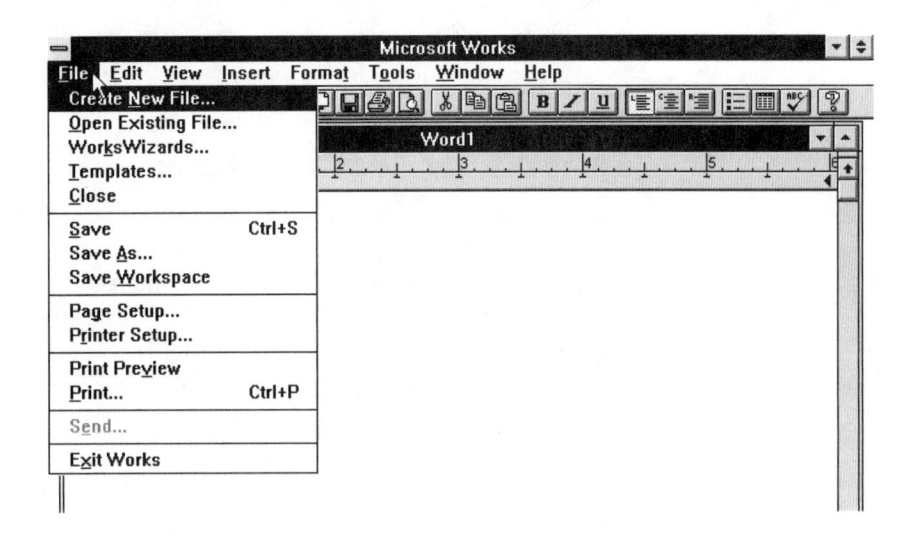

Making Menu Choices

Once you have a menu open, you can tell Works to execute a menu choice in three ways (please don't try them yet):

- ◆ Highlight the menu choice you want by pressing ↓ or ↑ until the choice you want is highlighted, and then press ↵.
- ◆ Click on the command.
- ◆ Press the underlined letter of the choice you want.

Tip Here is a quick way to learn what a menu command does: highlight the menu choice and read the short description in the message area. You can highlight a choice by pressing ↓ or ↑, or by dragging the mouse pointer down the menu.

These menu choices may seem a little confusing right now, but at this point you should only be concerned with learning the steps involved in opening menus and making choices, not with what the choices actually do. Menu names and menu commands are covered in detail in the chapters concerned with each productivity tool.

Symbols for Reading Menus

Some menus have special symbols that tell you more about the menu commands. For example, some commands in the File menu (see Figure 2.6) have ellipsis (three dots) after them, some have key combinations called *hot keys* next to them (Ctrl+S and Ctrl+P), and one is dimmed—that is, it appears in light gray. Other menus—look at the View menu, for example—have commands with check marks next to them. What do these symbols mean?

Dimmed command names When a command is shown as *grayed,* or *dimmed,* it means that this command is not available to you. Commands appear dimmed on the menu when the program doesn't have enough information or is unable to complete the command. For example, a command for changing type styles is dimmed when no text has been selected. If a window is already maximized, the Maximize command on the Control menu will be dimmed because maximizing the window wouldn't make sense.

Ellipses... An ellipsis (...) after a command name means that a dialog box will appear to prompt you for needed information after you after you choose the command. (Dialog boxes are discussed shortly.) Works displays a dialog box because it needs more information to execute the command.

✓Check marks A check mark (✓) before a command means that the command is a *toggle.* In computer lingo, a toggle is a command that is alternately turned on and off each time you select it, like a light switch. The check mark disappears when the command is inactive.

Hot keys Some menu commands show a hot key combination you can press to activate the command instead of clicking the command or pressing its underlined letter. For example, in the File menu you can choose the Save command by pressing Ctrl+S.

All about Dialog Boxes

A *dialog box* appears when you select a command with an ellipsis (...) after it. Dialog boxes pop up on your screen when Works needs more information in order to complete a command. Some dialog boxes ask you to type in information, others require you to check off options or make choices from a list, and some dialog boxes are quite complicated and do both. After you enter the information, you click OK or press ↵ so Works can execute the command.

This section of the chapter deals with dialog boxes. It explains how to

- Move the cursor to different parts of a dialog box.
- Enter information in a dialog box—that is, enter information using text boxes, check boxes, option buttons, command buttons, and list boxes.

Note Dialog boxes that pertain to saving, finding, and opening files can be tricky. See the next section of this chapter, "Dialog Boxes for Working with Files," if you're having trouble with file dialog boxes.

Tip There is another type of dialog box, an *alert* dialog box that alerts you to a problem with your system or an error you've made, or asks you to confirm a decision. Alert boxes often have a large letter *I* (for information) in them or an exclamation mark (!). With these boxes, you usually just read the message in the box and click OK (or click Cancel if you decide not to proceed). Some boxes only have an OK button.

CHAPTER 2 Works for Windows Fundamentals

Moving around in a Dialog Box

As you can see in Figure 2.7, dialog boxes often have several sections. You can move between the sections in three ways:

◆ Click on the section you want to go to.

◆ Press the Tab key until you arrive at the section you want to be in.

◆ Press Alt and an underlined letter in the section you want to go to or activate.

FIGURE 2.7

A typical dialog box

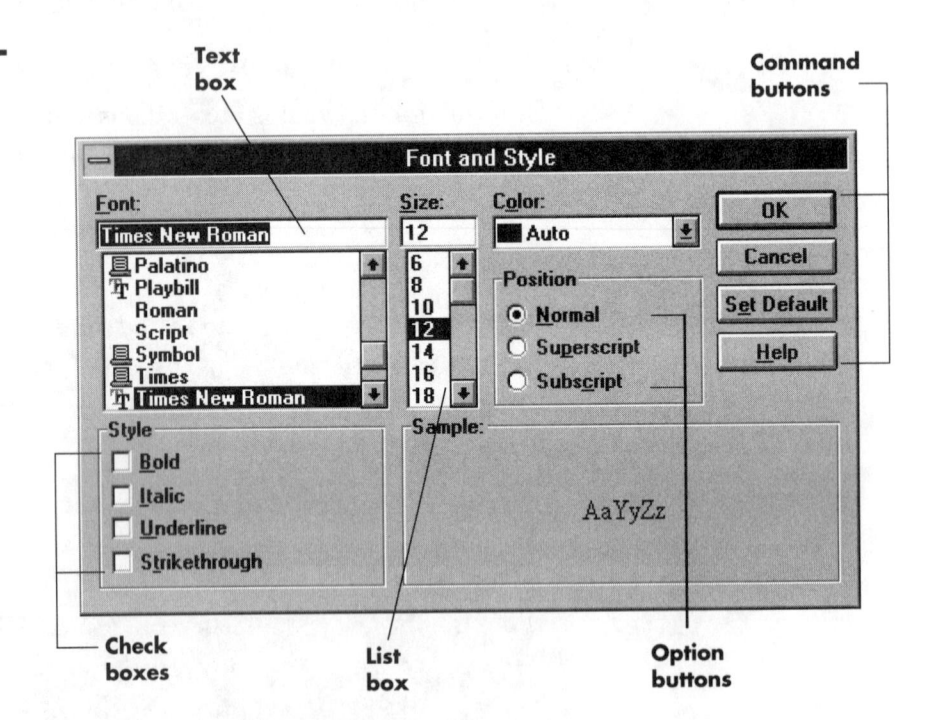

[Dialog box illustration labeled: Text box, Command buttons, Check boxes, List box, Option buttons. Dialog shows "Font and Style" with Font: Times New Roman (Palatino, Playbill, Roman, Script, Symbol, Times, Times New Roman), Size: 12 (6, 8, 10, 12, 14, 16, 18), Color: Auto, Position: Normal/Superscript/Subscript, Style: Bold/Italic/Underline/Strikethrough, Sample: AaYyZz, buttons OK/Cancel/Set Default/Help]

Filling In a Dialog Box

Now let's consider how to enter information in a dialog boxes. For entering information, there are six basic elements in dialog boxes: text boxes, check boxes, option buttons, list boxes, drop-down list boxes, and command buttons. Figure 2.7 above shows some of them. The rest are shown in Figure 2.8. Once you're in the correct section of the box, you enter the information. Following is a discussion of how to do this.

FIGURE 2.8

A dialog box. This one, which is used for opening or saving a file, includes a drop-down list box.

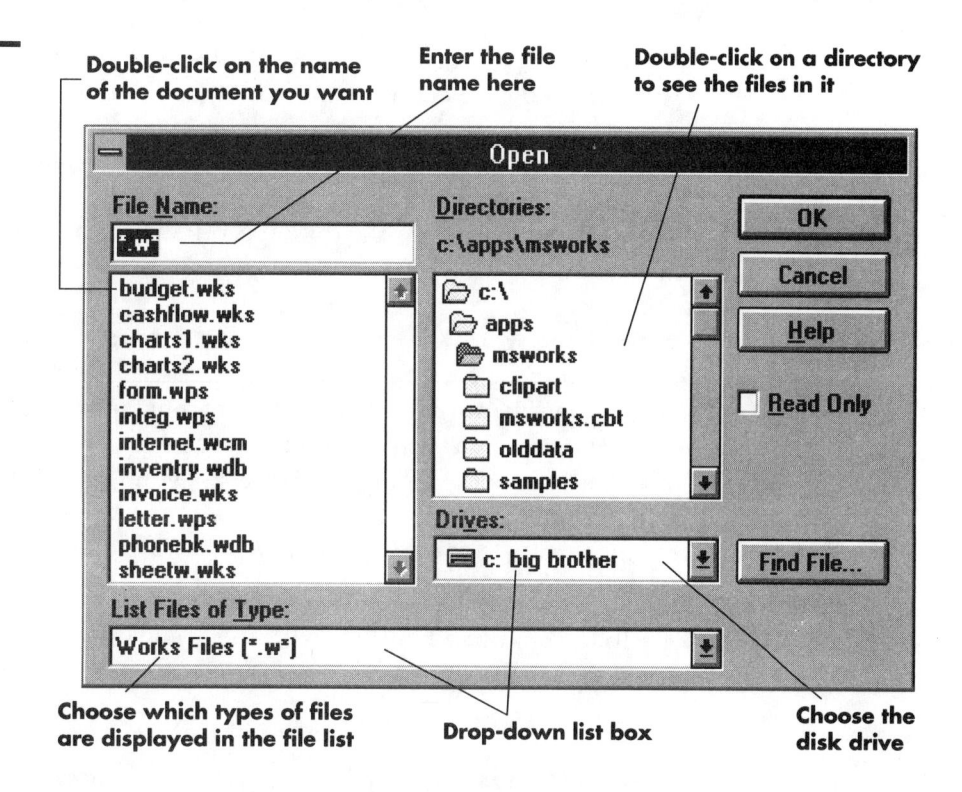

[Dialog box illustration with the following labels:]

- Double-click on the name of the document you want
- Enter the file name here
- Double-click on a directory to see the files in it

Open

File Name: *.w*

- budget.wks
- cashflow.wks
- charts1.wks
- charts2.wks
- form.wps
- integ.wps
- internet.wcm
- inventry.wdb
- invoice.wks
- letter.wps
- phonebk.wdb
- sheetw.wks

Directories:
c:\apps\msworks

- c:\
- apps
- msworks
- clipart
- msworks.cbt
- olddata
- samples

Drives:
c: big brother

OK
Cancel
Help
☐ Read Only
Find File...

List Files of Type:
Works Files (*.w*)

- Choose which types of files are displayed in the file list
- Drop-down list box
- Choose the disk drive

Text boxes *Text boxes* ask you to type in text with the keyboard. They are most often used for specifying file names when you are saving or loading documents and applications, and for specifying text to search for in a word processing document.

Sometimes text will be entered already. If you want to keep the text as-is, you can do so. To alter the text, simply type in new letters:

◆ If the text is already highlighted, just start typing. Works will erase the text immediately and replace it with what you type. You can also edit highlighted text. Click once on highlighted text to deselect it. The cursor (a vertical blinking bar) will appear where you put it in the text box.

◆ If the text is not highlighted, you can backspace over it to erase it, or edit it in any way you wish. Move the cursor by using the mouse or arrow keys. Press Del to delete text.

Check boxes *Check boxes* are the small square boxes (see Figure 2.7). They are used to select more than one option at once. For example, if you wanted a word to appear bold *and* underlined, you would select the Bold and Underline check boxes in the Font and Style dialog box. The boxes are toggle settings that you activate or deactivate by clicking on the box. When the box is empty, the option is off; when you see an *X* in the box, the option is on.

Option buttons Unlike check boxes, *option buttons* are exclusive settings—you can only select one at a time. (Option buttons are sometimes called *radio buttons* because they look like the buttons on an old-fashioned car radio.) Option buttons are round, not square, and you can choose only one at a time. For example, in Figure 2.7, you have to choose Normal *or* Superscript *or* Subscript, not a combination of two or three. Clicking on the button turns it on (the circle will be filled) and turns the previous selection off.

To use command buttons with the keyboard, move to the section by pressing Tab, use the arrow keys to select the button you want, and then press ↵.

Command buttons *Command buttons* are like option buttons except that they are used to execute a command immediately. They are shaped like rectangles, not boxes or circles. OK and Cancel are the most common command buttons and are found in almost every dialog box:

OK	Once you've filled in a dialog box to your liking, you click on the OK command button so Works knows to execute the settings you selected.
Cancel	If you change your mind and don't want the new choices on the dialog box executed, then click the Cancel command button. This closes the dialog box and cancels all settings you just entered.

The button that will be executed if you press ↵ always has a thicker border. Pressing the Esc key always has the same effect as clicking on the Cancel button—it closes the dialog box.

List boxes *List boxes* are like menus in that they show you a list of options or items you can choose from. You can see a list box for choosing type sizes in the Font and Style dialog box in Figure 2.7. To make a selection from a list box like this one, simply find the setting you want and click on it. With the keyboard, go to the list box by typing the first letter of its name, press the ↓ key until you've highlighted your choice, and press ↵.

When all the selections in a list box cannot be shown at once, a scroll bar appears on the right side of the box. Drag the scroll box up or down, or click on the small ↑ or ↓ and the bottom or top of the scroll bar to move the list up and down. The list will now scroll. When you've found the option you want, click on it.

Drop-down list boxes *Drop-down list boxes* have small underlined arrows on their right sides (see Figure 2.8). The current setting is displayed in the list box to the left of the small arrow. If this isn't the setting you want, click on the arrow to open the list and see more choices. Now you can treat the list like a normal list box. Find the choice you want and select it.

Dialog Boxes for Working with Files

The Open dialog box like the one in Figure 2.8 is an example of a *file dialog box.* This type of dialog box pops up whenever you open a document, save a document, or name a document. File dialog boxes are a little tricky to use at first, and saving, naming, and calling up files is probably the most confusing thing you'll have to do in Works. But once you get the hang of it, it's a cinch.

File dialog boxes are divided into two sections, one on the left for listing files and one on the right for listing directories. A *directory* is a place where groups of files are stored on disk. Directories are represented by folders, as you can see in the Directories section in Figure 2.8.

Finding a Directory and Opening a File

To move through the directories and find a file to open:

1. Make sure the correct disk drive is chosen in the lower-right side of the box. Open the Drives drop-down list box and select another drive if necessary.

2. Select a directory on the right side by double-clicking on its folder or name. All files in the directory you chose will appear in the list on the left side of the box.

Once you've found the directory you want, you can open a file or save a file—depending on what you want to do next. To open a file:

◆ Highlight the file you want in the File Name list box and click OK.

To save a new file, see "Giving a New File a Name" later in this section of the chapter.

Following is some advice for what to do if you can't find a directory, and how you can find files quickly with file dialog boxes.

If you can't find the right directory... If you don't see the directory you're aiming for, you need to "move down" or "go back up" the directory tree a level or two:

◆ To move up the directory tree and see what's in the directories there, double-click on a folder that has one less indent (such as C:\ in the graphic below).

◆ To move down the directory tree, double-click on a folder that has one more indent (such as clipart or msworks.cbt in the graphic below).

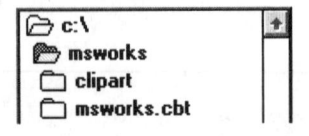

```
c:\
  msworks
    clipart
    msworks.cbt
```

To see certain types of files only You can limit the directory search to certain types of files only. This saves time and makes the search for a file go more quickly. Normally the List Files of Type box at the bottom-left of the dialog box shows

`Works Files (*.w*)`

This means that the file dialog box shows all files made in Works—that is, files with a *w* as the first letter in the file name extension. An *extension* is a three-letter name following the document name that identifies the application that made the document.

> **Note** See "Saving a File the First Time" later in this chapter for information about extensions and how they work.

To limit the search to certain types of files only:

1. Open the List Files of Type box, located at the bottom of the dialog box.
2. Highlight the type of files you want to see (such as word processor, spreadsheet, or database). The file types are, by extension:

EXTENSION	TYPE
.WPS	Word processor
.WDB	Database
.WKS	Spreadsheet
.WCM	Communications

3. Click OK.

Giving a New File a Name

When you save a file for the first time, the file won't exist on the drive yet, so it won't show up in a directory. You have to give a file a name before you can save or retrieve it.

To give a file a name:

1. Select the drive and directory where you want to save the file, as outlined above.
2. Move the cursor to the File Name area and type in the file name and extension. Make sure to delete any existing letters in the text area before you enter the name.

Working on Several Documents at Once

Notice the menu name Window on the right side of the menu bar. The Window menu offers an easy way to switch between open documents or view up to eight documents at once. For instance, you can jump from a letter to the database, then into a spreadsheet, create a drawing or a chart, then jump back to the word processor right where you left off writing your letter.

Try these steps to see how easy it is to jump back and forth between windows:

1. Open the Window menu. Notice the following line at the bottom of the menu:

    ```
    1 WORD1.WPS
    ```

    The bottom part of the Window menu always lists the names of open documents you can jump to.

Only one choice appears because you only have one document (WORD1) open.

2. Back out of the menu by pressing Esc twice or by clicking somewhere inside the workspace (but not on the menu).
3. Open a new file to jump to. Select File ➤ Create New File.
4. Choose Word Processor from the dialog box. The new document window opens up, covering the old one.

Notice that the title bar at the top of the window reads "Word2." It says that because this document is the second word processing file you've opened during this session. The old one is still available to you, as you'll soon see.

Working on Several Documents at Once

> **Note** "Select File ➤ Create New File" in step 3 above means to open the File menu and select the Create New File option. See the Introduction if you need to know about the ➤ and other conventions used in this book.

5. Open the Window menu again. It should now say you have two windows to choose from:

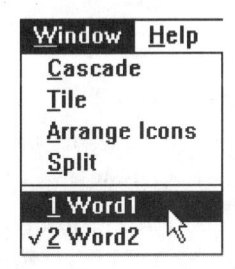

```
Window   Help
 Cascade
 Tile
 Arrange Icons
 Split
 1 Word1
√2 Word2
```

6. To go back to the first document:

- ◆ Type **1**,
- ◆ Click on Word1, or
- ◆ Highlight Word1 and press ↵.

You have just jumped from one window into a second window, then back again.

CHAPTER 2 Works for Windows Fundamentals

Tip

A quick way to jump through all the documents you have open is to press Ctrl+F6. Each press will move you in a round-robin fashion through the open documents. You have to keep your eye on the title bar, though, to see which document you've jumped to. The active window will become a brighter color (or dark gray on a monochrome screen) and will have Windows elements such as scroll bars, a Control menu, and a Minimize button.

Warning

You can have up to eight documents open at a time, but due to RAM and hard-disk-space limitations, the actual number and size of files you can open simultaneously depends on the size of the files. Works will warn you if one of your files is too large or you are running out of memory.

Managing Your Files

You need to save your work if you want to be able to use it in the future. When you store a document, it is placed on a floppy or hard disk drive. The important thing to know is that neither Works nor your computer saves files for you automatically. You must remember to save your files before leaving Windows or turning off your computer.

This part of the chapter explains how to

- Save a file for the first time
- Save a file on disk
- Open a file you worked with earlier
- Change the file extension of a file

Saving a File for the First Time

File names in the file dialog boxes have endings tacked to the end of them called extensions. In order for a file to be stored on your disk, it needs a name and extension. Without a file name, neither Works nor DOS would be able to find the file again on your disk. It would be like looking in a filing cabinet and finding no names on the folders.

File names have two parts, the name and the extension. You choose the name when you create a new file. Works adds the part after the period, the extension, for its own reference. Works adds the extension so that it can tell which tool a file belongs to.

Works file extensions You can tell which tool was used to make a file you see listed in the file boxes and on the Window menu because Works assigns the following extensions:

EXTENSION	TYPE
.WPS	Word processor
.WDB	Database
.WKS	Spreadsheet
.WCM	Communications

To save a document file for the first time:

1. Choose File ➤ Save. The Save As dialog box appears, as in Figure 2.9, with the current name of the file (such as word1) in the File Name box.

Obviously, a name like WORD1.WPS doesn't tell you anything about the file. It's better to use a descriptive name such as LETTER or INVOICE. Unfortunately, with only eight letters in a name, there isn't much room for description, but you have to do your best.

2. Enter a file name up to eight letters long in the File Name text box.

3. Click OK.

The Save As dialog box offers options for saving a file under a new directory and making backup copies of files. These options are explained below.

CHAPTER 2 — Works for Windows Fundamentals

FIGURE 2.9

The Save As dialog box. Use this dialog box to save a file for the first time or to rename a file.

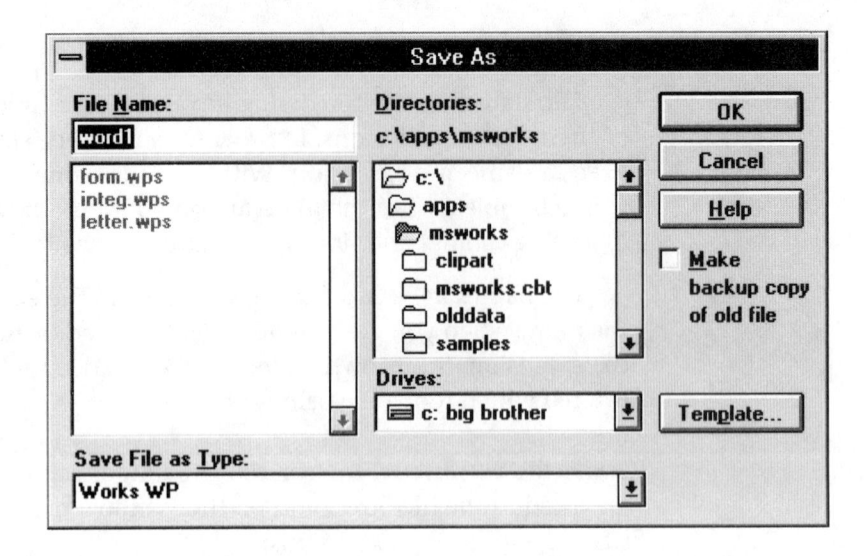

Saving to Other Drives and Directories

Save As and the other file dialog boxes let you choose other disk drives and directories to save your file on. To save a file to another directory:

1. Choose File ➤ Save to save the file.
2. Click on a new directory in the Directories box.
3. Click OK.

Making Backup Copies of Files Automatically

When the Make backup copy check box located below the Help button (see Figure 2.9) is checked, Works creates a subdirectory for storing backup copies of your documents. The backup file will have the same name and be in the same directory as the edited file, but its name will have a *B* as the first letter in the extension, like so:

FILE NAME	BACKUP FILE NAME
LETTER.WPS	LETTER.BPS

If you have the extra disk space, go ahead and use this feature. Then, if something catastrophic happens to a document, you can at least go back to the last edited version of it, the backup copy.

To open a backup copy of a file:

1. Select File ➤ Open Existing File.
2. Change the List Files of Type setting to All Files.
3. Set the drive and directory as necessary.
4. Choose the file from the list.

Saving a File

Saving a file you've saved already is quite easy. To do so:

◆ Choose File ➤ Save.

After you save a file, Works assumes that you want to use the name you saved it under for each subsequent save. Once a file is named the first time, Works won't bother asking you about the name (or present a dialog box) when you save it again.

Tip As you're working on a document, save it from time to time even if you're not finished working on it. That way, if the power is interrupted or the computer malfunctions, you'll lose only the work you've done since the last save.

Saving a File under a New Name

At times you'll want to save a document under a new name. For instance, if you wanted to make a copy of text you use often in your documents (sometimes called *boilerplate text*), or if you wanted to make a copy

CHAPTER 2 **Works for Windows Fundamentals**

of a document to experiment with, you could copy the existing document under a new name. To do so:

1. Open the document you want to make a copy of.
2. Choose File ➤ Save As. The Save As dialog box appears (see Figure 2.9).
3. Enter the new name of the file in the File Name text box.

Works will make a copy the file under the name you just gave and keep a copy of the old file under its old name. Moreover, it will automatically open the new file and put it on the screen. You can switch back to the original file via the Window menu.

> **Note** See "Working on Several Documents at Once" earlier in this chapter to see how the Window menu works.

Changing file formats You can save Works files in a variety of formats so that other programs can use them. Depending on the tool you're using, the Save File as Type list box at the bottom of the Save As dialog box will change. For example, you can save a Works spreadsheet in Lotus 1-2-3 format, or save a Works word-processing file as a "text only" file so that other programs such as Ventura Publisher can work with it. You can also save a text file in Word for Windows or WordPerfect format and work with the file from those programs.

> **Warning** Unless you are experienced with DOS, don't alter file extension when copying or renaming files. If you change file extensions, Works may not recognize them as Works files until you rename them properly. All Works documents should at least have a *w* as the first letter in the extension.

Opening a File

Opening files is very similar to closing them. To open a file:

1. Choose File ➤ Open Existing File. The Open dialog box appears (see Figure 2.8)
2. If necessary, tell Works what type of files to list with the List Files of Type drop-down list box at the bottom.
3. Select the file you want to open from the File Name list box.
4. Choose OK.

Alternatively, in the Open dialog box you can just type in the name of the file you want to open and press ↵.

> **Note** See "Dialog Boxes for Working with Files" earlier in this chapter if you need to know how the List Files of Type and Directories list boxes work.

Getting Help When You Need It

Notice the Help command on the right side of the menu bar. The Help command does just what its name implies—it helps you. If you get stuck in the middle of something and don't understand how it works, just open the Help menu and choose one of the commands. Or, from the keyboard, press F1.

For the most part, the help facility in all Windows programs works the same. Works' Help is *context-sensitive*, which means the program provides help for what you're doing at present. For example, if you didn't remember what the Save Workspace command on the File menu does, you could find out:

1. Open the File menu.
2. Press the ↓ key to highlight Save Workspace.
3. Press F1. Up comes an information screen about the Save Workspace command.
4. When you're done reading a help screen, press Alt+F4.

Many help screens and modules are built right into Works (and many other Windows programs for that matter). If you're not well-versed in the use of Help, this part of the chapter explains how it works.

Help Basics

To get help with what you're doing, open the Help menu and choose the kind of help you need:

- *How to Use Help* explains the basics of the help feature.
- *Contents* brings up a list of topics about the tool you're using.
- *Basic Skills* gives you a list of the elementary stuff covered here already.
- *Keyboard Shortcuts* lists hot key shortcuts for commands.
- *Tutorial* runs an interactive tutorial to teach basic skills for each tool (the same tutorial offered when you started Works).

Before moving ahead and really getting going with Works, you should play with the Help system. What you learn will come in handy later.

1. Switch to the Works window one way or another. (I use the Ctrl+Esc method to bring up the Task List, and then choose Works.)
2. Press F1 to start help. Initially, the overview for the tool you're using will come up. The Word Processor overview is shown in Figure 2.10.
3. To experiment, position the pointer on an underlined word, such as *tool*. Notice that the cursor changes to the shape of a hand pointing a finger, as shown in the figure.

Getting Help When You Need It

FIGURE 2.10

Pressing F1 while using the Works word processor brings up this screen if no dialog boxes or menus are open. (If a dialog box or menu is open, a help screen relating to the command or dialog box appears.)

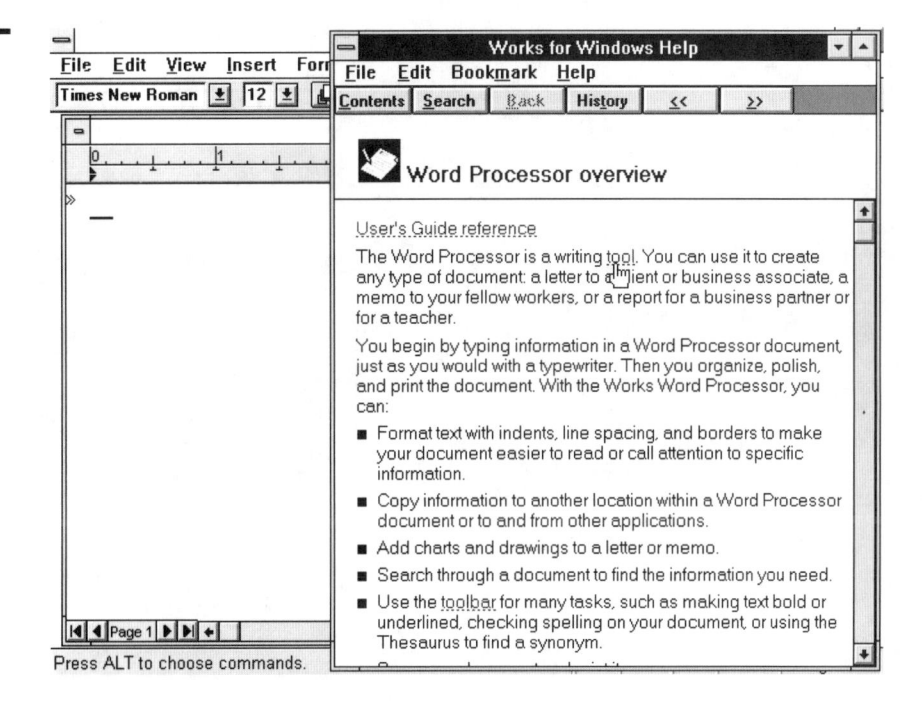

Reading a Help Screen

Here are some tips for reading and getting around in a Help screen:

- **Underlined words.** Any word or phrase in a list that appears lighter (or green, if you have a color monitor) and is underlined with a solid line is a *topic*. Click on a topic if you want information from the online manual (the documentation on your hard disk) pertaining to the underlined word. You will see a new Help window with information about the topic.

- **Light, or green, words with a dotted underline.** Some words in Help windows appear lighter (or green, on color monitors) and are underlined with a dotted line. These are called *hotspots*. You can read definitions of hotspot words. To see a definition, position the pointer on the term and click. The definition appears in a window like the one shown in Figure 2.11. To close the box, just click again, or press any key on the keyboard.

CHAPTER 2 Works for Windows Fundamentals

FIGURE 2.11
Words with a dotted underline are called hotspots. Click on a hotspot word to see its definition.

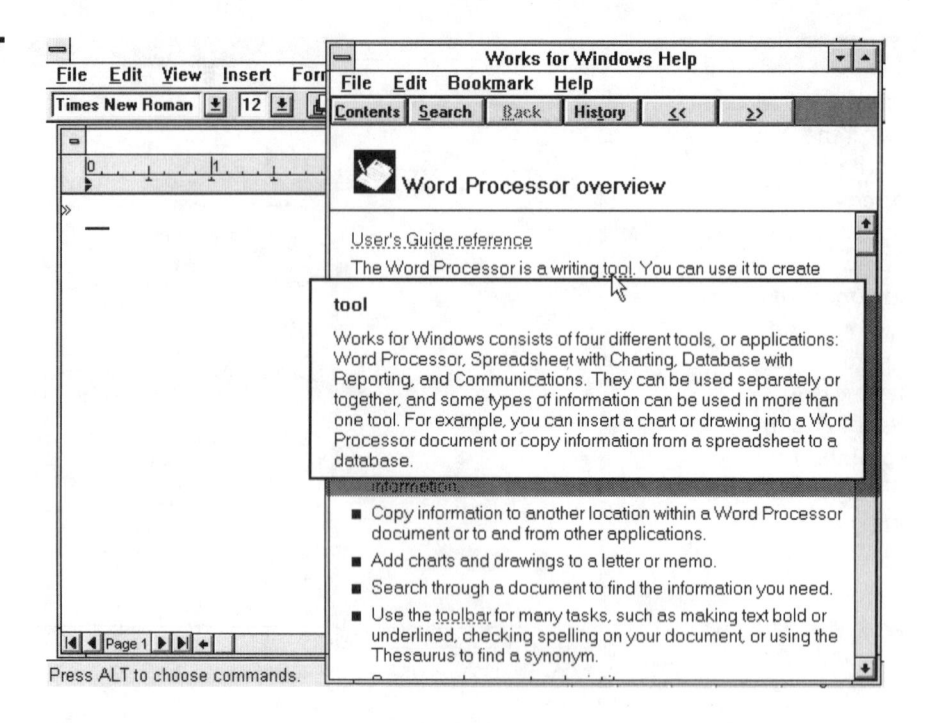

```
tool
Works for Windows consists of four different tools, or applications:
Word Processor, Spreadsheet with Charting, Database with
Reporting, and Communications. They can be used separately or
together, and some types of information can be used in more than
one tool. For example, you can insert a chart or drawing into a Word
Processor document or copy information from a spreadsheet to a
database.
```

Occasionally you'll encounter hotspots that display graphics instead of words. They don't look any different from other graphics in the Help windows, but the pointer turns into the hand icon when it's positioned over them. View information about hotspot graphics as you do other hotspots.

The Help Buttons

Beneath the title bar, each help screen has both a menu bar and a row of six command buttons:

Here's what the command buttons do when you click on them:

Contents Moves you directly to the Contents list. The Contents list is a good starting point for getting help and a good place to return to after reading Help on one item if you want to see more on another, unrelated item.

Search Displays a list of words from which you can choose a help topic. You can select the subject you want to read about, or you can type in a word and have Help look it up. As you begin typing, you will move down the list to the letter you typed first. When the topic you want help with is highlighted, click on Show Topics or press ↵. Another list of topics related to the one you just indicated appears in the lower box of the Search screen, as shown in Figure 2.12. Highlight the word you want to read and click on the Go To button (or press ↵). If you don't find the topic you want, click on the Cancel button (or press Escape).

Back Lets you back up through the Help topics you have already viewed in the reverse order that you viewed them.

History Brings up a little box within the current Help screen that lists the Help screens you've consulted in the reverse order that you viewed them.

<< This is the *Browse Backward* button. When Browse buttons appear on a help screen, it means that some topics related to the current one can be viewed one after another by pressing one of the Browse buttons. Each click on the Browse Backward button returns you to the previous topic in the series.

>> This is the *Browse Forward* button. It advances to the next in the series of related topics. When you reach the end of the series, the button is grayed.

FIGURE 2.12
Using the Search button in Help to look for a specific topic

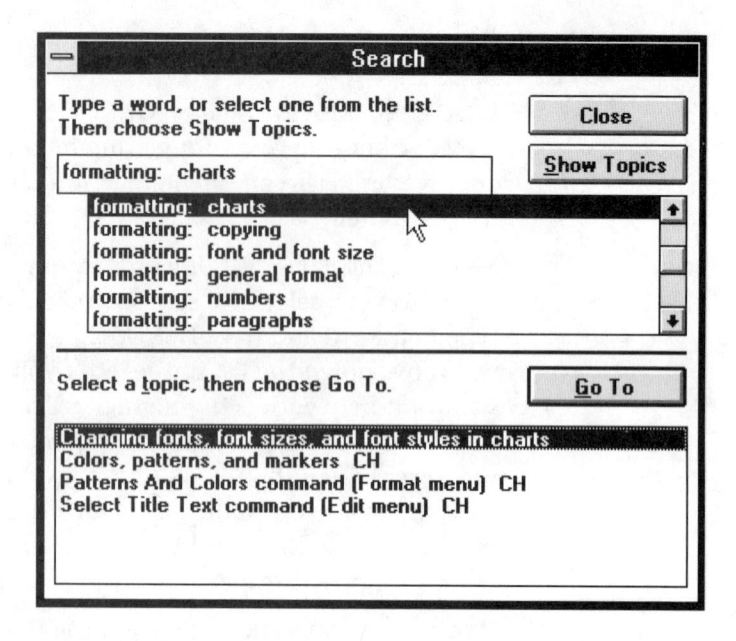

Keeping Help Information On-Screen while You Work

There are two ways to keep a help screen at hand:

- Shrink the Help window down to a size where you can still read it but it doesn't take up the whole screen.

- Turn in into an icon. To do this, click on the ↓ on the right side of the title bar. Be sure to leave enough space to see the icon on the desktop. When you need to read the help topic again, just double-click on the icon.

Exiting Works

To exit the Works program:

1. Choose File ➤ Exit.

Works presents you with a series of small dialog boxes, one for each open document. One box probably looks like this:

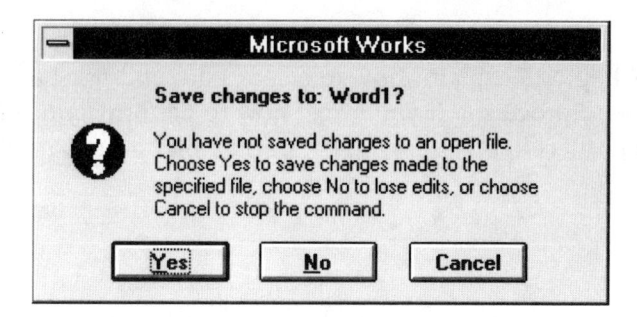

```
┌─────────────────────────────────────────────┐
│             Microsoft Works                 │
│                                             │
│   Save changes to: Word1?                   │
│                                             │
│  ?   You have not saved changes to an open  │
│      file. Choose Yes to save changes made  │
│      to the specified file, choose No to    │
│      lose edits, or choose Cancel to stop   │
│      the command.                           │
│                                             │
│    [ Yes ]    [ No ]    [ Cancel ]          │
└─────────────────────────────────────────────┘
```

2. In this case you haven't typed in anything worth saving, so you can click No.

However, if you were creating documents you wanted to save, you would click Yes. Yes is the default, so you could simply press ↵ to save the changes as well.

> **Tip** — **If you decide you don't want to either save the document or close it without saving, press Esc or click on Cancel. You'll be returned to the document so you can continue editing it.**

CHAPTER 2 Works for Windows Fundamentals

After you click Yes or No, Works closes and you are returned to Windows.

3. If you want to turn off your computer altogether, go to the Program Manager and choose File ➤ Exit Windows. Answer Yes to the question about ending your Windows session.

4. When the DOS prompt reappears (probably C:\>), turn off your computer.

Chapter 3 explains how to create, edit, and print a document using the word processor. If you forget how to perform some of the basics covered in this chapter, just flip back and look up the part you need help with.

PART two

Word Processing in Works

3

Introducing
the Word Processor

4

Advanced
Word Processing Skills

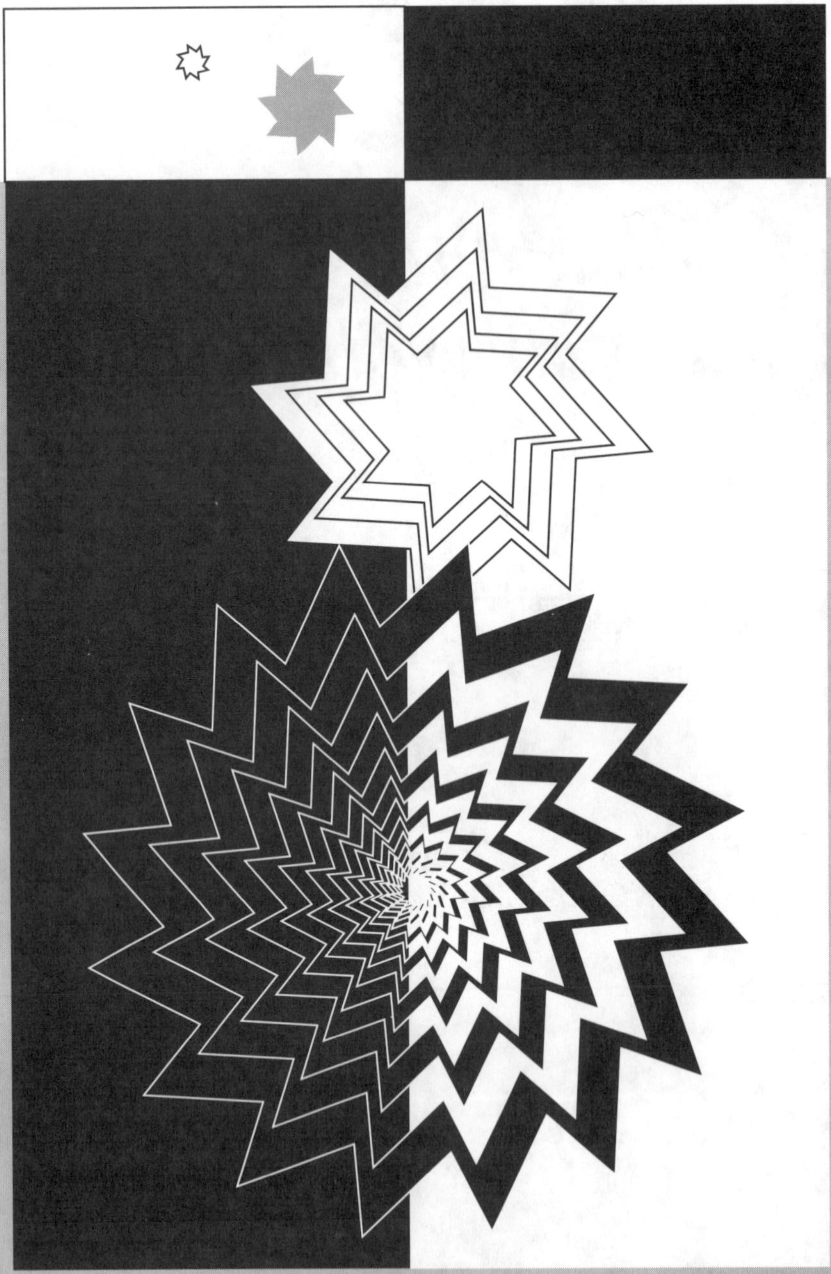

CHAPTER 3

Introducing the Word Processor

Fast Track

To begin creating a new word processing document,   **72**

either choose Word Processor from the Startup dialog box or choose File ➤ Create New Document and then choose Word Processor from the Startup dialog box.

To display the ruler,   **74**

choose Options ➤ Show Ruler. This is a toggle. When you want to turn the ruler off again, choose Options ➤ Show Ruler again.

There are many ways to move around in a document.   **82**

You can click anywhere with the mouse to reposition the cursor, use the arrow keys, press Ctrl and an arrow key, use the scroll bars, or press PgUp or PgDn.

To fix simple typing errors,   **86**

place the insertion point (the vertical blinking cursor) just after the typo and press the Backspace key.

You can select a block of text in several different ways.   **87**

You can drag the mouse over the area to be selected or drag down the left margin to select one line at a time. Using the F8 key, you can select a letter, word, sentence, paragraph, or the entire document. You can also press Shift and an arrow key, or click where you want to start selecting text, then press and hold down F8, and click again at the end of the text to be selected.

To cut or copy a block of text you've selected,   **93**

>choose Edit ➤ Cut or Edit ➤ Copy to move the text to the Clipboard. Next, place the cursor where you want the text block to go and choose Edit ➤ Paste.

You can also move text by dragging and dropping it.   **97**

>Select the text, click on the selection and hold down the mouse, drag the pointer where you want the text to go, and release the mouse button.

To center a title or line of text,   **97**

>click in the line to be centered and then click the Center button in the toolbar.

To save a document,   **99**

>choose File ➤ Save, alter the drive and directory if you need to, type a name in the File Name text box (do not enter an extension—Works will do that for you), and click on OK.

To print a document,   **101**

>choose File ➤ Print Preview to see what your document will look like when you print it, make sure your printer is on-line, and click on Print or press P on the Preview screen to start printing.

THE WORD PROCESSOR IS THE Works tool for writing letters, reports, and other text documents. You can create documents of any size, and you'll find the many built-in features indispensable. You can insert drawings, charts, pictures, and OLE objects such as video, sound, and drawings in your documents.

In this chapter you'll learn how to create, edit, and print a document. You'll experiment with all the most important procedures in word processing. You'll learn how to

- ◆ Enter text from the keyboard
- ◆ Edit text by deleting typos
- ◆ Move and copy sections of text
- ◆ Save a word processing document
- ◆ Print a document

If you took a break after Chapter 2, you'll have to bring up Works again before continuing.

Creating Your First Document

Follow these steps to open and create a new word processing document:

1. How to go about opening a new word processing document depends on whether you're just bringing up Works or Works is already running:

    - ◆ If you're just bringing up Works, choose Word Processor from the Startup dialog box.

◆ If Works is already running, choose File ➤ Create New File and choose Word Processor.

A new file with a blank screen opens for you, as shown in Figure 3.1.

3. Click the Maximize button in both the application (Microsoft Works) window and the document (Word1) window so both windows become as large as possible.

FIGURE 3.1
A blank word processing document

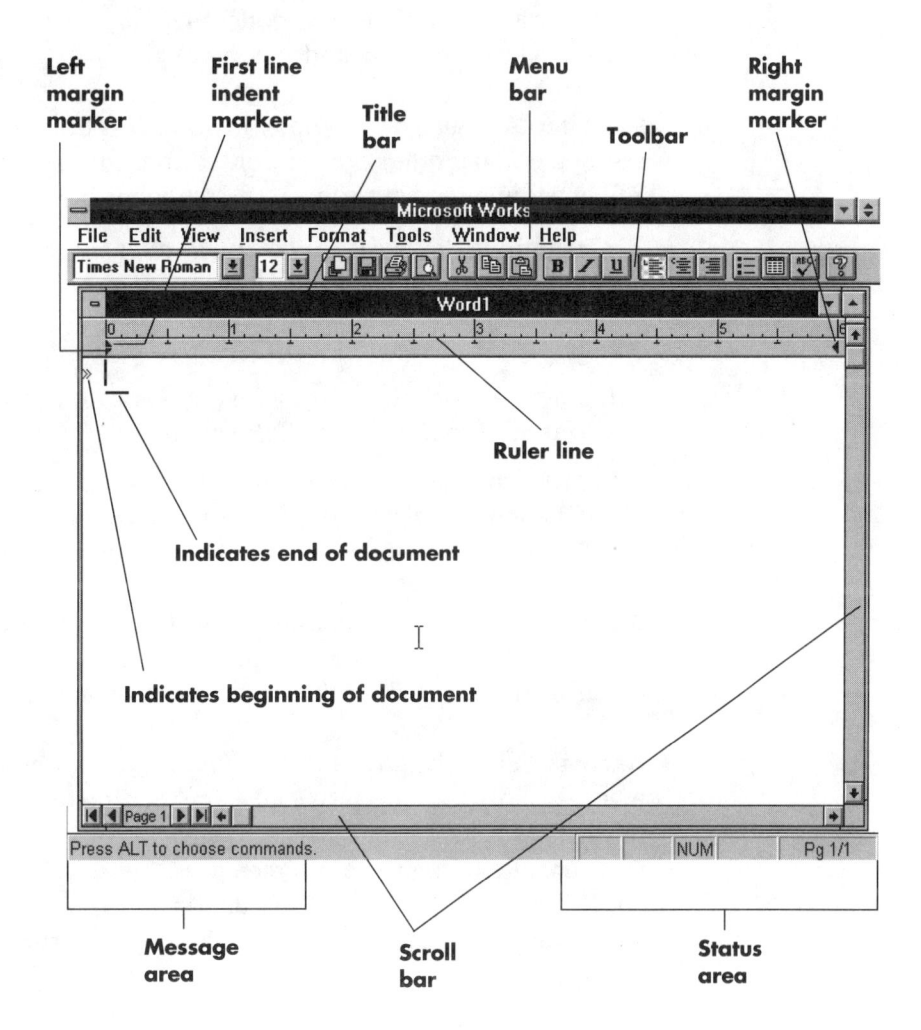

CHAPTER 3   Introducing the Word Processor

> **Note** See "The Parts of a Works Screen" in Chapter 2 for information about maximizing a window.

Finding Your Way around the Screen

There are several things to notice on your screen—the *menu bar*, toolbar, ruler, scroll bars, title bar, and >> symbol. Let's look at them one at a time.

Menu bar As usual, at the top of the screen is the *menu bar*. The word processing menu bar offers options for writing, editing, and formatting text. You experimented with some of these menus in Chapter 2.

Try pulling down each menu now to see the selections you have to choose from:

1. Open the File menu.
2. Press → to see the next menu and → again to see the choices on the one after that. Look at all the menus.
3. From the menus, choose an option that brings up a dialog box. (As Chapter 2 explains, these options have three dots after their name.) You can always press Esc (or click on Cancel) to back out of a dialog box.

Toolbar Below the menu bar is the *toolbar*. The toolbar offers various tools and drop-down lists for editing and formatting documents. You'll get familiar with these tools in this and the next chapter.

Title bar Below the toolbar is the *title bar*. You haven't named the document yet, so Works has provided a generic title for you, Word1.

Ruler line Referring to your screen or to Figure 3.1, notice that the *ruler line* lies immediately below the title bar. The ruler helps you keep track of where you are typing on the page. Normally the ruler is divided into inches.

Tip You can set the increments on the ruler to centimeters, picas, points, or millimeters. This is done with the Tools ➤ Options dialog box.

Notice the left- and right-pointing triangular markers at the edges of the ruler. These mark the left and right indents, or *margins*. Notice the tab settings every half inch. The ruler also shows paragraph indents, although paragraph indents are not shown on your screen or in Figure 3.1 because you haven't made this setting yet. Setting paragraph indents and tabs is explained later.

You can turn off the ruler and get more space for viewing and editing your documents:

◆ Choose Options ➤ Show Ruler.

When you want to bring the ruler back, choose Options ➤ Show Ruler again. Removing the ruler gives you an extra line of text, but as you'll see later, the ruler is useful to have around.

Scroll bars Notice the *scroll bars* on the right and bottom sides of the screen. As explained in Chapter 2, you can use scroll bars to move back and forth or up and down in a document.

Beginning and end document markers Next to the *cursor*, the vertical blinking line in the upper-left corner of your screen, are two other symbols:

>> The beginning marker. This symbol simply marks the beginning (top) of the document.

— The end marker. The underline marks the end (bottom) of the document.

Since you haven't typed in anything yet, the only thing between the top and bottom of the document is the cursor.

Message area The *message area,* as is the case in all Windows programs, gives you basic information about what the program is doing. It also tells you what menu commands do. Click on any menu command and look at the message area for a brief description of what it does.

Status area The *status area* at the bottom of the screen says Pg 1/1. In other words, you are on page 1 of a document that is one page in length. The word NUM means that Num Lock is on.

Entering Text in a Document

To see how to enter text, let's create a letter. When finished, it will look like the one in Figure 3.2. The letter gives us an opportunity to experiment with different word processing features, including tabs and line breaks.

However, instead of using Figure 3.2 as a guide, we'll use Figure 3.3. It has intentional errors in it that we can use later for learning about editing. Begin entering the text in the new file using Figure 3.3 as a guide. If you make unintentional mistakes as you type, use the Backspace key to back up and fix them. Otherwise, enter the letter in Figure 3.3, mistakes and all, following the directions below:

1. Begin by typing in the title on the first line. Don't bother trying to center it yet. You'll do that later.

2. Press ↵ three times to move down a couple of lines to prepare for typing the address. Notice that pressing ↵ is necessary for adding new blank lines in a word processing document.

FIGURE 3.2
The business letter in final form

Product Announcement for Microsoft Works for Windows

Efficient Chips
1000 West Goshen Lane
Walla Walla, Washington 98238

Dear Mr. Freud,

Microsoft Inc. announced today its new integrated productivity tool for the IBM PC and compatibles, Works for Windows. Works for Windows is an integrated product designed to run on computers that run Microsoft Windows. The key selling points of this program are ease of learning and immediate business productivity.

Works for Windows is a single program with word processing, spreadsheet, database, charting, and drawing built in. The word processor is quite capable, and is similar to Microsoft Word for Windows. Here are some of its features:

Feature	Notes
Document size	Unlimited
Undo	Yes, from menu
Character formatting	Bold, underline, italic, strikethrough
Fonts	Any Windows fonts
Alignment	Right, left, center, justified
Paragraph formats	Each paragraph has its own

Of course there are many other useful features included in the Works word processor that are worth your consideration as you will see once you try out the evaluation copy of the program enclosed. Please let us know if you have any questions.

Sincerely,

Harvey Fledgebog

Note Pressing the ↓ key at this point will not move the cursor down because there aren't any blank lines past the end of document mark. Even though the screen looks like a blank sheet of paper, you can't move the cursor down any further without entering blank lines. You can only enter blank lines by pressing ↵.

CHAPTER 3 — Introducing the Word Processor

FIGURE 3.3
The business letter with mistakes underlined. We'll use this letter to try out the word processing features.

Product Announcement for Microsoft Works for Windows

Efficient Chips
1000 West Goshen Lane
Walla Walla, <u>Wahshington</u> 98238

Dear Mr. Floyd,

Microsoft Inc. announced today its new integrated productivity tool for the IBM PC and compatibles, Works for Windows. Works for Windows is an <u>inegrated</u> product designed to run on computers that run Microsoft Windows. The key selling points of this program are ease of learning and immediate business productivity.

Works for Windows is a single program with word processing, spreadsheet, database, charting, and drawing built in. The word processor si quite capable, and is similar to Microsoft Word for Windows. Here are some of its features:

<u>Feeture</u>	Notes
Document size	Unlimited
Undo	Yes, from menu
Character formatting	Bold, underline, italic, strikethrough
Fonts	Any Windows fonts
Alignment	Right, left, center, justified
Paragraph formats	Each paragraph has its own

Of <u>coarse</u> there rae many other useful features included in the Works word processor <u>thatare</u> worth your consideration as you will see once you try out the evaluation copy of the program enclosed. Please let us know <u>is</u> you have any questions.

<u>Sinceerely,</u>

Harvey Fledgebog

---

3. Enter the first line of the address and press ↵ to move down to the next line. Do the same for the second and third lines of the address.

4. After typing the address, press ↵ twice to put in a blank line.

5. Type the salutation.

6. Press ↵ twice to skip another line.

7. Enter the body of the letter. Don't forget to leave in the spelling mistakes so that you can fix them later.

Word wrap As you type the body of the letter you don't have to worry about pressing ↵ at the end of each line—the word processor wraps the text for you automatically.

8. When you reach the end of the first paragraph, just move on down and begin the next one by pressing ↵ twice.

Now your letter should look like the one in Figure 3.4.

Creating columns with the Tab key The next part of the text is a simple table with two columns. Many letters, particularly business letters, require tables like this one. You use the Tab key to move from column to column.

1. Press ↵ to insert a blank line to separate the table from the previous paragraph.

FIGURE 3.4
The letter thus far—note the intentional misspellings

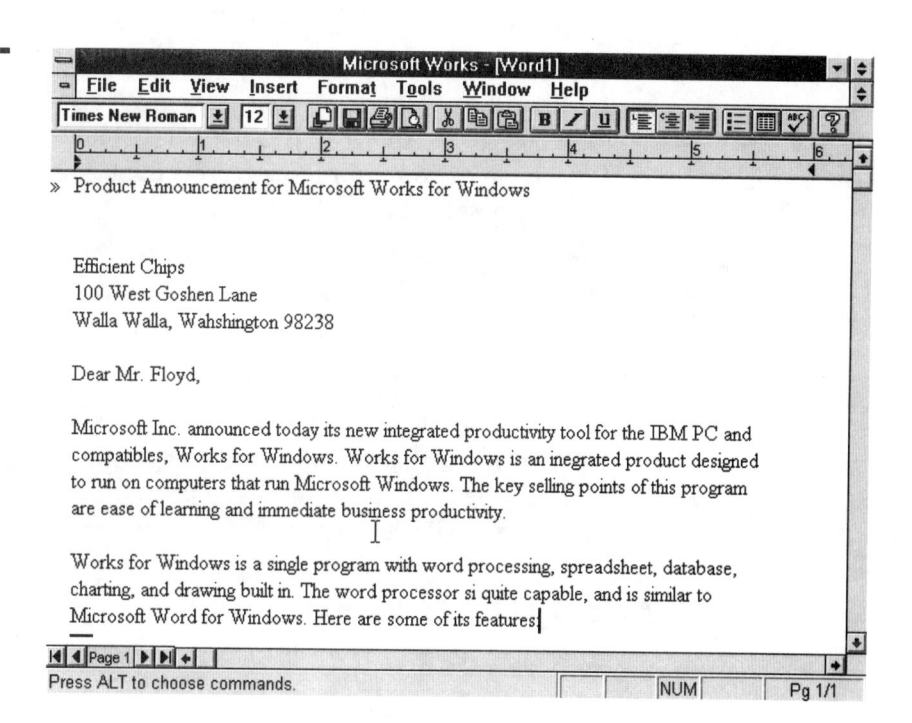

Notice that when you reach the bottom of the screen Works moves text up to make room for new text. But don't worry, the missing text is still there.

2. Type the word **Feeture**.

When you type the *F* the text and the cursor jump up to the middle of the screen. Most word processors only scroll the screen one line at a time, but not Works.

3. Press the Tab key (just above the CapsLock key on most keyboards) three times. Each press advances the cursor half an inch (the normal tab setting). You can set the Tab key to advance any amount of space, but for now we'll keep Tab settings on the half-inch marks of the ruler.

4. Type **Notes**.

5. Drop down to the next line by pressing ↵, and type in the dotted line as it appears in the letter. Remember that all the keys on the PC are repeating keys, so it's easy to type in this line. Just hold the hyphen key down. If you went too far, press the Backspace key to back up and erase some of the dashes.

6. Press ↵ again and begin entering the list. As shown in Figure 3.5, type in **Document size** and then press the Tab key two times. This moves the cursor to the Notes column.

7. Type in **Unlimited** and press ↵. This finishes the first line of the list.

8. Repeat the process for the remaining five lines, using Figure 3.5 as a guide. Notice that each line requires a different number of tabs to line up the Notes column. If you press too many tabs, press the Backspace key to delete them.

Adding the Ending

Now all that's left to type is the last paragraph and the closing:

1. Press ↵ twice to create one blank line before the last paragraph.

2. Type in the rest of the letter as shown in Figure 3.6. Again, enter the misspelled words because you'll correct them later as part of the tutorial.

FIGURE 3.5
The letter with the tabbed columns in place

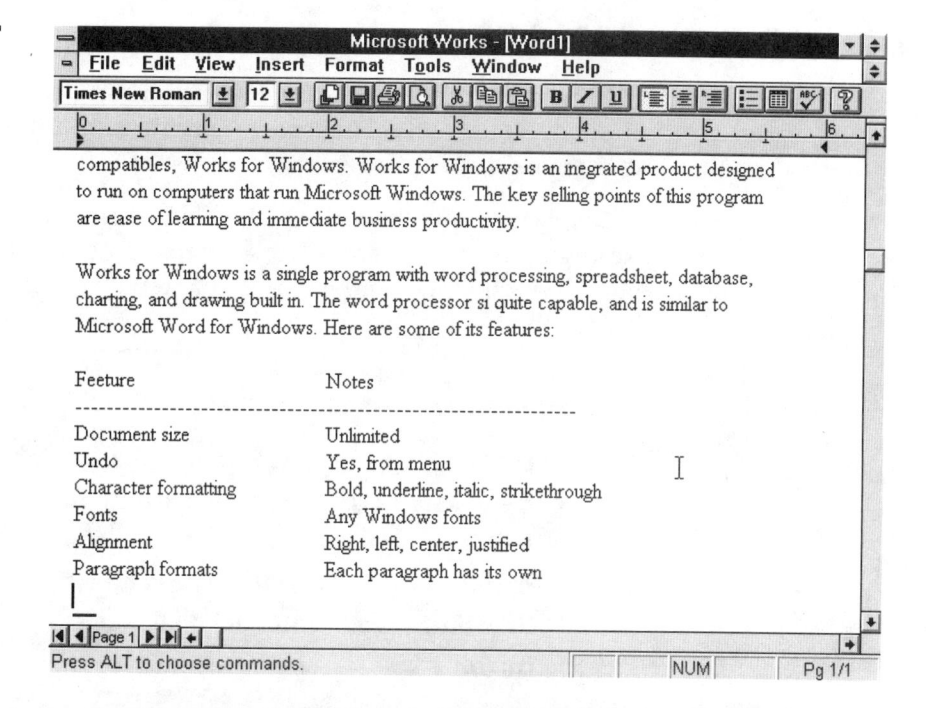

compatibles, Works for Windows. Works for Windows is an inegrated product designed to run on computers that run Microsoft Windows. The key selling points of this program are ease of learning and immediate business productivity.

Works for Windows is a single program with word processing, spreadsheet, database, charting, and drawing built in. The word processor si quite capable, and is similar to Microsoft Word for Windows. Here are some of its features:

Feeture	Notes
Document size	Unlimited
Undo	Yes, from menu
Character formatting	Bold, underline, italic, strikethrough
Fonts	Any Windows fonts
Alignment	Right, left, center, justified
Paragraph formats	Each paragraph has its own

FIGURE 3.6
Adding the last paragraph and closing the letter

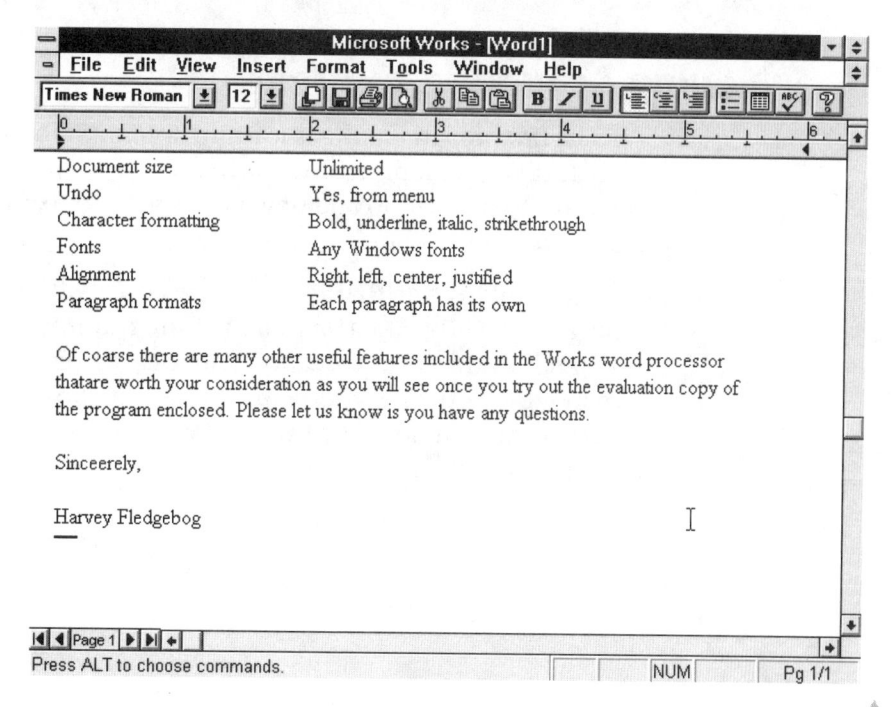

Document size	Unlimited
Undo	Yes, from menu
Character formatting	Bold, underline, italic, strikethrough
Fonts	Any Windows fonts
Alignment	Right, left, center, justified
Paragraph formats	Each paragraph has its own

Of coarse there are many other useful features included in the Works word processor thatare worth your consideration as you will see once you try out the evaluation copy of the program enclosed. Please let us know is you have any questions.

Sinceerely,

Harvey Fledgebog

Editing a Document

Now that you've typed the letter you can begin editing it. Even if you made your own mistakes while typing, you'll soon see how to fix those errors, too.

Editing is simply the process of making changes to a document for the sake of grammar and clarity. Works offers numerous editing features, only some of which we'll explore in this chapter. I'll discuss more advanced editing capabilities in Chapter 4.

> **Tip** Everyone who uses a word processor inevitably develops a style of editing. Some people like to print out a document, edit it on paper, fix the errors, and transfer the corrections on screen. Others prefer editing directly on the screen. Experiment with both techniques to see which works best for you.

Moving Around in the Text

The first step in editing is learning to move around in the text. As you enter text you seldom need to move the cursor, but for editing purposes you have to move it up and down quite a bit to fix misspelled words and make other corrections.

The blinking line that marks where letters will appear when you begin typing is called the *insertion point*. Editing text involves moving the insertion point to the correct location and then fixing the errors, and the first step in moving the insertion point is learning how to scroll. When there is more text in your document than can fit on one screen, you have to scroll to parts of the document you can't see.

Editing a Document

This part of the chapter explains how to

- Scroll with the keyboard
- Scroll with the mouse
- Move the cursor

Scrolling with the Keyboard

To scroll with the keyboard, you can use the following keys:

KEY	ACTION
PgUp	Moves the insertion point up one screen toward the beginning of your document.
PgDn	Moves the insertion point down one screen in the document.

Tip: When you use the scroll keys on the numeric keypad, make sure Num Lock is turned off. Pressing PgUp with Num Lock on, for example, will enter the number 9 instead of scrolling the text.

KEY	ACTION
Ctrl+End	Moves the insertion to the bottom of the document. To do this, press and hold down the Ctrl key while you press End.
Ctrl+Home	Moves the insertion point to the top of the document.

Scrolling with a Mouse

Scrolling with the mouse is somewhat different than scrolling with the keyboard. To scroll with the mouse, you use the vertical scroll bar, the bar along the right side of the document window. Notice the square button in the bar, called the *elevator*. The elevator shows you the relative position of the cursor in the document, from top to bottom. By moving the elevator up and down with the mouse, you can determine which part of the document appears on your screen.

To scroll using the mouse and the elevator, use these techniques:

◆ **Scrolling a line at a time:** Place the mouse pointer on one of the small arrows either at the top of the bar or at the bottom of the bar. When the pointer turns into an arrow, click the left button. Clicking the top arrow moves you toward the top of the document, and clicking the bottom arrow moves you toward the bottom. Each click shifts the screen one line in one direction. Holding the mouse button down longer scrolls several lines at once.

◆ **Scrolling one screen at a time:** Place the pointer somewhere in the scroll bar itself, either above or below the elevator, and click. Clicking above the elevator moves on screen at a time toward the top of the document; clicking below the elevator moves one screen the other direction.

◆ **Scrolling to a new position:** Place the pointer on the elevator, hold down the left mouse button, and drag the elevator up or down the document to roughly where you want to go. This is called dragging the elevator.

Think of the vertical scroll bar as a measuring stick for your document. The top of the bar represents the beginning and the bottom represents the end. By pulling the elevator to the relative position you want to scroll to, you can get close to where you want to be.

Tip The horizontal scroll bar works the same as the vertical bar, except it moves the document from side to side, not up and down. It is useful for working with wide documents.

Moving the Cursor with the Keyboard

Once you've scrolled to the screen you want, the next step is moving the cursor to the word or letter that you want to edit. Once the cursor is in the right position you can insert text, remove words, fix misspellings, or mark blocks of text for moving, copying, or deleting.

Keys and key combinations for moving the cursor are listed in Table 3.1. Try experimenting with all these keys, as they can be very handy.

TABLE 3.1: Shortcuts for Moving Around a Document

KEY(S)	MOVES THE INSERTION POINT
←	One character left
→	One character right
↑	One line up
↓	One line down
Ctrl+←	One word left
Ctrl+→	One word right
Ctrl+↑	One paragraph up
Ctrl+↓	One paragraph down
Home	To the beginning of the line
End	To the end of the line
Ctrl+Home	To the start of the document
Ctrl+End	To the end of the document
PgUp	One screen up
PgDn	One screen down
Ctrl+PgUp	To the top of the screen
Ctrl+PgDn	To the bottom of the screen

Moving the Cursor with the Mouse

Moving the cursor is particularly easy for mouse users. Simply move the arrow around the screen to the place you want to be and click.

> **Warning**
>
> Don't forget to click when you move the mouse to a new place. If you forget, you'll end up making changes in the wrong place. The text cursor doesn't move to a new location until you click on the mouse.

Fixing the Errors in the Sample Document

Now that you know how to get around, you can begin correcting the typos in our sample letter. Let's start with the third line of the address, where the word *Washington* is spelled wrong:

1. Using the arrow keys or the mouse, position the cursor just before the first *h* in *Wahshington*.
2. Press Del to remove the *h*. Notice that the space where the *h* was has been closed up.

> **Tip**
>
> Pressing the Del key deletes the letter to the right of the insertion point (cursor), while pressing the Backspace key removes the letter to the left of the insertion point.

Suppose you wanted to delete an entire word, sentence, or paragraph. You could move to the beginning or end of the text you wanted to delete and press Del or Backspace like mad, but this method is not only time-consuming, it is unpredictable—if you're not careful, you'll erase more than you intended to. A better way is to delete a whole block of text by selecting it and using the Delete command, as explained next.

Selecting Blocks of Text for Moving, Copying, or Deleting

Much of editing with a word processor involves manipulating blocks of text. A *block* is a portion of text, be it letters, words, paragraphs, or pages. Many of the commands in the productivity tools require manipulating blocks of information, whether they consist of text or other data, such as numbers.

But before a block can be worked with, it must be selected. *Selecting* a block of text means to mark, or highlight, the beginning and end of the block so it can be moved, copied, or deleted. The selected text is highlighted on the screen. When an area of a document is selected, it becomes the center of attention for the Works tool you are using and is usually treated differently than the rest of the document.

You can select a word, sentence, line, paragraph, or even a whole document with just a few key presses. We'll concentrate on what to do with selected text later in this chapter and in Chapter 4. For now, try these exercises to get the hang of selecting.

Selecting Text with F8

Here's how to select portions of text using the F8 key:

1. Put the cursor on the word *Works* in the first sentence of the second paragraph and press F8.

Extend mode On the status line located on the bottom right of your screen, notice the letters *EXT*. This means you are in *Extend mode* and you can extend your selection to include more letters, words, sentences, or paragraphs, or the whole document. The extension begins from the point or word where the cursor was when you pressed F8. This point is called the *anchor point*.

Once you get into Extend mode by pressing F8, there are several ways to increase the size of the selection. The first way is to press F8 repeatedly, like so:

2. Press F8 again to select the whole word you are on. Notice that the whole word, *Works,* is now highlighted.

CHAPTER 3 Introducing the Word Processor

3. Press F8 again to select the entire sentence, beginning with the word at the anchor point.

4. Press F8 again to select the entire paragraph. Your screen should now look like Figure 3.7.

5. Press F8 again to select the entire document.

Once you've pressed F8 for the fourth time and selected the document, pressing F8 again has no effect. However, you remain in Extend mode as indicated on the status line.

> **Tip** To leave Extend mode at any time, press Esc.

FIGURE 3.7
Pressing F8 three times selects the whole paragraph. Notice the EXT in the status line.

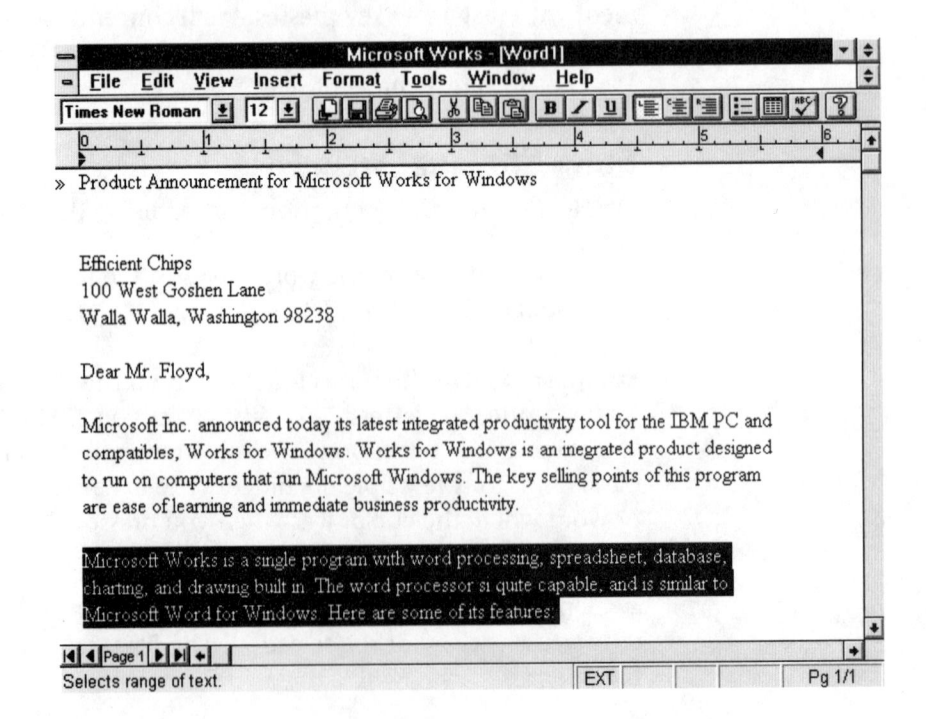

> **Warning**
>
> Once you've made a selection and you have highlighted text on screen, be careful not to press any keys except the navigation keys. If you press the A key, for example, the whole selection will be replaced by the letter *A*. If this happens accidentally, choose Edit ➤ Undo Editing immediately.

Shrinking the size of a selection In Extend mode you can decrease, or shrink, the size of the selection. This is done by pressing the Shift+F8 key combination and works in the reverse manner as extending a selection.

1. Press Shift+F8. The selection shrinks one level, down to just the paragraph.
2. Press Shift+F8 again, and you're back to just the first sentence.
3. Press Shift+F8 twice more and it looks like you're back where you started—that is, nothing seems to be selected. But the status line indicates that you are still in Extend mode. This is important, as you will soon see.

Selecting Text with F8 and the Shortcut Keys

A second way of selecting an area of text gives you more control than pressing the F8 key does. With this method, you press F8 and one of the Works shortcut keys for moving around in a document (see Table 3.1) to extend or shrink the selection. Try it out:

1. Press → several times. As you move the cursor over letters, they become selected. This is because you are still in Extend mode.
2. Press ↓ several times. Notice the similar effect.
3. Press ↑ and see the reverse effect.
4. Press Ctrl+→ and Ctrl+← to move the cursor, respectively, a word to the right and a word to the left.
5. Press and hold down the ← key for a bit.

As the cursor moves past the anchor point (in this case the letter *W* in Works), the selection starts upward from there. Now text in the first paragraph is being selected. The anchor point is the point from which text is selected either backward or forward in a document.

Selecting Text with the Shift Key

You can use the Shift key in combination with the arrow keys to select one letter or word at a time:

1. Deselect anything you have already selected by pressing Esc.
2. Move the cursor to the first word in the first paragraph, *Microsoft*.
3. Press Shift+→. The selection advances one letter with each press.
4. Press Shift+Ctrl+→. The selection advances a word with each press.
5. Release the Shift key.
6. Press Esc. The highlight disappears and the selection is now deselected.

Selecting Text with the Mouse

Selecting text is easy with the mouse. All you have to do is drag over the text:

1. Move the arrow pointer to the first *d* in the word *designed* in the first paragraph.
2. Hold the button down and move the pointer down several lines. As you move the mouse, the selection extends.
3. Let go of the button. The selection is finalized.
4. Click again anywhere to turn off the selection.

The anchor point works the same way it does when you use keyboard commands to select text:

1. Click in the middle of the first paragraph to establish the anchor point.
2. Press F8 to enter Extend mode.

3. Click on the first word of the paragraph. Now you have selected all text between the anchor point and the beginning of the paragraph.

4. Click on the last word of the paragraph to change the selection. Now you have selected all text from the anchor to the end of the paragraph.

5. Click anywhere to deselect the text and get ready for the next exercise.

> **Tip** Use these shortcuts to select text with the mouse. To select a word, double-click on it. To select a line, move the mouse pointer to the blank area in the left margin of the text window. The arrow pointer changes direction, angling to the right. Clicking at this point selects the line.

Selecting and Replacing Words

Now that you know how to select blocks of text, let's get back to editing the letter. We'll begin by selecting the misspelled word *si* in order to delete it and replace it with *is*. Before you begin this exercise press Esc if you have to in order to deselect highlighted text and get out of Extend mode.

1. Select the word *si* in the second line of the second paragraph.

2. Press the Del key. The selection disappears.

3. Type **is**, the right word. (You may have to add a space after the word, depending on how you selected *si*.)

Let's try another approach. For this exercise, assume that the addressee's name is really Mr. Freud, not Mr. Floyd. Here's a shortcut for replacing a word or selection with some other text. In this case you'll just change the name in the greeting.

1. Select the word *Floyd*.

2. With *Floyd* highlighted, type in the word **Freud**.

Notice that *Floyd* is deleted the moment you type in the first letter of *Freud*. This saves the extra step of pressing the Delete key or choosing Clear or Cut from the Edit menu.

Inserting Letters and Words in Documents

Now let's see how to insert letters and words in documents. The word *ingrated* in the first paragraph is missing a *t*. The missing letter will have to be inserted in the middle of a word:

1. Move the cursor between the *n* and *e* in *ingrated*. (Either click the mouse there or use the arrow keys to place the cursor.)
2. Type the letter **t**.

Notice that the word opened up to let the *t* in. Not only has Works readjusted the letters in the word, it has readjusted all the lines in the paragraph.

At this point you could insert any number of letters, words, or even paragraphs. Wherever you want to insert text in a document, the computer will accommodate you.

Entering Letters in Overwrite (OVR) Mode

Most word processors allow you to *overwrite* the text in a document as well as insert text. In *overwrite mode,* newly typed letters overwrite the old ones instead of pushing them to the right. Turn overwrite mode on and off by pressing the Ins key on your keyboard. When you are in overwrite mode, the status area displays the letters OVR.

Tip If the letters you are typing start wiping out letters you want pushed to the right, look at the status line to see if you are accidentally in overwrite mode. If OVR appears on the status line, press the Ins key to return to *insert mode*.

Editing a Document

Try fixing some errors in overwrite mode:

1. Move the cursor just before the *s* in the word *is*. This word is in the last line of the last main paragraph. It is supposed to be *if*.
2. Press the Ins key to change to overwrite mode.
3. Type the letter **f**. Notice how the *f* obliterates the *s*.
4. Do the same to repair to the word *Feeture* in the table heading. Place the cursor before the second *e* and press **a**, replacing the second *e* with an *a*.
5. Press the Ins key again to leave overwrite mode and return to insert mode.

Fixing the Other Typos

Now that you know how to repair most simple errors, go ahead and correct the remaining ones:

1. In the last paragraph, insert a space between the words *that* and *are*. Put the cursor before the second *a* and press the Spacebar. If the screen scrolls to the right when you're at the right end of the line, just press Home to get back after you make the correction. This will straighten out the screen.
2. In the same paragraph, the second word, *coarse*, should be spelled *course*. Make the necessary correction.
3. Delete the extra *e* in *Sinceerely* and you're finished editing.

Your letter now looks like Figure 3.2, except that the heading is not centered. (I'll get to centering in a moment.)

Moving and Copying Text Blocks in a Document

Editing often requires moving large portions of text, such as sentences and paragraphs, to new places in a document. Rather than inserting a block of text by retyping it, you can pick it up and move it from one place to another with the Cut or Copy commands on the Edit menu. Moving text this way can be a real timesaver and is easy to do.

93

To move a block of text, following these basic steps:

1. Select the text you want to move.
2. Choose the Cut or Copy command from the Edit menu.
    - Cut removes the block of text from the document and places it on the *Clipboard,* a temporary storage area that Windows maintains.
    - Copy copies the block of text to the Clipboard. The highlighted text you selected remains in the document. It has been copied, not cut out.
3. Move the cursor where you want to place the cut or copied text.
4. Choose Edit ➤ Paste.

Let's use the Cut command to reverse the order of the first two paragraphs in the letter:

1. Press Ctrl+Home to move to the top of the document.
2. Select the entire second paragraph using whatever technique you prefer.
3. Open the Edit menu and choose Cut. Your screen now looks like Figure 3.8.

How the Clipboard Works

You've just put the text on the Windows Clipboard. The Clipboard can hold pictures, charts, sounds, graphics, text, or numbers. When you use the Cut command from a Windows program such as Works, the cut text goes to the Clipboard.

You can copy it back into your document in as many different places as you wish by using the Paste command. In fact, you can drop what is on the Clipboard into several different documents. When you cut or copy new text to the Clipboard, however, the text that was there previously is removed. You can't get it back.

Editing a Document

FIGURE 3.8
Cutting out the second paragraph in order to move it elsewhere

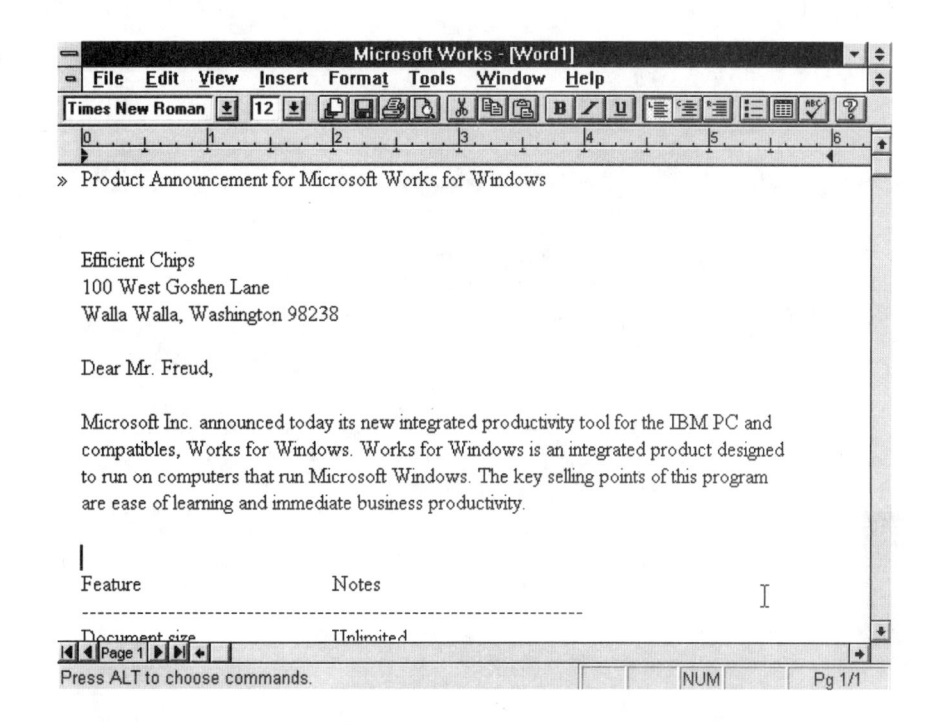

> » Product Announcement for Microsoft Works for Windows
>
> Efficient Chips
> 100 West Goshen Lane
> Walla Walla, Washington 98238
>
> Dear Mr. Freud,
>
> Microsoft Inc. announced today its new integrated productivity tool for the IBM PC and compatibles, Works for Windows. Works for Windows is an integrated product designed to run on computers that run Microsoft Windows. The key selling points of this program are ease of learning and immediate business productivity.
>
> Feature   Notes
> --
> Document size   Unlimited

Warning The Clipboard can hold only one thing at a time. Once you cut or copy something new to the Clipboard, what was there before is lost.

Pasting Text in a New Location

Now paste the paragraph on the Clipboard to a new location:

1. Move the cursor where you want to insert the paragraph, which happens to be just before the *M* in the word *Microsoft* that starts the first paragraph.
2. Choose Edit ➤ Paste. Your screen should look like Figure 3.9.

95

CHAPTER 3 Introducing the Word Processor

FIGURE 3.9
Pasting the paragraph in a new location

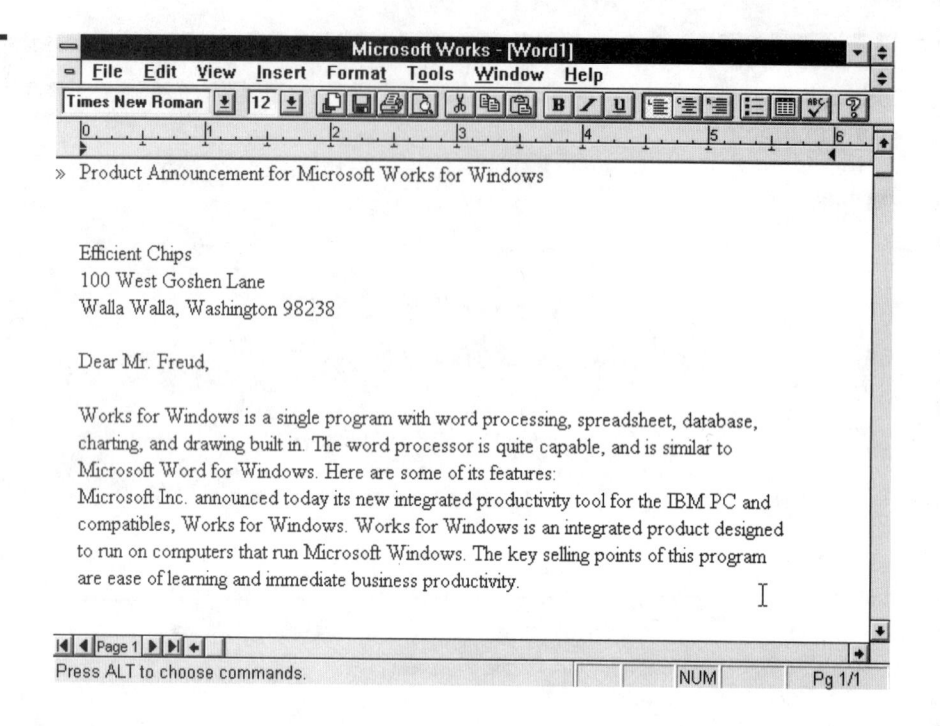

> Product Announcement for Microsoft Works for Windows
>
> Efficient Chips
> 100 West Goshen Lane
> Walla Walla, Washington 98238
>
> Dear Mr. Freud,
>
> Works for Windows is a single program with word processing, spreadsheet, database, charting, and drawing built in. The word processor is quite capable, and is similar to Microsoft Word for Windows. Here are some of its features:
> Microsoft Inc. announced today its new integrated productivity tool for the IBM PC and compatibles, Works for Windows. Works for Windows is an integrated product designed to run on computers that run Microsoft Windows. The key selling points of this program are ease of learning and immediate business productivity.

Notice that the paragraphs have run together. This sort of spacing problem is common when moving blocks of text. After you move a text block, you often have to do a little adjusting.

3. Move to the *M* in *Microsoft Inc.* and press ↵ to separate the paragraphs.

Tip To remove unwanted blank lines, place the cursor on the first space of the blank line (the far left margin) and press the Backspace key.

4. After you have things looking right, give yourself a little more practice by returning the paragraphs to their original positions.

Centering Titles and Other Text

Tip Ctrl+X (for Cut), Ctrl+C (for Copy), and Ctrl+V (for Paste) are very useful shortcut keys. To use these shortcuts, highlight some text and then press either Ctrl+X (Cut) or Ctrl+C (Copy) to move the text to the Clipboard. Next, reposition the cursor and press Ctrl+V (Paste).

Moving Text with the Drag-and-Drop Method

For short moves from one part of the screen to another, you can "drag and drop" text blocks to new positions. When you move the insertion point over a block of highlighted text, it changes to a pointer with the word *DRAG* under it, as shown in Figure 3.10. At this point you can drag the text block to a new location:

1. Select the new first paragraph and then move the insertion point over it. Your screen should look like Figure 3.10.

2. Click the mouse (and hold down the mouse button). The word changes to *MOVE*.

3. Drag the insertion point where you want the block to appear and release the mouse button.

Centering Titles and Other Text

Now there is only one thing to do before actually printing the letter—you have to center the first line in the document. Here's how to center titles and other text:

1. Put the cursor anywhere on the line you want to center. In our case, the line is the one that begins "Product Announcement…."

CHAPTER 3 Introducing the Word Processor

FIGURE 3.10
A selected block showing an arrow with the word DRAG below it. You can drag this block to a new location.

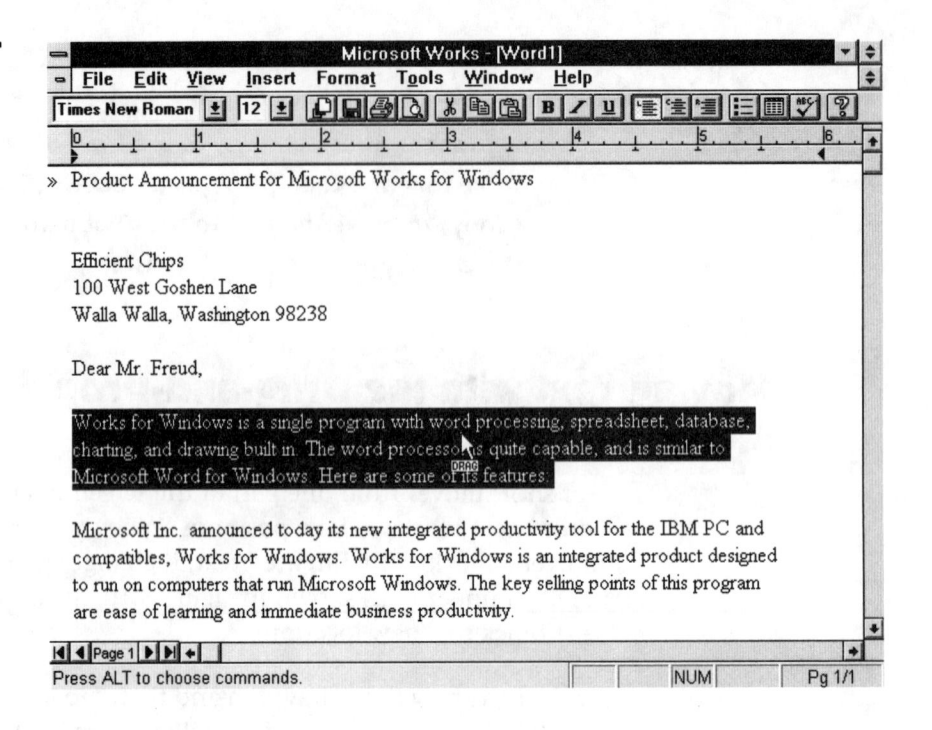

```
Microsoft Works - [Word1]
File  Edit  View  Insert  Format  Tools  Window  Help
Times New Roman  12

» Product Announcement for Microsoft Works for Windows

    Efficient Chips
    100 West Goshen Lane
    Walla Walla, Washington 98238

    Dear Mr. Freud,

    Works for Windows is a single program with word processing, spreadsheet, database,
    charting, and drawing built in. The word processor is quite capable, and is similar to
    Microsoft Word for Windows. Here are some of its features.

    Microsoft Inc. announced today its new integrated productivity tool for the IBM PC and
    compatibles, Works for Windows. Works for Windows is an integrated product designed
    to run on computers that run Microsoft Windows. The key selling points of this program
    are ease of learning and immediate business productivity.

Page 1
Press ALT to choose commands.                              NUM    Pg 1/1
```

2. Click on the Center button in the toolbar (the one the arrow is pointing to below):

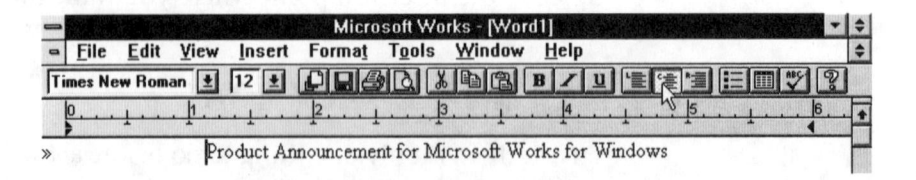

```
Microsoft Works - [Word1]
File  Edit  View  Insert  Format  Tools  Window  Help
Times New Roman  12

» Product Announcement for Microsoft Works for Windows
```

Notice that when you click on a button you seem to push it down and it changes color. Now the paragraph the cursor is in is centered. You don't have to select the whole line or paragraph to center a line or a title. Just place the cursor in the line or title.

98

Saving Your Work

You save your documents with the Save and Save As commands on the File menu. The first time you save a document, Works asks you to name it. After that, Works saves the document under the name you gave, but you can always save a document under a new name with the Save As command.

> **Note** See "Dialog Boxes for Working with Files" in Chapter 2 for detailed instructions about saving documents.

> **Tip** Save your work whenever you think that losing it would cause grief or consternation, or when you have done a fair amount of editing. I recommend saving every fifteen minutes.

To save a document:

◆ Choose File ➤ Save.

Because this is the first time you've saved the document and Works needs to ask you for a name, the Save As dialog box appears, as in Figure 3.11.

The file name The File Name line shows the default file name (word1). This is the temporary name that Works assigns to the document until you give it a permanent name. The name is highlighted so you can type in a new name from the keyboard without having to move to the File Name text box.

CHAPTER 3   Introducing the Word Processor

FIGURE 3.11
The Save As dialog box. This dialog box appears when you save a document for the first time.

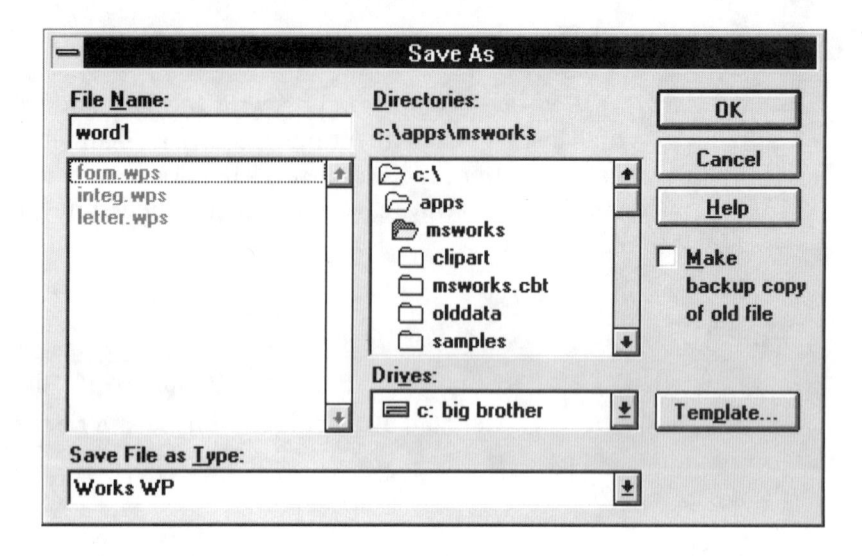

[Save As dialog box showing:
- File Name: word1
- File list: form.wps, integ.wps, letter.wps
- Directories: c:\apps\msworks
- Directory tree: c:\, apps, msworks, clipart, msworks.cbt, olddata, samples
- Drives: c: big brother
- Save File as Type: Works WP
- Buttons: OK, Cancel, Help, Template...
- Checkbox: Make backup copy of old file]

Disk drive and directory Before you provide a name, however, you want to be sure that you are going to store the file on the correct disk drive and correct directory. Notice, below the word *Directories*, the current directory name:

`c:\msworks`

This means that the file will be saved to the msworks directory on the C drive unless you switch to another directory or drive.

The Save File as Type box The Save File as Type box is automatically set to Works WP, since Works knows you're saving a word-processing file. Don't alter this setting unless you want to create a file that other word processors or other types of PC programs can read.

> **Note** With Works, you can create files for use with other word-processing programs and trade your Works files with colleagues and friends who don't use Works. See Chapter 12 and Appendix B for information.

In short, to save your work:

1. Choose File ➤ Save.
2. Adjust the Drive and Directory setting if necessary. (Usually this is not necessary.)
3. Move back to the File Name section (if necessary).
4. Type in the file name. For our example letter, enter the name **LETTER1** and press ↵. Your disk drive will make some noise and the file will be saved.

You are returned to the document. Notice that the title bar now says LETTER1.WPS.

Printing a Document

Assuming you have a printer connected to your PC, you can print the letter. However, before you print a document, consider *previewing* it first:

1. Choose File ➤ Print Preview to see your document before it is printed. Your screen should look like Figure 3.12.

By previewing the document, you won't have waste paper printing out bogus copies. If your document doesn't look right, click on Cancel, make corrections, and try again.

To actually print the document:

2. Click on the Print button on the Preview screen, or click on Cancel and choose File ➤ Print from the menu bar. In either case you'll see the Print dialog box shown in Figure 3.13.
3. Tell Works how many copies of the document you want to print. Since you only want to print one and there is already a 1 in the Number of Copies box, you're okay. If you wanted to print more than one, you would enter a number for how many copies you want to print.

CHAPTER 3 — Introducing the Word Processor

FIGURE 3.12
Previewing a document before you print it is a great way to see if you've made errors or omissions.

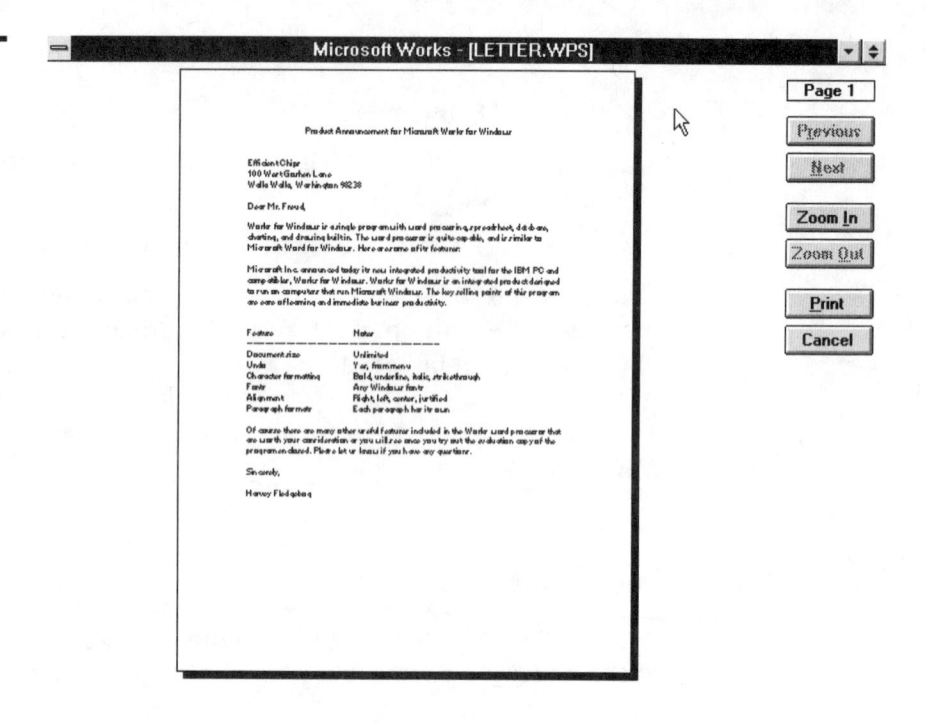

4. Tell Works which pages you want to print:

   All   Tells Works to print all the pages in the document.

   Pages   Lets you indicate which pages you want printed.

   All is selected by default. Your document is only one page long, so you can let this setting stand. But if you had a longer document, you could select Pages, click in the From box and enter the first page to be printed, and click in the To box and enter the last page to be printed.

5. Make sure your printer is on-line and check to see that it is connected to your computer.

6. Press ↵ or click on OK. Your letter should begin printing.

Printing a Document

FIGURE 3.13
The Print dialog box. This is where you tell Works how many copies you want printed and how much of the document to print.

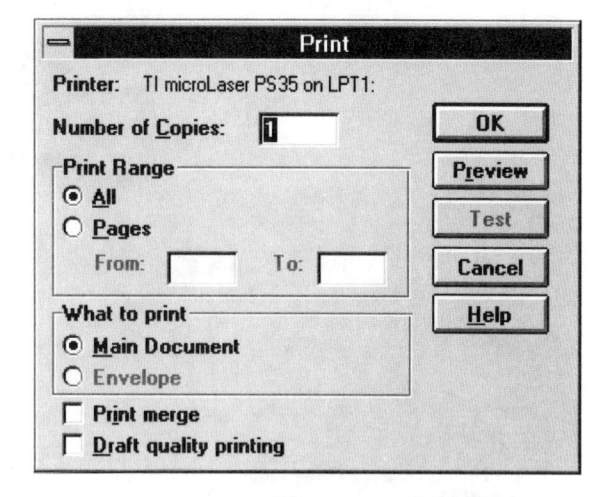

> **Note** *On-line* means the printer has been turned on and is ready to receive data sent to it by your computer. Most printers have a switch for putting the printer on-line. You take a printer off-line to advance the paper feed, change the paper, or make other adjustments.

Chapter 4 covers advanced features of the word processor, such as paragraph and character formats, fonts, undoing errors, checking spelling, and using the thesaurus.

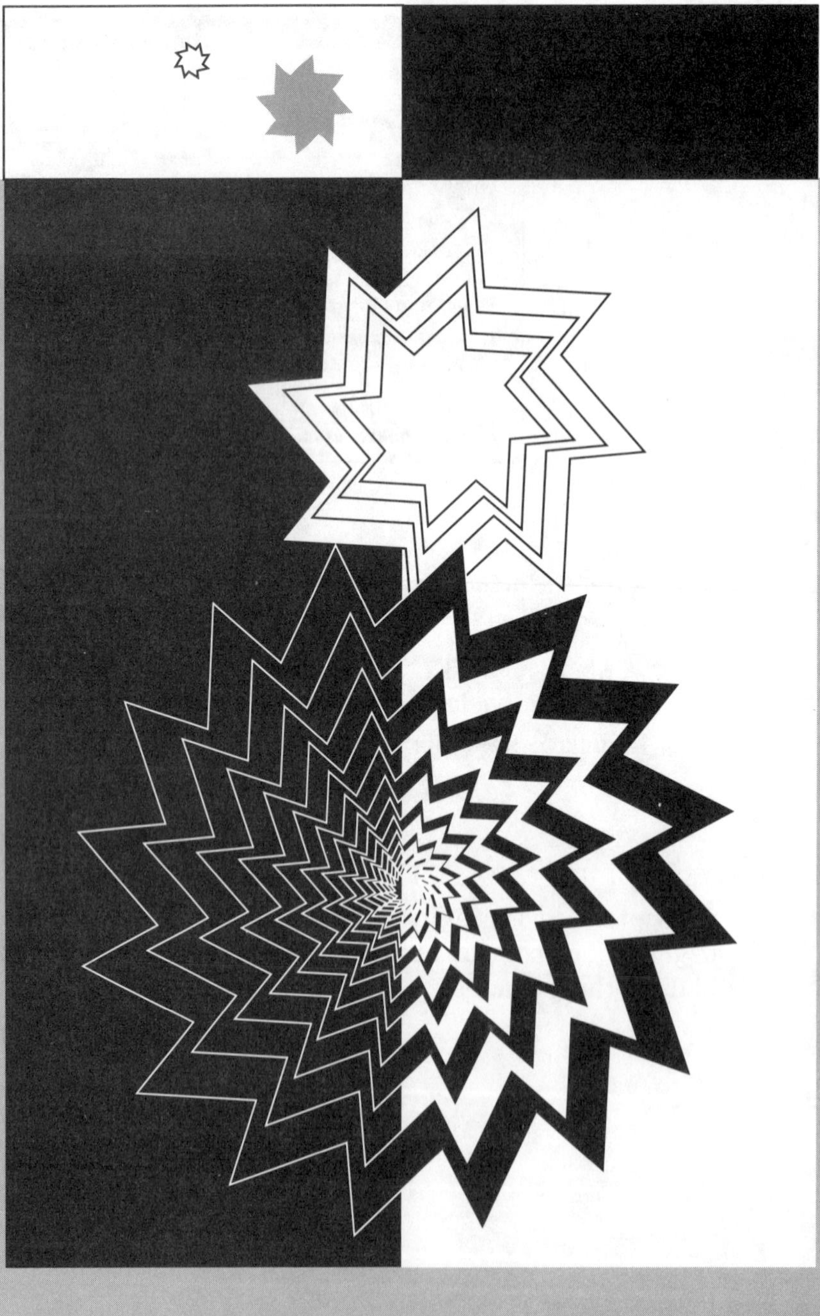

CHAPTER 4

Advanced Word Processing Skills

Fast Track

In Works, the paragraph is the essential formatting element.   **108**

    Each paragraph has its own settings, such as indents, tabs, and line spacing, and you can set these parameters for individual paragraphs. A "paragraph" is everything that comes before a press of the ↵ key, be it a blank space, empty line, single word, or sentence.

To align text on the margin,   **111**

    place the cursor in the paragraph or, to align several paragraphs at once, select at least a portion of several paragraphs. Next, click on the appropriate alignment button—Left, Right, Center—in the toolbar.

To indent a paragraph,   **112**

    place the cursor on the paragraph and drag a marker on the ruler. There are three markers, one for the first line indent, left indent, and right indent.

To make text single- or double-spaced,   **116**

    select the text whose spacing you want to change and choose Format ➤ Paragraph. Select the Breaks and Spacing tab, and enter a number (such as 1 or 2) in the Between Lines box in the Spacing area.

To change the font and style of text,   **124**

    select the text and click on the Font section of the toolbar. Scroll the list and click on the font you want to assign to the selected text, and then click on the Size section and change the size. You can click on the B, U, or I buttons to get bold, underline, or italics for the selected text if you want to.

To set tab stops in a document, **132**

> select the paragraphs where you want the new tabs to be in effect and click in the ruler at the location where you want a tab added. A little tab marker appears on the ruler and the text realigns itself. You can drag a marker to adjust tab locations.

To undo a mistake you have made, **137**

> choose Edit ➤ Undo.

To search for a word or phrase in a document, **139**

> choose Select ➤ Find and enter the text you're looking for. Set the other options if necessary and click OK.

To correct spelling errors in a document, **142**

> move to the top of the document and click on the ABC✓ button in the toolbar. A dialog box appears whenever Works finds a misspelling. Click on Ignore if you want the word left as-is and continue to the next misspelling, enter the correct spelling, or click on Suggest to find a correct spelling. Then click on Change.

To add clip art to your document, **152**

> place the insertion point where you want the clip art to go and select Insert ➤ ClipArt. Choose a category, highlight the clip art you want, and click OK.

IN CHAPTER 3 YOU LEARNED word processing basics. In this chapter you will expand on those skills and learn how to

- Format paragraphs and copy formats between paragraphs
- Format characters for bold, italic, and other typefaces
- Change type size and typeface
- Set the tab stops
- Use the Undo command
- Use the automatic find and replace feature
- Use the spell checker and thesaurus
- Split the window so you can see two parts of a document at once
- Copy text between documents
- Add headers, footers, and page numbers
- Add illustrations to a document

In this chapter you will use the LETTER.WPS file you created in Chapter 3. Open this file and put it on your screen in the active window.

The Importance of Paragraphs to Formatting

Formatting means to control the look of text. When it comes to formatting in Works, paragraphs are the most essential element. In Works, a *paragraph* is any text terminated by a carriage return—that is, a press of the ↵

key. So even a single letter, word, or line is treated as a paragraph if you press ↵ after it. In Works, each paragraph is a separate entity with its own formatting information. Formatting information is stored in the document along with each paragraph.

The default paragraph format When you created the LETTER.WPS file, you used Works' default paragraph format. In the default format

- The first line is not indented
- Paragraphs are separated from one another by blank lines
- The right margin is *ragged* (crooked) instead of *justified* (straight)

For most documents, the default format works fine.

In the example letter, Works applied the default format for you, carrying it from one paragraph to the next as you typed. You can change formats simply by altering the settings in a dialog box and typing away. Works will format everything you type according to the settings you made in the dialog box.

Changing Formats in a Document

This part of the chapter explains how to change formats in a document. You'll learn how to see what the format is for a paragraph, how to align and indent text, how to make indents with the ruler, how to "nest" paragraphs and create hanging paragraphs, and how to place a border around text.

Finding Out What the Paragraph Format Is

To see what the settings for a paragraph are and change them if necessary:

1. Place the cursor anywhere in the paragraph.
2. Choose Format ➤ Paragraph.

CHAPTER 4 — Advanced Word Processing Skills

For example, to see what the settings for the first paragraph in the LETTER.WPS document are:

1. Move the cursor to the top line of the document, the line you centered in Chapter 3.
2. Choose Indents and Alignment at the top of the dialog box. Now the Paragraph dialog box looks like Figure 4.1.

The Paragraph dialog box always shows the formats of the paragraph the cursor is in. In our case, the cursor is in the first line of the document, so the Center button in the Alignment option box is selected.

Tip
On the toolbar, notice that the Center button is pressed in. Another way to tell the format of a paragraph is to look at the toolbar. Seeing which buttons are pressed shows you how the paragraph is formatted.

FIGURE 4.1
The Paragraph dialog box with the Indents and Alignment tab selected

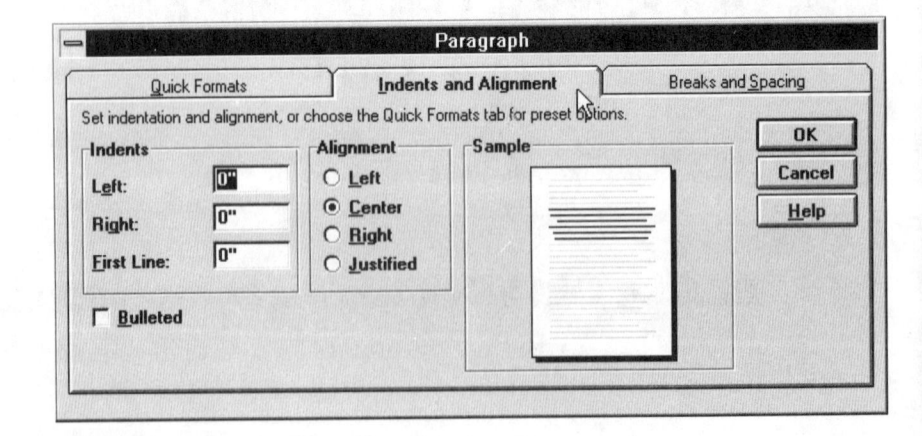

Tip — Look at the Sample box in the Paragraph dialog box to see a representation of what the formats you are dealing with will look like on the printed page.

Aligning Text on the Margins

Which Alignment button you select on the Indents and Alignment tab of the Paragraph dialog box determines how the paragraph is aligned. (To view this tab if you don't have it in front of you, select Format ➤ Paragraph and click the Indents and Alignment tab). You have four options:

BUTTON	ALIGNMENT
Left	Aligns the text along the left margin (the default alignment). Text on the right margin is ragged, or crooked.
Center	Centers text in the middle of the page.
Right	Aligns the text along the right margin. Text on the left margin is ragged. This is not a standard way to align text but it can be used to create interesting effects.
Justified	Aligns text on both the left and right margin. This is the standard for published books.

Note — You can choose Left, Center, or Right alignment with buttons on the toolbar, but if you want Justified alignment you must select it from the Paragraph dialog box.

CHAPTER 4 — Advanced Word Processing Skills

Shortcut keys for aligning text Following are some shortcut keys you can use to align text. Select the paragraph you want to align before pressing these keys:

KEYS	ACTION
Ctrl+E	Centers the text
Ctrl+L	Left-aligns the text
Ctrl+R	Right-aligns the text
Ctrl+J	Full-justifies the text
Ctrl+Q	Returns the text to normal paragraph specifications

Tip Pressing Ctrl+Q returns the text you selected to Works' default paragraph formatting specifications. Pressing Ctrl+Q with the cursor in a paragraph is an easy way to clear all the settings you've made and start from scratch.

Indenting Text

Works gives you several ways to indent text. You can use the Paragraph dialog box or the ruler. The ruler gives you the advantage of seeing on screen what your indent format look like. But with the dialog box you can get more exact settings. This part of the chapter explains how to

- Indent text by way of the Paragraph dialog box
- Indent text with the ruler
- Create nested indents
- Create hanging indents

The Paragraph Dialog Box for Indenting Text

Aside from the Alignment options on the Indents and Alignment tab (see Figure 4.1), there are three Indent settings—Left, Right, and First Line. (To view this tab if you don't have it in front of you, select Format ➤ Paragraph and click the Indents and Alignment tab.) The three settings require you to type in numbers, inches in this case.

Left A *left indent* is one made from the left margin. This indent refers, not to the first line of the paragraph, but to the entire thing (the First Line option is for indenting the first line). The number entered in the Left indent box determines how far (in inches, centimeters, or points) from the left margin the paragraph will be when you print it.

> **Tip** When you change the margin setting, you also change the indent, because the indent settings are relative to the margin.

Right The *right indent* determines how far from the right margin the paragraph will be when you print it.

First Line The First Line setting controls how far the first line is indented in the paragraph. The number you enter here is relative to the Left indent setting. For example, a setting of .5 indents the first line a half-inch in from the Left indent setting.

By entering a number in this box, you can indent the first line of the paragraphs in your document without having to press the Tab key.

113

CHAPTER 4 Advanced Word Processing Skills

> **Tip** Setting the First Line indent to a negative number such as –.3 creates a hanging indent, also called an outdent—a first line that hangs out in the margin. See "Hanging Indents" later in this chapter.

Changing Indents with the Ruler

The ruler is the quickest way to indent selected text or new text you are about enter from the keyboard. Notice the markings on the ruler:

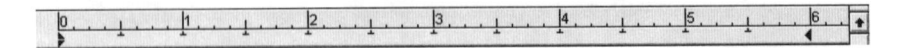

To quickly change paragraph indentation without having to fill in the dialog box and calculate distances in your head, just grab one of the triangular markers and drag it:

- ◆ The top-most triangle on the left controls the first-line indentation.
- ◆ The bottom triangle on the left controls the left margin indentation.
- ◆ The triangle on the right controls the right margin indentation.

When you release the mouse button, the paragraph will reposition itself.

> **Note** If your ruler isn't showing, turn it on by choosing View ➤ Ruler.

Nested Indents

In reports and books, quotes usually appear in nested paragraphs. A *nested paragraph* is indented from both the left and right margins. Works provides an easy way to create nested paragraphs:

1. Place the cursor in the paragraph. In our case, place it in the first main paragraph.
2. Press Ctrl+N.

The left margin moves to the next default tab stop, which in our case is five spaces in. The paragraph reformats itself to fit into the narrower margins. Notice that the left indent and first line indent markers in the ruler have moved.

3. Press Ctrl+N again. The left margin moves in five spaces again.
4. Press Ctrl+M. Now the margin moves five spaces back to the left.
5. Press Ctrl+M again to return the paragraph to its original left margin.

Hanging Indents

A *hanging indent* occurs when the first line of a paragraph is *outdented* instead of indented. An outdented line hangs out farther to the left than the rest of the paragraph does. Hanging indents serve to accent the first line of a paragraph. Hanging indents are useful for formatting numbered lists to make the numbers stand off to the left.

There are three ways to format outdents:

- You can set the first line indent to a negative number in the Indents and Alignment tab of the Paragraph dialog box. For this to work, there must be a Left indent as well. For example, you could set the Left indent to 1" and the First Line indent to −.5".
- You can use a preset "Quick Format" for hanging indents. Select Format ➤ Paragraph, click the Quick Format tab, click Hanging indent in the Style area, and click OK.
- You can press Ctrl+H.

CHAPTER 4 — Advanced Word Processing Skills

Let's try creating a hanging indent in our sample letter:

1. Put the cursor on the first main paragraph.
2. Press Ctrl+Q to return the paragraph to its "normal" unadulterated state.
3. Press Ctrl+H. The first line stays as it was, but all other lines in the paragraph move to the first tab stop.

Each time you press Ctrl+H, the paragraph moves to the right by one tab stop. However, the first line doesn't move.

4. Press Ctrl+G to reverse the outdent.

Controlling the Space between Lines and Paragraphs

To control how much space to put between the lines in your documents, you use the Breaks and Spacing tab in the Paragraph dialog box. To bring up this dialog box and tab if you have not already done so:

1. Choose Format ➤ Paragraph. The Paragraph dialog box appears.
2. Click the Breaks and Spacing tab on the right side of the dialog box. Now the Paragraph dialog box looks like Figure 4.2.

FIGURE 4.2

The Paragraph dialog box with the Breaks and Spacing tab selected. Use this tab to control the space between lines.

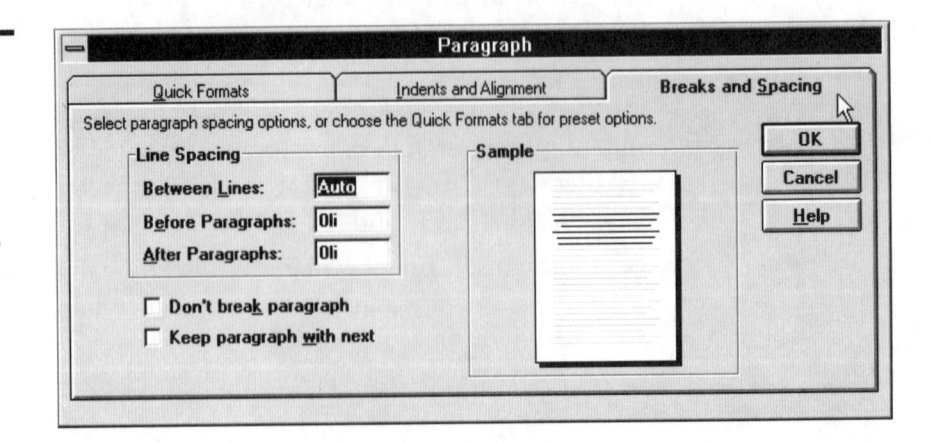

116

Space between Lines

Under Line Spacing there are three options. The first option, Between Lines, is the one for choosing how much space to put between lines of text in a paragraph. The amount of space between lines is called *line spacing*. Ordinarily you use single, double, or triple spacing, so you would enter a 1, 2, or 3 in the Between Lines box. You can also enter 0 or Auto here for *auto spacing*. With auto spacing, each line will be as tall as necessary to accommodate the largest font in the line.

Customized line spacing When you type a number in the Between Lines box, Works assumes you mean lines. However, if you want to enter a line spacing of your own, type a number and include a unit of measurement in inches, centimeters, picas, or points, like so:

2in

1cm

3pi

12pt

Works will convert the number you enter into lines but keep the measurement you entered.

> **Note** *Points* and *picas* are measurements used by typesetters. One point equals $1/72$ inch. One pica equals twelve points, or approximately $1/6$ inch.

> **Note** Some printers aren't capable of spacing lines in increments smaller than one line or more exact than a single line. In other words, some printers cannot handle spacings of .8 or 1.5 lines. If you enter an increment and find that the lines in your document are printing on top of one another, stick to whole numbers (1, 2, 3, and so on).

Shortcut keys for line spacing Here are some shortcut keys for controlling line spacing. Select the text before pressing these keys:

KEY	ACTION
Ctrl+2	Double-space
Ctrl+1	Single-space
Ctrl+5	1½-space

The 1½-space setting will look the same as double spacing on some systems but will print differently if your printer is capable of fractional line spacing.

Space Before and After Paragraphs

The Before Paragraphs and After Paragraphs boxes on the Breaks and Spacing tab are for controlling the amount of lines between paragraphs. Typically, the amount of space is in lines, but you can use other the units of measurement as explained above.

When you press ↵ to end a paragraph, Works moves the cursor to the next line. But by entering, for example, 1.5 in the Before Paragraphs box, you can make Works move down one and a half lines. Entering a number in the After Paragraphs box has the same effect, only it adds space at the end of the paragraph.

Controlling How Paragraphs Break across Pages

When a paragraph starts on one page and ends on the next, it *breaks* across the page. The Breaks and Spacing tab has two check boxes for keeping paragraphs from breaking:

- Check the Don't break paragraph box to keep a paragraph from being printed across two pages. Works will move the entire paragraph to the second page to keep the break from occurring.

- Check the Keep paragraph with next option to "glue" several paragraphs together to keep them from breaking. Before you can check this option, you must select the paragraphs first.

Tip Use the Keep paragraph with next check box to keep tables and lists of items from breaking across pages.

Using Works' Preset "Quick" Formats

The start of this chapter mentioned works default paragraph format, the so-called Normal format. Works offers another preset format with single-spaced text and a 1/2-inch first line indent. Try Works' "Quick" format on the first two paragraphs of our sample letter:

1. Select the first two paragraphs of the letter. (Actually, you only have to select a portion of each paragraph in order to change the format.)
2. Choose Format ➤ Paragraph.
3. Click the Quick Formats tab, the one on the left.
4. Click 1st line indent in the Style box.
5. Click OK or press ↵. The paragraphs reformat.

CHAPTER 4 Advanced Word Processing Skills

6. Deselect the paragraphs by pressing an arrow key or clicking outside the highlighted are with the mouse.

Your screen should look like Figure 4.3, with the first line of each paragraph indented.

Unfortunately, when you added the indent, you added it not only to the paragraphs but to the blank line between the paragraphs. Extra ↵ key presses can cause difficulties later on, because each time you press ↵ you are adding a paragraph as well as a blank line, and each format you apply to paragraphs will be applied to blank lines as well. The next section explains how to control the space between paragraphs without using extra ↵ key presses.

FIGURE 4.3
Applying a "Quick" format to the first line indent of the letter

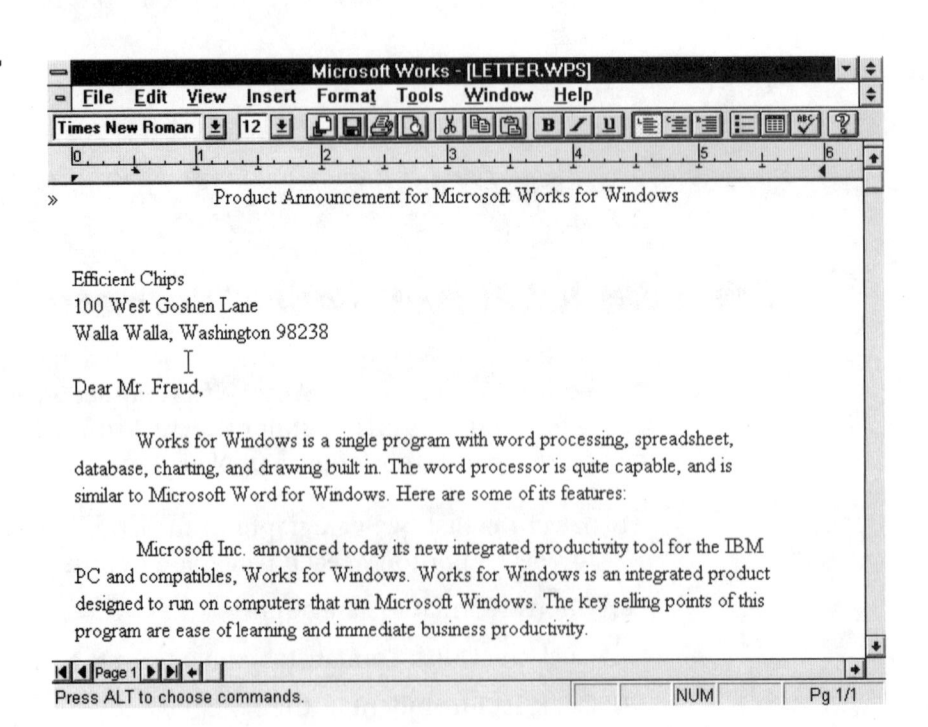

Warning If you plan to reformat paragraphs or change the spacing between them later on, don't press ↵ to enter a blank line between paragraphs. Use the Space After or Space Before settings in the Breaks and Spacing tab of the Paragraph dialog box instead.

Invisible Characters for Seeing How a Page Is Formatted

Works has a special feature so you can tell whether a blank line between paragraphs was put there by a press of the ↵ key or with the Before Paragraph or After Paragraph settings in the Paragraph dialog box. To make this distinction, you can chose the Show All Characters command on the View menu and see the invisible characters. You enter *invisible characters* whenever you press ↵ and the spacebar to enter a blank line.

Invisible characters With the invisible characters on screen, you can tell what's causing what and add or delete the characters as necessary. Figure 4.4 shows the invisible characters on screen:

¶   The paragraph symbol, which shows where paragraphs end.

·   The dot, which shows exactly where blanks spaces are.

→   The tab, which you enter when you press the tab key.

To display the invisible characters:

1. Choose View ➤ All Characters.
2. Notice the extra paragraph mark between the two main paragraphs. Delete this extra paragraph mark as you would a single letter by moving the cursor to the mark and pressing Del.

CHAPTER 4   Advanced Word Processing Skills

FIGURE 4.4
With the invisible characters on display, you can tell precisely where paragraphs break and where blank lines are.

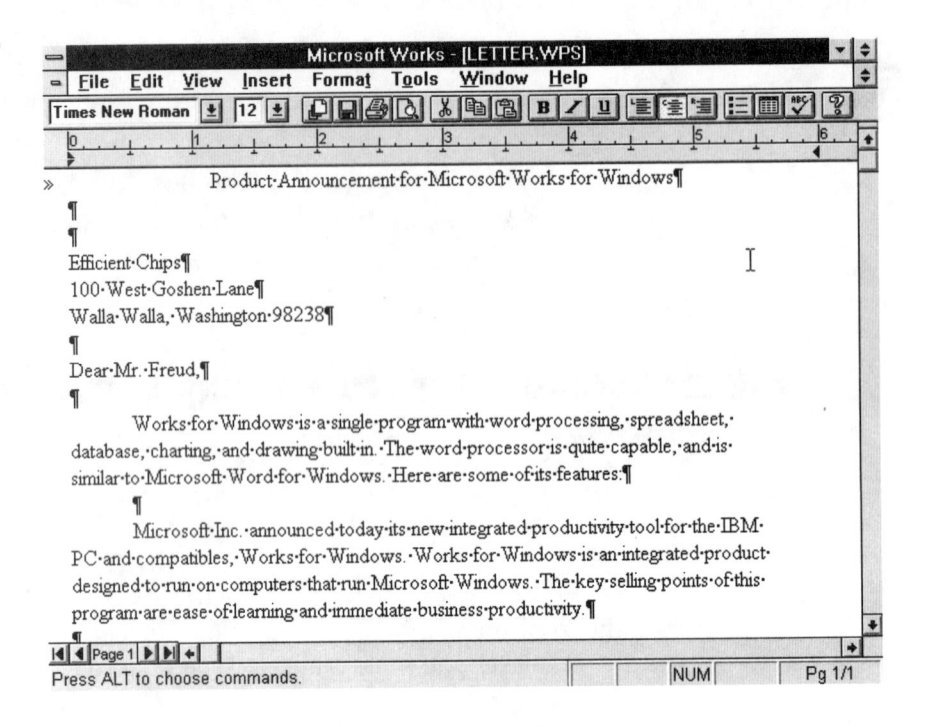

```
┌─────────────────── Microsoft Works - [LETTER.WPS] ──────────────┐
│  File  Edit  View  Insert  Format  Tools  Window  Help          │
├─────────────────────────────────────────────────────────────────┤
│ Times New Roman  12                                             │
├─────────────────────────────────────────────────────────────────┤
│                  Product·Announcement·for·Microsoft·Works·for·Windows¶
│  ¶
│  ¶
│  Efficient·Chips¶
│  100·West·Goshen·Lane¶
│  Walla·Walla,·Washington·98238¶
│  ¶
│  Dear·Mr.·Freud,¶
│      ¶
│           Works·for·Windows·is·a·single·program·with·word·processing,·spreadsheet,·
│      database,·charting,·and·drawing·built·in.·The·word·processor·is·quite·capable,·and·is·
│      similar·to·Microsoft·Word·for·Windows.·Here·are·some·of·its·features:¶
│           ¶
│           Microsoft·Inc.·announced·today·its·new·integrated·productivity·tool·for·the·IBM·
│      PC·and·compatibles,·Works·for·Windows.·Works·for·Windows·is·an·integrated·product·
│      designed·to·run·on·computers·that·run·Microsoft·Windows.·The·key·selling·points·of·this·
│      program·are·ease·of·learning·and·immediate·business·productivity.¶
│      ¶
│  Page 1
│ Press ALT to choose commands.                    NUM      Pg 1/1
└─────────────────────────────────────────────────────────────────┘
```

The paragraph mark is deleted and the extra line disappears, leaving the paragraphs formatted in normal letter style.

3. Choose View ➤ All Characters again to hide the invisible characters.

Placing a Border around Text

Works' borders feature lets you put lines called *borders* around paragraphs. You could use this feature, for example, to place a line above or below a page of text or draw a box around important text in a document.

To demonstrate how borders work, let's put a border around the Features section of our letter:

1. Select the list of features.
2. Choose Format ➤ Border. The Border dialog box appears, as shown in Figure 4.5.

FIGURE 4.5
The Border dialog box

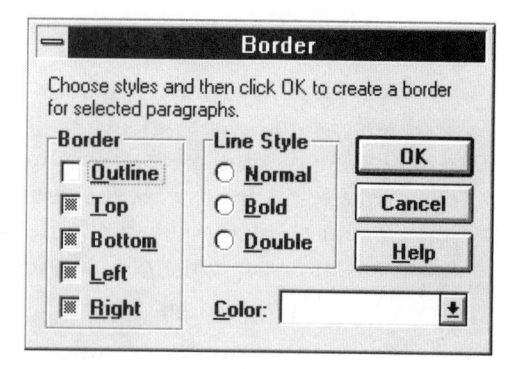

3. From the Border area, choose Outline.
4. Choose Bold from the Line Style area.
5. Click OK. Now the Feature list appears in a box.
6. Select Format ➤ Border again and uncheck all the options in the Border area (click each one twice until it's unchecked).
7. Click OK.

Using the Border dialog box is a simple way to highlight specific text or separate it from surrounding text.

Tip

When a bordered paragraph breaks over two pages, the border appears on each page. Works does not make compensations for borders that get broken. To keep a paragraph from breaking across two pages, bring up the Breaks and Spacing tab in the Paragraph dialog box and check the Don't break paragraph check box. See "Controlling the Space between Lines and Paragraphs" earlier in this chapter.

CHAPTER 4   **Advanced Word Processing Skills**

Working with Type Sizes, Type Styles, and Fonts

Works lets you change the look of type by giving it a different *style*. Bold text, underlined text, and italic text are all examples of type styles. You can also change the size of letters or their appearance by choosing a different font. A *font* is typeface such as Courier or Times Roman. Depending on your printer, you can choose from a variety of fonts and tailor the look of your documents to your audience and your liking.

You can change the formatting of individual letters, blocks of text, or an entire document. Works formats the characters in a standard (default) font, style, and line position, but you can change fonts and styles to your liking. All such changes are accomplished by way of the Font and Style dialog box.

This part of the chapter explains

- Changing the style of characters to bold, underline, and other styles
- Changing character size for headlines and other purposes
- Using different character fonts

Changing Character Styles

Changing the style of characters is useful when you want to emphasize text or a specific word. You can change character styles in three ways

- With the toolbar
- With the Font and Style dialog box (bring up this box by selecting Format ➤ Font and Style)
- With shortcut keys

How to apply a new style   You can apply styles to existing text by selecting it and choosing a new style, and you can apply styles to text you haven't entered yet by choosing the style before you start typing.

Styles you can use Here are the styles you can use in your documents along with their shortcut keys:

STYLE	SHORTCUT KEY	EXAMPLE
Bold	Ctrl+B	**Use Bold Text in Headlines!**
Italic	Ctrl+I	*Use italics for emphasis and with foreign words.*
Underline	Ctrl+U	<u>Use underline for emphasis too.</u>
Strikethrough	Ctrl+S	~~Use strikethrough to show where text is to be striken from a document.~~
Superscript	Ctrl+Shift+=	Superscript (raised letters and numbers) is used often in math and science: πr^2.
Subscript	Ctrl+=	Subscript (lowered letters and numbers) is also used in math and science: $x - y_2 = z$.

Works provides two more shortcut keys for use with character styles:

◆ Press Ctrl+spacebar to remove all styles.

◆ Press Shift+F7 to apply your last formatting command to the text you just selected. The new text will be formatted just as the previous text was. This is an easy way to make multiple changes with a single keystroke.

Changing Fonts and Type Sizes

You can change fonts and type sizes with the Font and Style dialog box or with the toolbar. Either way, you begin by selecting the text you want to change or, if you haven't entered the text yet, going to the place in your document where you want to enter text in a new font or type size.

CHAPTER 4   Advanced Word Processing Skills

> **Tip**   Be cautious when using fonts. Amateur designers usually use far too many different fonts and styles. Most documents require no more than two font families, such as Times and Helvetica. Bold and italic should be used meaningfully, which often means they should be used sparingly. Notice that this book has a font for headings and another for text, and that italics and bold are used occasionally, not often. You don't want to overtax or confuse the reader.

Using the Font and Style dialog box   To change fonts or type sizes with the dialog box:

1. Select the text or move the cursor where you want to enter new text.
2. Choose Format ➤ Font and Style to open the Font and Style dialog box.
3. Make font and type size selections in the dialog box.
4. Click OK.

Using the toolbar   If the toolbar is showing, making font and size changes is even easier: You just select some text, click on the drop-down list in the Font area in the toolbar, and select the font. Here Times New Roman is being selected:

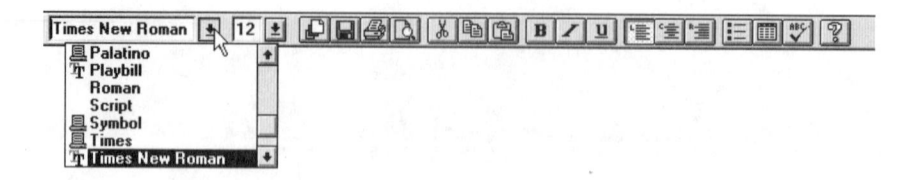

126

Working with Type Sizes, Type Styles, and Fonts

Tip To quickly move to the Font area of the toolbar without using the mouse, type Ctrl+F.

Change the font size in the same manner—by clicking on the type size drop-down list and either clicking on a size or entering a new one in the text box. Here 12-point type is being selected:

Warning The size you enter in the font box may not print correctly if you printer doesn't support a font of that size.

Measuring type in points Works measures character sizes in points. In most documents, characters range in size from 9 to 14 points. A point equals 1/72 of an inch, so 72-point type is one inch high. The type in the book you're reading is 10-point type. Headlines can be as high as 60 points. Here are some examples of actual point sizes:

12 point

18 point

24 point

60 point

127

How You Can Tell What Character Formats You're Using

Works shows you character formats on the screen. However, some of the subtler nuances will escape you from time to time, you have to print a document before you can really see what it looks like and, moreover, sometimes you forget what font size and name you've given characters.

To see what formats you've given characters, use one of these techniques:

♦ Place the cursor on a letter or text in question, open the Font and Style dialog box, and look at the settings. The dialog box will show you a complete list of settings, including font style and type size.

♦ Look at the toolbar. It will tell you the setting for the text that the cursor is on.

> **Tip** With some fonts it's difficult to see if the text is in bold. Just click on the text in question and look at the toolbar. The Bold button will be pressed in if the text is bold.

Trying Out Some Formatting Changes

Now, using the letter, let's practice changing character formats:

1. Select the top line of the letter.
2. Click the B button in the toolbar or press Ctrl+B. The letters on screen change to boldface.
3. Select the top line of the table (the words *Feature* and *Notes*).
4. Choose Format ➤ Font and Style. The Font and Style dialog box appears, as in Figure 4.6 (yours may look a little different).
5. Press Alt+B or click on the Bold box to turn on the Bold style.
6. Press Alt+I or click on the Italic box to turn on the Italic style.

Working with Type Sizes, Type Styles, and Fonts

FIGURE 4.6
The Font and Style dialog box

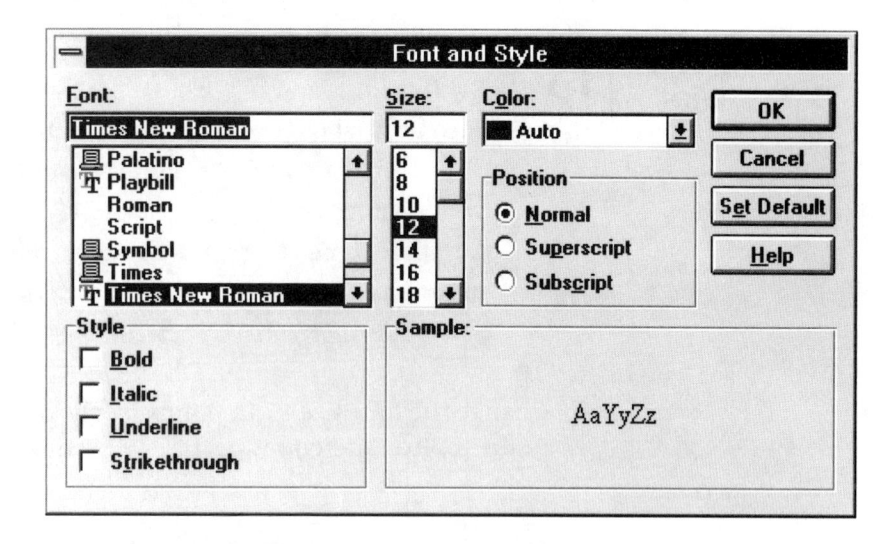

> **Note** Notice that the Normal, Superscript, and Subscript boxes are option buttons. Only one can be selected at a time.

7. Press ↵ or click on OK. The result appears immediately.

Feature Notes

Now try changing the font and font size. Typically, headings, headlines, titles, legends, and so on require font changes. Let's change the heading of the letter.

1. Select the top line of the letter, the one that begins "Product Announcement...."

2. Click on the ↓ in the toolbar's Font area—the area that lists typeface names—and select another font. Use Arial if you have it on your system. I've chosen AvantGarde.

129

CHAPTER 4 — Advanced Word Processing Skills

> **Tip**
>
> For headings and other large text, choose a *sans serif* font such as Arial or Univers. Sans serif (the term means "without stroke" in French) fonts do not have short lines at the upper and lower ends. They are plainer and more straightforward. Compare Times Roman, a *serif* font, and Arial to see the difference between serif and sans serif fonts.

3. Change the font size to 14 points by clicking on the ↓ in the Size list in the toolbar and choosing 14. Notice how the headline changes:

> Product Announcement for Microsoft Works for Windows

Reusing Paragraph and Character Formats in a Document

Suppose you are working on a document that has several types of character and paragraph formats. For example, your document has indented quotations, tabular columns, and paragraphs formatted a particular way. Rather than reentering these formats each time you need them, you can copy them from elsewhere in your document and reuse them.

Copying a format to a new place in a document is very similar to copying and moving text. The general steps are as follows:

1. Place the cursor in the text where the formatting specifications you want to copy are located.

2. Choose Edit ➤ Copy.

3. Place the cursor in the paragraph or word you want to format.

Reusing Paragraph and Character Formats in a Document

   4. Choose Edit ➤ Paste Special.

   5. Choose an option in a dialog box and click OK.

To see how the Paste Special command works, let's copy the hanging indent format you assigned to the first paragraph to the last paragraph:

   1. Place the cursor anywhere in the first paragraph.

The first paragraph should have a hanging indent of one-half inch. If it doesn't, follow the instructions in "Hanging Indents" under "Indenting Text with the Dialog Box and Ruler" earlier in this chapter.

   2. Choose Edit ➤ Copy. Nothing appears to happen, but the formatting characteristics of the paragraph (or selection if you had made one) are copied to the Clipboard.

   3. Move the cursor anywhere in the last paragraph.

   4. Choose Edit ➤ Paste Special. The Paste Special dialog box appears:

```
┌─────────────────────────────┐
│       Paste Special         │
│                    ┌──────┐ │
│                    │  OK  │ │
│  ○ Character Style └──────┘ │
│                    ┌──────┐ │
│  ◉ Paragraph Format│Cancel│ │
│                    └──────┘ │
│                    ┌──────┐ │
│                    │ Help │ │
│                    └──────┘ │
└─────────────────────────────┘
```

   5. The dialog box asks which characteristic of the format you want to copy to the new cursor location. There are two choices:

   ◆ Character Style copies the character format to the target text.

   ◆ Paragraph Format copies the paragraph format, including tab settings, to the target text (tabs are covered in the next section of this chapter).

   6. We want to copy paragraph formats, so select the Paragraph Format option and press ↵ or click on OK. The paragraph now has a hanging indent.

131

CHAPTER 4 Advanced Word Processing Skills

Tip You can copy a format to more than one paragraph (a table is considered more than one paragraph). To do so, select at least part of all the paragraphs you want to copy the format to (the paragraphs must run together). When you click OK in the Paste Special dialog box, the format will be applied to all the paragraphs.

Tip If you have complex formats you use often, make a "master" document with all your formats on it. Then, when you need to enter a format, go to your master document, copy the format you want, switch to the original document, and place the format copy there with the Paste Special command.

Working with Tabs

You can vary the tab settings to suit your needs. By default, tabs are set every half inch, but you can change that. You can also use different types of tabs—left, center, right, and decimal. When you entered the table in our example letter, you had to press the Tab key several times to get to the second column. You could have pressed Tab only once if you had set the tabs where you wanted them. When you create complex, multicolumn tables, you will have to set up your own tab stops.

This part of the chapter explains

◆ The different kinds of tabs you can use
◆ How to set tab stops
◆ How to change tab stops

The Different Types of Tabs

As shown in Figure 4.7, Works offers four different types of tabs:

TAB TYPE	DESCRIPTION
Left	Text in the tab column lines up on the left, beginning at the tab.
Center	Text is centered between the beginning of the tab and the beginning of the next tab to the right.
Right	Text in the tab column lines up on the right (as defined by the beginning point of the next tab column to the right)
Decimal	Text flanks the decimal point.

FIGURE 4.7
The four tab types

```
LEFT         CENTER       RIGHT        DECIMAL

January      January      January      January
July         July         July         July
October      October      October      October
123          123          123          123
13,579.1     13,579.1     13,579.1     13,579.1
$45.95       $45.95       $45.95       $45.95
```

Using leaders You can have a *leader* character fill in the blank spaces in a tab column. A leader character appears in text between tab stops. Leaders are useful in tables of contents and other documents that refer to page numbers. In the following example, a period is used as the leader between a chapter title and the page on which the chapter starts:

Chapter 2: Doris Gets Her Oats..24

Creating and Rearranging Tab Stops

To create tab stops, use the Format ➤ Tabs command or the ruler. Once you've created tab stops, you can rearrange them as you wish. To see

CHAPTER 4 — Advanced Word Processing Skills

how tabs work, we will create a small table at the end of our sample letter with right tabs, decimal tabs, and a leader:

```
Pistons      26.................24.90
Rings        45..................3.50
Filters      10..................5.85
Plugs        45..................1.98
```

> **Tip** You can copy tab formats from one place to another with the Paste Special command. To see how this command operates, see "Reusing Paragraph and Character Formats in a Document" earlier in this chapter.

Creating new tabs with the Tabs dialog box To create the table and tab stops:

1. Press Ctrl+End to move to the end of the document.
2. Press ↵ to insert a new paragraph.
3. Choose Format ➤ Tabs. The Tabs dialog box appears, as in Figure 4.8.

Notice that current default tab stops are set to 0.5". We'll set tab stops at 1.5, 2.5, and 3.5 inches.

FIGURE 4.8
Set tab stops with the Tabs dialog box.

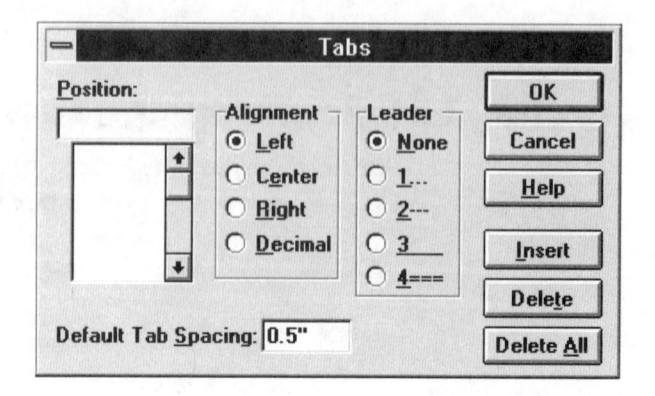

Working with Tabs

4. Type **1.5** into the Position area and click on Insert.
5. Type in **2.5**.
3. Click on the Right option button to make this tab a right-aligned tab.
4. Click on Insert.
5. Repeat the procedure, setting the third stop at 3.5 inches. Choose Decimal as the alignment option, and as the Leader option choose the 1... setting.
6. Click on OK to close the Tabs dialog box.

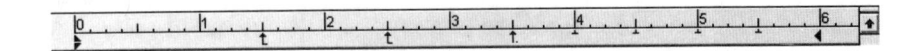

If everything went according to plan, your ruler now looks like this:

Notice the tab markers, and how the decimal tab at 3.5 inches is different from the other two.

Entering the text after you've created tab stops Now you can begin entering text into the columns:

1. Press ↵ to move down a line. Even though you're moving down a line, the formatting we just set for the tabs moves along with the new text.
2. Press Tab once to move to the first tab location.
3. Type **Pistons**.
4. Press Tab to move to the second tab.
5. Type **26**. Notice that the numbers appear to slide sideways to the left as you type. This is because this tab is right-aligned.
6. Press Tab again to get to the next column. A line of periods—the leader you asked for in the Tabs dialog box—fills the gap to the next tab.
7. Press the Backspace key. The periods disappear because they are just filler for the tab. A tab is only one character wide, even though it appears to be longer.
8. Press Tab again. The periods reappear.

9. Enter **24.90** as the price of the pistons.
10. Enter the rest of the table as you see here:

Pistons	26	24.90
Rings	45	3.50
Filters	10	5.85
Plugs	45	1.98

Rearranging Tab Stops

Changing the tabs in a table or list is an easy way to play with the look and size of a layout without having to retype the table, or add or delete spaces between columns. You just select all the lines you want to reformat, bring up the Tabs dialog box, and change the tab settings.

> **Tip** — To see where the tabs are in your document, choose View ➤ All Characters. The arrows that appear in your document mark where tabs are located.

In our example letter, let's move the second tab a bit to the right:

1. Select the whole table.

Remember that selecting one line or putting the cursor on one line of the table does not select it. You have to select the whole table.

2. There are two ways to change tabs once you've selected the table:

   ◆ Choose Format ➤ Tabs, clear the tab at position 2.5 and create a new one at, say, 3.0.

   ◆ Use the ruler. Click on the second tab marker and drag it to the right until it is under the 3, and release the mouse. The column moves over.

> **Tip** You can clear all the tabs (and restore the defaults) by choosing Delete All from the Tabs dialog box.

The ruler is the easiest method. Use it to move the third tab:

3. Move the third tab (the decimal one) under the 4. Your columns are now evenly spaced.

Removing a tab on the ruler To remove a tab on the ruler, simply drag it out of the ruler and into the work area. It will disappear. When you remove a tab stop by dragging it this way, it may be replaced by a default tab stop. This only occurs if there are no manually created tab stops to the right of the one you're removing.

Correcting Mistakes with the Undo Command

The Undo command on the Edit menu is very useful. If you make a mistake whether large or small, you can correct it with the Undo command. To use it, you just choose Edit ➤ Undo. You don't have to position the cursor anywhere first.

> **Warning** The Undo command can only reverse the *last action* you did with your word processor. To use Undo, you must catch your mistake before you do something new, such as entering or deleting other text. Undo can only reverse your last action.

What you can fix with Undo Undo can reverse these actions:

- ◆ Block deletes made with the Cut command on the Edit menu or the Del key on the keyboard. The deleted text will reappear where it was before.

CHAPTER 4 Advanced Word Processing Skills

- Letter or groups of letters you erased by pressing Del or Backspace. Undo will return the last letter or series of letters erased.
- Selected text blocks deleted and replaced by with new text you entered with the keyboard.
- Character and paragraph formatting changes, including font, size, alignment, indents, and spacing adjustments.
- Search and replace procedures done with the Select ➤ Replace command.
- Words replaced by the thesaurus.
- Words replaced by a spelling check.

To see how Undo works:

1. Select some text.
2. Press Del to erase it.
3. Select Edit ➤ Undo. The text is restored.
4. Select Edit ➤ Undo to delete it again.
5. Select Edit ➤ Undo to restore it.

Undo always reverses your last action.

What cannot be undone Not all commands can be undone. Undo will not return a section of text to its original location once it has been pasted to a new location. You can use Undo after cutting text, but once it is pasted, Undo only undoes the pasting—it doesn't return the text to its original location. If you move a block of text and then decide you liked it better where it was, you have to reverse the procedure step by step.

Finding and Replacing Text

Works offers Find and Replace commands so you can look for specific letters, words, or series of words in a document and replace them if necessary. Find and Replace are very useful commands. If you were writing a novel and you decided to change the heroine's name from Addie to

Laurie, you could do it in a snap with Find and Replace. If you were working on a twenty page document and you needed to find the passage discussing penguins, you could find the word *penguin* immediately with the Find command and in so doing arrive at the passage you were looking for.

This part of the chapter explains

- Locating text or a word with the Find command
- Finding and replacing text

The Find Command for Locating a Word or Phrase

To see how the Find command works, here's how to use the Find command to locate the word *data*:

1. Move to a place in the document *above* where you think the word appears. Works only searches in a downward direction (toward the bottom of the document).

2. Choose Edit ➤ Find. The Find dialog box appears:

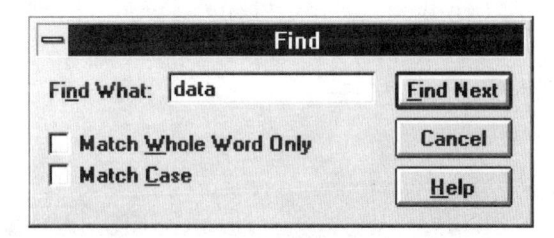

3. Type in **data** and press ↵.

4. The cursor moves to the word *database* because the letters *data* are part of this word.

5. Click Cancel.

6. Choose Edit ➤ Find again. The Find dialog box appears again, with the word *data* already typed in.

Works always remembers the last word you searched for, which makes it easier to repeat a find operation.

7. Press ↵ or click Find Next to find another instance of the word *data* in the document.

A dialog box appears with the message "No match found" and other information. Works is telling you that *data* only appeared once in the document and it could find no other occurrences of the word.

8. Press ↵ or click on OK.

Matching the whole word in searches   To speed up searches, you can look for whole words only. In the exercise above you looked for the word *data* and Works came up with the word *database*. By choosing the Match Whole Word Only box, you can have Works search for whole words only. In our case, Works would find the word *data* if it existed in the document but would skip over the word *database*.

Matching the case of the word in searches   If you click the Match Case check box in the Find dialog box, Works will search for instances of the word that match the *case* of the word in the Find What box. For example, if you had entered the word *Data*, it would not have found *data* because the *D* in *data* is uppercase.

Tip   The Find command starts looking for words at the current cursor location and searches to the end of the document. It doesn't wrap around to the beginning. If you want to search the whole document, press Ctrl+Home before doing the search.

Replacing Text with Find and Replace

To see how to replace a word, let's replace the words *Works for Windows* with *Microsoft Works*:

1. Place the cursor at the beginning of the document again.
2. Choose Edit ➤ Replace. The Replace dialog box appears, as shown in Figure 4.9.

Notice that the settings from the last Find command show up in this box too.

3. Type **Works for Windows** in the Find What box.
4. Press Tab.
5. Type **Microsoft Works** in the Replace With box.
6. Check Match Case so that, for example, the words "works for windows" in the phrase "Pledge window cleaner works for windows" is not replaced. With this box checked, only "Works for Windows" with initial capital letters will be replaced.
7. Click on Find Next or press ↵.

The first occurrence of *Works for Windows* is highlighted on the top line of the screen. Now you have these choices:

Find Next — Skips to the next occurrence without replacing the phrase.

Replace — Replaces the phrase with the Replace With text.

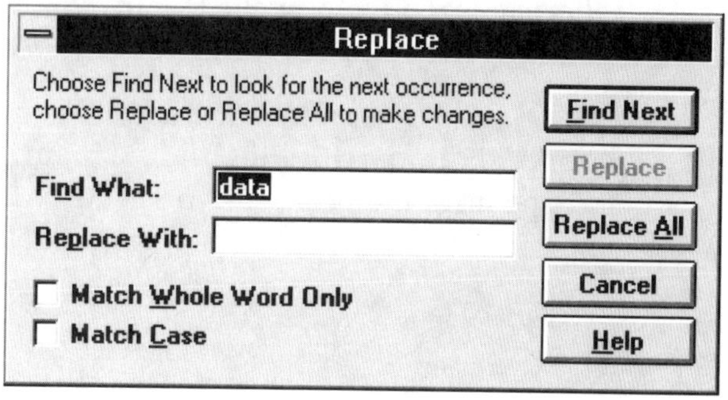

FIGURE 4.9

The Replace dialog box. Enter the text to be replaced in the Find What box and the replacement text in the Replace With box.

Replace All	Replaces all occurrences of the Find What text in the document.
Cancel	Ends the search.
Help	Provides help concerning the Replace dialog box.

8. Click Replace. The change is made quickly by Works.

9. The second occurrence of Works for Windows now gets highlighted. Click Replace again. Repeat this several times.

You are returned to the top of the document when all instances of the Find What text have been found.

10. Click Close.

> **Tip** Find and replace operations can be limited to a selected text block. Just highlight the selection before doing the search and replace.

Checking the Spelling in a Document

Before printing a document, check its spelling. Works' built-in spelling checker will methodically compare your spellings to the entries in its 120,000-word dictionary to see whether each word is spelled correctly. When it comes across a misspelled word, Works will point it out and offer alternative, correctly spelled words to use in its place. At that point you can keep the word as-is or use one of Works' replacement words.

Of course, your documents will likely include words not found in Works' dictionary. Telling the program that these words are really not misspellings is a bore, so Works lets you enter words of your own in its

Checking the Spelling in a Document

dictionary. You can also call upon custom dictionaries when using the spelling checker.

During a spell check, Works also looks for incorrect capitalization, incorrect hyphenation, and accidentally repeated words (such as *the the*), and alerts you to these errors.

To use the spell checker:

1. Move to the top of the document. In our LETTER.WPS document, move to the top of the file and retype the word *for* in the title as *frr*.
2. Make sure the cursor is on *frr*.
3. Choose Tools ➤ Spelling or click on the ABC✓ button in the toolbar. The Spelling dialog box appears, as in Figure 4.10.

FIGURE 4.10

The Spelling dialog box. Click the Change button if you want the word in the Change To box to replace the one highlighted in your document.

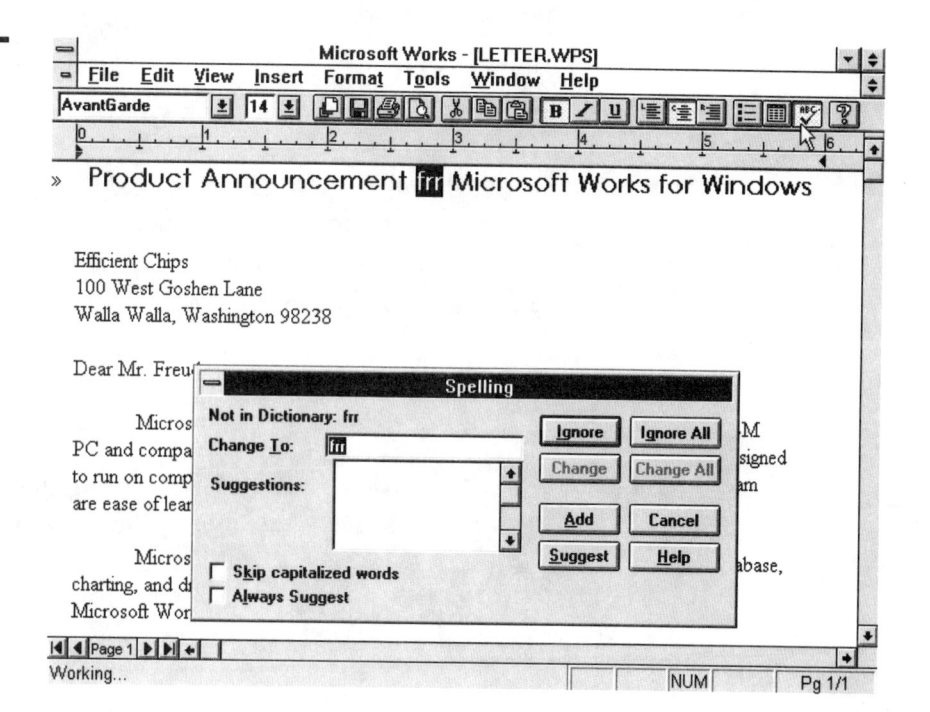

143

The Suggestion button The dialog box reports it has found a misspelled word. The word is highlighted in the document and highlighted as well in the Change To text box so you can begin retyping it if necessary. The Suggestions box is empty. If you want suggestions for correct spellings, click on the Suggest button.

4. It's easier to retype *frr* than look it up by clicking Suggestions, so just type **for** and press ↵.

The spelling checker places the word *for* in your document and checks this new word's spelling before moving on. If you were to type in a misspelling again, it would be caught and reported, just as *frr* was.

> **Tip** If you want Works to always make suggestions for misspellings, select the Always Suggest check box at the bottom of the Spelling dialog box. This way you don't have to click on the Suggest button when you want Works to suggest spelling corrections. However, keeping the Always Suggest check box off speeds up spell checking since Works doesn't have to rummage through as much of its dictionary to find the suggestions.

> **Tip** You can check a single word for accuracy as you're typing along: Select the word and run the checker. Whenever a selection is active, the checker looks only at words in the selection.

Repeated words Now the next suspect word *Microsoft* appears in the Spelling dialog box because it is a repeated word. When you completed the exercise with the Replace command, the word *Microsoft* was accidentally repeated. The Change To box contains nothing, which means the program is suggesting that the repeated word simply be axed, and replaced with nothing.

1. Click on Change to eliminate the repeated word.

If you wanted to ignore the repetition and let the two words stand, you would press the Ignore button. The Ignore button is the default (it has a darker border around it), so pressing ↵ would also ignore the repeated words.

2. The next detected misspelling is *Goshen*, the name of a street. It doesn't make much sense to add this to the dictionary, so click on Ignore to ignore it.
3. Click on Ignore a few times until you get to the end of the document.
4. Click Cancel when you're done.

Skipping capitalized words In a spell check, you can have Works skip the checking of capitalized words. This can make spell checks go faster. To skip capitalized words, place a check in the Skip capitalized words check box.

The Thesaurus for Improving Your Writing

We aren't all geniuses when it comes to vocabulary. More often than not, people rely on the same war-torn turns of expression day in and day out. Luckily, Works offers a built-in *thesaurus* that not only makes looking up synonyms easy, it makes replacing one word with another easy as well. A *synonym* is a word that has the same or nearly the same meaning as another word.

To see how the thesaurus works, let suppose you wanted to use another word in place of *new* in the first paragraph of the sample letter:

1. Click on the word *new*. You don't have to select it—the cursor just has to be somewhere on the word.
2. Select Tools ➤ Thesaurus. The Thesaurus dialog box appears as in Figure 4.11.

CHAPTER 4 Advanced Word Processing Skills

FIGURE 4.11
The Thesaurus dialog box. Here is where you can find synonyms to help with your writing.

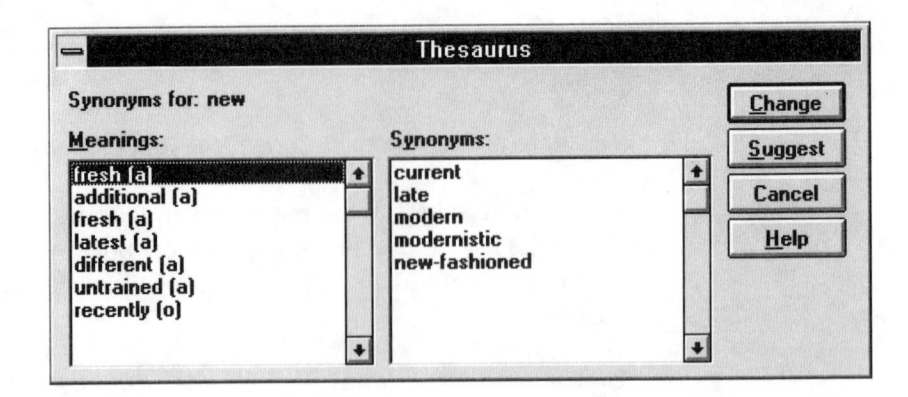

```
Thesaurus
Synonyms for: new
Meanings:                    Synonyms:              Change
fresh (a)                    current                Suggest
additional (a)               late
fresh (a)                    modern                 Cancel
latest (a)                   modernistic
different (a)                new-fashioned          Help
untrained (a)
recently (o)
```

The Meanings box The Meanings box on the left side of the dialog box shows alternative words for *new*. These words have meanings different but similar to new. Notice the letters next to the words indicating what part of speech they are—adjectives, nouns, verbs, or adverbs. When you click on a word in the Meanings box, synonyms for it appear in the Synonyms box on the right side.

The Synonyms box The right side of the Thesaurus dialog box lists synonyms. These words are more closely related to the word in question than the words in the Meanings box are.

Tip If you don't like any of the meanings or synonyms, click on either a meaning word or a synonym and then click on Suggest. A related list of words will appear.

You can replace your word with either a meaning or a synonym.

3. Click on *latest* in the Meanings box to highlight it.

4. Click the Change button.

The dialog box disappears and the word *new* is replaced in your document with the word *latest*.

If no meaning words or synonyms are to your liking, click on the word most similar to the one you want and then click on Suggest. The thesaurus might come up with something useful. The part of speech may not be correct in the context of your document, but you can change that manually in your text.

Splitting the Window to View Different Parts of a Document

Works lets you divide the screen into two horizontal sections so you can, for example, view and edit the first and last page of a large document. The advantage here is that you can move or copy text from one part of a document to another, and you can keep one part a document on screen as a reference while you work on another part.

To split the screen:

1. Choose Window ➤ Split. A line appears across the middle of the window.

2. To determine where the *split line* dividing the windows appears:

    ◆ Press ↑ or ↓ to adjust the split.
    ◆ Drag the split line with the mouse. In Figure 4.12, the pointer is on the split line. Drag the split line down into the work area.

    Press ↵ or release the mouse when the split is in the right place.

Regardless of how you achieve the split, a second ruler appears in the bottom window. At first you see the same part of the document in both windows. Think of the split screen as a way to scroll through the document using two separate windows. You're still only editing a single document, not two documents. You can scroll the windows independently and edit in either window.

All changes made in one window will show up in the other one when you scroll to the section involved. The cursor is in the lower window now.

CHAPTER 4 Advanced Word Processing Skills

FIGURE 4.12
Splitting the window to see two sections

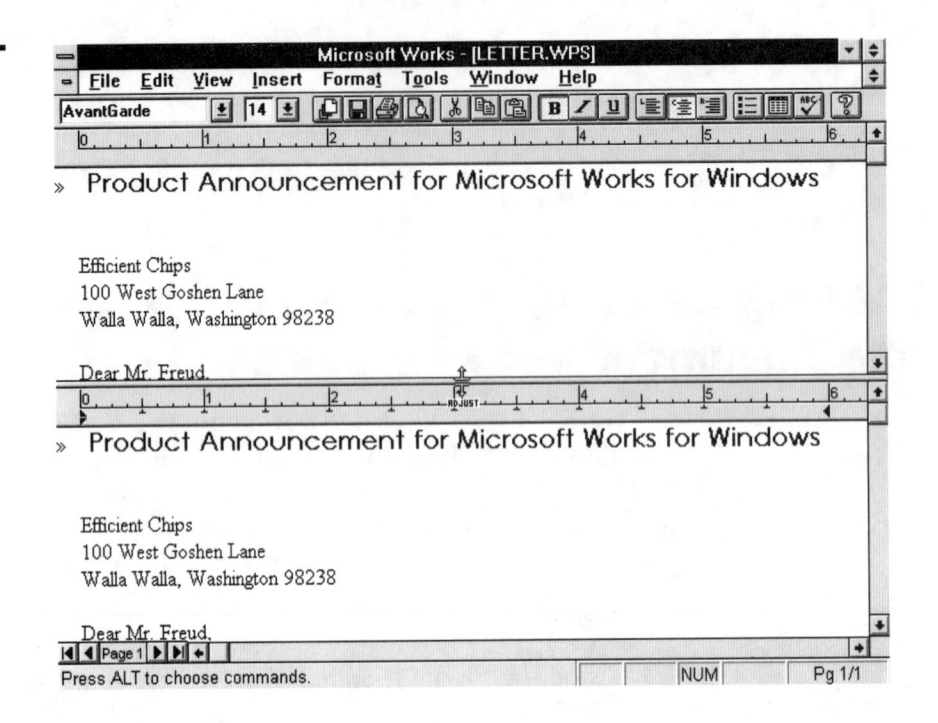

3. Change the company name in the sample letter. The changes you make in the lower window are made as well in the top one.
4. Retype the original name. It now appears in both windows.
5. Press PgUp and PgDn. The text in the lower window, but not the upper one, scrolls up and down.

> **Tip** You can tell which window is the active one by looking at the ruler. The ruler in the active window has the usual indent and tab markers in it. The inactive window doesn't.

Moving the Cursor between Windows

To move the cursor back and forth between windows so that you can enter and edit text, do the following:

- With the keyboard, press F6. Each time you press F6, you move the cursor to the other window.

- With the mouse, position the pointer anywhere in the other window and click the left button. Now you can scroll, edit, use commands, or do whatever else you'd like.

Works remembers the cursor positions in each window so that you don't lose your place when going back and forth.

"Unsplitting" the Windows

To see a single "unsplit" window again, either

- Select Window ➤ Split again, or
- Click the horizontal bar and drag it all the way to the top of the screen.

Creating Headers and Footers

Once you've edited you document, it's time to consider adding headers and footers. This part of the chapter explains this.

A *header* is a line of text that appears at the top of every printed page, such as a page number or chapter title. *Footers,* which print at the bottom of the page, typically contain similar text. Works lets you include headers, footers, or both in each document. Headers and footers can even include more than one line of text and drawings.

To create a header or footer or both:

1. Select View ➤ Headers and Footers. The Headers and Footers dialog box appears, as in Figure 4.13.

FIGURE 4.13
The Headers and Footers dialog box

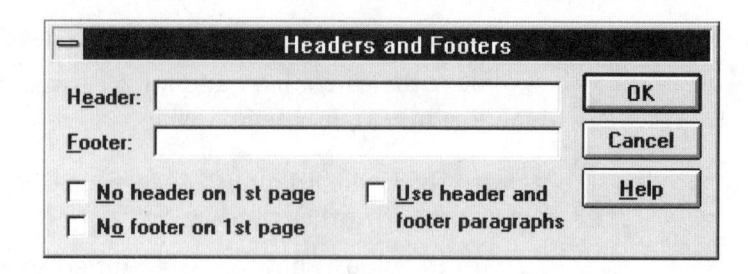

2. If you want a simple header or footer, type in the appropriate text and choose whether you want the text to appear on the first page or not.

Complex Headers and Footers

If you want a complex footer or header with more than one line or a picture:

1. Select View ➤ Headers and Footers.

2. Click on the Use header and footer paragraphs check box.

3. Click OK.

4. Scroll to the top of your document. Two lines have been added to the document:

```
H
F                                    Page - *page*
»  Product Announcement for Microsoft Works for Windows
```

The H line is the header line, and the F line is the footer line. This is where you enter new text for headers and footers.

The default footer As a default footer, Works inserts the word *Page* followed by *page*, the code necessary to print a page number on the footer of each page. Thus, you will always see something like

Page - 3

at the bottom of each printed page unless you change this default footer. If you don't want a page number at the bottom of the page, you can delete the code as you would any text.

Entering the header and footer text Use these steps to put the header and footer text in your document:

5. Move to the top of your document—the LETTER.WPS file in our case—by pressing Ctrl+Home.
6. Move to the appropriate header or footer line and enter your text.
7. When you finish, move the insertion point into the document.

Headers and footers can include anything that normal text can. You can choose alignments, fonts, and type sizes for your text. You can also insert special characters.

Multiline headers and footers To create headers or footers more than one line long, end each line by pressing Shift+↵ instead of ↵. Works will create an additional footer or header line. However, if you enter multiline headers, you have to increase the Header Margin and/or Footer Margin settings in the File ➤ Page Setup dialog box to make room for the larger header or footer. Unfortunately, there is no easy way to calculate how much extra space is needed, since it is hard to tell how the font size of the footer and header text and number of lines per page will affect margins. You may have to experiment.

Tip The header and footer paragraphs that Works automatically generates when you choose Use Header and Footer paragraphs from the Headers and Footers dialog box have preset tabs for centering text and for aligning text on the left or right margin. Press Tab once to center text; press Tab twice to align text to the right before typing it.

Adding Illustrations to Documents

Works includes Microsoft Draw, a drawing feature for creating and inserting simple pictures. Works drawings are *object-oriented*. Object-oriented drawings are similar to collages in that you place objects such as lines, circles,

CHAPTER 4 Advanced Word Processing Skills

and text on top of each other to create images. These objects can later be moved, sized, cut, copied, and altered without affecting the rest of the picture. Objects can be moved around on the screen after they are drawn, grouped together and moved *en masse,* or copied, cut, or deleted.

With Microsoft Draw, you can do many things, such as the following:

- Create signs
- Create technical drawings
- Design letterheads with pictures
- Load and edit clip art and drawings from other programs
- Create illustrations for printed matter
- Design invitations that include a map

On the other hand, if you'd rather leave the artwork to professionals, you can select from a gallery of clip art supplied with Works.

This part of the chapter explains

- Inserting clip art in documents
- Making drawings of your own
- The various drawing tools
- Editing pictures
- Positioning drawings in a document

Inserting Works Clip Art in Documents

Works comes with a variety of generic artwork for illustrating documents and publications. Here's how to take a look at what's available:

1. Open the Letter document. If you don't have that document, open a new word processing document.
2. Position the cursor on the blank line below the title (or on the first line if it's a new document).
3. Select Insert ➤ ClipArt. The Microsoft ClipArt Gallery dialog box appears, as in Figure 4.14.

Adding Illustrations to Documents

FIGURE 4.14

The Microsoft ClipArt Gallery. Select a category of art and then scroll through the examples.

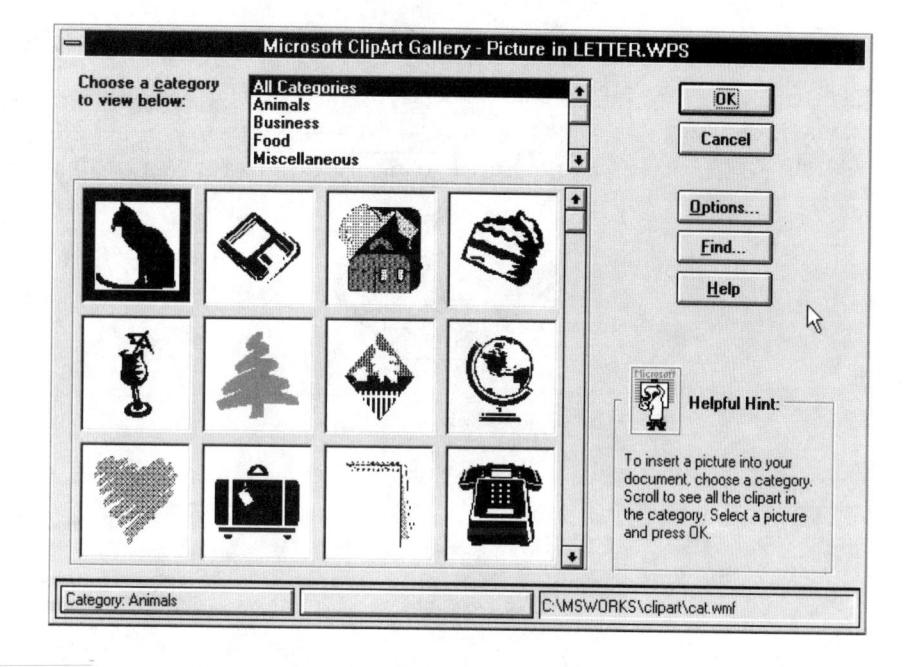

You can select clip art by category and then click OK to insert an illustration in your document.

4. In the box at the top of the gallery, select the different category choices one after another to see the clip art grouped by category.

5. Select Business.

6. Select the illustration of a diskette (it should already be selected).

7. Click OK.

The gallery disappears and the clip art you chose is inserted in your document, as in Figure 4.15. Once you've inserted a drawing, you can select, delete, cut, copy, or paste it as you would text.

8. Press Del to erase the drawing you just inserted.

CHAPTER 4 Advanced Word Processing Skills

FIGURE 4.15
The Letter document with clip art inserted

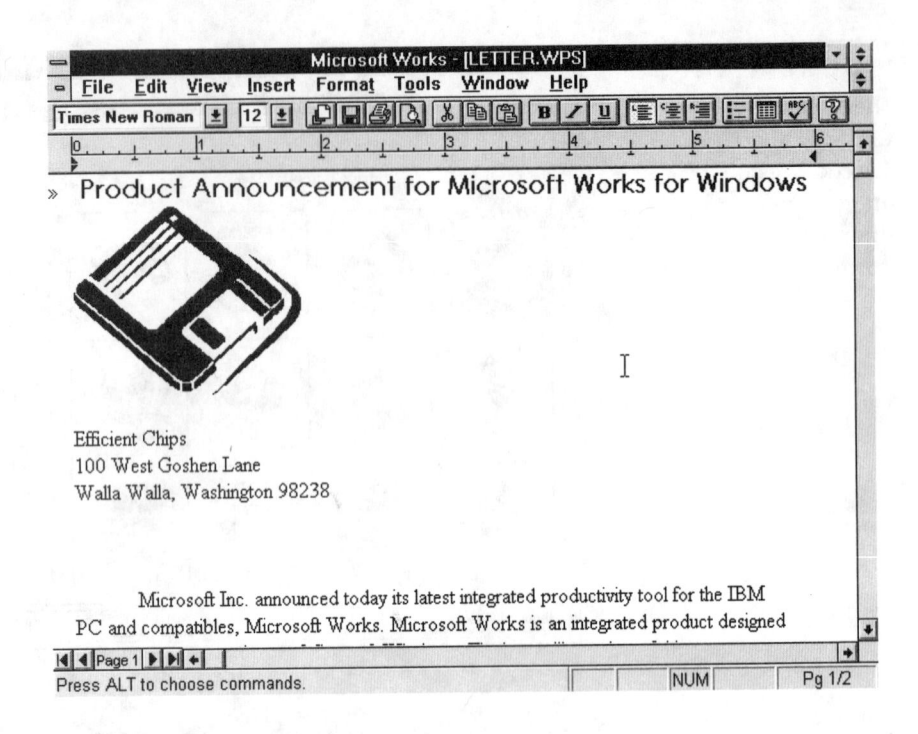

Making a Drawing of Your Own

Inserting original art is a little more complicated than inserting Works clip art. You have to make the drawing yourself for one thing! The process of inserting your own art, however, is somewhat similar.

To make a drawing of your own, you bring up a separate program called Microsoft Draw. You use Draw's tools to create your drawing. When you are finished with Draw, it places a drawing into the word processing document you're working on and closes down. Try it now:

◆ Choose Insert ➤ Drawing. The Microsoft Draw window appears on top of the Works window, as in Figure 4.16.

The work area is where you do your drawing. You use the tools in the toolbox along with selections from the Line and Fill color selectors to create drawings.

FIGURE 4.16

The Microsoft Draw screen with its component parts

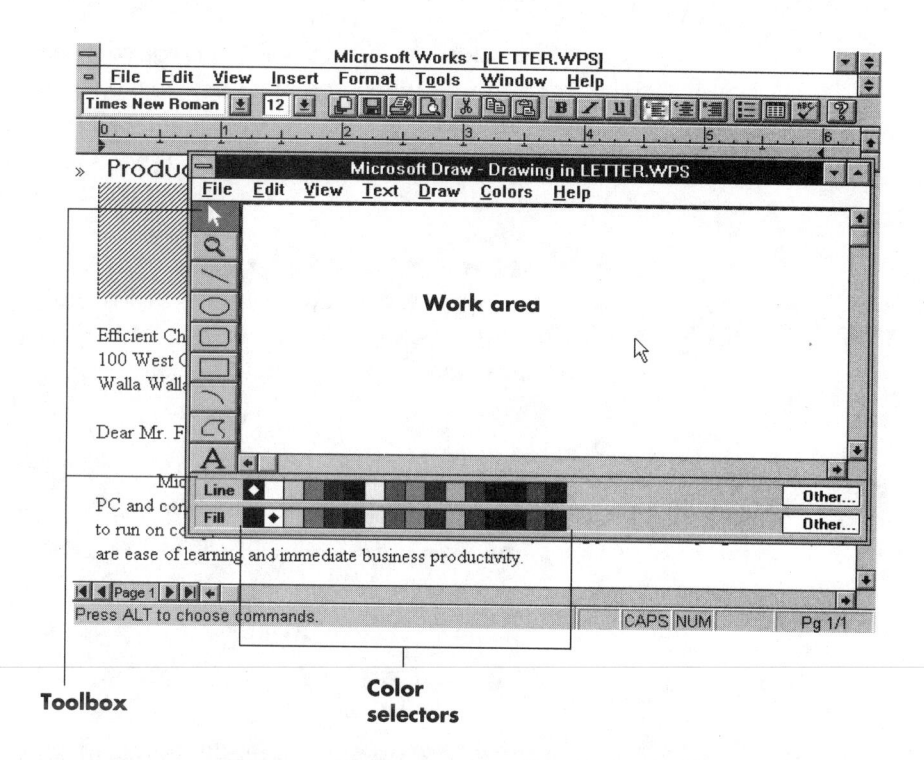

(screenshot showing Microsoft Draw window with labels: Toolbox, Color selectors, Work area)

> **Tip**
>
> When drawing, maximize the Draw window to make your drawing area as large as possible. To do this, click the Maximize button in the upper-right corner. You need as much space as you can get for drawing.

Setting Up the Colors for a Drawing

If you intend to make colored drawings, the first step in creating a new picture is to set the foreground and background colors selected from the palette. In draw programs, the term *color* describes either a color or a colored pattern selected from the color palette. If you are using a black-and-white screen (or you have a black-and-white printer), shades of gray and varying densities of dot patterns will appear in the palette.

CHAPTER 4 — Advanced Word Processing Skills

Fill and line colors The *fill color* is the color you want the inside of an object to be. For example, when you draw a circle, you assign a specific color to it. It's like deciding which color of paint to put on the brush before painting a stroke. The *line color* effects the outline color of circles, squares, and enclosed polygons, and the color of text. The default colors are black on white.

Establishing line and fill colors for objects To set the line and fill colors, point to the color in the palette and click. The color you chose will appear in the drawing if you've selected one, or in the drawing you are about to make if that's what you're going to do.

> **Warning** Changing the line and fill colors after you've loaded a multicolor drawing will wipe out its colors and convert it to a two-color boring mess. You'll have to reload it or use the Edit ➤ Undo command to restore the line and fill colors.

Microsoft Draw does try to render colors in shades of gray, although it doesn't do this as well as some other programs do. Experiment with your printer to determine what happens when you try to print colors. If the results aren't satisfactory, stick with the default foreground and background colors of black on white.

Setting the Line Width

Probably the next thing you'll want to do is choose a line width for the drawing. The line width determines how thin or fat lines are. This includes lines around boxes and circles, curvy lines, and so on. To change the line width:

1. Choose Draw ➤ Line Style.
2. From the cascading list, choose the size and style of line you want.

Using the Drawing Tools

Once you've chosen a line width and fill and background colors, you can begin working. Using Microsoft Draw is largely a matter of trial and

Adding Illustrations to Documents

error. All you really need to know is the basics of using each tool, a few tricks concerning menu options, and how to save a file and print it. The rest is up to you and your imagination.

This section describes each of the tools and suggests tips and tricks for using them. You might want to sit at your computer and work with each of the tools as you read, changing colors (if you have color) and line widths along the way. Pretty soon you'll have a good high-tech mess on your screen, at which point you can just select everything and press Del or choose Edit ➤ Clear to clear the screen and be ready for more experimentation.

Figure 4.17 shows what you can do with the toolbox, and Figure 4.18 shows the tool's icons and their names.

Choosing a tool To choose a tool:

◆ Click on its icon in the toolbox.

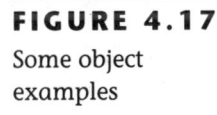

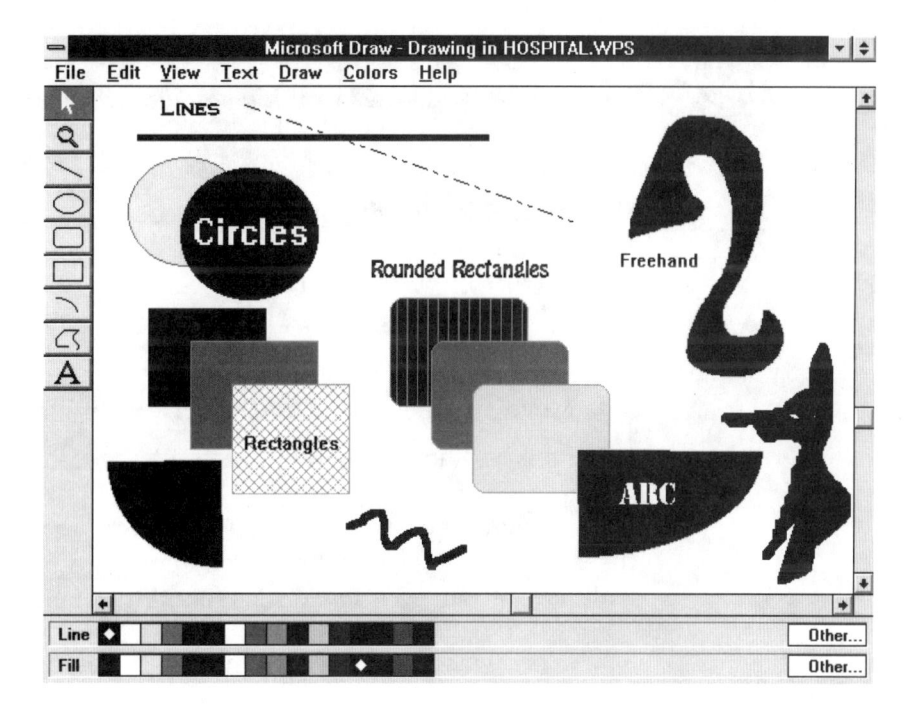

FIGURE 4.17

Some object examples

| CHAPTER 4 | **Advanced Word Processing Skills** |

FIGURE 4.18
The Microsoft Draw toolbox

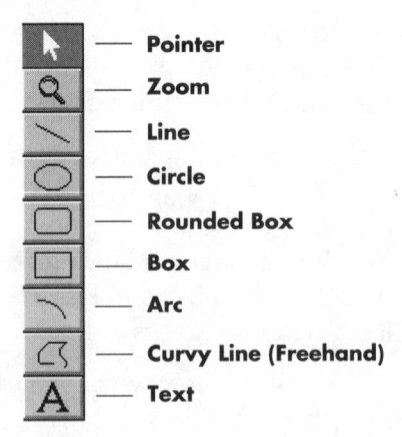

- Pointer
- Zoom
- Line
- Circle
- Rounded Box
- Box
- Arc
- Curvy Line (Freehand)
- Text

The tool is then activated (highlighted), and the cursor changes shape when you move back into the work area. The tool stays selected until you create an object with it. Then it deselects.

Tip To erase the last thing you did, just choose Edit ➤ Undo.

The Line tool for drawing straight lines Use the Line tool (see Figure 4.18) to draw straight lines:

1. Set the color and line style.
2. Select the Line tool.
3. Move into the work area. The cursor becomes a cross hair.
4. Press and hold the left button as you move the mouse.

A straight line will appear between the beginning (anchor) point and the end point. You can move the end point around until you are satisfied with its location, even in a circle around the anchor point.

5. When you are happy with the line, release the mouse button.

Adding Illustrations to Documents

> **Tip** Use the Shift key along with the line tool to constrain the line to vertical, horizontal, or 45° angle lines.

The Circle, Box, and Rounded Box tools Use these tools (see Figure 4.18) to draw circles, ovals, boxes, and rectangles. Try drawing a box:

1. Select the box tool.
2. Set the fill and line colors you want.
3. Click where you want one corner of the box to start. This sets the anchor.
4. Drag the cross hair down and to one side. As you do, a flexible frame appears.
5. Release the mouse button when the size is correct.

> **Tip** If you want a single-color object, make the line and fill colors the same color.

> **Tip** If you want to give your objects a texture, use the Pattern settings from the Draw menu. Not only will objects have a fill color, they'll also have a pattern.

The Arc tool Drawing with the Arc tool (see Figure 4.18) is similar to drawing with the Box and Circle tools. However, as you draw, an arc appears. Two examples of arcs are shown in Figure 4.17. To draw with the Arc tool:

1. Select the Arc tool.
2. Set the line and fill color.

CHAPTER 4 — Advanced Word Processing Skills

3. Click where you want one corner of the arc to start. This sets the anchor.

4. Drag the cross hair down and to one side. As you do, a flexible arc appears.

5. Release the mouse button when the arc is the right size.

The Curvy Line tool for freehand drawings The Curvy Line tool (see Figure 4.18) works like a paintbrush, pen, or marker. Use this tool to create freehand drawings. The Curvy Line tool is sometimes called the Freehand tool. To use it:

1. Select the Curvy Line tool.

2. Select the fill color and line width.

3. Press the left button and start drawing. Hold the button down as long as you want to continue the line.

4. Release the button when you want to stop drawing the line.

5. Click on the starting point again to fill the object with color.

> **Tip** If you just want a wiggly line, not an enclosed object such as a lake, double-click at the end point. This will complete the line. Use this technique for drawing road maps.

The Text tool for adding labels to drawings The Text tool (see Figure 4.18) lets you add instructions, directions, or other labels to your drawings. In Figure 4.17 I used the text tool to label the various objects I drew. Notice that some of the text is white on black, while most of it is black on white. I modified some of the text in the figure to give it a larger point size.

Adding Illustrations to Documents

Tip Text made with the Text tool can be resized. You can change the font, style, and point size of text at any time. All you have to do is click on the object and access the appropriate menu command or color bar.

To use the Text tool:

1. Choose the Text tool (the *A*).
2. Choose the style of type from the Text menu. You might also want to set the alignment. Bold, italic, and underline can all be on at one time.
3. Choose the color for the text from the Color Palette. The Line (upper) color bar is the operative one.
4. Pick the type size and typeface you want to use from the Text ➤ Font and Text ➤ Size cascading menus.
5. Place the cursor where you want to start typing and click.
6. Enter the text. Erase mistakes with the Backspace key if you need to.
7. Press ↵ when you are done.

Warning The Draw program doesn't wrap text. Pressing ↵ finalizes the text, it doesn't move you down a line.

Placing Your Drawing in the Document

When you've finished with your drawing and you want to place it in the *destination document*—the document you were in when you started the Draw program—choose one of these commands:

◆ File ➤ Update if you want to place the drawing in the word processing document and keep playing with it.

161

◆ File ➤ Exit, at which time you'll be asked if you want to update the destination document and export the drawing there *in toto*.

Let's try the second technique:

1. Choose File ➤ Exit and Return to LETTER.WPS.
2. Click Yes to the dialog box about updating. This switches you back to the Works document.

Notice that your artwork has been pasted into the document at the cursor location, just as the clip art was.

3. Click anywhere on the picture in the word processing document. It becomes highlighted.
4. Choose Format ➤ Picture/Object. A dialog box, as in Figure 4.19, comes up for scaling the picture in the word processing document.
5. Experiment with the dimensions of the picture. For example, if you want it to be half as large, enter **50** and **50** in the Width and Height Scaling area. The Size area shows the original dimensions of the picture.
6. After experimenting, return the Scaling to **100** and **100** (full size).
7. Unless your drawing is brilliant, select it and delete it now.

Tip You can also scale the picture in Draw by using the mouse. If you would rather have manual control over the scaling process, do the scaling in Draw instead.

FIGURE 4.19
Scaling a picture in a word-processing document

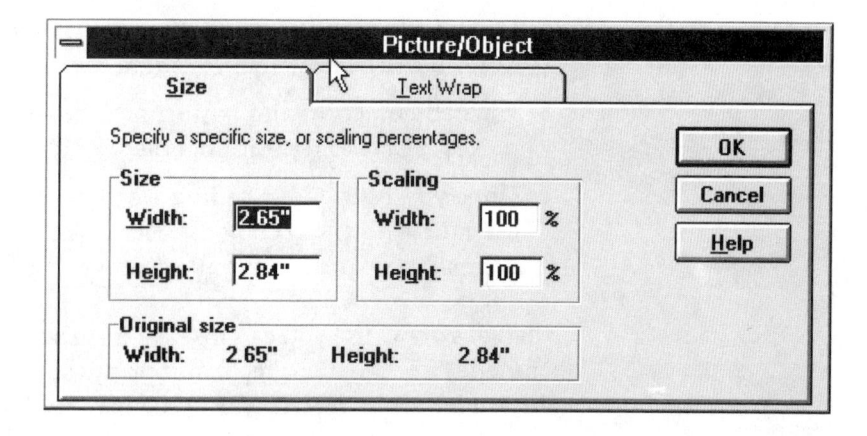

> **Warning** If you try to scale a picture while the source document (in this case Draw) is open, you'll get an error message. You have to close the source program before you can scale the picture from the Works word processor. Just exit Draw.

Editing a picture in a word processing document Once the embedded picture is in the document, you can edit it. To do so, double-click on the drawing. The Draw program will start up again so you can edit the picture. Click File ➤ Exit and Return to... when you are finished editing the drawing.

Positioning the Picture in a Document

When the picture is in your word processing document, use these techniques to position it:

◆ Works treats a picture like text. To push the picture to the right, place the insertion point on its left and either hit the Tab key or enter blank spaces. The picture will move to the right.

- Format the picture Left, Right, or Centered. This will affect its location on the page, just as if it were text.

- You can cut, copy, and paste a picture anywhere in a document. This makes it easy to reposition a piece of clip art.

- Once you're in Draw or in a word processing document, you can use Edit ➤ Copy to copy the picture into many other Windows programs. Many programs will accept graphics.

Besides drawings, you can insert spreadsheet charts in a word-processing document. You can also create and print customized forms, mailing labels, and form letters using the word processor tool in conjunction with data files in the database tool. These techniques, since they involve the use of two or more Works tools at once, will be covered in Chapter 12.

Chapter 5 explains how to use the Works spreadsheet for making business calculations, for accounting, and for budgeting.

PART three

The Works Spreadsheet Tool

5

Using the Spreadsheet

6

Advanced Spreadsheet Skills

7

Graphing and Charting

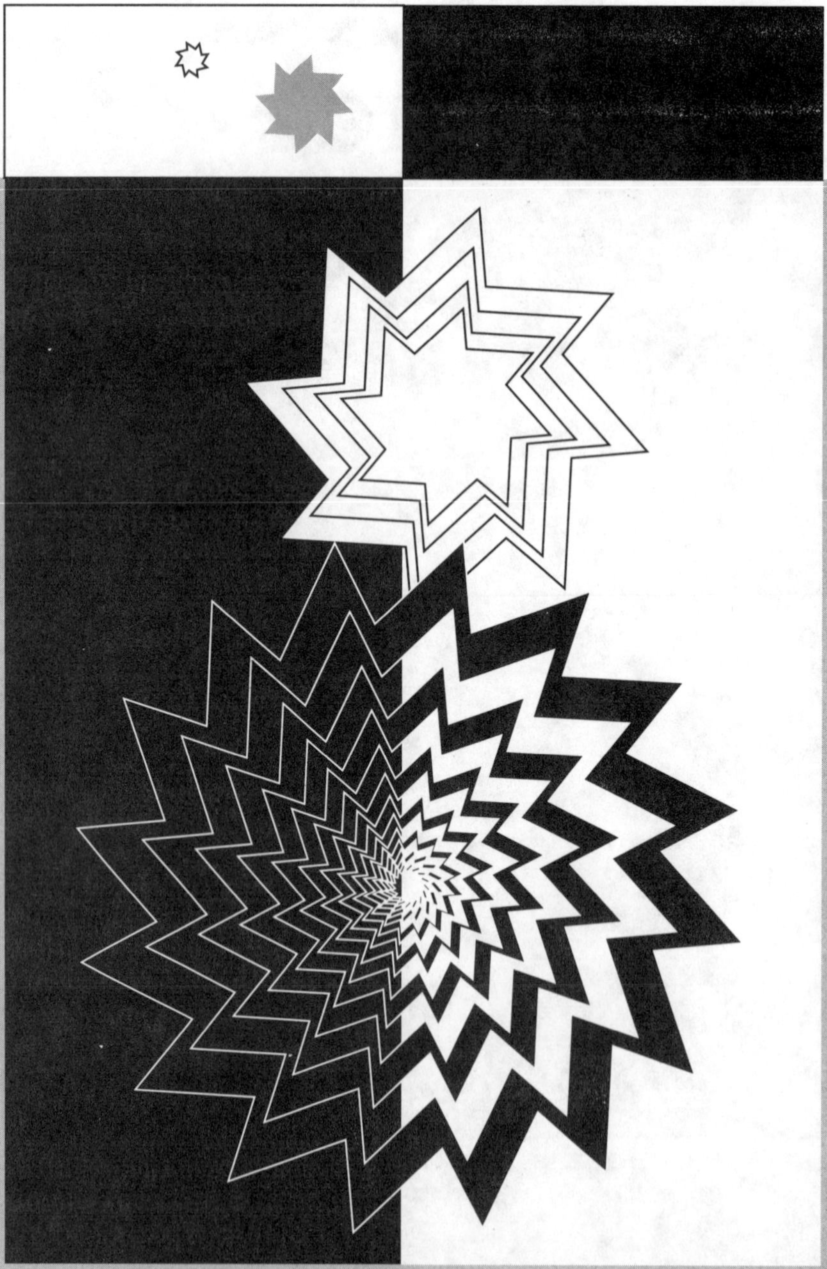

CHAPTER 5

Using the Spreadsheet

Fast Track

To start a new spreadsheet,   **172**

choose Spreadsheet from the Startup dialog box, or choose File ➤ Create New File and choose Spreadsheet.

The highlighted cell is the active cell.   **176**

Only one cell can be the active cell—the one ready to receive data. The active cell's formula, value, or label appears in the formula bar.

To enter a label or value in a cell,   **177**

click on the cell or move to it with the arrow keys and begin typing. What you type appears in the cell and on the formula bar. Press ↵ or click on the check mark in the formula bar when you are finished.

To format a cell as Bold, Italic, Currency, Percent, and so on,   181

select the cell or group of cells you want to format, and then either click on the appropriate button in the toolbar or open the Format menu and choose an option.

To align spreadsheet cells in columns,   187

select the cells whose alignment you want to change and then either click the L (Left), C (Center), or R (Right) alignment button on the toolbar, or choose Format ➤ Alignment command and click on an alignment option.

To print a spreadsheet,   200

select the portion you want to print and then choose File ➤ Set Print Area, turn on your printer and check the paper, click on Print, and click on OK.

WORKS' SPREADSHEET IS THE ELECTRONIC equivalent of an accountant's ledger pad, pencil, and calculator. Spreadsheets are used for keeping track of and organizing business expenses and household expenses. Works can perform a variety of mathematical, statistical, and financial computations quickly on the numbers in a spreadsheet. Once you've entered the numbers, changing them is easy. Here are the business documents you can generate with the Works spreadsheet:

- Annual reports
- Budgets
- Tax statements
- Invoices
- Accounts payable and receivable
- Production schedules

Spreadsheets are often used in business to run what-if calculations—in other words, to experiment with the effects of altering selected variables. For example, if a business wanted to see what effect hiring a new employee or increasing its inventory would have on annual profits, it could do so by making what-if calculations on a spreadsheet.

Scientists and engineers use spreadsheets for storing data and for calculation purposes. Teachers use them for keeping track of students' grades and for other activities. At home you can use a spreadsheet to keep track of everyday household finances, to total your monthly expenses, and to keep track of mortgage and other payments. You can also draw bar, line, pie, and scatter charts with the Works spreadsheet.

This chapter explains how to

- Open the spreadsheet productivity tool
- Start a new spreadsheet
- Enter numbers in cells
- Format cells
- Use calculation functions to add up data
- Change the contents of cells
- Save a spreadsheet
- Print a spreadsheet

More advanced spreadsheet information is covered in Chapters 6 and 7.

Note See "Spreadsheet Basics" in Chapter 1 for a quick rundown of what a spreadsheet does and how one operates.

Up and Running with the Spreadsheet Tool

Before you even open the spreadsheet tool and start working, you need to consider what you want your spreadsheet to do—and therefore how you want to lay out your spreadsheet. This part of the chapter explores how to treat spreadsheets in the planning stage. It explains the basics of spreadsheet use, how to open the productivity tool, and how to enter data in a spreadsheet.

Why Planning the Layout of a Spreadsheet Is Important

Because spreadsheets are powerful and can be complex, some careful consideration is necessary in the planning stages. Before you start work, ask yourself the following questions:

- What kind of information do I intend to put in my spreadsheet?
- How should the information be arranged?
- What types of solutions am I attempting to find with the calculations I'll put in my spreadsheet?
- What types of reports do I need to produce with my spreadsheet?

These are all questions you should ask yourself as you create a new document.

Note In spreadsheet terminology, a *report* is a form with summary information about the data in a spreadsheet.

Once you've answered the above questions, next determine which formulas and/or mathematical functions you'll need and where to put them in your spreadsheet. By considering these matters before you open a new spreadsheet, you'll save yourself a lot of trouble later on.

Starting a New Spreadsheet

Once you've sketched out your plan for a spreadsheet and you know what you want it to accomplish, it's time to open a new spreadsheet document:

1. If you are already in Works, choose File ➤ Create New File to open the Create New File dialog box. If you're just loading Works, the box appears by itself.

Up and Running with the Spreadsheet Tool

2. Click on Spreadsheet in the dialog box.

3. A new blank spreadsheet document appears on your screen as shown in Figure 5.1.

When maximized, most screens show twenty rows and eight columns (A through H). Getting to other columns and/or rows requires using the PgUp and PgDn keys, the arrow keys, or the mouse to scroll through the spreadsheet.

FIGURE 5.1
A new spreadsheet

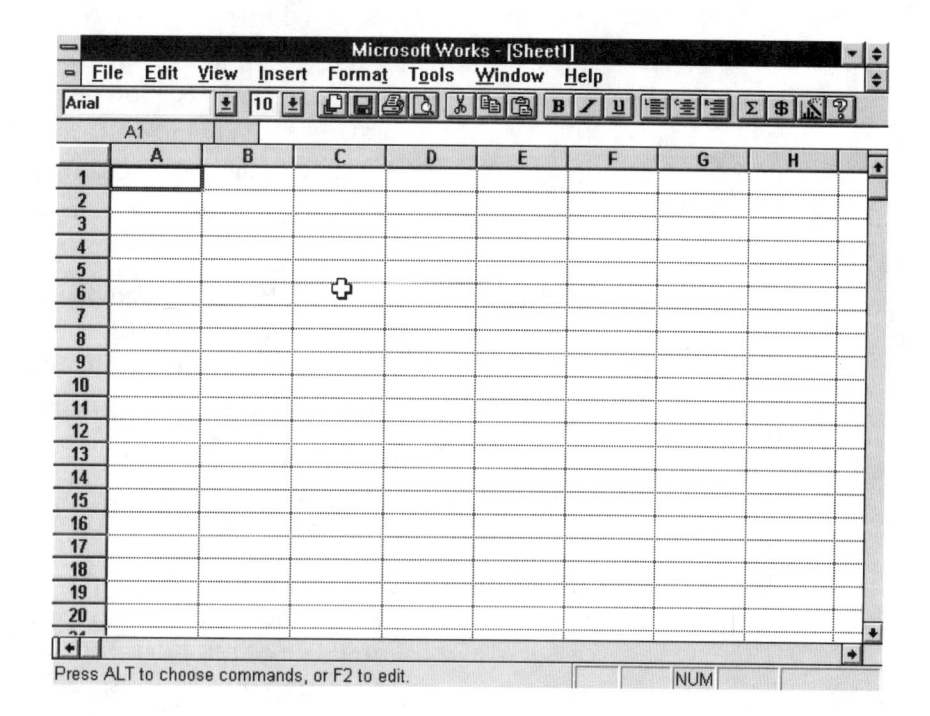

The Basic Elements of a Spreadsheet

Figure 5.2 shows the elements of a typical spreadsheet. Let's look at them one at a time:

Columns Columns are numbered across the top of a spreadsheet. In the figure you can see columns A–G. After reaching column Z, the columns are named AA, AB, AC, and so on to the last column, column IV. A spreadsheet consists of vertical columns and horizontal rows.

Rows Each row is numbered along the left side of the spreadsheet. Works allows up to 256 columns and as many as 16,384 rows in each spreadsheet.

Active cell listing The active cell is the one where the cell pointer is located. The active cell listing tells you which cell this is (the active cell is explained below).

Formula bar The formula bar, located below the menu bar, is where you enter and edit the contents of cells. You'll learn more about the formula bar later.

Labels Labels provide text information in a table (see below for more information).

Values Values are the numeric entries in the cells (see below for more information).

Cells The place where a column and row intersect on a spreadsheet is called a *cell*. Cells are where you enter data or formulas. Each cell is referenced by its location on a spreadsheet. For example, the cell in the first row, first column is cell A1 (column A, row 1). The cell is the third row, seventh column is G3 (column G, row 3). Cells can hold text, a value, or a formula.

With 16,384 rows and 256 columns, a spreadsheet in theory can have up to 4,194,304 cells. However, the number of possible cells is determined

Up and Running with the Spreadsheet Tool

FIGURE 5.2

The elements of a spreadsheet

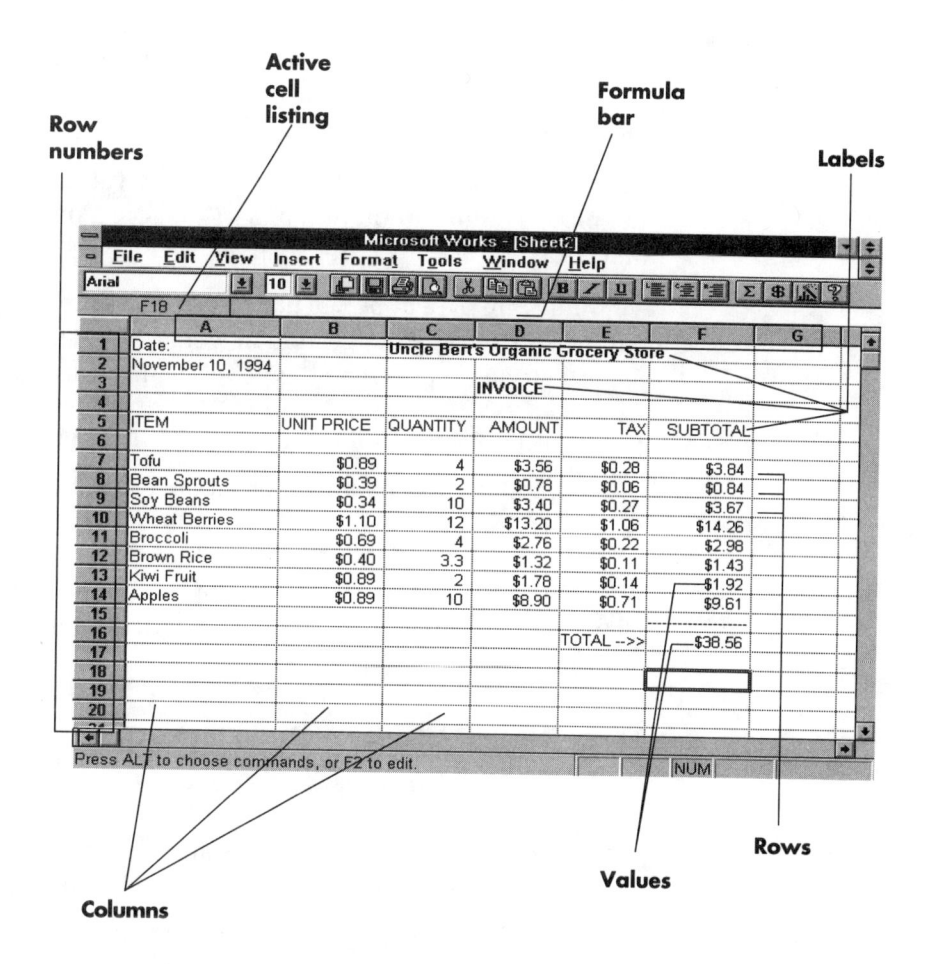

(Screenshot of Microsoft Works - [Sheet2] spreadsheet window with callouts: Row numbers, Active cell listing, Formula bar, Labels, Columns, Values, Rows)

Spreadsheet contents:

	A	B	C	D	E	F	G
1	Date:			Uncle Bert's Organic Grocery Store			
2	November 10, 1994						
3				INVOICE			
4							
5	ITEM	UNIT PRICE	QUANTITY	AMOUNT	TAX	SUBTOTAL	
6							
7	Tofu	$0.89	4	$3.56	$0.28	$3.84	
8	Bean Sprouts	$0.39	2	$0.78	$0.06	$0.84	
9	Soy Beans	$0.34	10	$3.40	$0.27	$3.67	
10	Wheat Berries	$1.10	12	$13.20	$1.06	$14.26	
11	Broccoli	$0.69	4	$2.76	$0.22	$2.98	
12	Brown Rice	$0.40	3.3	$1.32	$0.11	$1.43	
13	Kiwi Fruit	$0.89	2	$1.78	$0.14	$1.92	
14	Apples	$0.89	10	$8.90	$0.71	$9.61	
15							
16					TOTAL -->>	$38.56	

by the amount of memory in your computer, the number of other documents you have open in Works, the amount of information you put in each cell of your spreadsheet, and the available storage space on your disk.

Labels and Values

Labels consist of nonmathematical information and cannot be used in calculations. Labels are typically used to make a spreadsheet easier for the viewer to comprehend. Row and column names are typical examples of labels, as are the words SUBTOTAL and TOTAL in Figure 5.1. Though labels more often consist of letters, they can consist of numbers as well. For

175

example, the dates 1994, 10/12/92, and July 4 could be either labels or values, since Works performs calculations on dates but dates can also be used for data-identification purposes.

As you'll learn when you start entering values on spreadsheets, you can place a double quotation mark (") before a numeric entry to tell Works that the entry is a label, not a value.

Values are data to be calculated or the results of calculations. A list of numbers to be added to get a total would be considered a value, as would the total itself. There are two types of values, *constants* and *formulas:*

- Constants are numbers such as 149 and $369.99.
- Formulas are equations that produce numbers. For example, A1+A2+A3 is a formula—it adds the contents of cells A1, A2, and A3.

Whether a constant or a formula, the cell holds a numeric value, which explains why formulas are considered values even though they may not look like values.

How Formulas Are Constructed

Formulas have three possible parts:

- *Operators:* The mathematical statements that perform calculations, such as addition, subtraction, multiplication, and division.
- *Functions:* The "canned" equations that perform common calculations for you, such as trigonometry, financial, and date calculations. Works comes with 76 built-in functions to make performing complex calculations easier.
- *Cell-references:* Notations that refer to the values in other cells. For example, the formula A1+A2+A3 uses references (joined by operators) to sum the values stored in cells A1, A2, and A3.

The Active Cell

In the spreadsheet you just opened, notice that cell A1 is highlighted, is another color, or has a box around it. This means that Cell A1 is the *active cell*. The active cell is the one where the cursor is located. Its address always appears in the active cell listing to the left of the formula bar. Unless a given cell is active, you cannot enter data into it.

Moving Around a Spreadsheet

Usually you use the arrow keys to move around a spreadsheet, but there are other techniques as well. You will learn them throughout this chapter and in Chapter 6. Meanwhile, try these basic techniques for moving the cell pointer in a spreadsheet:

- Move the cell pointer around the spreadsheet by pressing the ↑, ←, →, and ↓ keys. With the mouse, you can just move the large cross pointer and click on the cell you want to activate.

- Press Ctrl in conjunction with →, ←, ↑, and ↓ to go to the far corners of the spreadsheet.

- Choose Select ▶ Go To on the menu bar, type **C4** when the Go To dialog box appears, and press ↵ or click OK. The highlight moves to cell C4 and C4 becomes the active cell. (You can also press F5 to go directly to the Go To dialog box.)

Tip When entering cells to move to in the Go To dialog box, or when entering cell addresses anywhere in the spreadsheet, you can enter lowercase letters such as c4 or b3, or uppercase letters. Remember to type the letter first. If you type a number first, you will either get an error message or nothing will happen.

Entering Data in Cells

The following exercises will show you how to enter values and labels into cells. You'll also see how formulas work in spreadsheets.

CHAPTER 5 — Using the Spreadsheet

1. Move to cell A1.

2. Type in the words **This is a test to see what can be typed into a cell** (do not press ↵ yet).

As you type the words, they appear in the formula bar and in Cell A1, although the sentence gets cut off. Notice the check mark to the left of the formula bar. In step 3, you will officially enter the data in the formula bar in cell A1:

3. Press ↵ or click on the check mark with the mouse.

The ✓ and X next to the formula bar Now cell A1 grows longer so the whole sentence can fit inside the cell. Moreover, the check mark next to the formula bar turns into an *X*. If you change your mind and don't want to enter the data, clicking on the *X* to the left of the formula bar cancels the entry. The check mark and *X* only appear when you are entering or editing data. When you simply click on a cell they don't appear.

Entering double quotes for labels Assuming you haven't entered anything in the other cells in row 1, the sentence you typed should appear across the top line of the spreadsheet. Notice that a double quotation mark (") now appears before your words in the formula bar. Works has assumed rightly that you intend this cell entry to be a label, not a value. It assumes this because you typed in words, not numbers. If you had entered numbers and you wanted the numbers to be treated as a label, not a value, you would have had to enter the double quotation yourself. For example, to enter a label such as 1994, you would have to enter:

"1994

> **Note** Works will always try to display the contents of a cell, regardless of how long the contents are. The entire contents of a cell will display on-screen as long as the contents don't run into a cell that contains data.

178

Up and Running with the Spreadsheet Tool

The sentence you entered was longer than the cell and thus it now overlaps columns B, C, D, E, and F. Works displays the entire contents of A1 because none of the cells adjacent to A1 have any entries in them. Let's see what works will do when you make an entry in cell B1:

4. Move to cell B1.

5. Type **25** and press ↵.

Notice that a double quotation mark does not appear in the formula bar. Word understands this to be a numeric entry. Meanwhile, cell A1 now shows the words *This is a tes*, not the complete sentence. The contents of cell A1 are not lost, however.

6. Select cell A1 again and look at the formula bar. It shows the entire contents of cell A1.

Entering a formula Let's try entering a formula in one of the cells:

7. Move to C1.

8. Type in **=B1*4** (don't press ↵ yet).

This formula means "calculate this cell to equal the contents of cell B1 times 4." The equal sign means that you want this cell to be calculated by Works.

9. Now press ↵.

Notice that Works calculates the cell as soon as you press ↵. The number 100 (the result of multiplying 25 times 4) appears in cell C1.

10. Move to B1, type **35**, and press ↵. In an instant, C1 recalculates to 140 because one of the cells in its formula, B1, was altered.

11. Move to cell D1, type in **=C1*4**, and press ↵. The value 560, or 140 times 4, appears.

12. Go back to cell B1, type in different numbers and press ↵. Cells C1 and D1 will recalculate to reflect the changes you make. This is the basis of "what-if?" calculations.

Notice that the formula bar shows a formula when you move to cell C1 or D1, not the value of those cells, but that when you move to cell B1 the value of the cell appears. That happens because B1 does not contain a formula, whereas the other two cells do.

Clearing a spreadsheet In the next part of this chapter you'll create an invoice spreadsheet. To prepare for this exercise, close the spreadsheet you've been working on:

1. Close the current spreadsheet by choosing File ➤ Close.
2. When Works asks if you want to save the changes, type **N** or click on No.

Example Exercise: Building an Invoice Spreadsheet

In the next part of this chapter, you'll build a spreadsheet to be used for invoicing clients of a fictitious company we'll call "Uncle Bert's Organic Grocery Store." This spreadsheet will automatically calculate subtotals and totals for customer invoices.

In this part of the chapter, you'll get practice with the

- Cutting, copying, and pasting data from cell to cell
- Applying styles such as boldface and underline to data
- Aligning cells in spreadsheet columns
- Entering formulas—and copying formulas so they can be used in other parts of a spreadsheet

To begin with, you have to bring up a new spreadsheet to work with:

1. Choose File ➤ Create New File to open a new spreadsheet. A new, blank spreadsheet called SHEET2.WKS appears.
2. Maximize the sheet by clicking on its Maximize button.
3. Move to cell C1, type **Uncle Bert's Organic Grocery Store**, and press ↵.
4. Move to D2, type **INVOICE**, and press ↵.

Cutting and Pasting Spreadsheet Data

On second thought, those two lines are too close together, so we'll move the word *INVOICE* down a line. To cut and paste spreadsheet data:

5. Highlight what you want to move. In our case, D2 is still highlighted.

6. Choose Edit ➤ Cut.

7. Move to the cell where you want to paste the data. In our case, press ↓ once to highlight cell D3.

8. Choose Edit ➤ Paste. This moves the contents of cell D2 into cell D3. You can always use this technique to move the contents of a cell or cells to another location.

> **Tip**
>
> You can also move or copy the contents of a cell to another cell with the drag-and-drop method. To do this, move the insertion point to the *left* edge of the highlighted cell or block of cells. The word DRAG will appear below the pointer. Click and drag the cell contents to a new location to move them there. To copy the contents of a cell, hold down the Ctrl key before you click and drag.

Applying Boldface and Other Styles to Data

To make our spreadsheet easier to read and understand, we can apply styles to the data in the spreadsheet. Let's make the headings bold:

1. Click on the cell whose contents you want to apply a style to. In our case, click on C1.

2. Click on the B (for Bold) button in the toolbar.

If you wanted to, you could click on the I (for italics) button or the U (for underline) button.

181

3. Click on D3, which contains the word *INVOICE*.

4. Click the B button again to make this word bold.

Entering the Spreadsheet Data

Now that you have a nice-looking title and heading in place, enter the first row of the spreadsheet:

5. Move to cell A5.

6. Type **ITEM**.

Arrow-key shortcuts for entering cell contents As you know, pressing ↵ enters data in a spreadsheet. The spreadsheet tool offers a shortcut for entering data: By pressing ↑, ↓, ←, or →, you can enter the contents of a cell as well as move the cell pointer. Try it out:

7. Press ↓ twice. Notice how pressing ↓ enters the data *and* moves down a cell.

8. In cell A7, type **Tofu** and press ↓.

9. Type in the following list in the same way you entered the word *Tofu*, by moving down one cell at a time in the same column. When you are done, your spreadsheet should look like Figure 5.3.

CELL	ENTER
A8	**Bean Sprouts**
A9	**Soy Beans**
A10	**Wheat Berries**
A11	**Broccoli**
A12	**Brown Rice**
A13	**Kiwi Fruit**
A14	**Apples**

Example Exercise: Building an Invoice Spreadsheet

FIGURE 5.3

The spreadsheet with the item list and title entered

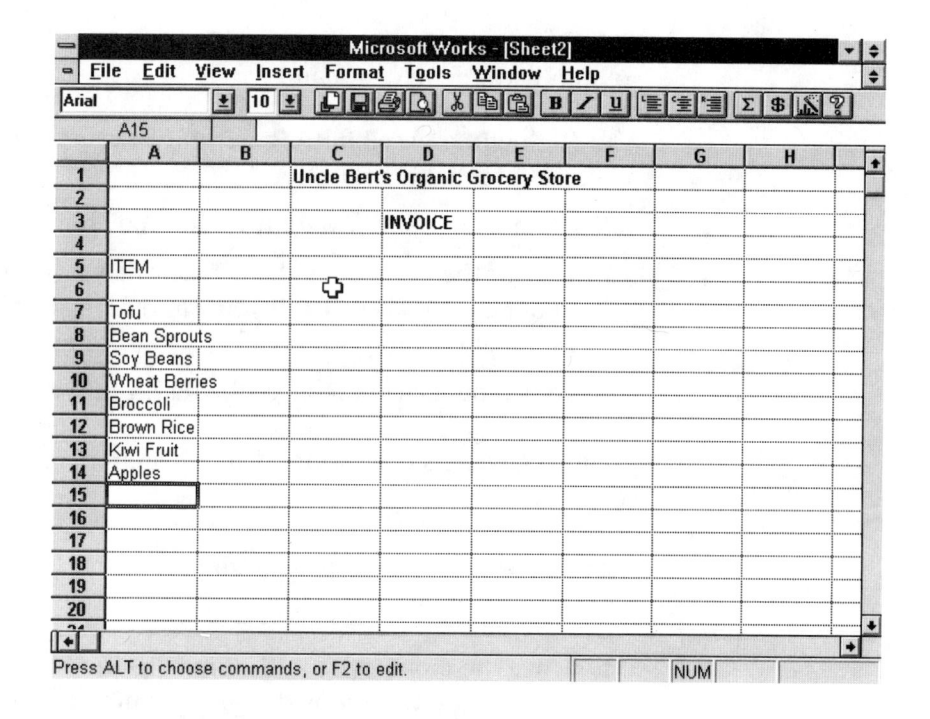

	A	B	C	D	E	F	G	H
1			Uncle Bert's Organic Grocery Store					
2								
3				INVOICE				
4								
5	ITEM							
6								
7	Tofu							
8	Bean Sprouts							
9	Soy Beans							
10	Wheat Berries							
11	Broccoli							
12	Brown Rice							
13	Kiwi Fruit							
14	Apples							

Widening and Narrowing Spreadsheet Columns

Next you'll put in the second column, which will list the price per unit. When you do this you will find it necessary to widen column A—and you will find out how to do this.

1. Move to B5.
2. Type **UNIT PRICE** and press ↓ twice.

Whoops! It looks like this column is going to cut off some labels in the ITEM column if you keep going. You could move the UNIT PRICE column to column C, but it would be easier to simply widen column A. You can widen a column either with menu commands or with the mouse.

183

Widening or narrowing a column with the menus To widen (or narrow) a column with menu commands:

1. Highlight any cell in the column you want to widen (or narrow). In our case that is column A.

2. Choose Format ➤ Column Width. A dialog box appears.

3. Type in the number of characters wide you want the column to be. In our case, make it **14**. If you wanted to narrow the column, you would enter a lower number.

4. Press ↵ or click OK to close the dialog box.

Column A widens to accommodate the item names without running into column B.

Widening or narrowing a column with the mouse You can also widen a column with the mouse:

1. Move the mouse cursor (the cross) to the dividing line between the column you want to widen and the next column. The *dividing line* is located at the top of the spreadsheet. In our case you would put the mouse cursor on the line between the A and the B at the top of the columns. When you have the cursor in the right position, it changes to a two-headed arrow with the words ADJUST below it:

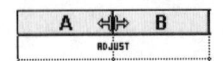

```
  A  ⇔  B
     ADJUST
```

2. Drag the mouse to the right to widen the column or to the left to narrow it.

3. Release the button when the column is the right width.

   Now that column A has been widened, let's enter the data in column B:

4. Move back to B7, the Tofu unit price cell.

5. Type **.89** and press ↓. Notice that Works puts in the leading 0 (zero) to display 0.89.

Example Exercise: Building an Invoice Spreadsheet

6. Finish entering the unit prices in column B:

CELL	ENTER
B8	.39
B9	.34
B10	1.10
B11	.69
B12	.40
B13	.89
B14	.89

Formatting Cells for Currency

Notice that some of your entries have two digits after the decimal point and others have only one. Works doesn't know that you have entered monetary figures here; it assumed you entered plain numbers. To tell Works that you want the numbers in column B to be monetary figures, you have to *format* the column. Here's how:

1. Click on the B at the top of column B. The column is highlighted to let you know it has been selected.

> **Tip** The letters at the top of the columns are called the *column selectors*. Click on a column selector to select the entire column directly below it. The column will be highlighted.

2. To give column B the Currency format, either:

   ◆ Click on the dollar sign ($) in the toolbar, or

   ◆ Choose Format ➤ Number, click Currency in the dialog box, and click OK.

Your column B should look like column B in Figure 5.4 (you'll enter the quantity figures in column C shortly).

CHAPTER 5 — Using the Spreadsheet

FIGURE 5.4
Formatting the spreadsheet so that column B numbers are dollar-and-cents figures

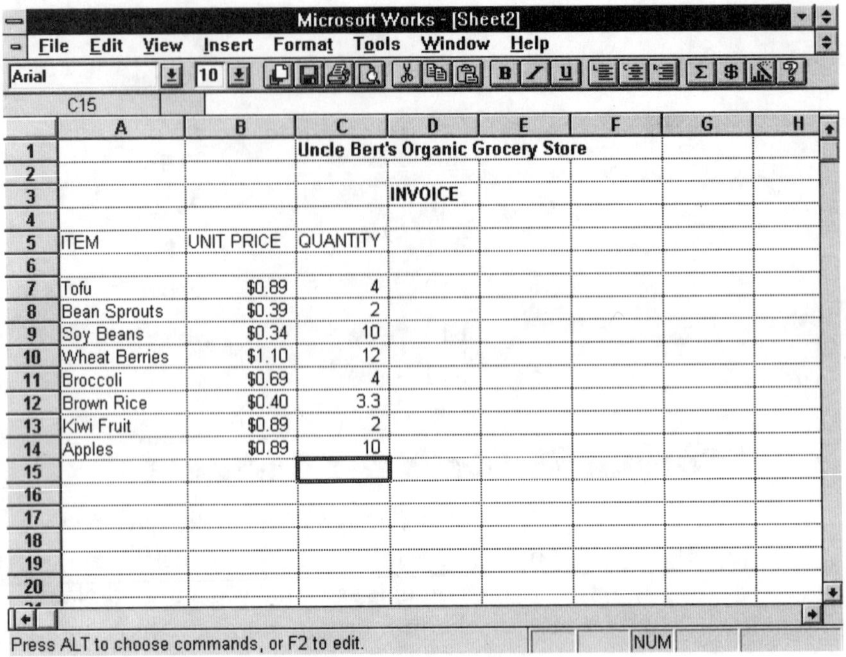

	A	B	C	D
1				Uncle Bert's Organic Grocery Store
2				
3				INVOICE
4				
5	ITEM	UNIT PRICE	QUANTITY	
6				
7	Tofu	$0.89	4	
8	Bean Sprouts	$0.39	2	
9	Soy Beans	$0.34	10	
10	Wheat Berries	$1.10	12	
11	Broccoli	$0.69	4	
12	Brown Rice	$0.40	3.3	
13	Kiwi Fruit	$0.89	2	
14	Apples	$0.89	10	

3. Click on any cell to deselect column B.

You can format individual cells or groups of cells as well. You don't have to format an entire column or row. Just select the cells you want to format by dragging the mouse over them.

Now let's enter the figures in column C, the Quantity column:

1. Move now to C5.

2. Type **QUANTITY** and press ↓ twice.

Notice that the word *QUANTITY* runs right up against *UNIT PRICE*, like so:

`UNIT PRICQUANTITY`

This is because column B is too narrow.

3. Widen column B using either the mouse or menu commands. Use Figure 5.4 as a guide.

Example Exercise: Building an Invoice Spreadsheet

> **Note:** If you need to know how to widen a column, see "Widening and Narrowing Spreadsheet Columns" earlier in this chapter.

4. Enter the quantity information in column C. Column C shows how many pounds of each item were purchased. Unlike columns A and B, this column will change with each customer order.

CELL	ENTER
C7	4
C8	2
C9	10
C10	12
C11	4
C12	3.3
C13	2
C14	10

Now your spreadsheet looks like the one in Figure 5.4.

Aligning Spreadsheet Cells in Columns

The next column, AMOUNT, will reflect the unit price times the ordered quantity. Obviously this column will be comprised of *calculated* cells. Calculated cells are cells with formulas in them.

1. Move to D5.
2. Type **AMOUNT**.

Notice that AMOUNT, like the other column headings you entered, is running up against the column to the left. Instead of widening a column to solve this problem, you can change a cell's *alignment*—you can left-align the cell, center it, or right-align it.

CHAPTER 5   Using the Spreadsheet

To change cell alignments, highlight the cells whose alignment you want to change and then either:

- Select an alignment button on the toolbar. These buttons are marked with a tiny L (Left), C (Center), or R (Right).

- Select the Format ➤ Alignment command and select an Alignment option.

By right-aligning the word *AMOUNT*, we can shift the word to the right a tad:

3. With the cursor still in column D5 (the cell we want to realign), choose Format ➤ Alignment. The Alignment dialog box appears, as in Figure 5.5.

Note Unless you select a row, column, or group of cells, only the active cell will be formatted in the style you choose from the Format menu.

FIGURE 5.5
The Alignment dialog box. Make an alignment selection to realign data in columns.

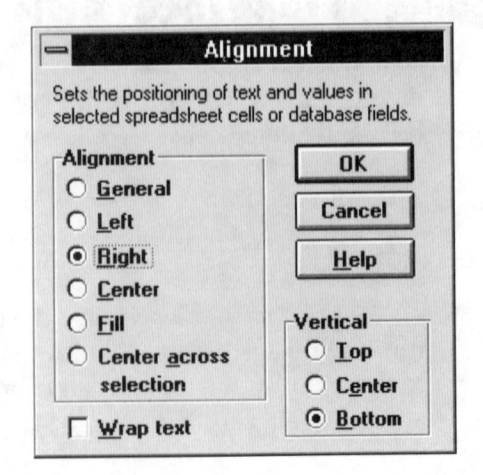

Alignment

Sets the positioning of text and values in selected spreadsheet cells or database fields.

Alignment:
- General
- Left
- ◉ Right
- Center
- Fill
- Center across selection
- ☐ Wrap text

Vertical:
- Top
- Center
- ◉ Bottom

[OK] [Cancel] [Help]

The different types of alignments As shown in Figure 5.5, Works offers the following kinds of alignments:

ALIGNMENT	DESCRIPTION
General	Words are *left-justified* (aligned along the left side of the cell); and numbers are *right-justified* (aligned along the right side of the cell). This is the default style for all cells.
Left	Lines up the contents with the left side of the cell.
Right	Lines up the contents with the right side of the cell.
Center	Centers the contents of the cell.
Fill	Fills the cell with the contents, repeated if necessary.
Center across selection	Centers the contents across all the selected cells.

4. In the Alignment dialog box, click on Right to open up a little space between the headings (and incidentally align the heading with the numbers below).

You could also right-align the word *AMOUNT* by clicking on the R button on the toolbar or by pressing Ctrl+R.

Entering and Copying Formulas in Cells

Here you'll begin to see the real advantages of spreadsheets. In the AMOUNT column we will enter a formula for calculating the amount, which is equal to the unit price times quantity. By entering a formula we save ourselves the trouble of having to make numerous calculations.

1. Move to cell D7. The formula for this cell should be B7 times C7.
2. Enter **=B7*C7** and press ↓.

Don't forget to use an asterisk (*) and not a small letter *x* to indicate multiplication. To enter the asterisk, you can press either Shift+8 or press

PrtSc (the Print Screen key) by itself. You don't have to use uppercase letters for the cell references. In step 2 you could just as well have entered b7*c7.

The number 3.56 shows up in cell D7. Works did the calculation.

3. In D8, you need a similar, slightly modified formula, since the numbers you want to multiply here are in row 8 instead of row 7. Type **=B8*C8** and press ↓.

Copying Formulas down a Column

Instead of entering formulas in the rest of the column, you can use a shortcut and simply copy the formula down the column. When you copy a formula, Works automatically changes the row or column references—called *relative references*—to compensate for their new locations in the spreadsheet.

Here is how to copy the formula you already entered in D8 to cells D9 through D14:

1. Make D8 the active cell.
2. Select the cells you want to copy the formula to. In our spreadsheet, press and hold down the Shift key as you press ↓ six times. The rest of the column should be highlighted.
3. Release the Shift key.
4. Choose Edit ➤ Fill Down.

The column suddenly fills itself in and calculates the amounts for each item. If you want to make sure the formulas were adjusted correctly, press the arrow keys and move to a few of the cells between D8 and D14. You will see that they have been appropriately modified. Remember, however, that the cell at the top of the highlighted selection is the one whose formula has been duplicated.

Let's change number formats in column D to the Currency format, since these are monetary figures:

5. Select Column D by clicking on the D at the top.
6. Click on the $ button in the toolbar. Your screen should look like Figure 5.6.

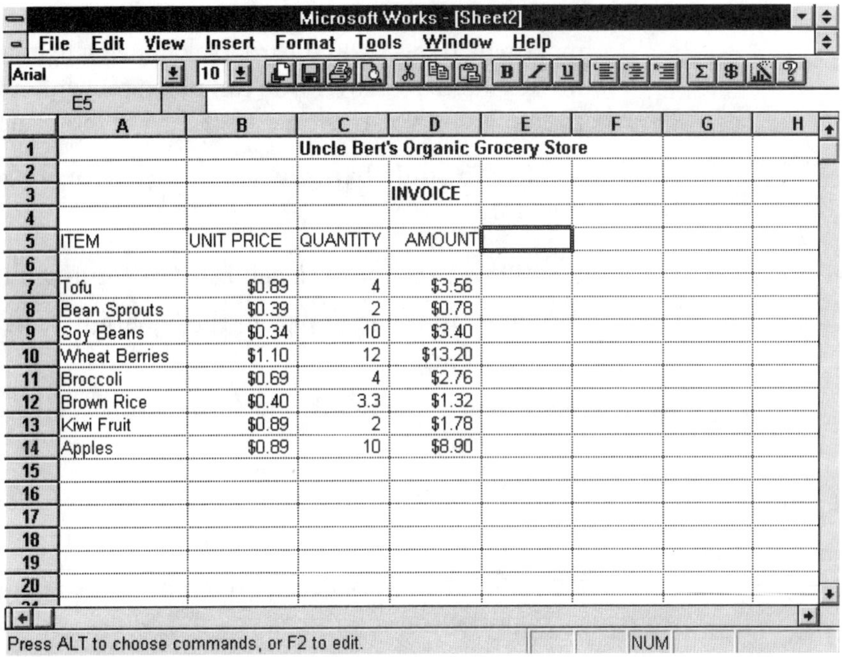

Example Exercise: Building an Invoice Spreadsheet

FIGURE 5.6
The four columns in place, formatted, and aligned

	A	B	C	D
1		Uncle Bert's Organic Grocery Store			
2				
3				INVOICE
4				
5	ITEM	UNIT PRICE	QUANTITY	AMOUNT
6				
7	Tofu	$0.89	4	$3.56
8	Bean Sprouts	$0.39	2	$0.78
9	Soy Beans	$0.34	10	$3.40
10	Wheat Berries	$1.10	12	$13.20
11	Broccoli	$0.69	4	$2.76
12	Brown Rice	$0.40	3.3	$1.32
13	Kiwi Fruit	$0.89	2	$1.78
14	Apples	$0.89	10	$8.90

Notice that the one non-numerical entry in column D, the word *AMOUNT*, is not formatted for currency. Numerical formats only affect values, not labels.

Calculating the Tax on Spreadsheet Items

Suppose our store is located in a state with an 8 percent sales tax on groceries. We'll add a column to the spreadsheet to calculate tax on each item.

1. In cell E5, enter **TAX**, and right-align the cell by pressing the Right-Align button in the toolbar.

2. In cell E7, just enter = (an equal sign). Don't press anything else yet.

Point mode for entering cell addresses in formulas Notice when you pressed the equal key that the cell name and the word *POINT* showed up in the status bar. When you press the equal key you enter *Point mode*. In

CHAPTER 5 Using the Spreadsheet

Point mode, you can use the arrow keys to point to a cell to enter it in a formula, which saves you the trouble of having to enter the cells contents with the keyboard. Moreover, you can pick a cell without having to find out what its address is—all you have to do is see it and move the cursor to it.

The formula bar now reads =D7 with the cursor waiting up there for more.

3. Press ← to move to cell D7. The formula in cell E7 now reads =D7.

4. Type in the next part of the equation, ***.08** (assuming a sales tax of 8 percent).

5. Press ↵ to enter the equation and leave Point mode. The equation should read

   =D7*0.08

6. Select the rest of the column by pressing Shift+↓.

7. Use the Edit ➤ Fill Down command to copy the equation down the rest of the column as you did before.

Notice that some of the numbers in column E have more than two decimal places. Most financial transactions do not permit more than two decimal places, so you need to change column E to the currency format:

8. For column E, set the format to the Dollar type. If you haven't moved the cursor since using the Fill Down command, cells E7 to E14 should still be selected. Therefore, all you have to do is click the $ button to change to the currency format.

> **Note** When formatting numbers as currency, Works rounds off the displayed figures to the nearest penny. However, the actual numbers are kept in memory, and when you make calculations the actual numbers are used.

Example Exercise: Building an Invoice Spreadsheet

Creating the Subtotal Column

Now let's create another column showing a subtotal for each item. When you're done entering this column, your screen will look like Figure 5.7.

1. In F5, type **SUBTOTAL**.

2. Right-align the column and enlarge its size a bit so the headings don't run together.

3. In F7, enter the formula **=D7+E7**.

4. With F7 as the active cell, select all cells from F7 to F14 and choose Edit ➤ Fill Down to copy the formula down the column. (If you use the dragging method to select the cells, be sure to start with F7 and drag down. This makes F7 the active cell.)

5. While the cells are still highlighted, choose Format ➤ Number ➤ Currency to reformat the numbers. This saves you the step of selecting the cells again.

Now your screen looks like that shown in Figure 5.7.

FIGURE 5.7
All six columns in place

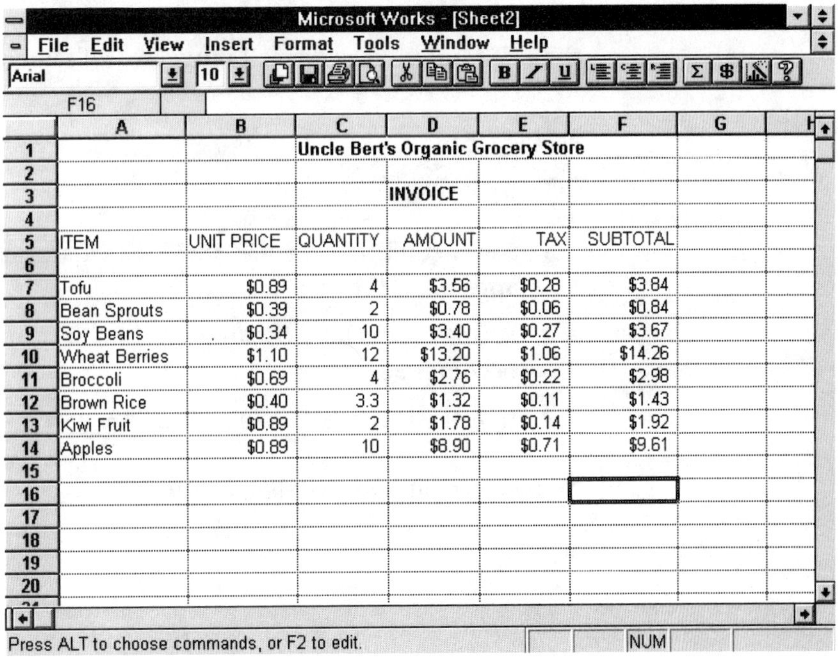

	A	B	C	D	E	F	G
1			Uncle Bert's Organic Grocery Store				
2							
3				INVOICE			
4							
5	ITEM	UNIT PRICE	QUANTITY	AMOUNT	TAX	SUBTOTAL	
6							
7	Tofu	$0.89	4	$3.56	$0.28	$3.84	
8	Bean Sprouts	$0.39	2	$0.78	$0.06	$0.84	
9	Soy Beans	$0.34	10	$3.40	$0.27	$3.67	
10	Wheat Berries	$1.10	12	$13.20	$1.06	$14.26	
11	Broccoli	$0.69	4	$2.76	$0.22	$2.98	
12	Brown Rice	$0.40	3.3	$1.32	$0.11	$1.43	
13	Kiwi Fruit	$0.89	2	$1.78	$0.14	$1.92	
14	Apples	$0.89	10	$8.90	$0.71	$9.61	

Using Cell Ranges in Formulas

Now we'll add up the figures in the Subtotal column by using the SUM function. In this way we will get a grand total for all items on the Invoice. This part of the chapter also introduces cell ranges.

To get the grand total, we will add up the figures in column F by using a SUM function which will be entered in cell F16. But how should we enter the formula? One way would be to enter it like this:

`=F7+F8+F9+F10+F11+F12+F13+F14`

You could enter this formula either by pointing at the cells one by one and pressing **+** after each one, or by typing the whole thing.

An easier way, however, would be to enter the SUM function and a range indicating which cells to total up. A *range* is a series of cells to be used in formulas or other commands.

Range notation To tell Works which cells to include in a range, you list the upper-left cell first (the topmost cell if the range is only one column wide), then a colon (:), and then the lower-right cell (or the bottom cell if the range is only one column wide). For example, the grand total formula we enter in cell F16 will add up all cells from F7 to F14. Therefore, using the SUM function and a cell range, we will enter the formula in cell F16 like so:

`=SUM(F7:F14`

Let's try it out:

1. Select cell F16, type **=SUM(F7:F14)**, and press ↵. The number 38.556 appears in the cell.

2. Format the cell by clicking on the $ button on the toolbar. The total becomes $38.56.

3. In cell E16, enter the label **TOTAL** -->>.

Your screen should look like Figure 5.8.

Example Exercise: Building an Invoice Spreadsheet

FIGURE 5.8
The grand total added to the spreadsheet and formatted

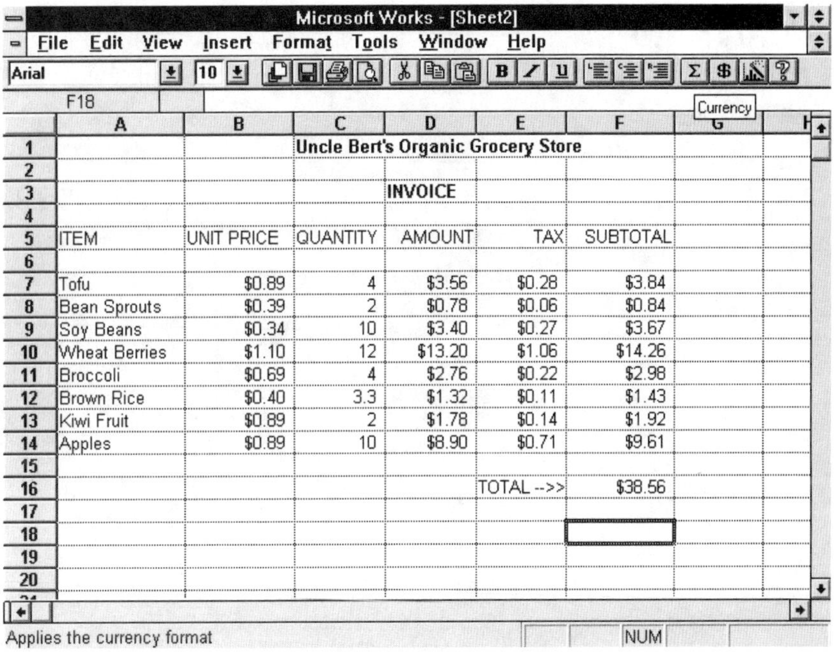

	A	B	C	D	E	F
1				Uncle Bert's Organic Grocery Store		
2						
3				INVOICE		
4						
5	ITEM	UNIT PRICE	QUANTITY	AMOUNT	TAX	SUBTOTAL
6						
7	Tofu	$0.89	4	$3.56	$0.28	$3.84
8	Bean Sprouts	$0.39	2	$0.78	$0.06	$0.84
9	Soy Beans	$0.34	10	$3.40	$0.27	$3.67
10	Wheat Berries	$1.10	12	$13.20	$1.06	$14.26
11	Broccoli	$0.69	4	$2.76	$0.22	$2.98
12	Brown Rice	$0.40	3.3	$1.32	$0.11	$1.43
13	Kiwi Fruit	$0.89	2	$1.78	$0.14	$1.92
14	Apples	$0.89	10	$8.90	$0.71	$9.61
15						
16					TOTAL -->>	$38.56

Applies the currency format

How Works Handles Dates in Spreadsheets

Let's add the finishing touches to the spreadsheet. As shown in Figure 5.9, we'll add a place for recording the transaction date—something every invoice should have—in the upper-left corner:

1. In A1, enter the label **Date:**.

2. In A2, type **11/10/94**.

Works is capable of some interesting date manipulations. To see what they are:

3. With the cursor still in cell A2, select Format ➤ Number. The Number dialog box appears, as in Figure 5.10.

Works has assumed that A2 contains a date and has highlighted the Date button. In the options area, there's a Date box that lists many date formats.

195

CHAPTER 5 — Using the Spreadsheet

FIGURE 5.9
The finished spreadsheet

FIGURE 5.10
The Number dialog box with Date format options

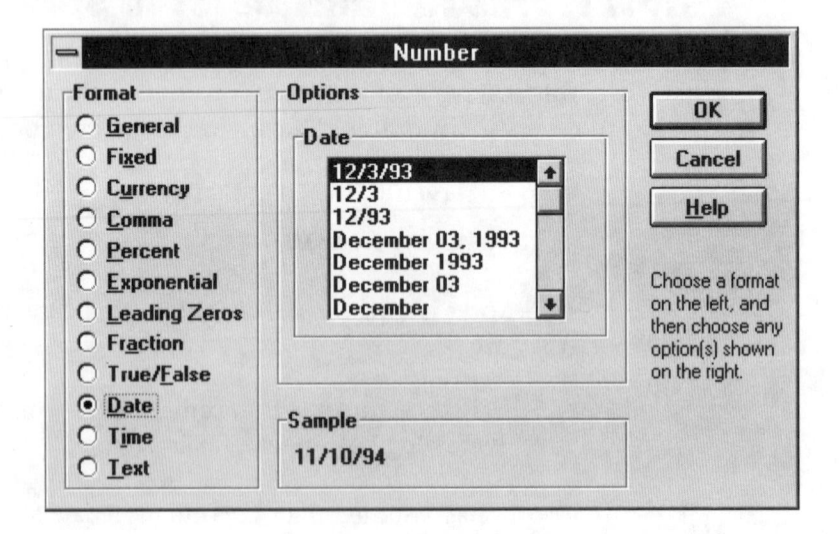

196

4. In the Date area, select the fourth option, the longest one with the month and year spelled out.

5. Click OK.

The # in spreadsheet cells On your spreadsheet, the cell the date is in now changes to #######. Where you see a row of pound symbols, it means that the numeric information in the cell is too long to be displayed.

6. Widen the column a bit until the #'s disappear and the date appears. You should see November 10, 1994 in its entirety on your spreadsheet.

7. Try typing in any date in the *xx/xx/xx* format and watch Works translate it to the long, spelled-out format.

As shown in Figure 5.9, let's add a line to cell F15 to show that the numbers in the Subtotal column are added to achieve a grand total:

8. Move to F15 and enter

   "--------------------

   Don't forget the quotation mark. If you forget it, Works will think you are trying to subtract something and you will get an error message.

> **Note** Remember to enter a quotation mark before numbers and mathematical symbols if you want Works to treat the cell contents as a label and not a value or numerical formula.

The F2 Key for Speeding Up Editing

Before printing out or saving spreadsheets on disk, you will likely edit—that is, change—the contents of certain cells. In our example grocery store invoice, you did most of your editing by highlighting the cell in question, retyping the data or formula, and pressing ↵ or an arrow key. This part of the chapter describes shortcuts you can use when editing a spreadsheet.

The easiest way to edit a cell is to highlight the cell you want to edit and press F2. When you press F2:

- The word *EDIT* appears in the status line to inform you that you've entered *Edit mode*
- The contents of the cell appears in the formula bar
- You can edit the cell contents in the formula bar

Use these keys when editing the cell contents in the formula bar:

KEY	ACTION
←	Moves the cursor left on the formula bar
→	Moves the cursor right on the formula bar
Backspace	Erase letters to the left of the cursor
Del	Deletes the letter the cursor is on
Home	Moves the cursor to the beginning of the line
End	Moves the cursor to the end of line

To see how editing is done, let's drop the word *Uncle* from the grocery store's name in cell C1 in order to give the store a more modern name:

1. Move to C1. The cell contents appear in the formula bar, as usual.

2. Press F2. The blinking cursor now appears at the end of the line in the formula bar. From here you can edit the cell using the keys listed above.

3. Press Home to get to the beginning of the line.

4. Press Del seven times to delete the word *Uncle*. (The quotation mark will also be deleted, but Works will insert a new one when you press ↵.) Now your invoice title is:

   ```
   Bert's Organic Grocery Store
   ```

5. Press ↵.

Saving Spreadsheets on Disk

Before printing your spreadsheet, it's always a good idea to save it on disk. This way, if something goes wrong with your printer or your computer "hangs up" for some reason, you won't lose any data.

To save a spreadsheet:

1. Choose File ➤ Save. Works wants to know what file name and drive you want to save your spreadsheet in.
2. Select the correct drive and directory if you want to change them. If you want to use the current drive and directory, don't make any changes.
3. Type in the name **INVOICE** and press ↵.

Works does the rest. It adds the extension .WKS to the name you give.

Note See "Dialog Boxes for Working with Files" in Chapter 2 if you need help with saving a file in Works.

Tip Save your spreadsheet every fifteen minutes or so. This way you won't lose very much work if the power fails or your computer hangs up. You can just go back to the last version of the file you saved.

Creating a "Model" Spreadsheet You Can Use Over and Over

Many spreadsheet layouts are designed to make repetitive bookkeeping tasks such as monthly income and progress reports, invoices, and inventory details easier. Once you've created a spreadsheet with a layout, formats, labels, and formulas, you can make it a "model" spreadsheet and use it again for other projects without having to re-enter the data. Here's how:

1. Create a basic layout, complete with formulas, but leave out any data that will change from month to month. In other words, create a blank spreadsheet.

2. Save the spreadsheet on disk under a generic name such as BLANKINV (Blank Inventory), or use some other name that is easy to remember and understand.

3. When you need to create a real spreadsheet from the template, choose File ➤ Open, and open BLANKINV, or whatever you have named your model spreadsheet.

4. Modify the spreadsheet template by typing in your data or making any other changes.

5. Choose File ➤ Save As and save the spreadsheet under a new name—but not the old one, or you will erase the template!

> **Note** Works supplies a number of templates, including some prepared spreadsheet models with formulas and formatting already set up. Templates are covered in Chapter 11.

Printing a Spreadsheet

Printing a spreadsheet is simple. There are only a few steps to follow, although printing large spreadsheets gets a bit more complex. To print a spreadsheet:

1. Select the range of cells you want to print. To select the range, you could drag over them with the mouse, but the easiest way is to press F5 and type in the range using standard range notation. For example, to print our spreadsheet, you would press F5 and enter **A1:F16**.

2. Choose Format ➤ Set Print Area and click OK. This tells Works to print only the selected cells.

3. Choose File ➤ Page Setup ➤ Margins and set the page dimensions and the right paper size.

4. Choose File ➤ Page Setup ➤ Other Options if you want to select printing options for your spreadsheet:

    ◆ Turn on the Row and Column Headers check box if you want your printout to include line numbers and column letters.

    ◆ Turn on Print Gridlines if you want to see the lines that divide the cells from one another.

5. Preview the printout to make sure it looks all right by choosing File ➤ Print Preview. Click OK when you're done.

6. Make sure your printer is on, connected, and has enough paper.

7. Choose File ➤ Print and press ↵.

Note When you print a large spreadsheet, Works divides the printed document into page-sized pieces. The size of these pieces is determined by the dimensions you choose from the Print ➤ Page Setup ➤ Margins dialog box.

In this chapter, you've learned the rudiments of designing, creating, editing, and printing a modest-sized spreadsheet. Of course, many spreadsheets are larger and more complex, but even with the beginner's skills you have learned here, you can probably think of some everyday spreadsheets to build for yourself. Try experimenting on your own. When you're done, save the Invoice spreadsheet as it is now for use in Chapter 6.

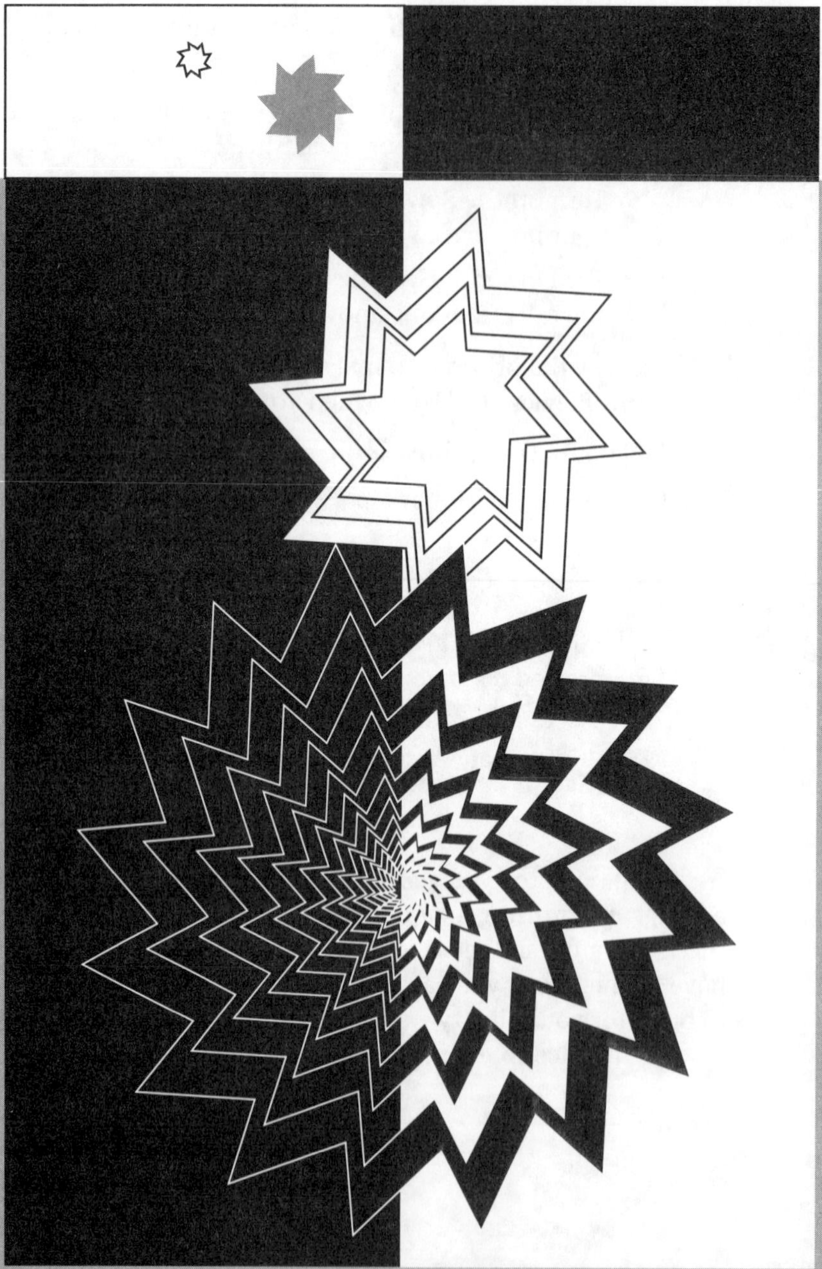

CHAPTER 6

Advanced Spreadsheet Skills

Fast Track

To select a range of cells, — 210

press F8, the Extend key, and press arrow keys to extend the selection. Press Esc to exit Extend mode.

To enter labels, values, or formulas into multiple cells, — 211

select the range of cells you want to enter the data in, type in the value, label, or formula, and press Ctrl+↵ instead of ↵. The data is copied to each cell, and in the case of formulas, the cell addresses are adjusted accordingly.

To insert a row or rows into a spreadsheet, — 219

select the row below where you want the new row to go, choose Insert ➤ Row/Column, select Row, and click OK. A new row is inserted just above the row you had selected. To insert more than one row, select more rows before choosing the Insert command.

To split a spreadsheet into two or four panes, — 222

drag the vertical split line to the right for a vertical split and release the mouse button; for a horizontal split, drag the horizontal split line and release the mouse button. To move the cursor between panes, click within the pane or press F6.

Formulas can have absolute or relative cell references.   225

Unlike relative references, absolute references are not adjusted by Works when you copy a formula. Absolute references refer to one cell or one group of cells only, no matter where the formula is copied. To enter an absolute reference, include dollar signs, like so: =3*$C$20. Absolute references allow you to "borrow" key values from specific cells elsewhere in the spreadsheet.

To quickly add up a column or row of numbers,   228

move to the cell at the bottom or right of a contiguous column or row of values, click on the Summation button in the toolbar, and press ↵.

To "freeze" rows and columns so they don't scroll,   229

drag the split bars(s) to the bottom and right of the rows and columns you want to freeze and choose Format ➤ Freeze Titles. Now all rows above and columns to the left of the active cell will not scroll.

To prevent the alteration of any cell's contents,   236

choose Format ➤ Protection, check Protect Data, and click OK.

IN CHAPTER 5 YOU CREATED, edited, and printed a simple invoice spreadsheet. But spreadsheets are most often used for budgeting, and in this chapter you'll create a budget for a fictitious company called "Bob's House of Gadgets." As you build this spreadsheet, you'll learn about

- Entering and copying formulas
- Viewing different parts of a spreadsheet at the same time
- "Freezing" row and column headings so you can see them wherever you go on a spreadsheet
- Setting up cell formatting
- Keeping cells from being erased
- Controlling the recalculation of your data
- Setting up a typical budget

Example Exercise: Building a Budget Spreadsheet

Suppose our fictitious retail chain, Bob's House of Gadgets, is doing so well that we are considering adding a new store in another part of the city. Obviously, we'll want to consider a lot of variables before committing to such a business venture. What will the new monthly expenses be? How much income can the new location generate? What are the start-up costs? A spreadsheet model can help you budget a venture, experiment with variables, and keep track of a store's finances.

Dividing the Spreadsheet into Assumption Data and Projected Data

Figure 6.1 shows the budget as it will look when you are finished building it. Notice that it is divided into two sections labeled "Givens" and "Budget":

- The Givens section includes all the assumptions upon which you will base your budget. Factors such as the number of employees and their salaries, the expected growth per quarter, and fixed expenses, including rent and utilities, are found in this section.

- The Budget section uses the numbers from the Givens section to project data concerning the cost of the store's first year of operation. Each quarter of the year is broken out separately to show the numbers resulting from the estimated quarterly growth rates. The TOTAL column adds up the yearly figures for each category on the left side of the sheet. The percentage of net sales that each category accounts for is displayed in the SALES column.

Why setting assumption data apart is important Of course, all the "givens" could be stored in the body of the spreadsheet instead of the top, but in a large, complex spreadsheet like the one we are about to create, making a change to a "given" that is widely referenced could end up being a very time-consuming task. You might have to change formulas in as many as ten or twelve cells. Moreover, if you overlooked one of the references and failed to update it, the result would be an inaccurate bottom line somewhere.

It is much easier to derive formulas from a small group of *assumption* cells—or "given" cells—that hold changeable values such as taxation rates or salaries. When one of your "assumptions" changes, all you have to do is update the cell in which the assumption is stored. All formulas that refer to the assumption cell will be recalculated automatically.

For example, rather than using a formula such as D7*0.05 to calculate sales tax, you could use the formula D7*E4, where E4 is the cell that stores that sales tax rate. This way, if the tax rate went up, all formulas that refer to the tax rate in cell E4 would automatically be recalculated.

CHAPTER 6 Advanced Spreadsheet Skills

FIGURE 6.1

The finished budget. You will create a spreadsheet exactly like this one in this chapter.

Bob's House of Gadgets
Budget for New Store

================= =====Givens=== ====== ====== ====== ======

EMPLOYEES	Number	Salaries	1st Grth	8.0%	Rent	2000
STORE MANAGER	1	2,500	2nd Grth	12.0%	Util	400
FLOOR MANAGER	1	2,000	3rd Grth	12.0%	Maint	500
TAILOR	1	1,600	4th Grth	15.0%	Deprec	750
SALES PERSON	4	1,200	Returns	2.0%	Insur	250
			COS	63.0%	Phone	150
TOTAL SALARIES		10,900	P/R Tax	15.0%	Misc	150
			Fringe	7.0%		
			Post/Fgt	1.0%		
			Exc.Tax	0.5%		

================= =====Budget=== ====== ====== ====== ======

BUDGET CATEGORY	QTR 1	QTR 2	QTR 3	QTR 4	TOTAL	SALE
REVENUE						
SALES	113,400	127,008	142,249	163,586	546,243	102.0%
RETURNS	2,268	2,540	2,845	3,272	10,925	2.0%
NET SALES	111,132	124,468	139,404	160,315	535,318	100.0%
COST OF SALES	70,013	78,415	87,825	100,998	337,251	63.0%
GROSS PROFIT	41,119	46,053	51,579	59,316	198,068	37.0%
EXPENSES						
SALARIES	32,700	32,700	32,700	32,700	130,800	24.4%
PAYROLL TAXES	4,905	4,905	4,905	4,905	19,620	3.7%
FRINGE BENEFITS	2,289	2,289	2,289	2,289	9,156	1.7%
Subtotal labor	39,894	39,894	39,894	39,894	159,576	29.8%
STORE RENT	6,000	6,000	6,000	6,000	24,000	4.5%
UTILITIES	1,200	1,200	1,200	1,200	4,800	0.9%
MAINTENANCE	1,500	1,500	1,500	1,500	6,000	1.1%
DEPRECIATION	2,250	2,250	2,250	2,250	9,000	1.7%
ADVERTISING	4,500	2,000	1,750	1,500	9,750	1.8%
POSTAGE & FREIGH	1,111	1,245	1,394	1,603	5,353	1.0%
INSURANCE	750	750	750	750	3,000	0.6%
TELEPHONE	450	450	450	450	1,800	0.3%
EXCISE TAXES	556	622	697	802	2,677	0.5%
MISCELLANEOUS	450	450	450	450	1,800	0.3%
Subtotal nonlabor	18,767	16,467	16,441	16,505	68,180	12.7%
TOTAL EXPENSES	58,661	56,361	56,335	56,399	227,756	42.5%
NET PROFIT	(17,542)	(10,308)	(4,756)	2,918	(29,688)	-5.5%

Formatting Cells before You Enter Data

In Chapter 5 you didn't format the cells to look a particular way until you had entered most of the data. Actually, formatting the cells beforehand is a little easier, since numbers will then appear in the correct form as you enter them. Follow the instructions below to format the cells in the spreadsheet.

> **Note** See "Widening and Narrowing Spreadsheet Columns" and "Aligning Spreadsheet Cells in Columns" in Chapter 5 for detailed information about these formatting features.

Making Columns the Right Width

1. Open a new spreadsheet document by selecting File ➤ Create New File.

Notice in Figure 6.1 that all the columns except column A fit into an eight-character-wide space. To get as many columns on screen as possible, you need to cut the width of the columns down to 8 spaces from the default of 10. Column A will require more space, though.

The Go To key, F5, for selecting a range We need to select range B1:G1 in order to change the column widths of columns B through G. To select this range, you can use the mouse or the Go To key, F5. Let's try the Go To key:

2. Press the Go To key, F5. The Go To dialog box appears. Here you can quickly enter a cell range.

3. Type **B1:G1** and in the Go To section of the dialog box and press ↵. The range is selected.

4. Choose Format ➤ Column Width. Type in **8** as the width and press ↵.

5. To change the width of column A, select cell A1. Set the width of column A to 20 to accommodate the lengthy labels in that column.

CHAPTER 6 Advanced Spreadsheet Skills

In the case of both column A and columns B through G, the entire column changed width even though only one cell in each column was selected. You only have to select one cell in a column to alter the column's width.

Formatting with Commas and Percentages

Now we want to set up a large section of the spreadsheet (cells B20 to F48) to display numbers with commas but not with decimal places. Although these are dollar figures, we will eschew the decimals because we want to round off the numbers to the nearest dollar.

1. Press F5 to display the Go To dialog box and select cells **B20:F48**.
2. Choose Format ➤ Number and select Comma on the Number dialog box.
3. Type **0** to set Number of decimals to 0.
4. Click OK.

The Extend key, F8, for selecting a range Two ranges on the spreadsheet display their contents in percent format:

- The "Givens" section of column E, with growth and tax figures
- The "Budget" section of column G (the percentage of net sales that each category accounts for)

This time we'll use the Extend key, F8, to select the range. When you press F8, you enter *Extend mode*. In this mode you can press arrow keys to automatically enlarge a range area. Try it out:

1. Move the cursor to cell E5.
2. Press F8.
3. Press ↓ nine times, or until the area to the left of the formula bar reads E5:E14.
4. Press Esc to exit Extend mode.
5. Choose Format ➤ Number, select Percent, and set one decimal place.

210

Example Exercise: Building a Budget Spreadsheet

6. Now set the same percent formatting (with one decimal place) for range G20:G48.

7. Choose File ➤ Save and save the file under the name BUDGET.

> **Tip** To select a cell range, you can press Shift and an arrow key, press the Go To key (F5), press the Extend key (F8), or use the mouse. Depending on how many cells you need to select, one technique will be easier than another.

Entering the Data

Since most of the Givens section consists only of labels and numbers (not formulas), start entering data into the Givens cells first:

1. Referring to Figure 6.1, start by entering the title and main heading, **Bob's House of Gadgets**, in cell B1.

2. In cell B2, enter two spaces (by pressing the spacebar) followed by the words **Budget for New Store**. The extra spaces help center this heading below the store name.

3. Now move the cursor to A4 and type twenty equal signs:

    "====================

You must begin the row with double quotation marks or else Works will think you are trying to create a formula.

Ctrl+⏎ for entering the same data across several cells That puts a bunch of equal signs into cell A4, but it doesn't create a line all the way across the screen. To create such a line, you could keep holding down the equal sign and enter one long line into cell A4, but then the word *GIVENS*, when entered into cell B4, would overwrite the right half of the line. You could also select each adjacent cell one at a time and enter equal signs into all of them, but there is an easier way: press Ctrl+⏎ to enter identical data into multiple cells.

CHAPTER 6 — Advanced Spreadsheet Skills

1. Move the cursor to B4.
2. Select B4 to G4.
3. Press " and then = eight times to fill the length of one cell (8 spaces).
4. Press Ctrl+↵ to enter the equal signs into all the selected cells.

Now your spreadsheet should look like Figure 6.2.

FIGURE 6.2
The first four lines entered

> **Tip** You can also press Ctrl+↵ to copy formulas into a range of cells. Works will automatically adjust the formulas to their relative references in the process.

Now let's put the word *Givens* in the middle of the line of equal signs:

1. Move to B4, type "=====**Givens**====== (that's five equal signs before and six after), and press ↵.

However, the word has been cut off. The equal signs in cells C4 and D4 are preventing the rest of the word from being seen.

2. Move to C4, and clear out its contents by pressing the Del key. Now you should be able to read the word.

Example Exercise: Building a Budget Spreadsheet

Entering the "Given" Employee Information

Our spreadsheet assumes that the number of employees will stay constant, and that their salaries will, too. Employees are categorized by type. The number of each type employee is listed, and so is the monthly salary. By multiplying the number of employees in each salary type by the salary and then summing the results, you can calculate the total salary outlay per month.

1. Type in the following information in column A (don't forget to skip a line at cell A10):

CELL	ENTER
A5	EMPLOYEES
A6	STORE MANAGER
A7	FLOOR MANAGER
A8	TAILOR
A9	SALES PERSON
A11	TOTAL SALARIES

Tip: You can press an arrow key to enter a value into the current cell and move to the next cell in one key press. This makes entering numbers in columns easier.

2. Move to column B and enter the following information:

CELL	ENTER
B5	Number
B6	1
B7	1
B8	1
B9	4

CHAPTER 6 — Advanced Spreadsheet Skills

3. Move down to B11, but don't type in the number 10,900 as you see it in Figure 6.1.

    Cell B11 is a calculated number that reflects the sum of the salaries in column C multiplied by the number of employees in column B.

4. In cell B11, enter the formula

    =(B6*C6)+(B7*C7)+(B8*C8)+(B9*C9)

    and press ↵.

    Notice that a zero appears in cell B11. This is because there is currently nothing in the cells referenced by the formula you just entered. Don't forget the equal sign at the beginning of the formula, or Works will think you are creating a label instead of a formula.

> **Tip** If you forget to enter the equal sign at the start of a formula, press F2 to switch to Edit mode, press Home to get to the beginning of the formula, and then press Del to delete the quotation mark. Then enter an equal sign and press ↵.

5. Enter the following in column C:

CELL	ENTER
C5	Salaries
C6	2500
C7	2000
C8	1600
C9	1200

Notice that the number in cell B11 is recalculated with each entry you make in the column. It should now read 10900.

Example Exercise: Building a Budget Spreadsheet

6. To format the salary figures, select C6 to C9, select Format ➤ Number, choose Comma, set the Number of decimals to 0, and click OK.

7. Do the same for cell B11.

Entering the "Given" Percentage Information

Percentage Givens break down as follows:

◆ The first four entries list what the store's income growth percentages are expected to be by quarter.

◆ A 2 percent allowance for customer returns of goods sold to be calculated against the store's revenues.

◆ The cost of sales (COS), which we assume is 63 percent. The cost of sales is essentially the gross sales minus inventory costs and selling expenses.

◆ Payroll tax (P/R Tax), fringe benefits (Fringe), postage and freight (Post/Fgt), and excise tax (Exc. Tax).

To enter the percentage "givens":

1. Enter these ten labels in column D:

CELL	ENTER
D5	1st Grth
D6	2nd Grth
D7	3rd Grth
D8	4th Grth
D9	Returns
D10	COS
D11	P/R Tax
D12	Fringe
D13	Post/Fgt
D14	Exc.Tax

CHAPTER 6   Advanced Spreadsheet Skills

Notice that the left edge of column D and right edge of column C seem to run together. You can fix that:

2. Select D5 to D14 and click on the Right Align button in the toolbar. Now your screen should look like Figure 6.3.

3. Enter the following in column E. Don't forget to include the percent (%) sign. As an alternative to using the percent sign, you can enter .08, .12, and so on. You formatted these cells for percentage, so Works will convert such data entries to 8 percent, 12 percent, and so on.

CELL	ENTER
E5	8%
E6	12%
E7	12%
E8	15%
E9	2%
E10	63%
E11	15%
E12	7%
E13	1%
E14	.5%

Entering the "Given" Fixed Expenses

Now it is time to enter the fixed expenses. These are the expenses that are not expected to change each month. Actually, salaries could fit into this category, but for the sake of clarity it's better to break salaries out as you have done. The fixed expenses include rent, utilities, maintenance, depreciation, insurance, telephone costs, and miscellaneous odds and ends, all of these rounded to the nearest dollar.

FIGURE 6.3
The first four columns entered

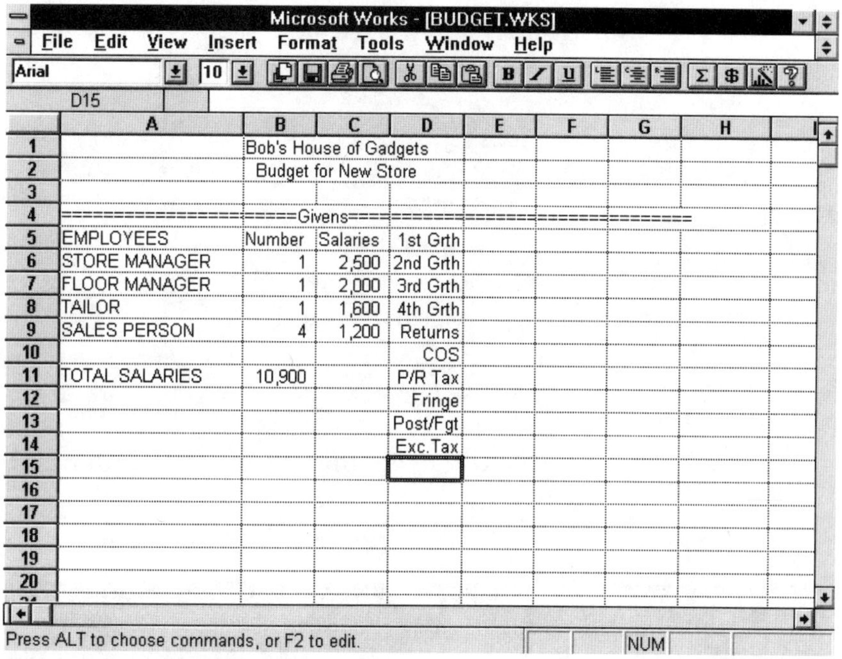

	A	B	C	D	E	F	G	H
1		Bob's House of Gadgets						
2		Budget for New Store						
3								
4	=====	======	=====Givens====	=====	=====	=====	=====	======
5	EMPLOYEES	Number	Salaries	1st Grth				
6	STORE MANAGER	1	2,500	2nd Grth				
7	FLOOR MANAGER	1	2,000	3rd Grth				
8	TAILOR	1	1,600	4th Grth				
9	SALES PERSON	4	1,200	Returns				
10				COS				
11	TOTAL SALARIES		10,900	P/R Tax				
12				Fringe				
13				Post/Fgt				
14				Exc.Tax				

To enter the "given" fixed expenses:

1. Enter the following in column F:

CELL	ENTER
F5	**Rent**
F6	**Util**
F7	**Maint**
F8	**Deprec**
F9	**Insur**
F10	**Phone**
F11	**Misc**

These labels are running up against the neighboring column again.

2. Select F5 through F11 and format it using the toolbar's Right Align button.

CHAPTER 6 Advanced Spreadsheet Skills

3. Enter the following in column G:

G5	2000
G6	400
G7	500
G8	750
G9	250
G10	150
G11	150

4. Choose File ➤ Save to save your work so far and continue.

That completes the Givens section. Your screen should look like Figure 6.4.

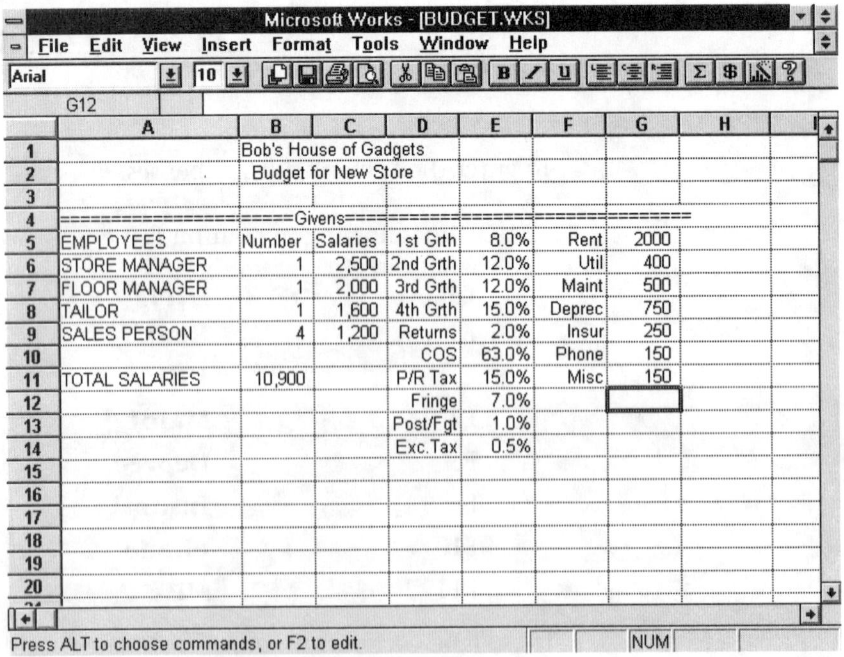

FIGURE 6.4

The "Givens" section completed

	A	B	C	D	E	F	G	H
1			Bob's House of Gadgets					
2			Budget for New Store					
3								
4	========	======	======	==Givens==	======	======	======	======
5	EMPLOYEES	Number	Salaries	1st Grth	8.0%	Rent	2000	
6	STORE MANAGER	1	2,500	2nd Grth	12.0%	Util	400	
7	FLOOR MANAGER	1	2,000	3rd Grth	12.0%	Maint	500	
8	TAILOR	1	1,600	4th Grth	15.0%	Deprec	750	
9	SALES PERSON	4	1,200	Returns	2.0%	Insur	250	
10				COS	63.0%	Phone	150	
11	TOTAL SALARIES		10,900	P/R Tax	15.0%	Misc	150	
12				Fringe	7.0%			
13				Post/Fgt	1.0%			
14				Exc.Tax	0.5%			

Entering the Budget

Now you can move ahead to enter the budget itself, along with the formulas. During this process, you'll learn several new techniques, mostly pertaining to how you use a spreadsheet that's larger than your screen.

First you'll enter the heading line, the column names, and the line of single dashes that separates the Budget section from the Givens section. Refer to Figure 6.1 to refresh your memory during the following steps.

1. Select A15 and enter twenty equal signs in it. (Don't forget the quotation mark at the beginning.)

2. Select B15 and enter "=====**Budget**==== (that's five equal signs before and four after).

3. Select D15 to G15, enter "======== (eight equal signs, the width of the column) and press Ctrl+↵.

Inserting Rows in a Spreadsheet

It looks as though the dividing line was supposed to be one row lower, in row 16, not 15, at least according to Figure 6.1. To correct this, we'll insert a new row:

1. Position the mouse cursor on the 15 at the far left edge of the window. (This is the selector button for the row.)

2. Click on the row number directly below where you want to insert the row or rows. In our case, click on row number 15. This selects the whole row.

3. Choose Insert ➤ Row/Column and click on Row if it is not already selected. A new row is inserted just above the row you had selected.

Tip

To insert more than one row, select more rows before choosing the Insert command. Selecting two rows inserts two rows, selecting three rows inserts three rows, and so on.

CHAPTER 6 Advanced Spreadsheet Skills

Let's continue with our spreadsheet:

1. Enter the seven column headings across row 17. Press the Caps Lock key as you make the entries (since they are all in uppercase letters) and press → to move to the next column after each entry.

CELL	ENTER
A17	**BUDGET CATEGORY**
B17	**QTR 1**
C17	**QTR 2**
D17	**QTR 3**
E17	**QTR 4**
F17	**TOTAL**
G17	**% SALES**

   After you've entered the final column heading, press ↵.

2. Center the headings (except the first one) by selecting B17 through G17 and clicking on the Center Align button in the toolbar.

3. Enter the row of single dashes in row 18 to set off the headings from the body of the budget. This can be done in one fell swoop by typing

   "--

   and pressing ↵. (Don't forget the quotation mark.) If the line length isn't correct, press F2, edit it by adding more dashes or pressing the Backspace key, and press ↵ again.

Entering the Row Labels

Now you can type in the row labels, or *headings*. Note that there are 24 headings to be typed in and that some of them are bold. There are also six blank rows in the Budget section. Don't forget the blank rows or put them in the wrong places. If you do, things won't line up correctly.

Example Exercise: Building a Budget Spreadsheet

4. Use Figure 6.1 as a guide and enter the following row labels (REVENUE, EXPENSES, TOTAL EXPENSES, and NET PROFIT should be in bold):

CELL	ENTER
A19	**REVENUE**
A20	SALES
A21	RETURNS
A22	NET SALES
A23	
A24	COST OF SALES
A25	
A26	GROSS PROFIT
A27	
A28	**EXPENSES**
A29	SALARIES
A30	PAYROLL TAXES
A31	FRINGE BENEFITS
A32	Subtotal labor
A33	
A34	STORE RENT
A35	UTILITIES
A36	MAINTENANCE
A37	DEPRECIATION
A38	ADVERTISING
A39	POSTAGE & FREIGHT
A40	INSURANCE
A41	TELEPHONE
A42	EXCISE TAXES
A43	MISCELLANEOUS
A44	Subtotal nonlabor

CHAPTER 6   Advanced Spreadsheet Skills

CELL	ENTER
A45	
A46	TOTAL EXPENSES
A47	
A48	NET PROFIT

Splitting the Screen to See More of a Spreadsheet

When you entered the row labels, your screen scrolled upwards when you reached row 20 or 21. At times you will want to keep parts of a spreadsheet on screen as you move around. For example, if you were entering data in row Z, you would want to see the column labels in row A so you could make sure you were entering data in the right places.

Works lets you divide your screen into *panes,* with each pane displaying a different part of the spreadsheet. You can split the screen in a horizontal direction, a vertical direction, or both ways at once to see four panes at one time. Dividing the screen into panes is especially helpful when you need to refer to a set of values, such as a list in the Givens section of our budget spreadsheet, while entering formulas or checking your work.

Let's create two panes, one for the Budget section and one for the Givens section:

1. Move to the top of the spreadsheet by pressing Ctrl+Home.

2. Click on the horizontal *split line*. It is located just above the scrolling arrow in the upper-right corner of the work area:

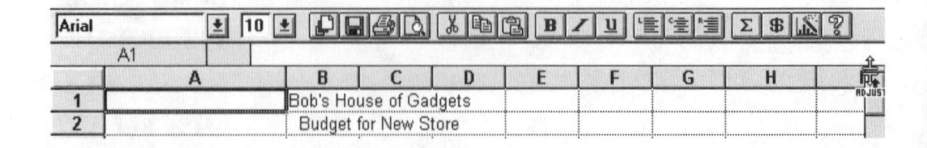

3. When you click on the small horizontal line, the cursor changes to a two-headed arrow and a line appears across the window.

222

Example Exercise: Building a Budget Spreadsheet

4. Drag the line down between rows 12 and 13, and release the mouse button. This sets the split and exits Split mode.

> **Tip**
> To split the screen vertically, locate the vertical split button in the lower-left corner of the window and drag it right. Another option, if you don't have a mouse, is to choose the Window ➤ Split command and press the arrow keys.

5. You want to work with the Budget section only, so move the cursor down into that pane by pressing the Pane key, F6. (If you had four panes, pressing F6 would move you through them in sequence.) Position your panes so that your screen looks like that in Figure 6.5.

FIGURE 6.5
Splitting the screen into two panes

223

Working in a pane is really no different than working in a window, except you can't see as much of your work at one time.

Entering the Formulas in the Spreadsheet

In our spreadsheet, each quarter's growth in sales revenue is arrived at by multiplying the prior quarter's sales by the projected growth factor (in cells E5 through E8) for the quarter plus 100 percent. The formula has to increase the growth percentages listed in E5 through E8 by 100 percent because, for example, the second quarter sales revenues will be 112 percent and not 12 percent of the first quarter sales.

Follow these steps to enter the sales formulas in row 20:

1. In the lower pane, move to cell B20, the sales for the first quarter.
2. Let's assume the sales will be about $113,400 during the first quarter. Enter the value **113400** (no need to enter commas) and press →.

Now you're on C20, the second quarter sales, where things start to get complex. The formula for this cell should multiply the previous quarter's sales (in cell B20) by the growth factor for the second quarter (in E6) plus 100, as explained above.

3. In cell C20, enter the formula =B20*(1+E6) and press →. Here you are telling Works to multiply first quarter sales (cell B20) by 112 percent, which is the second quarter growth rate of 12 (in cell E6) plus 100 percent.
4. For the third and fourth quarter sales, the formulas are almost the same. Enter the following formulas:

CELL	ENTER
D20	=C20*(1+E7)
E20	=D20*(1+E8)

Absolute vs. Relative and Mixed Cell References

In Chapter 5 you copied formulas and had Works adjust the references in the formulas as necessary for their new locations. For example, suppose the formula in B4 was

=B1+B2+B3

and you copied it (using the Edit ➤ Copy command) to cell C4. Works would adjust the formula to

=C1+C2+C3

> **Note** See "Entering and Copying Formulas in Cells" in Chapter 5 for advice about copying formulas with relative references.

But suppose you didn't want Works to make these adjustments. Works has assumed that the cell names in the formula are *relative* references and they should be adjusted when copied. Relative references are the most common type of reference used in electronic spreadsheets because, more often than not, the formulas in a row or column refer to other cells in the same row or column.

However, there is another type of reference called an *absolute reference*. You use absolute references when copying formulas to tell Works *not* to adjust the cell addresses in the formulas, but rather to leave them as they are. This way you can "borrow" key values from specific cells elsewhere in the spreadsheet. In an absolute reference, the cell address in the formula always refers to a specific cell, no matter where the formula is copied or moved.

The $ sign for entering absolute references You indicate an absolute reference in a formula by placing a dollar ($) sign before each part of the cell's address you want to reference. For example, if the formula

=B1+B2+$B$3

were copied to cell C4, Works would adjusts the first two cell references but leave the last one absolute. The copied formula in C4 would be:

=C1+C2+$B$3

Here, the absolute reference to cell B3 remains intact.

Using Mixed References

There is a third type of reference called the *mixed reference*. A mixed reference includes both absolute and relative references in a single cell address. For example, the pointers B$3 and $B3 are both mixed references:

- B$3 means the column is relative and the row is absolute.
- $B3 means the column is absolute and the row is relative.

However, mixed references are rarely used in spreadsheets and will not be covered here. When you use the Edit ➤ Fill command to copy mixed references, Works adjusts the relative part of the formula and leaves the absolute part unaltered.

Most of the remaining formulas in the budget example use absolute references, so you'll get lots of exercise in learning to use them.

Copying Formulas with Absolute References

Consider these two candidates for absolute references: the quarterly calculations for returned merchandise, a figure calculated by using the value in cell E9 (2 percent), and the quarterly Cost of Sales calculation, which repeatedly calls upon cell E10 (63 percent).

To get the Copy command to duplicate the absolute reference (to E9) in the Returns row (row 21), you'll manually enter the formula for the first quarter and then copy it to the remaining quarters:

1. In cell B21, enter the formula **=B20*$E$9**.

2. Make sure the cursor is in B21 and press Shift+→ three times to select the range B21:E21.

3. Choose Edit ➤ Fill Right.

The formulas—including the absolute references to cell E9—are copied into the remaining columns, and the cells' values are calculated and displayed.

The figure for net sales (row 22) is nothing more than the sales minus the returns. Calculating the net sales should be easy, since there are no absolute references here, only relative ones. Follow these steps to fill in B22 through E22.

1. Move to B22, enter **=B20–B21**, and press ↵.
2. Select B22:E22 and choose Edit ➤ Fill Right. That's it for net sales.

The cost of sales for each quarter (row 24) is calculated by multiplying net sales (row 22) by COS (cell E10), the gross sales minus inventory costs and selling expenses. When copying these formulas, we'll make cell E10 an absolute reference:

1. Move to B24, enter **=B22*$E$10**, and ↵.
2. Select B24:E24 and choose Edit ➤ Fill Right.

The copied formula retains the absolute reference to cell E10.

3. Move to B26 to begin filling in the gross profits. Gross profit is calculated by subtracting the cost of sales from the net sales.
4. In B26, enter **=B22–B24**, and press ↵.
5. Select B26:E26 and choose Edit ➤ Fill Right.
6. Save your work now before moving on.

Filling In the Total and Percent of Sales Columns

The revenues section isn't quite finished, since you haven't filled in the columns for totals and percent of sales.

Adding column or row cells with the Summation button The Total column is nothing more than the sum of the columns to the left. In F20, you want the sum of the values in the four cells to the left:

=SUM(B20:E20)

You could enter this formula directly or you could use the Summation button, the button shaped like a Greek letter sigma on the toolbar:

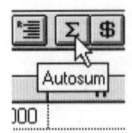

This useful button adds the values in the closest adjacent cells either in a row or column. For the Summation button to work, the active cell has to be at the bottom of a column or at the end of a row of cells.

To enter the totals in column F:

1. Select cell F20, click on the Summation button, and press ↵. The value 546,243 appears in cell F20.

Net sales and gross profit totals are calculated the same way, so you can use the Edit ➤ Fill Down command to enter these formulas. In fact, since the Total column will use the same formula all the way down to the last row—row 48—why not copy the formula in F20 all the way down? All the references are relative, so no dollar signs are required in the source cell.

2. Press F5 and select F20:F48.
3. Choose Edit ➤ Fill Down.

All the totals you wanted (and more) are calculated. For rows you haven't completed yet, the totals show up as zero, for obvious reasons. In addition, some rows that you didn't want anything in got zeros too. Don't worry about them now. The zeros will change as you add more data, and later you can use the Clear command to erase cells that should be blank.

To enter the sales percentages in column G, you have to calculate the percentage of total net sales that each budget category accounts for. Thus, sales (F20) divided by net sales (F22) will yield the proper answer for the Sales percentage column:

1. Move to G20 and enter **=F20/$F$22**. The net sales figure is an absolute reference.

The figure 102.0% appears, which makes sense since we expected returns of 2 percent.

2. Select G20:G48 and copy this formula all the way down to G48 with the Edit ➤ Fill Down command.

As expected, lots of zeros followed by percent signs (0.0%) appear. Most of these will be recalculated as you add data. The rest you can remove later.

"Freezing" Row and Column Names to Make Data Entry Easier

Works offers a special feature so you can tell where you are entering data in a spreadsheet. With the Format ➤ Freeze Title command, you can *lock* selected rows or columns and keep them from moving as you scroll through a spreadsheet. Being able to freeze column and row titles is especially useful in accounting work, where spreadsheets typically have at least twelve columns for the twelve months. You can lock columns, rows, or both at once.

Let's lock rows 17 and 18 so we can see which quarter we're working on in the bottom pane:

1. Move the split bar to row 18.
2. Move to cell A19.
3. Choose Format ➤ Freeze Titles to freeze all the rows above A19.

CHAPTER 6   **Advanced Spreadsheet Skills**

Now as you scroll down to enter the rest of the budget, anything above A19 will stay in view. Try it now to see the effect:

4. Press ↓ and hold it down for several seconds to scroll down.
5. Press ↑ and scroll up.

Freezing rows and columns   For your future reference, here are instructions for freezing columns, rows, and columns and rows:

TO FREEZE	ACTION
Rows	Move the split bar to the row you want to freeze. Then select Format ➤ Freeze Titles. All rows above the split bar will freeze.
Columns	Move the vertical split bar to the column you want to freeze. Then select Format ➤ Freeze Titles. All columns to the left of the split bar will freeze.
Rows and Columns	Move both split bars into place. Then select Format ➤ Freeze Titles to freeze all rows above the horizontal split bar and all columns to the left of the vertical split bar.

"Unfreezing" rows and columns   When you are done entering data and you no longer need to see "frozen" columns and rows, select Format ➤ Freeze Titles again. This will turn off the freezing feature.

> **Tip**   If you accidentally freeze the wrong rows or columns, select Format ➤ Freeze Titles again to turn off the freezing option and start all over again.

Example Exercise: Building a Budget Spreadsheet

Entering the Expenses

With the Revenue portion of the spreadsheet finished, you can begin entering the expenses formulas. This first section is relatively uncomplicated. It involves fixed, nonfluctuating expenses, so all you have to do is multiply numbers in the Givens section by three (because there are three months in a quarter):

1. Move to B29 (the first quarter salaries), enter **=3*$B$11**, and press ↵. Cell B11 is the TOTAL SALARIES cell, visible in the upper pane.
2. Select range B29:E29 and choose Edit ➤ Fill Right.
3. Repeat this process for the other cells using constants listed in the Givens section of the spreadsheet. After you enter the formula in column B, copy it across columns B through E (the last three quarters) for each of the fixed expenses below:

CELL	EXPENSE CATEGORY	ENTER
B34	STORE RENT	=3*$G$5
B35	UTILITIES	=3*$G$6
B36	MAINTENANCE	=3*$G$7
B37	DEPRECIATION	=3*$G$8
B40	INSURANCE	=3*$G$9
B41	TELEPHONE	=3*$G$10
B43	MISCELLANEOUS	=3*$G$11

Make sure that you enter the dollar signs (to indicate the absolute reference) before copying each formula to the last three quarters. Don't worry about the TOTAL or % SALES columns since these cells have already been entered and will recalculate as you progress.

At this point, if you were to remove the split and adjust the sheet to see the expenses details, your spreadsheet would look like Figure 6.6.

CHAPTER 6 Advanced Spreadsheet Skills

FIGURE 6.6

The spreadsheet with most of the budget formulas entered

	A	B	C	D	E	F	G
28	EXPENSES						0.0%
29	SALARIES	32,700	32,700	32,700	32,700	130,800	24.4%
30	PAYROLL TAXES					0	0.0%
31	FRINGE BENEFITS					0	0.0%
32	Subtotal labor					0	0.0%
33						0	0.0%
34	STORE RENT	6,000	6,000	6,000	6,000	24,000	4.5%
35	UTILITIES	1,200	1,200	1,200	1,200	4,800	0.9%
36	MAINTENANCE	1,500	1,500	1,500	1,500	6,000	1.1%
37	DEPRECIATION	2,250	2,250	2,250	2,250	9,000	1.7%
38	ADVERTISING					0	0.0%
39	POSTAGE & FREIGHT					0	0.0%
40	INSURANCE	750	750	750	750	3,000	0.6%
41	TELEPHONE	450	450	450	450	1,800	0.3%
42	EXCISE TAXES					0	0.0%
43	MISCELLANEOUS	450	450	450	450	1,800	0.3%
44	Subtotal nonlabor					0	0.0%
45						0	0.0%
46						0	0.0%
47	TOTAL EXPENSES					0	0.0%

Entering Fluctuating Expenses

There is only one fluctuating expense in the budget: advertising. Because this expense fluctuates from month to month, it is not included in the Givens section.

◆ Enter the following values for advertising for each quarter:

CELL	QUARTER	ENTER
B38	QTR 1	4500
C38	QTR 2	2000
D38	QTR 3	1750
E38	QTR 4	1500

Entering Formulas Using Functions

The remaining cells in the Budget section of the spreadsheet use functions in their calculations and draw upon values in other budget categories.

1. In B30, the row for payroll taxes, enter **=B29*$E$11** (the first-quarter salaries in B29 multiplied by the payroll tax rate in E11).

2. Copy this formula to the rest of the quarters using Edit ➤ Fill Right.

3. In B31, enter **=B29*$E$12** (the first-quarter salaries in B29 multiplied by the fringe benefit percentage in E12) to calculate the fringe benefits for the first quarter.

4. Copy the formula to the rest of the quarters using Edit ➤ Fill Right.

The labor subtotal in row 32 is the sum of salaries, payroll taxes, and fringe benefits.

5. In B32, enter **=SUM(B29:B31)**.

6. Copy the formula to the rest of the quarters in row 32 with Edit ➤ Fill Right.

Postage and freight are calculated by multiplying the net sales (B22) by the percentage in the Post/Fgt cell (E13):

7. Move to B39, type in **=B22*$E$13**, and press ↵.

8. Copy the formula to the rest of the quarters with Edit ➤ Fill Right.

Calculating excise taxes in row 42 is done the same way. In cell B42, you multiply the Net sales (cell B22) by the percentage in E14 (.5 percent):

9. In B42, enter **=B22*$E$14**.

10. Copy the formula to the rest of the quarters.

The nonlabor subtotal in row B44 is the sum of rows B34 to B43—in other words, all the expenses in this section.

11. In B44, enter **=SUM(B34:B43)**, and press ↵.
12. Copy the formula to the rest of the quarters.

Now it's time to enter the first quarter formulas for total expense and net profit. For the moment, we won't copy these formulas to the other quarters—we'll just enter them.

13. In cell B46, enter **=B32+B44**. This is the sum of the two subtotals (labor and nonlabor).
14. In cell B48, enter **=B26–B46** (the gross profits minus total expenses).

Copying Several Formulas at Once

You've been copying formulas across columns on a line-by-line basis, but there is a much faster way to copy formulas. Works lets you copy a block of formulas from left to right. For the copy procedure to work, the formulas being copied must be in the leftmost column of the block. When the copy is made, the formulas adjust across the whole block.

To copy several formulas at once:

1. Select both the cells to be copied and the cells to which you want to make the copies. In our case, select B44:E48 (the cells to be copied must be in the leftmost column of the selection):

43	MISCELLANEOUS	450	450	450	450	1,800
44	Subtotal nonlabor	18,767				18,767
45						0
46	TOTAL EXPENSES	58,661				58,661
47						
48	NET PROFIT	(17,542)				
49						

2. Choose Edit ➤ Fill Right.

Now you are done entering the data in the spreadsheet. Incidentally, the numbers in parentheses indicate negative values. Thus, it appears your new store will lose money in the first three quarters after opening.

Example Exercise: Building a Budget Spreadsheet

The Finishing Touches...

With all the data entered, you can go ahead and do a little cleaning up. Some rows have zeros in them. We could make these cells blank instead. The first thing to do is to remove the split so you can see the whole spreadsheet better:

1. Choose Format ➤ Freeze Titles to unfreeze the rows at the top.

2. Delete the cells that just have zeros in them with either of these methods:

   ◆ If zeros are all on one row, drag across the cells to select them and choose Edit ➤ Clear or press Del.

   ◆ If you're dealing with just one cell, move to the cell, press Backspace, and press ↵ or one of the arrow keys.

3. Make cells A28, A46, and A48 bold (if you haven't already). To do this, click on each cell—you have to choose them one at a time—and then click on the B button in the toolbar. This will help these important cell labels stand out.

4. Select B1:B2 (the title and subtitle) and click on the Bold button *and* the Italic button. Now the title and subtitle of the spreadsheet stand out more.

5. Try altering the character font and type size. Choose a new font on the toolbar and a new type size (such as 12-point instead of the default 10). Notice that the entire spreadsheet changes font, not just the active or selected cells.

Tip When working with a small spreadsheet, increase the point size to make doing your work on screen easier. For larger spreadsheets, decreasing the point size and using a sans-serif font such as Arial lets you see more data at one time.

235

Tips and Tricks for Using Spreadsheets

Once you have entered the data in a spreadsheet, you will likely want to perform what-if experiments on it, change the formulas if necessary, protect certain cells from being changed, insert page breaks, sort the data, search for data in a spreadsheet, and use names for cell ranges instead of cell addresses. This part of the chapter explains how to do these things.

Protecting Cell Contents from Being Erased

After you've done hours of laborious planning, experimenting, and keypunching to enter a spreadsheet and figure its formulas, you don't want any cells to be accidentally erased or altered. Works lets you protect cells so that no one deletes them, clears them, or copies data into them. You can protect all the cells in a spreadsheet or protect some of them.

All cells are locked by default, but this doesn't mean that they are protected. Locked cells are protected only when Protect Data is checked in the Protection dialog box. Therefore, to protect all the cells in a spreadsheet, all you have to do is select Format ➤ Protection and check Protect Data.

To protect specific cells while leaving others cells unprotected, you must unlock the cells you don't want protected before checking Protect Data.

Protecting the entire spreadsheet To protect your entire spreadsheet from alteration:

1. Choose Format ➤ Protection. The Protection dialog box appears, as in Figure 6.7.
2. Click Protect Data in the Protection area and click OK.

Now all of the locked cells—that is, all the cells in the spreadsheet—are protected and none can be altered. Moreover, the commands on the Format and Edit menus that have to do with changing data will no longer work with your spreadsheet.

Tips and Tricks for Using Spreadsheets

FIGURE 6.7
The Protection dialog box. Here, you can lock the entire spreadsheet or lock some cells so no one can alter them.

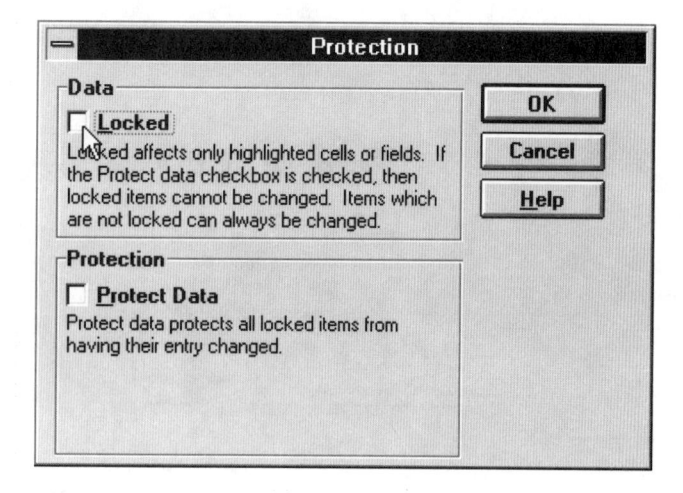

> **Protection**
>
> **Data**
> ☐ **Locked**
> Locked affects only highlighted cells or fields. If the Protect data checkbox is checked, then locked items cannot be changed. Items which are not locked can always be changed.
>
> **Protection**
> ☐ **Protect Data**
> Protect data protects all locked items from having their entry changed.
>
> [OK] [Cancel] [Help]

Protecting specific cells in a spreadsheet Chances are you'll want to be able to alter some cells and not others in a spreadsheet. To lock some cells but not others:

1. Select Format ➤ Protection and make sure Locked and Protect Data are checked (see Figure 6.7).

2. Select the range you want to be able to alter.

3. Choose Format ➤ Protection and uncheck Locked. Now the cells you selected are not locked and can be altered.

4. Check Protect Data to turn protection on for the rest of the cells.

Let's say you want to be able to alter the number of employees and their salaries in the Givens section of your budget spreadsheet:

1. Make sure Protection is off. (Select Format ➤ Protection and uncheck Protect Data Locked in the Protection dialog box, if necessary.)

2. Select the range you want to be able to alter. In our case, select B6:C9.

3. Choose Format ➤ Protection and uncheck Locked (see Figure 6.7).

CHAPTER 6 Advanced Spreadsheet Skills

4. Check Protect Data to turn protection on again. Now, whenever you try to type into any one of the protected cells, the following message appears:

> **Microsoft Works**
>
> Cannot change: locked.
>
> This data has been protected. For information on how to turn off protection, look up Protection in the User's Guide index.
>
> OK

Tip To see whether a cell is unprotected, move to it and choose Format ➤ Protection. Locked will be checked if the cell is protected.

Tip If you want to hide columns so no one can seem them, choose Format ➤ Column Width and set the column width to 0. When you want to see the column again, just widen it.

Viewing the Formulas in a Spreadsheet

By choosing View ➤ Formulas, you can see the formulas on your spreadsheet instead of the values they generate. This command is very

Tips and Tricks for Using Spreadsheets

valuable for those times when your spreadsheet is not calculating right and you need to find out where you entered a formula incorrectly.

To see the formulas:

◆ Choose View ➤ Formulas.

The columns double in width so you can see the formulas in their entirety. You will likely have to use the horizontal scroll bar at the bottom of the screen to see the cells on the right side of your spreadsheet. With the formulas showing, your screen will look something like Figure 6.8.

FIGURE 6.8

A spreadsheet with the formulas showing

	B	C	D	E	F	
20	113400	=B20*(1+E6)	=C20*(1+E7)	=D20*(1+E8)	=SUM(B20:E20)	=F2
21	=B20*$E$9	=C20*$E$9	=D20*$E$9	=E20*$E$9	=SUM(B21:E21)	=F2
22	=B20-B21	=C20-C21	=D20-D21	=E20-E21	=SUM(B22:E22)	=F2
23						
24	=B22*$E$10	=C22*$E$10	=D22*$E$10	=E22*$E$10	=SUM(B24:E24)	=F2
25					=SUM(B25:E25)	=F2
26	=B22-B24	=C22-C24	=D22-D24	=E22-E24	=SUM(B26:E26)	=F2
27						
28						
29	=3*$B$11	=3*$B$11	=3*$B$11	=3*$B$11	=SUM(B29:E29)	=F2
30	=B29*$E$11	=C29*$E$11	=D29*$E$11	=E29*$E$11	=SUM(B30:E30)	=F3
31	=B29*$E$12	=C29*$E$12	=D29*$E$12	=E29*$E$12	=SUM(B31:E31)	=F3
32	=SUM(B29:B31)	=SUM(C29:C31)	=SUM(D29:D31)	=SUM(E29:E31)	=SUM(B32:E32)	=F3
33						
34	=3*$G$5	=3*$G$5	=3*$G$5	=3*$G$5	=SUM(B34:E34)	=F3
35	=3*$G$6	=3*$G$6	=3*$G$6	=3*$G$6	=SUM(B35:E35)	=F3
36	=3*$G$7	=3*$G$7	=3*$G$7	=3*$G$7	=SUM(B36:E36)	=F3
37	=3*$G$8	=3*$G$8	=3*$G$8	=3*$G$8	=SUM(B37:E37)	=F3
38	4500	2000	1750	1500	=SUM(B38:E38)	=F3
39	=B22*$E$13	=C22*$E$13	=D22*$E$13	=E22*$E$13	=SUM(B39:E39)	=F3

239

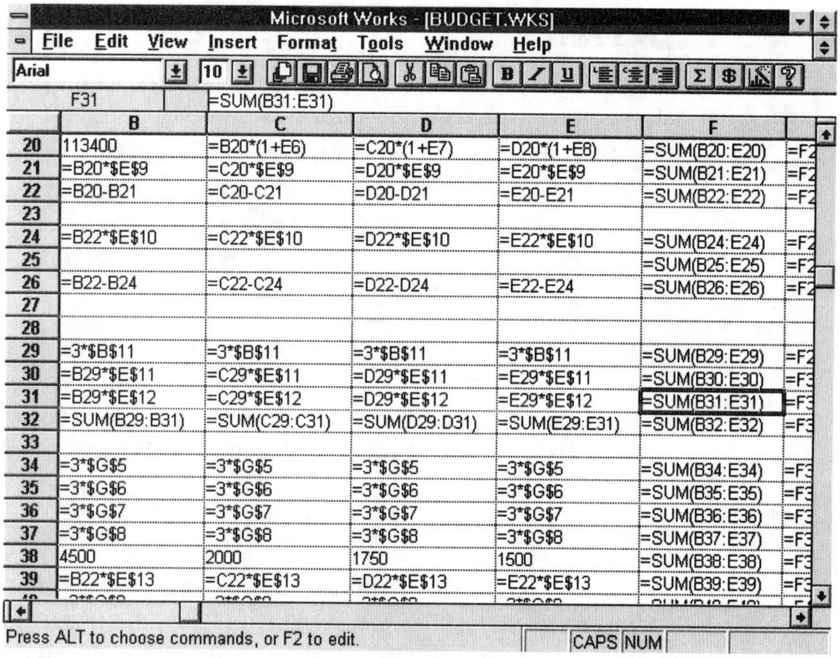

CHAPTER 6   Advanced Spreadsheet Skills

> **Tip**
>
> Printing a copy of your spreadsheet with formulas showing is a good idea because finding errors on the paper copy is easier than looking for them on screen. However, the column widths double when you show formulas, so Works will probably break up your printout across several pages. Try printing in a smaller font to avoid having this happen.

Manual Calculation for Faster "What-If" Experiments

One of the big advantages of spreadsheets is the speed with which you can tinker with variables. In the sample budget you created earlier in this chapter, try altering a few of the Givens at the top of the spreadsheet. Works recalculates formulas whenever you alter a variable that is referenced by a formula. It takes a while for the computer and Works to recalculate the numbers after you make a change, especially if the change alters values in a large number of cells.

Suppose you would like to do what-if experiments but you don't want to wait while Works recalculates formulas each time you alter a variable. Instead of waiting for the spreadsheet to recalculate all the formulas, you can postpone the recalculation. To do so:

◆ Choose Tools ➤ Manual Calculation.

The word *CALC* appears in the status area. When you see this word, it means that Works has yet to recalculate the formulas whose variables you are changing. The word appears after you make a cell change that will alter another cell's value.

When you have altered the variables and you are ready to calculate again:

♦ Choose Tools ➤ Calculate Now.

Inserting Page Breaks in a Spreadsheet

Large spreadsheets are usually larger than a standard page. When printing pages, Works automatically breaks pages at row and column borders as it deems necessary. Works divides pages on the basis of information in the File ➤ Page Setup dialog box and on its knowledge about your printer and the font you've selected.

However, you have some say in where page breaks occur. The Page Break and Delete Page Break commands on the Insert menu let you control the location of page breaks.

Inserting a page break in a spreadsheet To insert a page break in a specific location:

1. Select the column or row after which you want the page break to occur.
   - ♦ If you select a column, Works assumes you're creating a vertical page break—that is, a break between columns.
   - ♦ If you select a row, Works assumes you want a horizontal page break.
2. Choose Insert ➤ Page Break. A dotted line appears where the page break falls.

Deleting a page break To delete a page break:

1. Select the column or row with the page break.
2. Choose Insert ➤ Delete Page Break.

CHAPTER 6 — Advanced Spreadsheet Skills

> **Tip:** If you need more columns and rows on each page, narrow the page margins and eliminate the headers and footers.

Sorting the Data in a Spreadsheet

You can *sort* the rows of a spreadsheet alphabetically or numerically. You would do this, for example, if you had a large inventory spreadsheet with information concerning part numbers, prices, stocks on hand, and so forth, and you needed to print this information in a new order for employees in the store.

The Tools ➤ Sort Rows command makes rearranging rows pretty easy. As an example of how sorting works, let's use the grocery store invoice spreadsheet we created in Chapter 5. (If you don't have it anymore or you never created it, just check out the following figures to see how sorting works.)

> **Warning:** Before you sort a spreadsheet, make either a backup copy or a new copy of the original spreadsheet, since you can't undo a sort once it is completed.

Figure 6.9 shows the invoice as it stood at the end of Chapter 5. Suppose you wanted to sort this sheet so that the items were listed in alphabetical order. To do this, you select the rows to be sorted, choose Tools ➤ Sort Rows, and then you click off options in the dialog box, like so:

1. Bring up the INVOICE.WKS spreadsheet if you still have it.
2. Select the rows you want to sort. The easiest way is to select the column you want the sort based on. As shown in Figure 6.10, you would select A7:A14 in the Invoice spreadsheet.

Tips and Tricks for Using Spreadsheets

3. Choose Tools ➤ Sort Rows. The Sort Rows dialog box appears:

FIGURE 6.9
The invoice spreadsheet ready to be sorted

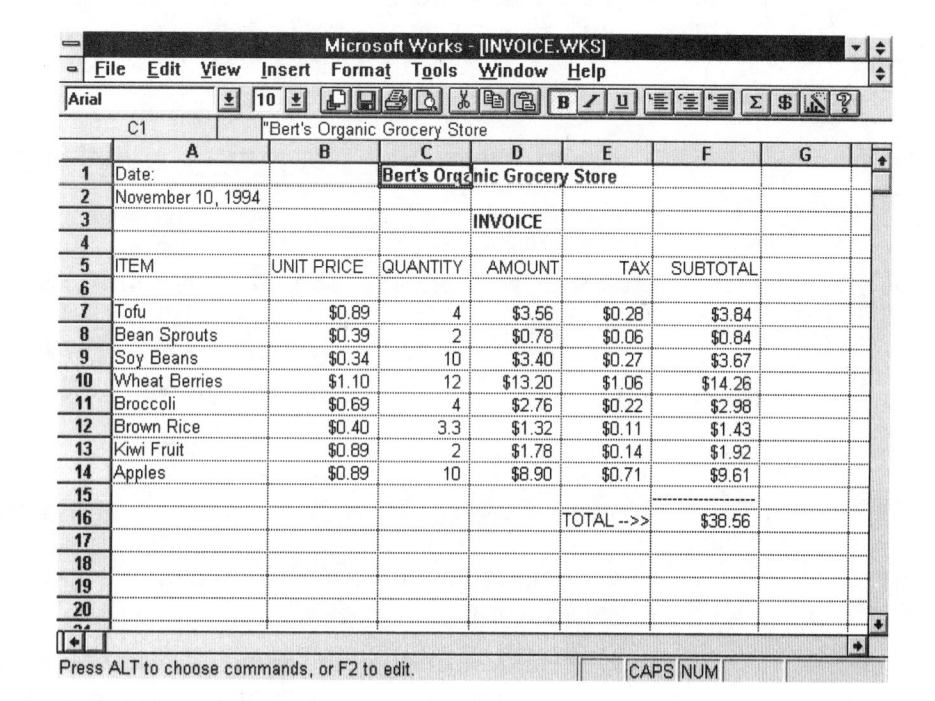

CHAPTER 6   **Advanced Spreadsheet Skills**

FIGURE 6.10

Preparing to sort by selecting rows to sort, and columns to base the sort on

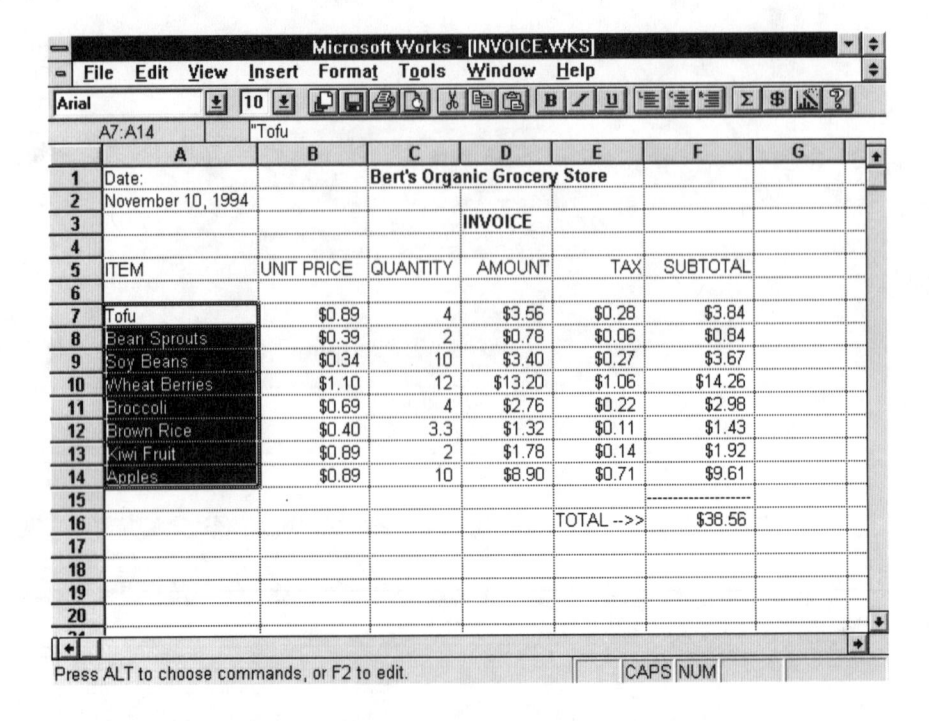

```
                Microsoft Works - [INVOICE.WKS]
 File  Edit  View  Insert  Format  Tools  Window  Help
Arial        10        B I U           Σ $
   A7:A14        "Tofu
              A           B          C          D          E          F          G
 1  Date:                      Bert's Organic Grocery Store
 2  November 10, 1994
 3                                        INVOICE
 4
 5  ITEM              UNIT PRICE  QUANTITY  AMOUNT      TAX     SUBTOTAL
 6
 7  Tofu                  $0.89       4      $3.56     $0.28     $3.84
 8  Bean Sprouts          $0.39       2      $0.78     $0.06     $0.84
 9  Soy Beans             $0.34      10      $3.40     $0.27     $3.67
10  Wheat Berries         $1.10      12     $13.20     $1.06    $14.26
11  Broccoli              $0.69       4      $2.76     $0.22     $2.98
12  Brown Rice            $0.40      3.3     $1.32     $0.11     $1.43
13  Kiwi Fruit            $0.89       2      $1.78     $0.14     $1.92
14  Apples                $0.89      10      $8.90     $0.71     $9.61
15
16                                                   TOTAL -->>  $38.56
17
18
19
20
Press ALT to choose commands, or F2 to edit.                  CAPS NUM
```

Ascending vs. descending sorts As a default, Works sorts in *ascending* order. Ascending sorts arrange the data in alphabetical order in the case of letters, and from one to infinity in the case of numbers. In descending sorts, Z comes before A and the highest numbers come before the lowest ones.

You can choose a descending or ascending sort. In the Sort Rows dialog box, column A is already selected (in the 1st Column box) and Ascend is already checked off. So all you have to do is click OK.

4. Click on OK. The rows are sorted by alphabetical order, as shown in Figure 6.11.

5. If you actually used the Invoice spreadsheet for this example, close the spreadsheet now, but don't save the changes. This way, the original order won't be altered.

"Sorts within sorts" As the Sort Rows dialog box shows you, you can sort on as many as three different rows to conduct a "sort within a sort." To

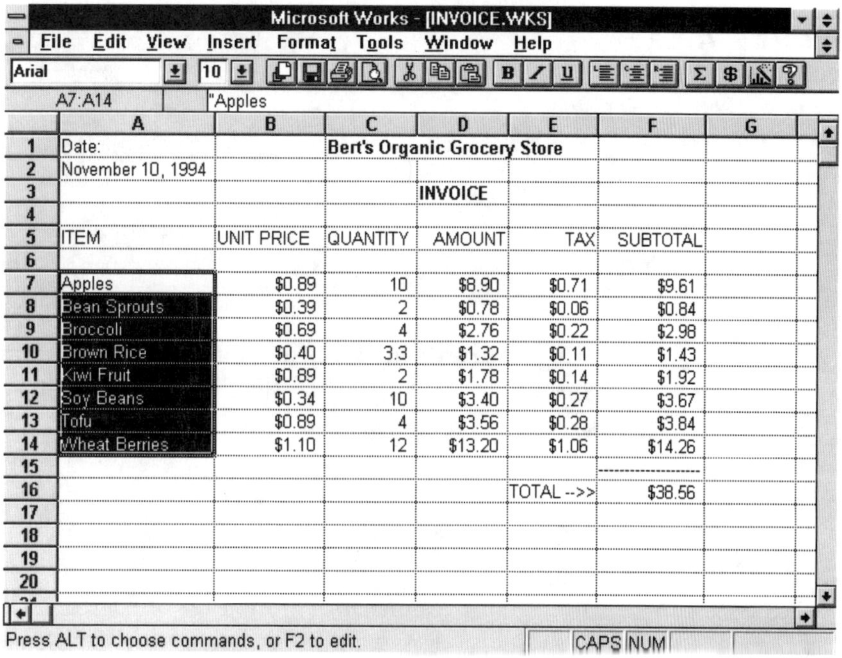

Tips and Tricks for Using Spreadsheets

FIGURE 6.11
The rows sorted in alphabetical order according to item

see why you would do this, consider what would happen if you were sorting a list of last names and two people on the list had the last name Jones. Raul Jones would come before Steve Jones in an ascending sort, but Works wouldn't know to put Raul before Steve unless you chose a second column—the first name column—to sort by in the Sort Rows dialog box. To break the tie, Works would look in the second column to sort by, in this case the first name column, and put Raul Jones before Steve Jones on the list.

Searching for Data in a Spreadsheet

In large spreadsheets, finding a specific cell can be a hassle. Fortunately, Works provides the Find command for searching for a cell value or, if the formulas are displayed, for a formula or portions of formulas.

To conduct a search in a spreadsheet:

1. Choose Edit ➤ Find. The Find dialog box appears as in Figure 6.12.
2. Enter the data you're looking for in the Find What field.

FIGURE 6.12

The Find dialog box

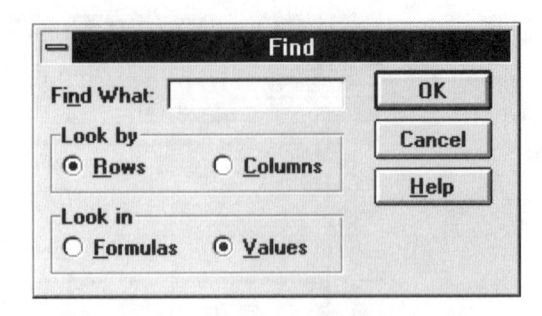

Using wildcards in searches You can enter normal text, such as the word *Broccoli*, in the Find What field, or you can enter wildcards to assist in the search. There are two wildcards:

?   Represents a single letter or numeral in a search. For example, entering Sm?th would find the names Smith and Smyth.

*   Represents more than one letter or numeral in a search. For example, entering Wall* finds both Waller and Wallbanger.

Next, in the Look by box, you must choose whether you want Works to search through the spreadsheet by rows or by columns. It doesn't matter much which you choose, so you don't have to worry about it. They both take about the same amount of time. On the other hand, if you are combing through a huge spreadsheet and know the general vicinity of the data you're looking for, you may save time by choosing the option that will lead Works to the target area more quickly.

3. Choose Rows or Columns in the Look by area.

4. Click on OK.

Works stops on the first cell that meets the match criterion. If it can't find a match, a dialog box appears telling you so.

5. Press F7 to move to the next cell that matches if you need to.

Range Names to Make Entering Formulas Easier

When entering formulas, sometimes it is easier to refer to cells by *range names* than it is to type in the cell addresses. After you give a group of cells a range name, you can refer to the name in formulas instead of entering the cells' addresses. For example, instead of entering

```
SUM(A1+A2+A3+A4)
```

in our example spreadsheet, you could give the range A1:A4 the name "quarterly sales" and enter the formula like so:

```
SUM(quarterly sales)
```

Range names eliminate the hassle of having to remember the addresses of important cells and important cell ranges. You just have to remember the names you've preassigned to certain ranges.

Giving cells a range name Here's how to assign a range name to a group of cells so that formulas can refer to the cells by name:

1. Select the cell(s) you want to name. In the Invoice spreadsheet (see Figure 6.11), choose range C7:C14, the Quantity column.
2. Choose Insert ➤ Range Name to bring up the Range Name dialog box.
3. Type in a name for the range. Range names must not exceed fifteen characters (including spaces). In this case, name the range **quantity**.
4. Click OK. The range is named and added to the list.

Using a range name in a formula Now you can refer to this range name in formulas having to do with the total number of items in the Quantity column. For example, you could sum the range using the formula SUM(quantity). Try it:

5. Move to cell C16 and enter **=SUM(quantity)**.
6. The total number of items in the Quantity column, 47.3, appears in cell C16.

247

CHAPTER 6 — Advanced Spreadsheet Skills

Renaming a range To rename a range:

1. Choose Insert ➤ Range name to open the Range Name dialog box.
2. In the lower box, click the range you want to rename.
3. Edit the name in the upper box, changing it to the new name.
4. Click on OK.

Deleting a range name After you rename a range, you'll probably want to delete its old name. If you don't, you'll have a duplicate range, which can cause confusion later on. To delete a range name:

1. Choose Insert ➤ Range Name to open the Range Name dialog box.
2. Select the old range name and click on Delete.
3. Click on OK.

Giving a range name a new cell address To give an existing range name a new cell address:

1. Select the range whose address you want to give to the existing range name.
2. Choose Insert ➤ Range Name.
3. In the dialog box, click on the range name whose address you want to change.
4. Click on OK.

Tips and Tricks for Using Spreadsheets

Note The Works spreadsheet contains numerous "canned" formulas for use in complex spreadsheets. For more details on the functions, operators, menu commands, and special keys used with the Works spreadsheet, see Appendix C.

You can create charts from your spreadsheet data for presentation purposes, for business reports, and to clearly see trends. Chapter 7 explains how to make various types of charts. Chapter 12 explains how to incorporate charts into other types of documents.

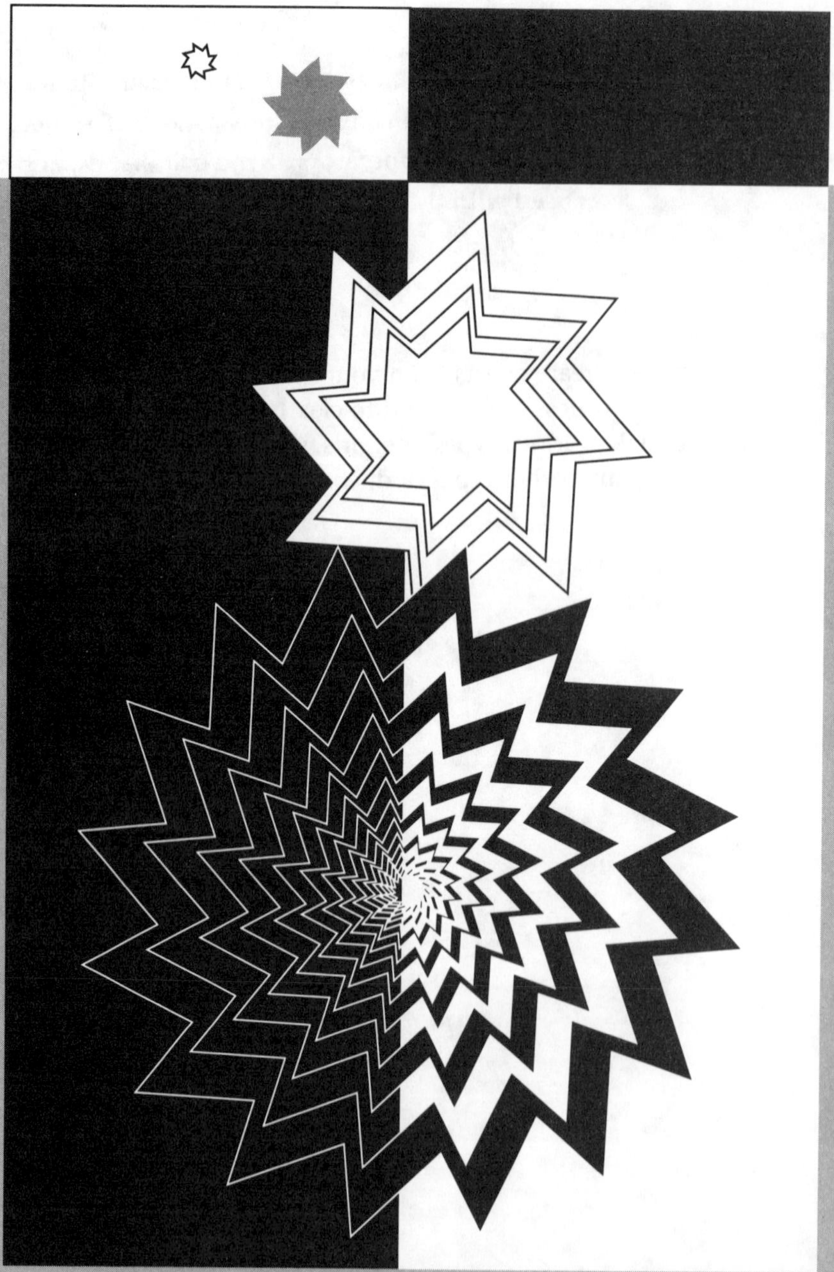

CHAPTER 7

Graphing and Charting

Fast Track

Works lets you create twelve types of charts.   **255**

    The basic types are area, bar, line, pie, stacked line, X-Y (scatter), radar, combination, 3-D area, 3-D bar, 3-D line, and 3-D pie.

You can change the chart type as you're creating a chart.   **255**

    Click in the toolbar on the type of chart you want, or open the Gallery menu and choose the chart type. From the dialog box, choose a look for the chart you want.

To start a new chart,   **260**

    select a series of cells in your spreadsheet with values you want to chart, and then click on the New Chart button in the toolbar or choose Tools ➤ Create New Chart.

To add titles to a chart,   **262**

    choose Edit ➤ Titles and enter the chart title, chart subtitle, names of the X and Y axes and right vertical axis as you see fit. You can leave some boxes blank if you want to.

To name and save a chart,   **265**

    choose Tools ➤ Name Chart. In the dialog box, click in the Name section and type the new name, click on Rename, and click OK. Choose File ➤ Save to save the spreadsheet and its new chart. Charts are saved as part of the spreadsheet.

To delete a chart from a spreadsheet, 267

choose Tools ➤ Delete Chart. This can be done either from the spreadsheet that contains the chart, or from any of the charts associated with a spreadsheet. From the resulting list, click on the chart you want to delete, click on Delete, and click OK.

To "explode" slices of a pie chart, 279

activate the chart's window, choose Gallery ➤ Pie, and choose option 2 or 3. To individually choose which slice of the pie to explode, choose Format ➤ Patterns and Colors, select the number of the slice, and check Explode Slice. Then click on Format and click on Close.

To change a chart's fonts (except for the title font), 294

choose Format ➤ Font and Style, select the font and type size you want, and click OK.

To alter the scaling of a chart, 295

choose Format ➤ Vertical (Y) Axis and fill in the Minimum, Maximum, and Interval settings. If you are working on an X-Y chart, the Format ➤ Horizontal (X) Axis command's dialog box will have a similar option.

CHARTS CONVEY THE MEANING OF the numbers in a spreadsheet far better than the spreadsheet itself does. Besides conveying the basics in a novel and graphical manner, plotting the numbers in a chart helps reveal trends, relationships between factors, and patterns within numbers.

Before computers, making charts was an expensive and tedious job that required special skills, tools, and personnel. Moreover, revising a chart after it was made was a nightmare. With Works, however, you can whip up charts with the spreadsheet tool as you build the spreadsheet or after the spreadsheet is completed. When you alter the data in the spreadsheet, the chart is altered as well.

In this chapter you'll learn how to

- Design a chart that suits your needs and presents your data in the best possible way
- Create all twelve of Works' chart types
- Attach legends, data labels, and other identifiers to charts
- Copy charts
- Adjust the fonts and scale on charts
- Print a chart

The Twelve Types of Charts You Can Create

Works lets you create twelve types of charts, as shown in Figure 7.1. The twelve types of charts are:

CHART TYPE	DESCRIPTION
Area	A business chart that uses shading to demonstrate the difference between a set of data points plotted on one line and a set of data points plotted on another. Usually area charts are used to compare one set of figures in proportion to another.
Bar	The bar chart, sometimes referred to as the *histogram,* consists of vertical boxes or bars arranged side by side. The height of each bar corresponds to the value it represents.
Line	The line chart shows related information as a series of horizontal lines in a "connect the dots" fashion. Typically, line charts are used to display changes over a period of time.
Pie	The old, familiar pie chart is simply a circle sliced into wedges, each representing a value in a single list of numbers.
Stacked Line	The stacked line chart creates a series of horizontal lines superimposed over each other. It is usually used for comparing data.
X-Y	Sometimes called a *scatter chart,* this type of chart plots points against an X and a Y axis to display the relationships between pairs of numbers.
Radar	The radar chart arranges values in a ring around a central axis.
Combination	The combination charts superimposes two other kinds of charts (bar and line, by default).

CHAPTER 7 Graphing and Charting

FIGURE 7.1

The twelve types of Works charts. You can also create variations on these charts.

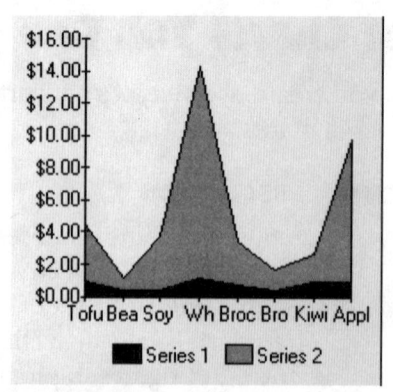

Area chart

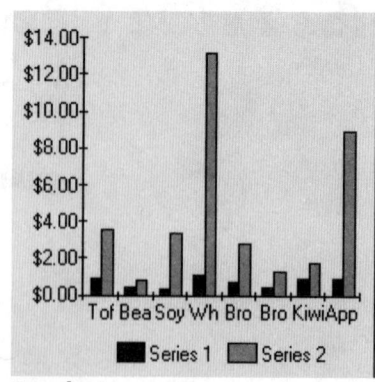

Bar chart

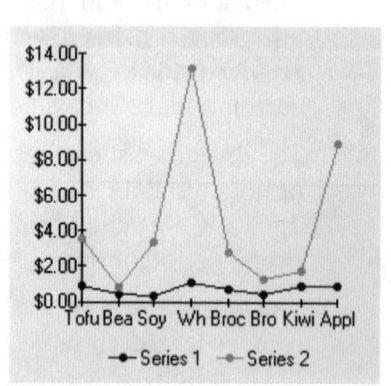

Line chart

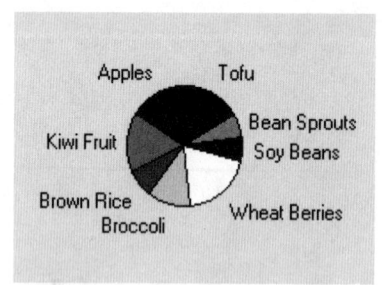

Pie chart

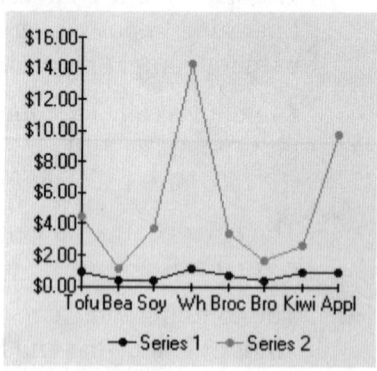

Stacked Line chart

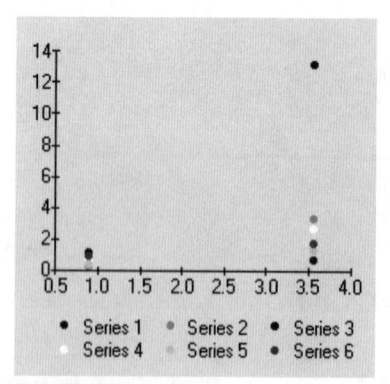

X-Y (Scatter) chart

The Twelve Types of Charts You Can Create

FIGURE 7.1
The twelve types of Works charts. You can also create variations on these charts. (continued)

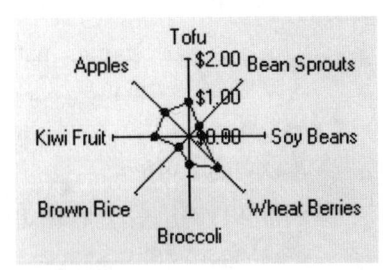

Radar chart

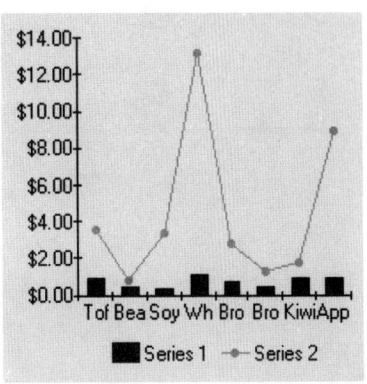

Combination chart

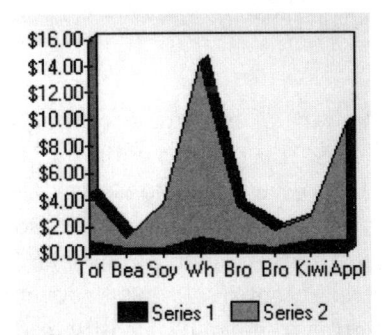

3-D Area chart

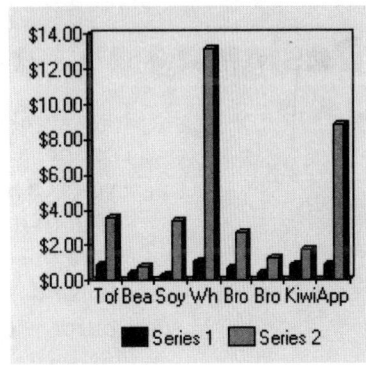

3-D Bar chart

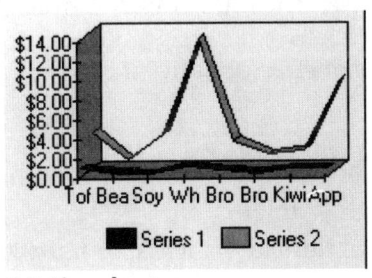

3-D Line chart

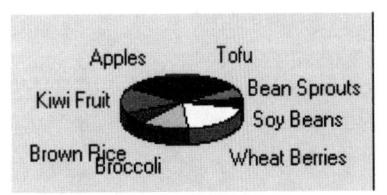

3-D Pie chart

CHART TYPE	DESCRIPTION
3-D Area	The 3-D area chart is a stylistic variation on the normal area chart with 3-D visual effects.
3-D Bar	The 3-D Bar chart is just a normal bar chart with 3-D visual effects.
3-D Line	The 3-D Line chart is just a normal line chart with 3-D visual effects.
3-D Pie	The 3-D Pie chart is just a normal pie chart with 3-D visual effects.

Designing a Chart

Designing a chart takes some forethought, just as creating a database or spreadsheet does. You need to consider in advance just what message your chart should convey to the observer. Generally speaking, it's a good idea to make charts as simple as possible. Don't try to include too much data or other information (such as labels) in a single chart. If you have a lot of data to present, consider making several charts instead of one. The purpose of a chart is to make data easily understood.

The best way to start designing a chart is with a piece of paper and a pencil. Ask yourself the following questions:

- What type of chart should it be? Pie, bar, X-Y, or one of the other kinds?
- What data will be displayed?
- Who will be looking at the chart?
- What should the increments, or units, of the chart be?
- What should the labels, titles, or other explanatory markings be and where should they be placed?

Figure 7.2 shows an example of a freehand rendering of a chart in the planning stages.

Once you have a sense of what you'd like your chart to look like, go back to the computer, load the spreadsheet with the data you want to chart, and dig in. All the data you want to chart must be in your spreadsheet. If it isn't, you must enter it before you can create a chart.

To be charted, your data must be organized into ranges that can be easily selected in groups. That is, each group of numbers you want to chart must be contiguous. Works cannot jump around your spreadsheet to find data for the chart.

FIGURE 7.2
Draw a sketch of your chart before you start creating it. This will save time and trouble later on.

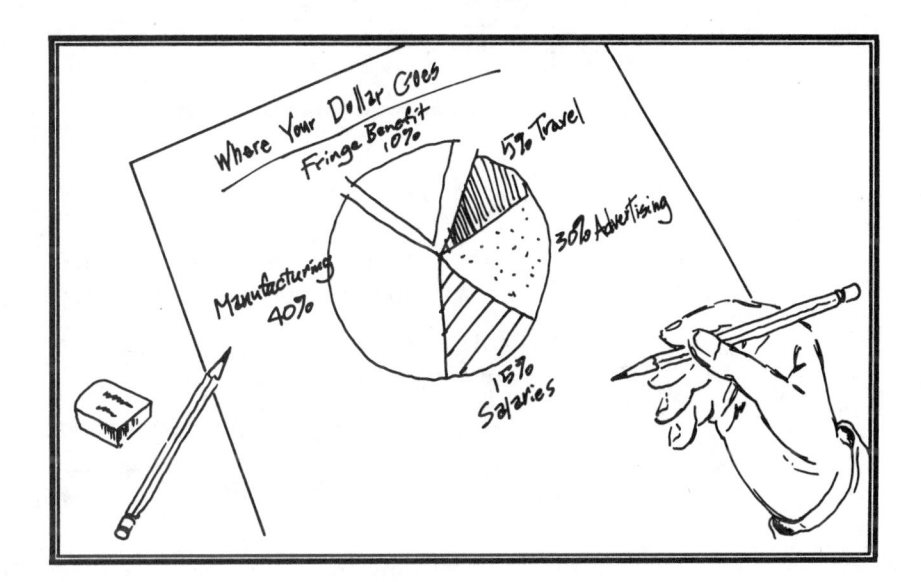

Creating a Bar Chart

To begin with, we'll create a bar chart, since this is one of the simplest charts to make. The chart will demonstrate estimated gross profits over four quarters. It will be based on the BUDGET spreadsheet you created in Chapter 6. If you did not create the spreadsheet in Chapter 6, follow along with a spreadsheet of your own. In the bar chart, time will be plotted horizontally from left to right, and the profits will be charted vertically, as shown in Figure 7.3.

CHAPTER 7   **Graphing and Charting**

FIGURE 7.3

A sketch of the bar chart. The chart will plot the four quarters horizontally. Profits will be plotted vertically.

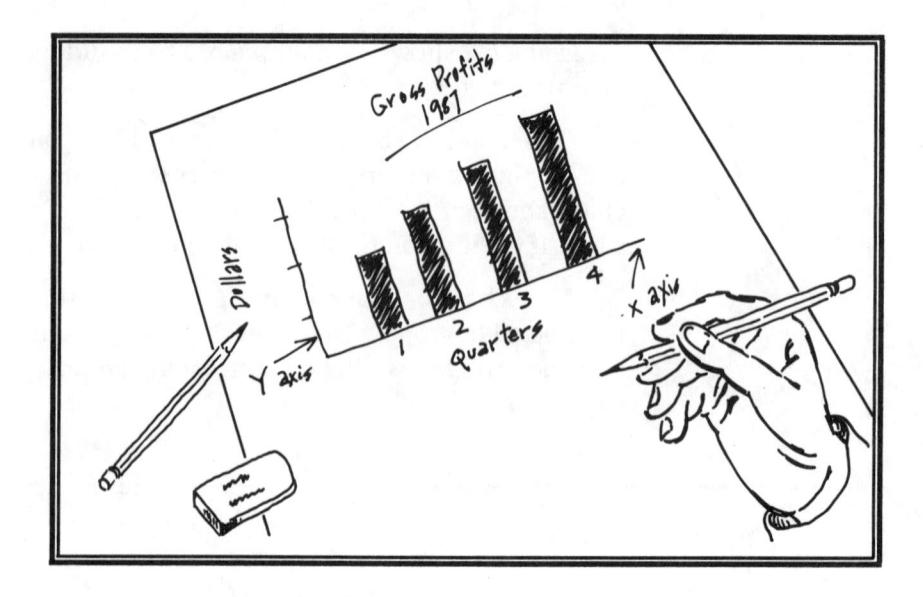

To create a bar chart:

1. Open the spreadsheet from which the data for the chart will come. In our case, open the BUDGET spreadsheet.

2. Select B26:E26, the gross profit for each of the four quarters. This is the range you want to chart.

3. Choose Tools ➤ Create New Chart (or click the New Chart button in the toolbar, the one that shows a bar chart and a magic wand). As in Figure 7.4, the New Chart dialog box appears.

In the New Chart dialog box, Bar already appears in the What type of chart do you want? scroll box. Bar is the default chart type. Notice the sample bar chart in the lower-right corner.

4. Click OK, since you want to create a bar chart. In place of the spreadsheet, a full-screen view of a bar chart appears, as in Figure 7.5. Notice that this screen has a different toolbar.

Creating a Bar Chart

FIGURE 7.4
The New Chart dialog box showing a sample bar chart

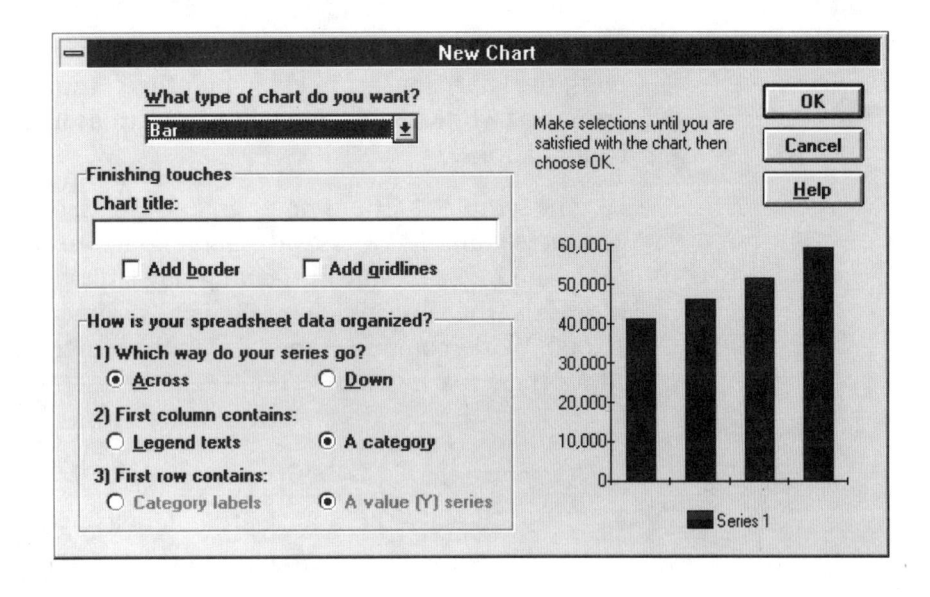

FIGURE 7.5
A basic, no-frills bar chart. Notice that the toolbar has changed.

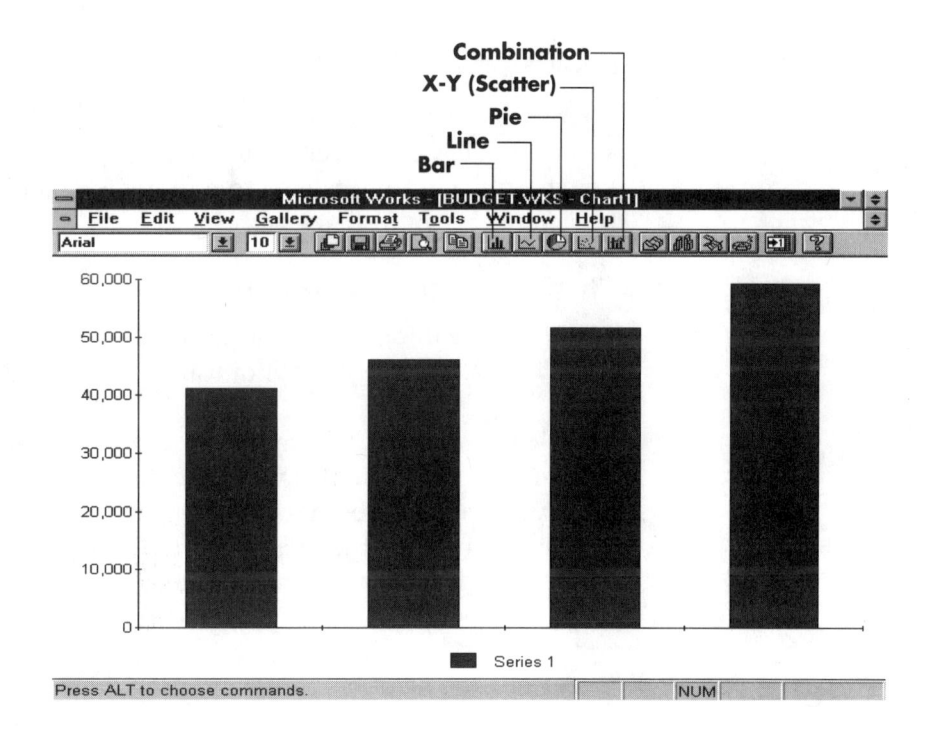

261

Exactly how the chart looks depends on your hardware. On some systems, the chart appears in color, on others it appears in black and white, green and white, amber and white, or various intensities of these color combinations.

The sample chart has no titles, axis labels, or data labels. You have to add these yourself. Works was smart enough to scale the chart. The lowest value and highest value in the range are a reasonable distance apart. On the Y-axis (the vertical line on the left), tick marks appear in increments of 10,000. Works computed and labeled these marks automatically. You can adjust these marks later.

> **Note** To make the chart a little bigger so you can see it better, choose View ➤ Toolbar to turn off the toolbar.

Adding Labels to the Chart

You can see from glancing at this chart that the first year's growth has been relatively steady over the four quarters. To the casual observer, though, this chart means next to nothing without some labels to clarify the significance of the axes.

1. Choose Edit ➤ Titles. A Titles dialog box appears, as in Figure 7.6.

2. Fill in the information you see in the figure. (Leave Right Vertical Axis blank, since you're not using a right Y axis.)

The right vertical axis The right vertical axis adds another vertical axis to the right side of the chart. This is sometimes useful on complex charts, or where you want to show, for example, one type of currency on one Y axis and another on the other Y axis.

3. Click OK in the Titles dialog box. Now your chart looks like Figure 7.7.

Creating a Bar Chart

FIGURE 7.6
The Titles dialog box for adding labels to a chart

FIGURE 7.7
The bar chart with the labels and titles you entered in the Titles dialog box

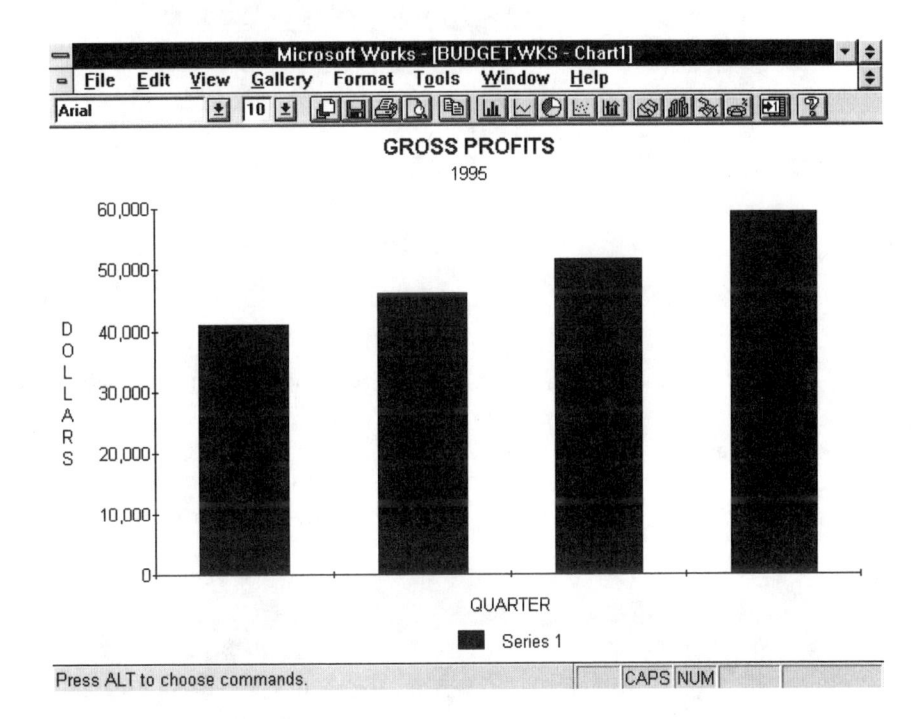

Using spreadsheet cells to label the bars in the chart Let's label each bar in the chart with the exact monetary figure it represents. Here's how to do that:

1. Choose Window ➤ BUDGET.WKS to get back to the Budget spreadsheet. Make sure cells B26:E26 (the gross profit per quarter) are still selected.

CHAPTER 7   Graphing and Charting

We'll use the actual cell data in our data labels:

2. Choose Edit ➤ Copy to put a copy of the selected cells onto the Windows Clipboard.

3. Choose Window ➤ BUDGET.WKS–Chart1 to get back to the chart.

4. Choose Edit ➤ Data Labels. The Data Labels dialog box appears:

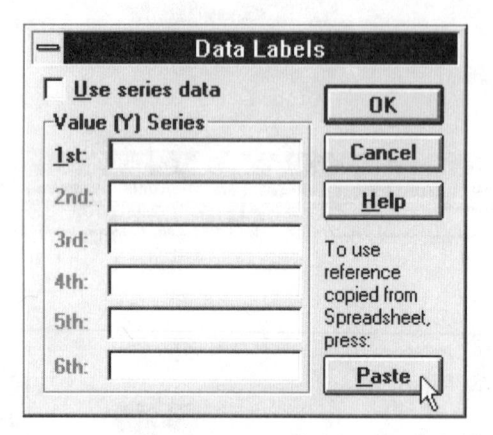

The first line of the dialog box under Value (Y) series, 1st, should be highlighted.

5. Click on the Paste button on the lower-right corner of this dialog box. This plugs the selected range of cells (B26:E26) into the chart's Y-series.

> **Note** A *Y-series* is simply a number of associated data elements (numbers) that you want to chart. In this chart, you plotted only one series of values (gross profits for four quarters), so you only have one Y-series. Works automatically plugged the selected cells' values into the 1st Y-series, but, as you will see later, you can plot up to six Y-series on a single graph.

Creating a Bar Chart

6. Click on OK to view the chart again. Now your chart shows the exact dollar amounts of each bar, as shown in Figure 7.8.

FIGURE 7.8
Placing data labels on the bars of the chart. These labels came directly from the spreadsheet.

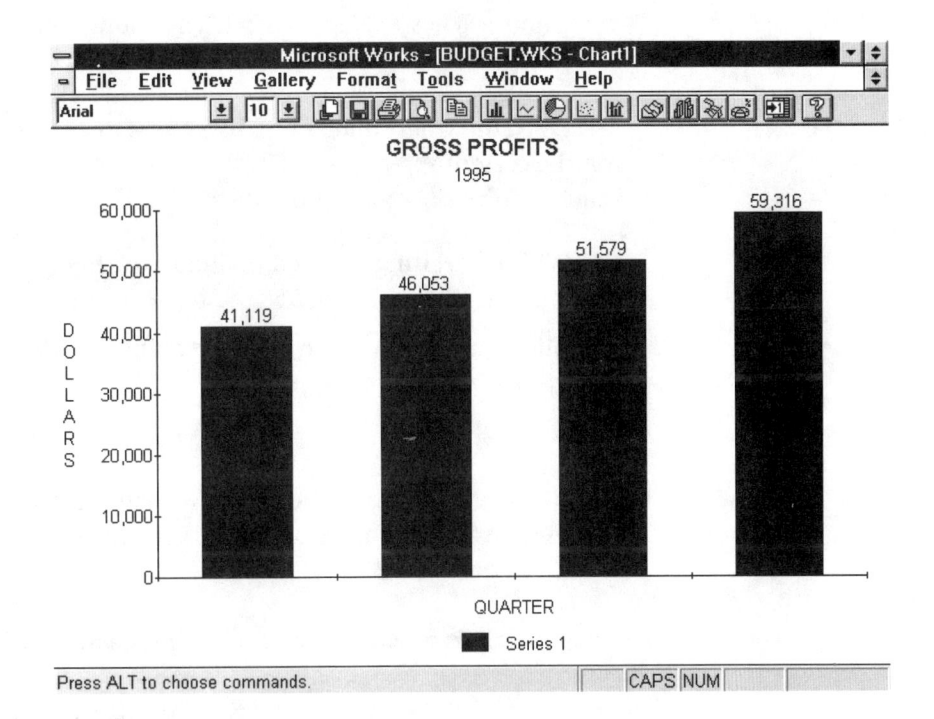

Naming and Saving a Chart

Once you've created a chart, it is updated and stored on disk whenever you save your spreadsheet. All aspects of the chart are saved, including a descriptive name that you can assign. Each spreadsheet can have as many as eight charts stored along with it. You switch between charts by using the Window menu.

Giving the chart a name Works assigns a default name to each chart you create, so you don't have to name a chart if you don't mind the default names (Chart1, Chart2, and so on). But if you use the default names, you'll have to view each chart to determine what it contains. To avoid

265

CHAPTER 7 Graphing and Charting

that inconvenience, name your charts descriptively. In this case, we'll name the chart *Profits, Bar*, like so:

1. Choose Tools ➤ Name Chart. The Name Chart dialog box appears, as in Figure 7.9.

The Name Chart dialog box lists the names of all the charts associated with the current spreadsheet. Only Chart1 appears, as shown in Figure 7.9, because you've only made one chart.

2. With Chart1 highlighted (it should be highlighted since it's the current chart), click in the Name text box and enter **Profits, Bar**.

3. Click on Rename to change the name of Chart1 to Profits, Bar. Notice the title bar change.

4. Click OK.

Now when you open the Window menu, the new name appears at the bottom with a check mark beside it. The check mark tells you that this is the active chart.

Saving the chart on disk Saving a chart is easy. To save the chart on disk:

◆ Choose File ➤ Save to save the spreadsheet and the newly created and named chart.

FIGURE 7.9

The Name Chart dialog box. Click on a chart and enter its new name in the Name text box.

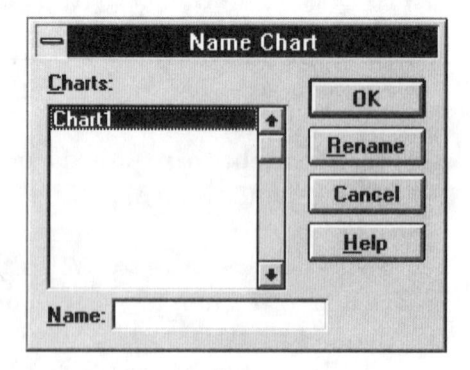

266

> **Warning**
>
> Make a habit of saving your charts regularly as a precaution against a hardware or software malfunction. If your data is lost but you've saved the chart recently, you can go back to the version you saved last without losing too much work.

Deleting an Unwanted Chart

At times you will want to delete unwanted or outdated charts to eliminate confusion when selecting which charts to view. Here are the steps for deleting a chart (don't follow them, as you still need the bar chart you just created):

1. From either the chart or spreadsheet window, choose Tools ➤ Delete Chart.
2. In the list box, select the name of the chart you want to delete.
3. Click on the Delete button.
4. Click OK.

The chart you deleted will no longer appear in the Chart list, making room for other charts. Remember, only eight charts per spreadsheet are allowed.

Copying Charts for Later Modification

Once you've finished defining a chart, you can start experimenting with it. You can present the data in a different format (pie chart, line chart, or another chart), or alter the titles and labels, or make other modifications. The best way to do this is to copy the existing chart to a new chart and fiddle with the copy. This way, your original chart stays intact if you need it.

CHAPTER 7 Graphing and Charting

Let's copy the Profits, Bar chart to a new chart we'll call "Net Sales vs. Profits":

1. Choose Tools ➤ Duplicate Chart. The Duplicate Chart dialog box appears.
2. Highlight Profits, Bar.
3. Move to the Name area and type in **Net Sales vs. Profits.**

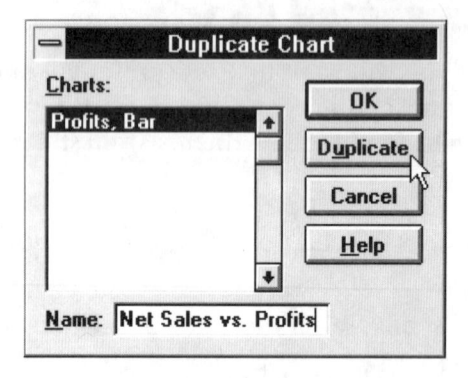

[Duplicate Chart dialog box shown with Charts: Profits, Bar; buttons OK, Duplicate, Cancel, Help; Name: Net Sales vs. Profits]

4. Click on Duplicate and then on OK.
5. Select View ➤ Charts.

Notice that a new chart called "Net Sales vs. P" has been created by Works. The chart is named "Net Sales vs. P" because the name you entered in the Duplicate Chart dialog box was too long to display. No matter, we'll use the chart you just copied to learn about modifying a chart.

> **Tip** Since chart names can't be longer than fifteen characters, you have to be creative in your naming conventions.

Adding a Second Y-Series to a Bar Chart

We'll modify the copy of the chart by adding another set of bars to display net sales for each quarter. This way we'll be able to see the relationship between net sales and gross profits on a single chart.

1. Choose View ➤ Charts, select Net Sales..., and click OK to activate the new copy of the chart.

2. Choose Window ➤ BUDGET.WKS to get back to the spreadsheet.

3. Select cells B22:E22 (net sales for the four quarters), and copy them to the Clipboard with the Edit ➤ Copy command (or by pressing Ctrl+C if you prefer the keyboard).

4. Return to the chart by selecting Window ➤ Net Profits vs. P.

To make the values you just selected show up as a second set of bars, you have to assign them to a second Y-series. To do this:

5. Choose Edit ➤ Paste Series. The Paste Series dialog box appears:

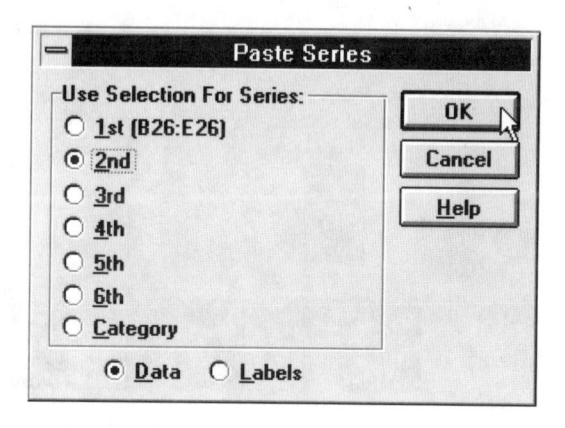

CHAPTER 7 Graphing and Charting

The 2nd range button is already selected, so all you have to do is click on OK to add the new data to the chart. In the dialog box, notice the options for pasting the data as labels rather than as data.

6. Click OK to assign the data to a new Y-series.
7. Choose Edit ➤ Titles, change the Chart title to **Net Sales vs. Profits** and press ↵.

Leave everything else in the Titles dialog box the same. Don't worry about the quote marks that Works puts in front of each title. It just does that for its own internal purposes.

8. Press ↵. The chart should now look like Figure 7.10.

FIGURE 7.10

A bar chart with a second Y-series

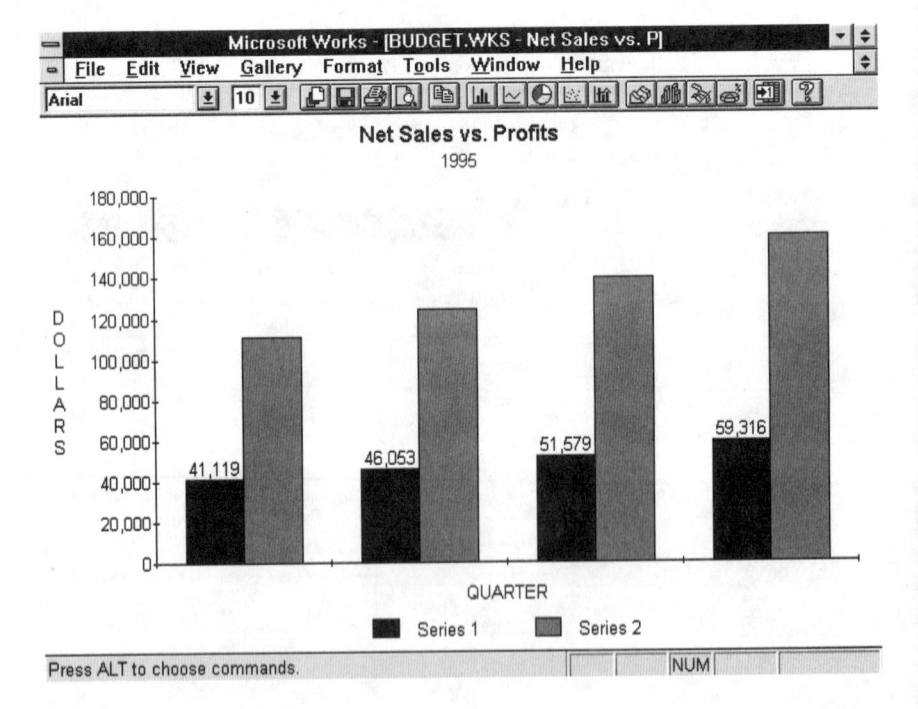

> **Note** You can enter very long titles in the Titles dialog box. When you do, the title will scroll to the left. If you enter a long title, consider how much of it will fit on the screen and on your printouts as well. A lot depends on the font sizes you use in your chart.

Adding Legends to a Chart

Not a bad-looking chart, only you can't tell what each of the sets of bars represents. Instead of adding data labels, this time we'll add legends to the chart. *Legends,* sometimes called *keys,* are the little patterned or colored boxes at the bottom of the chart used to clarify what the various bars represent.

Before we add the legends, let's remove the data labels:

1. Choose Edit ➤ Data Labels.

In the Data Labels dialog box, the first line of the series shows the data labels you entered earlier:

```
1st Y (B26:E26)
```

2. Press Del to remove these labels from the chart.

3. Press OK to close the Data Labels dialog box.

Next, to clarify what each set of bars is for, you'll add the legends:

1. Choose Edit ➤ Legend/Series Labels. A dialog box appears.

2. Uncheck Auto series labels.

Now add the two legends:

3. In the 1st Value Series area, type **Gross Profits**.

CHAPTER 7 Graphing and Charting

4. In the 2nd Value Series area, type **Net Sales.**
5. Click OK.

When you view your chart, it will look like Figure 7.11.

Tip — Instead of typing in a legend for each Y-series yourself, you can enter a cell address with the label you want to use. Just type in a cell name such as A15 in the Value Series text area of the Legend dialog box. Works will use the label in that cell as the legend.

Your new chart shows that gross profits have risen slightly in comparison to net sales. Also, you can see from the chart that gross profits appear to equal approximately 50 percent of net sales.

FIGURE 7.11
The Chart with two legends added

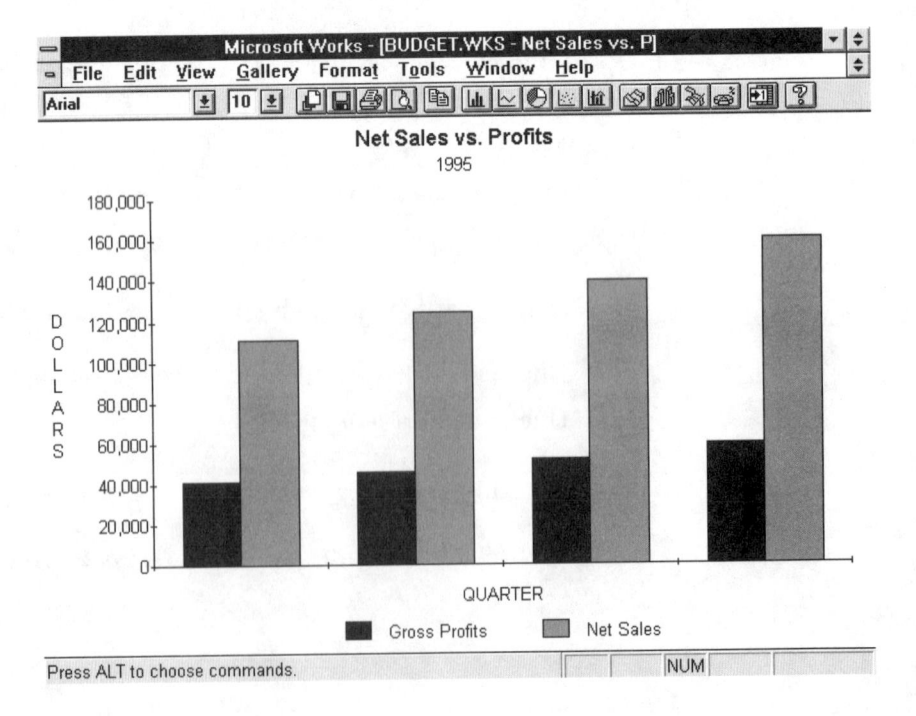

272

Creating a Line Chart

Works makes moving from one chart format to another simple. In this part of the chapter we'll view the currently displayed data in a line chart instead of a bar chart:

1. Copy the existing chart to a new one and name it **Profits, Line**.

> **Note** If you need to know how to copy an existing chart, see "Copying Charts for Later Modification" earlier in this chapter.

2. Switch to your new Profits, Line chart by choosing View ➤ Chart and selecting it from the Charts dialog box.

3. Click on the Line Chart button in the toolbar (the second one from the left in the first group of five chart buttons) to change the type of chart. The Line dialog box appears, as in Figure 7.12.

4. Six types of line charts are displayed here. We'll be exploring them in a bit. But in the meantime, just click OK to select the first chart.

FIGURE 7.12
The Line dialog box. From this box you can choose among six different kinds of line charts.

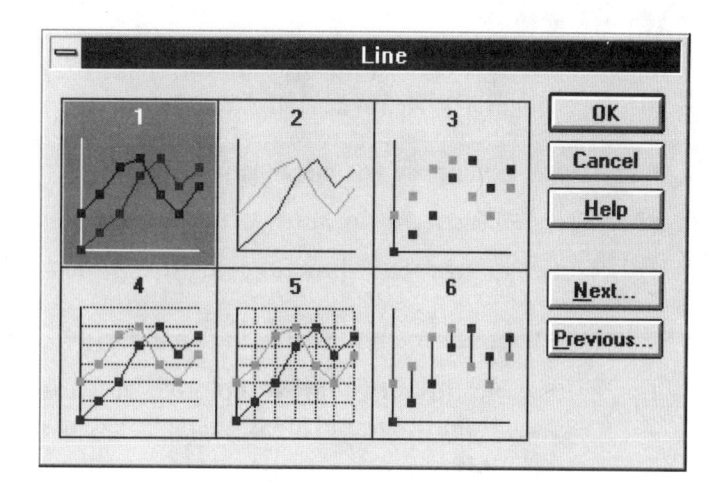

Adding More Lines to the Chart

The data is represented as points along two lines. Let's fill out the picture a little by adding another line representing Cost of Sales to the chart:

1. Switch to the Budget spreadsheet again and select B24:E24 (the cost of sales across four quarters).
2. Choose Edit ➤ Copy to put the data on the Clipboard.
3. Return to the chart window by selecting it from the Window menu.
4. Choose Edit ➤ Paste Series.

In the Paste Series dialog box, the 3rd button is already selected.

5. Click OK so that the cost of sales data you just selected in the spreadsheet will be used to add a new, third line to the chart.
6. To add a legend for the new line, choose Edit ➤ Legend/Series Labels, click in the third section, and enter the legend **Cost of Sales**.
7. Click OK.

Now you have three lines and three legends in your line chart.

Adding Grid Lines to Make the Chart Easier to Read

Let's add some grid lines to make the chart easier to understand. We'll change the title as well.

1. Choose Format ➤ Horizontal (X) Axis. A dialog box appears.
2. Turn on the Show Gridlines check box and click OK.
3. Repeat the process using the Format ➤ Vertical (Y) Axis command.

Your screen should now look like Figure 7.13.

In this gird chart you plotted only three sets of data, but as you can see from the Data Labels dialog box, you can plot up to six Y-Series if you want to.

Creating a Pie Chart

FIGURE 7.13
The line chart with the grid showing

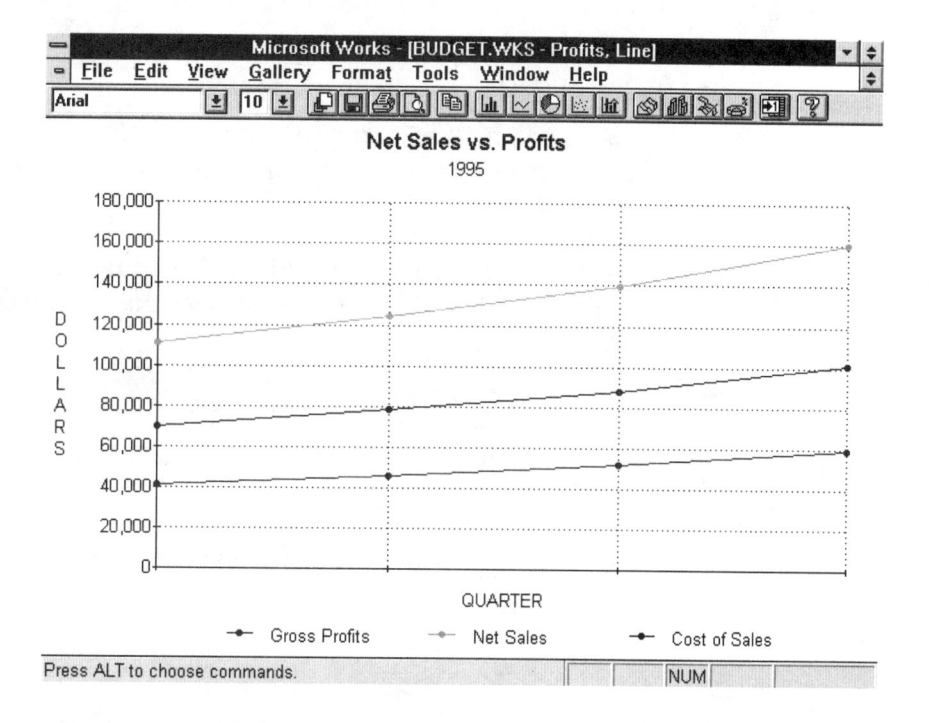

Creating a Pie Chart

Next to bar charts, pie charts are probably the most popular display format, particularly when the intention is to portray parts as a percentage of the whole. Pie charts can only display a single Y-series, however, so there are certain limitations to this type of chart.

To see how pie charts work, we will make a pie chart from the Budget spreadsheet showing the store's labor expenses to get an idea of the relative proportions of each category.

1. Open the Window menu and return to the spreadsheet.

2. Select the cells from which you want to plot the data. In our case, select cells F29:F31, the salaries, payroll taxes, and fringe benefits figures.

3. Choose Tools ➤ Create New Chart. The New Chart dialog box appears with a bar chart showing (see Figure 7.4).

CHAPTER 7 Graphing and Charting

4. Select Pie in the What type of chart do you want? scroll box and click OK. The pie chart appears.

5. Click the Pie Chart button on the toolbar (the one shaped like a pie chart) to see the gallery of pie chart options, as shown in Figure 7.14.

Observe the types of pie charts you can create. The main differences between these charts have to do with whether you see percentages or data labels, and whether slices are *exploded*—that is, pulled out of the pie slightly.

6. Select choice 5, the Percentage option.

7. Click OK.

Notice that percentages are shown around the circle's perimeter. Pie charts show a Y-series as portions (percentages) of a whole, which of course equals 100 percent.

> **Tip** Pie charts are excellent for depicting percentages. However, for data comparisons, you are better off choosing a bar chart or line chart.

FIGURE 7.14
The Pie chart options. From here you can choose which type of pie chart you want.

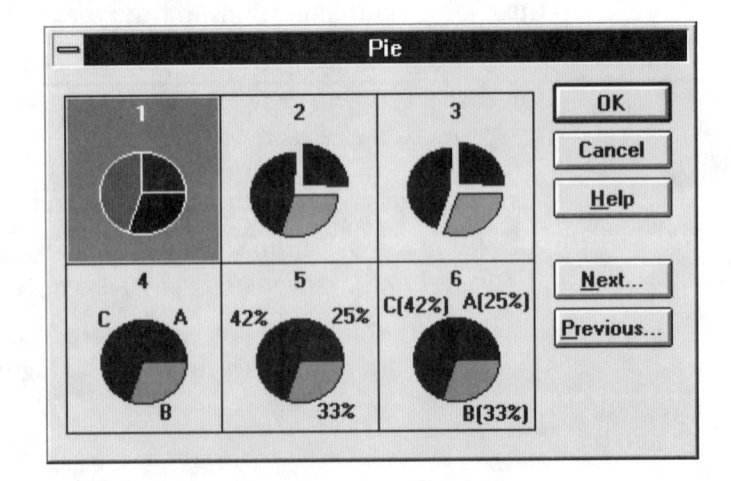

276

Adding Labels to a Pie Chart

We should add labels to the chart to explain what each slice represents. Since you already have the labels in the spreadsheet (in column A), you don't have to type them in yourself. Just select the cells with the labels you want to use and assign them to the X-axis. (Actually an X-axis doesn't really exist in a pie chart, but this technique does the trick anyway.) We'll use the Edit ➤ Data Labels dialog box to make the assignment.

1. Select the labels you want to use from the worksheet. In our case, select A29:A31 (the Salaries, Payroll Taxes, and Fringe Benefits labels).
2. Copy these cells by using the Edit ➤ Copy command.
3. Switch to the chart and choose Edit ➤ Data Labels.
4. Click in the cell range and click on Paste to use the labels you just copied.
5. Set the 2nd Label to Cell Contents and the 1st label to Percentages:

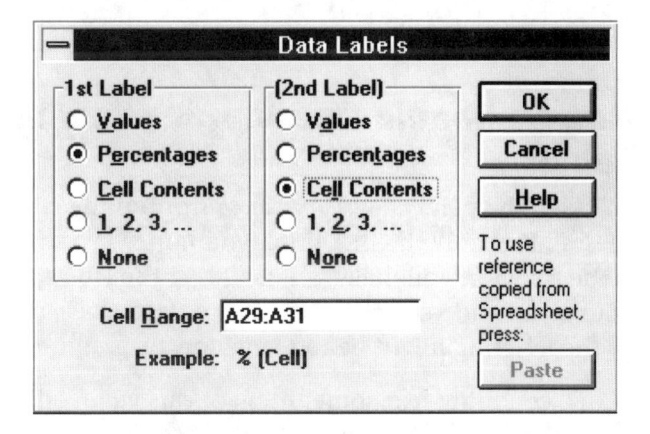

6. Click OK.

Now we'll add a few finishing touches:

7. Choose Edit ➤ Titles and for the chart title, type in **Labor Expenses**.
8. Add a border around the perimeter of the chart. To do this, choose Format ➤ Add Border. Now your chart should look like Figure 7.15.

CHAPTER 7 Graphing and Charting

FIGURE 7.15
The pie chart with a border and labels

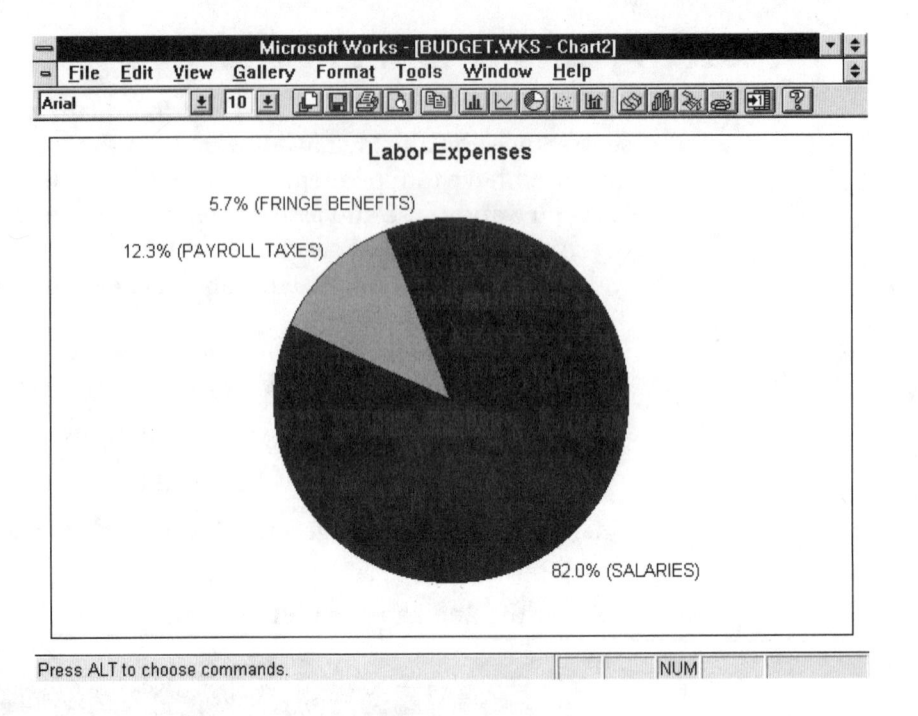

[Screenshot of Microsoft Works - BUDGET.WKS - Chart2 showing a pie chart titled "Labor Expenses" with slices labeled 5.7% (FRINGE BENEFITS), 12.3% (PAYROLL TAXES), and 82.0% (SALARIES)]

How to Handle Overlapping Text in Labels

Now the percentages appear in front of the labels (which are in parentheses). Probably the first thing you noticed was that the pie shrank. This is the trade-off you make when adding the labels. Moreover, depending on your setup and your chart, the percentage labels may overlap one another, or the lettering might be too large for the graph.

Overlapping text sometimes appears when adjacent pie sections are small and their labels end up very close to each other. To keep text from overlapping, use a smaller font for the labels. See "Changing the Fonts in Labels, Legends, and Titles" later in this chapter.

Another solution is to rearrange the data in the spreadsheet so that small slices aren't next to each other in the pie. The program starts drawing a pie chart at the 12 o'clock position and works clockwise. By entering the data into a series in such a way that the smaller values are interspersed with the larger ones, the pieces of the pie chart will be more evenly distributed.

A final solution is to explode one of the slices, which moves it out of the pie a little bit. You can try that next.

"Exploding" Slices of a Pie Chart

Occasionally you'll want to emphasize a slice of a pie chart by exploding it—that is, pulling it slightly out of the circle. You do this just by choosing another Pie chart style from the Pie Chart dialog box. Say you want to emphasize the Fringe Benefits slice in our pie chart:

1. Choose Format ➤ Patterns and Colors. The Patterns and Colors dialog box for establishing the appearance of each slice of the pie appears:

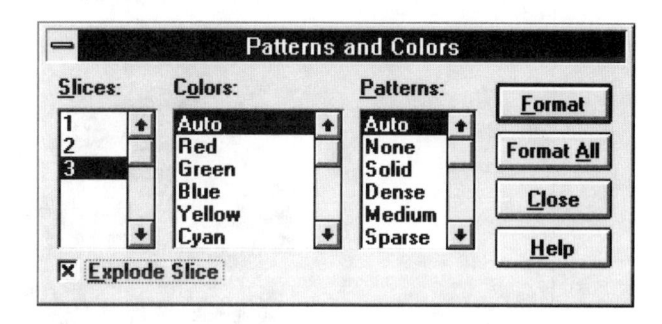

2. Since Fringe Benefits is the third cell in our selection (from top to bottom), it corresponds to slice three of the pie. Click on 3 in the Slices scroll box.

3. Check the Explode Slice box at the bottom of the dialog box.

4. Click on Format (but not Format All, since you don't want to explode all the slices) and then choose Close.

CHAPTER 7   Graphing and Charting

Putting the percentages, not the labels, in parentheses In our current pie chart, labels are in parentheses and percentages are not. Let's reverse that:

5. Open the Edit ➤ Data Labels box.

6. In the 1st Label section, click on Cell Contents, and in the 2nd Label section, click on Percentages. Then click OK.

   Now you have reversed the situation. Your chart should now look like Figure 7.16.

7. Using the Tools ➤ Name Chart command, name your pie chart **Labor, Pie** for future use.

FIGURE 7.16

The pie chart with a section exploded and parentheses around the percentages, not the labels

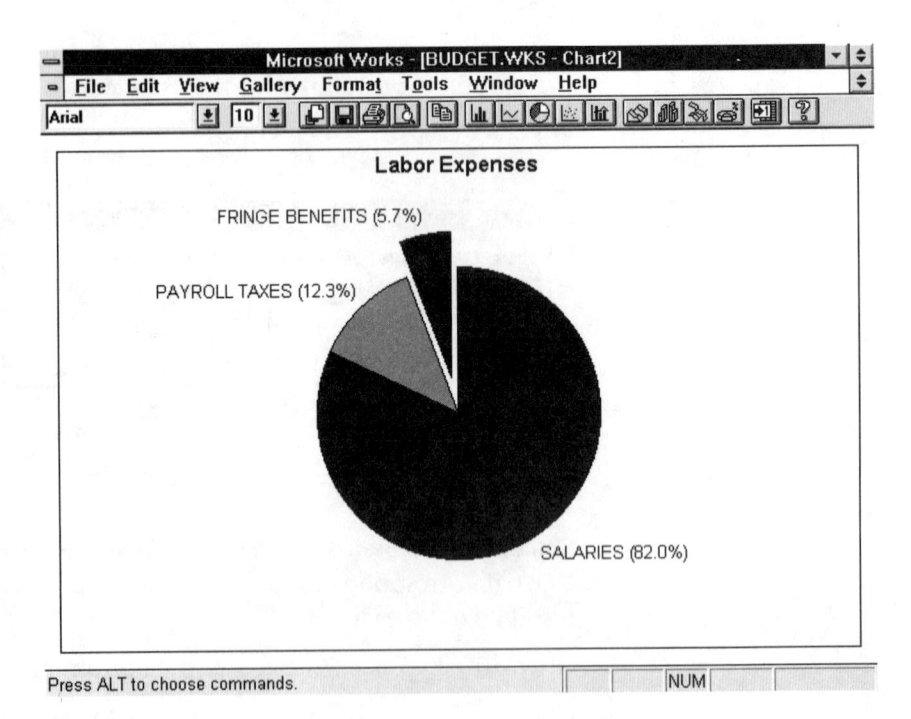

> **Tip** If you are creating color printouts or making presentations on screen, selecting vibrant and contrasting colors in the Patterns and Colors dialog box will add to your presentation.

Creating Different Chart Types

The next part of this chapter explains how to create the other types of charts with Works—that is, how to create all the charts except for bar charts, line charts, and pie charts, which are explained above.

Making a 100% Bar Chart

The 100% bar chart is a bit like a pie chart in that values are displayed as a percentage rather than as individual units of measurement. Thus, the scale on the Y-axis lists percentage, not units such as dollars, days, or pounds. Think of 100% bar charts (and of stacked bar charts, covered in the next section) as grouped bars on top of one another instead of next to one another. Unlike pie charts, 100% bar charts plot multiple Y-series, not a single one, so you need at least two series to convey any relevant information.

The big advantage of this type of chart is that more than one bar can be plotted at a time. It's like being able to plot multiple pie charts simultaneously. The 100% bar chart is most useful for transforming an existing multiple-bar bar chart into a form that conveys percentage relationships of grouped bars instead of their absolute values.

As an example, let's convert the Net Sales vs. P chart to the 100% bar format:

1. From the View ➤ Chart dialog box, select the Net Sales vs. P chart.
2. Click on the Bar button in the toolbar (the first one in the group of five) or choose Gallery ➤ Bar. The Bar dialog box appears:

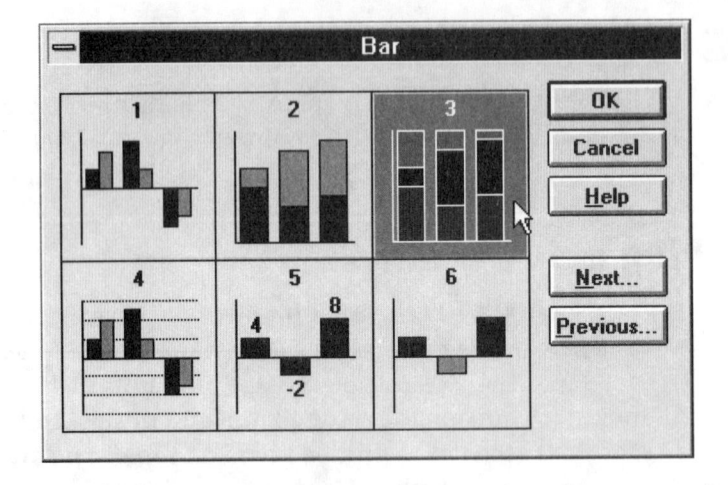

3. Choose option 3 from the Bar dialog box and click on OK.
4. Choose Format ➤ Vertical (Y) Axis and set Show Gridlines on. The chart should look like Figure 7.17.

Just glancing at this chart provides all kinds of useful information. For example, you can see that profits were about 27 percent of net sales every quarter.

Tips for using 100% bar charts You may want to add labels to each section of each bar. To do this:

1. Select and copy the appropriate cells.
2. Choose Edit ➤ Data Labels, select the Y-series, and then click the Paste button.

A label will appear at the top of each bar in the series you select.

Creating Different Chart Types

FIGURE 7.17

A 100% bar chart. This kind of chart conveys the percentage relationships of grouped bars instead of their absolute values.

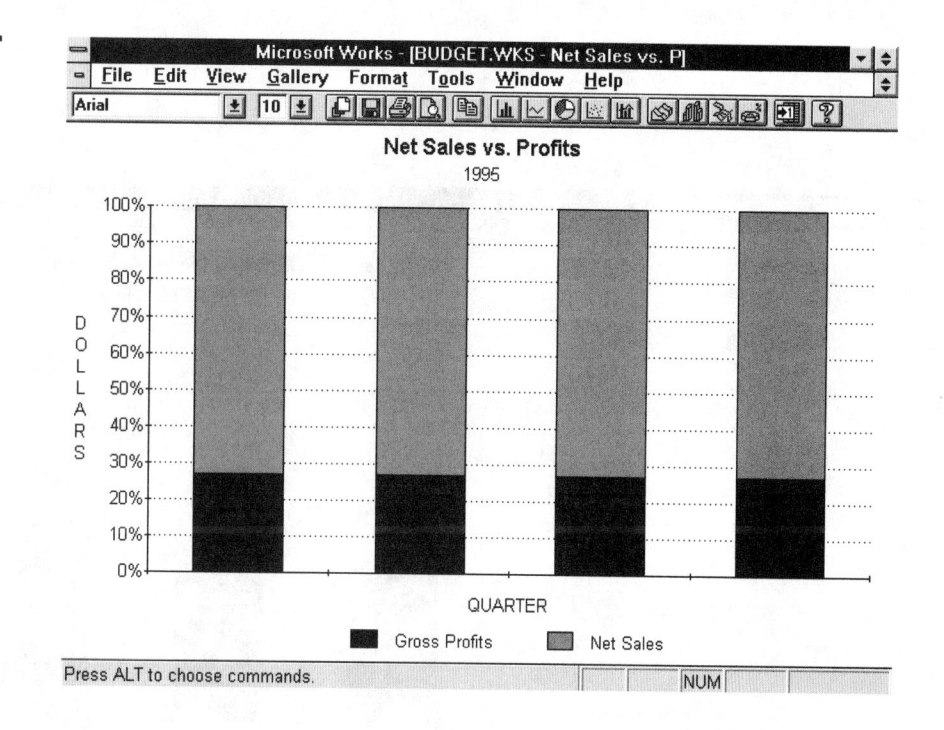

[Screenshot of Microsoft Works - [BUDGET.WKS - Net Sales vs. P] showing a 100% bar chart titled "Net Sales vs. Profits 1995" with Y-axis labeled DOLLARS (0% to 100%) and X-axis labeled QUARTER. Legend shows Gross Profits and Net Sales.]

Try labeling the actual numerical value of each section of the bar. This way, the Y-axis will indicate percentages and the label will report actual amounts. Another use for a label would be to convey what's represented by each section, such as "Salaries" or "Expenses."

Making a Stacked Bar Chart

The stacked bar chart is similar to the 100% bar chart, but in this type of chart, actual values of Y-series elements are displayed rather than their relative percentage of a whole. In effect, each bar displays a grand total of each set of associated bars. And instead of using the X-axis as the starting point for each new Y-series, Works uses the top of the bar that is being built upon. Thus, two grouped Y-series elements of sizes 300 and 500 result in a bar that shows a grand total of 800. Here's how to redisplay the 100% bar chart you just created in the form of a stacked bar chart:

1. With the last chart on screen, choose Gallery ➤ Bar (or click on the leftmost chart button in the toolbar).

283

CHAPTER 7 Graphing and Charting

2. Choose option 2 from the dialog box.
3. Click on OK. The chart should look like Figure 7.18.

FIGURE 7.18
This bar chart is stacked.

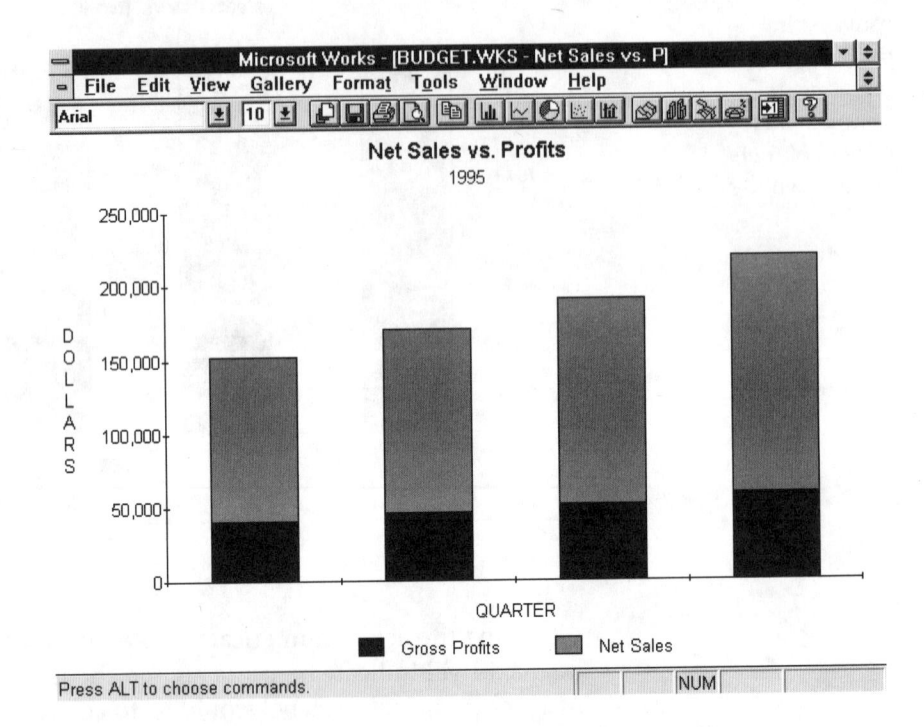

Making a Stacked Line Chart

A stacked line chart works much the same way as a stacked bar chart: each Y-series is computed and plotted using the line below it as its X-axis. The line below it is the plot of the previous Y-series of data. The result is a cumulative or grand-total effect, with one Y-series adding to the previous one. The only significant difference is that data values are displayed as points along a line instead of as bars.

Try switching the last chart to stacked line format:

1. Choose Gallery ➤ Stacked Line and choose the first chart style.
2. Click on OK. The chart should look like Figure 7.19.

Creating Different Chart Types

FIGURE 7.19
A stacked line chart. These charts are usually used for comparing data.

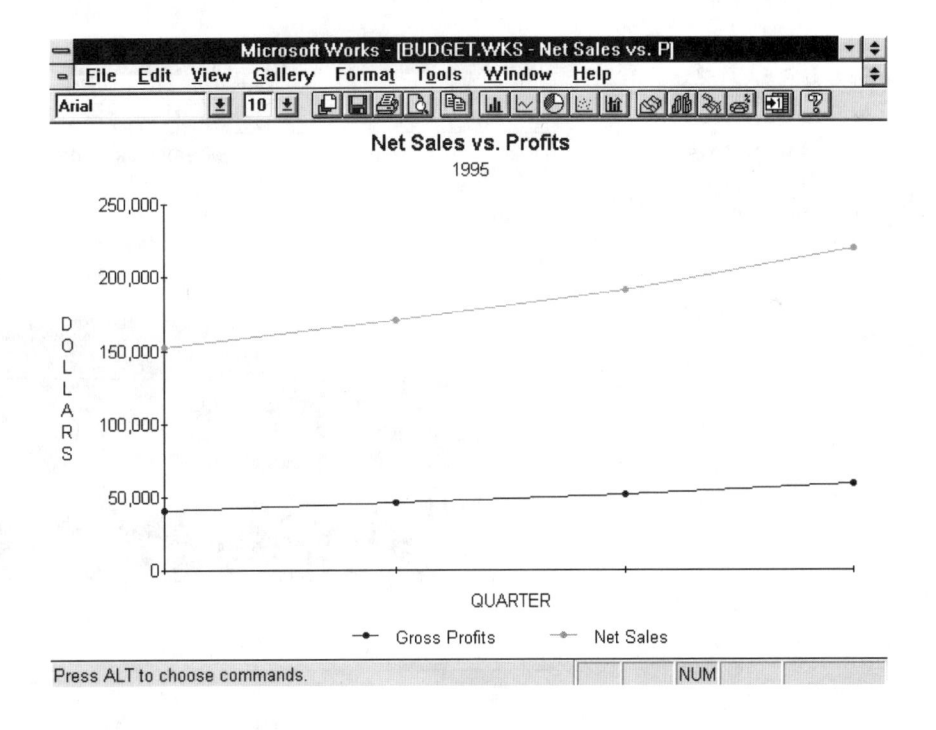

Making an Area Chart

An area chart is a kind of stacked line chart with some of the visual impact of a bar chart. The area under each line is colored in. The lines can be stacked up to totals or as percentages. Let's see how our chart would look as an area chart:

1. Choose Gallery ➤ Area and choose the fourth chart style.
2. Click on OK. The chart should look like Figure 7.20.

Making a High-Lo-Close Chart

High-lo-close charts are typically used to report the selling prices of stocks, commodities, and mutual funds. As the name implies, this type of chart normally displays three Y-series of data corresponding to an item's highest trading price, lowest trading price, and closing price. Works

CHAPTER 7 Graphing and Charting

FIGURE 7.20
An area chart. Use area charts to see one set of figures in proportion to another.

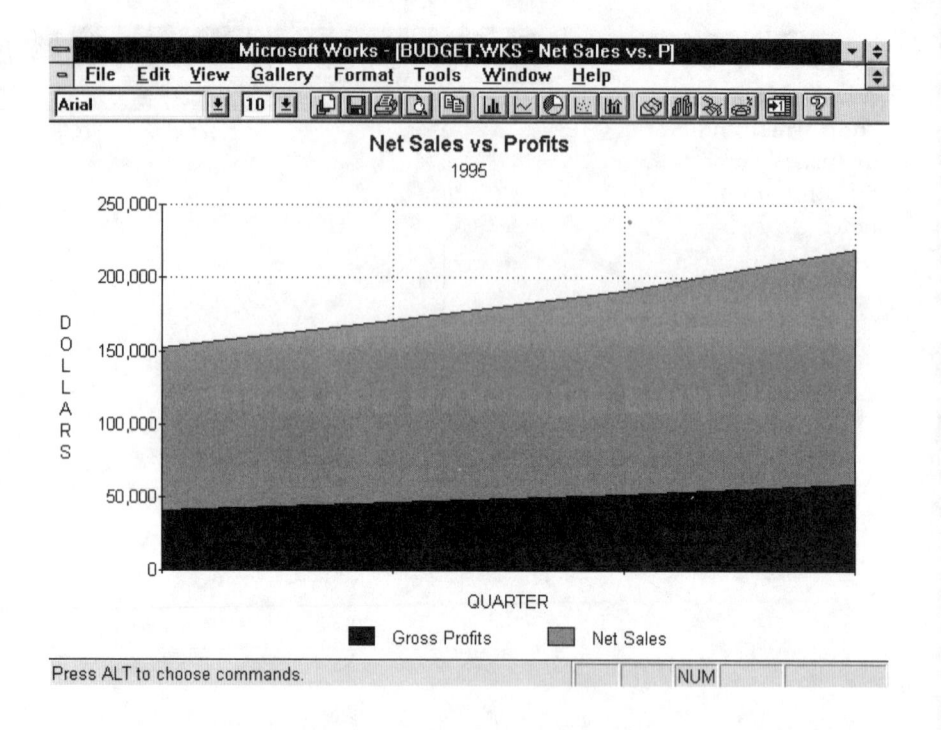

displays the three values as points, tying them together with a vertical line. You use markers and legends to indicate which points represent high, low, and close.

You need at least two Y-series to draw this type of chart, and you'll probably want to use three. If you use only two, you can plot low and high prices, high and low temperatures for the day, and so on, but not closing values.

You'll have to create a new spreadsheet to experiment with this type of chart, since appropriate data doesn't appear in the ones you've been working with.

Creating Different Chart Types

1. Choose File ➤ Create New File and choose Spreadsheet.
2. In the blank spreadsheet, enter the following data chronicling the trading price of Frazmus stock over a five-day period:

	A	B	C	D	E	F
1		Monday	Tuesday	Wednesday	Thursday	Friday
2	High	9	10	13	12	11
3	Low	7	5	8	7	6
4	Close	8	9	12	10	11

3. Select the range B2:F2.
4. Choose Tools ➤ Create New Chart or click the New Chart button.
5. Select Line in the What type of chart do you want? box and click OK.
6. Choose Gallery ➤ Line or click the Line chart button (the second one) on the toolbar.
7. Choose style 6, the Hi-Lo-Close chart and click OK.

What you get is five dots, because only one Y-series has been assigned. Now you have to assign the other series:

8. Return to the spreadsheet (Window ➤ Sheet1), select the range B3:F3 (the low figures), and copy it with Edit ➤ Copy.
9. Return to the chart and choose Edit ➤ Series. Click in the 2nd Y-series area and then click on Paste. Then click OK. This assigns the 2nd Y-series.
10. Back in the spreadsheet, select the range B4:F4 and copy it.
11. Switch to the chart again, and using Edit ➤ Series, click in the 3rd Y-series and click Paste again. This assigns the 3rd Y-series.
12. Select the range B1:F1, copy it, and assign it to the X-series by clicking in the X-series box and then on Paste. This will create weekday labels on the horizontal axis.

If you view the chart now, you'll see five vertical lines on the screen, each one with three dots on it. Well, actually the line on the far right only seems to have two. This is because the High and Close values are identical (11). Now enter legends to show what the dots correspond to:

1. Choose Edit ➤ Legend/Series Labels.
2. Uncheck Auto series labels.
3. Enter **High** as the legend for the first Y-series.
4. Repeat the process for the two other series, entering the legends **Low** and **Close** for 2nd-Y and 3rd-Y, respectively.
5. Add titles if you want to with the Edit ➤ Titles command.
6. View the chart. It should look something like Figure 7.21.

FIGURE 7.21

A hi-lo-close chart. This type of chart displays three Y-series of data—an item's highest trading price, lowest trading price, and closing price.

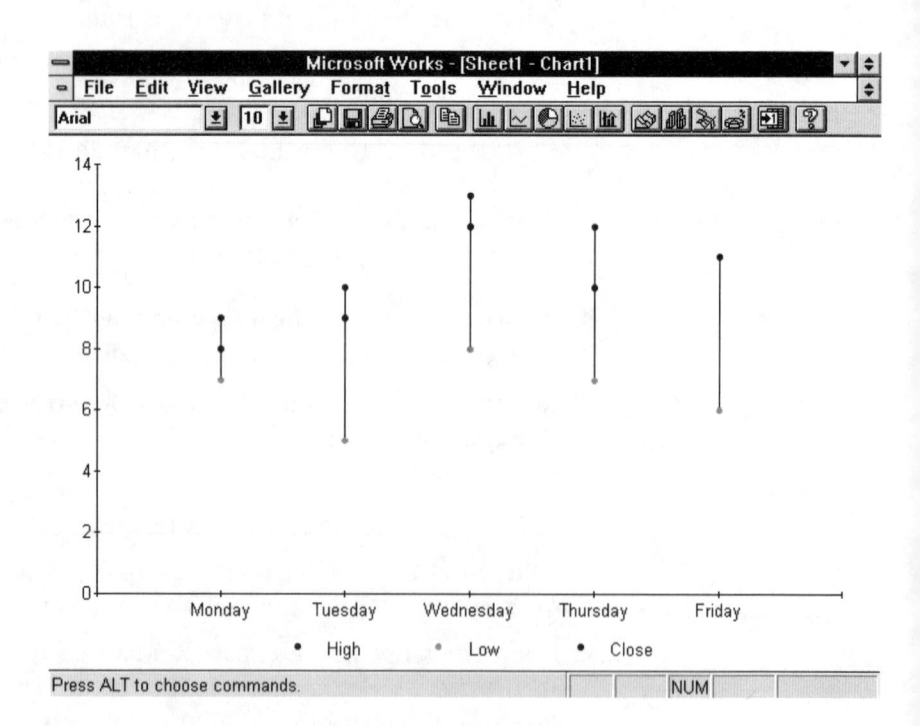

Making an X-Y Chart

X-Y charts, often called scatter charts, are used for statistical analysis because they can depict correlations between two sets of data. For example, you might want to show auto insurance rates as a function of drivers' ages, or a company's stock prices as correlated to its profits. Of course, there are many other applications, notably in scientific studies where cause-and-effect relationships in experimental environments are analyzed.

To plot an X-Y graph, you need two sets of data whose relationship you want to display. One set of data is plotted against the Y-axis, the other against the X-axis. Each value is plotted as a dot, or data point, on the chart. If there is perfect positive correlation between the X and Y data, the data points form a line at 45 degrees starting in the lower-left corner of the chart. Perfect negative correlation results in the opposite effect, a 45-degree line starting in the lower-right corner and rising toward the upper-left. If there is very little correlation, the data points are evenly distributed across the chart. Other types of correlation, such as logarithmic, have their own characteristic patterns such as arcs or S-curves.

Let's create an X-Y chart showing the correlation between wolf and deer populations as they change over time. We'll use data from a fictitious research study.

1. Open a new spreadsheet and enter the following data:

	A	B	C	D	E	F	G	H
1		December	January	February	March	April	May	
2	Wolves	20342	20021	17505	14996	10005	7412	
3	Deer	7521	10301	15231	18021	19547	20500	
4								

2. Select range B2:G2.
3. Choose Tools ➤ Create New Chart.
4. Choose X-Y (Scatter) and click OK.

Works uses the selected cells for the first Y-series. Now you have to declare the second Y-series:

5. Return to the sheet, select B3:G3, and choose Edit ➤ Copy to put this range on the Clipboard.

CHAPTER 7 Graphing and Charting

> **Tip** If you remember the cell addresses you want to assign to a series, you don't have to go back to the spreadsheet to select them. Simply choose Edit ➤ Series, and type in the cell addresses. This can save time. As another alternative, you can adjust the spreadsheet and chart windows so they both fit on the screen. Then you can switch between them just by clicking on a window.

   6. Back on the chart, choose Edit ➤ Series, click on 2nd, and click Paste. The range B3:G3 is inserted in the box. Click on OK.

   Now you have two sets of dots on the scatter chart.

   7. Enter the following information for the titles:

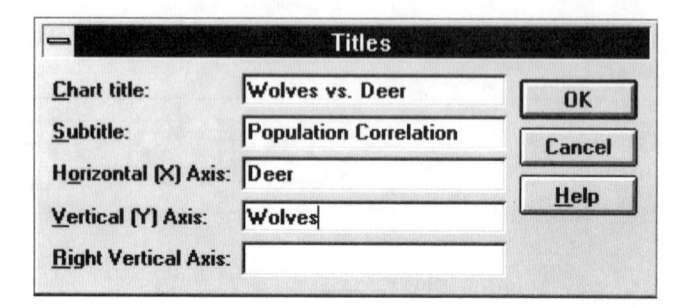

Titles	
Chart title:	Wolves vs. Deer
Subtitle:	Population Correlation
Horizontal (X) Axis:	Deer
Vertical (Y) Axis:	Wolves
Right Vertical Axis:	

   8. Click OK and view the chart. It should look like Figure 7.22.

   The chart clearly indicates the correlation between wolf and deer populations. As the wolf population increases, the deer population decreases.

Creating Different Chart Types

FIGURE 7.22

An X-Y chart with plotted data. Use this kind of chart to plot points against an X and a Y axis to display the relationships between pairs of numbers.

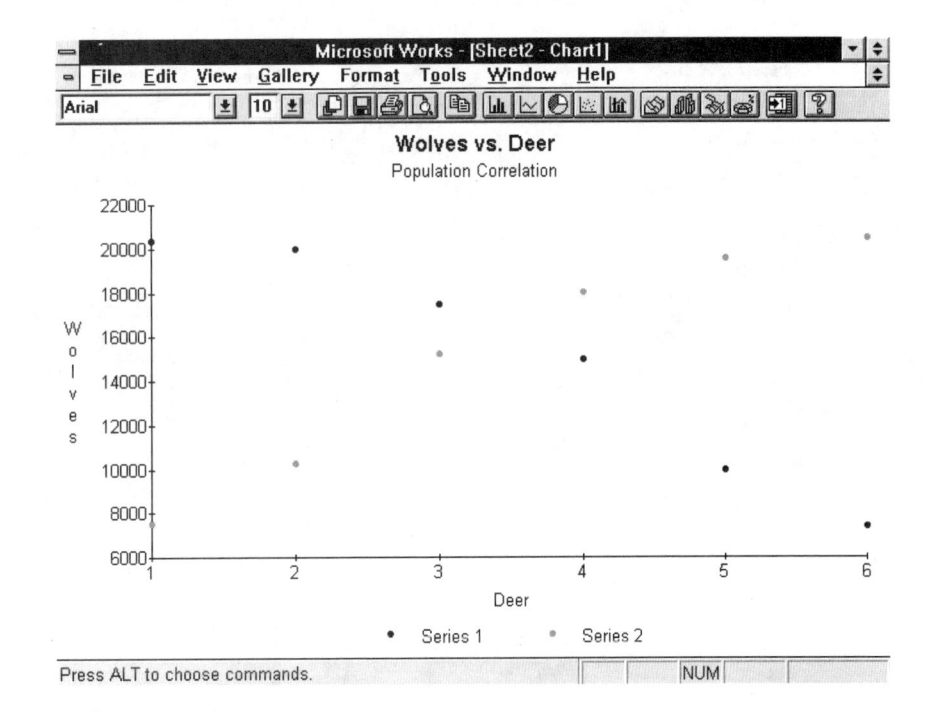

Making a Radar Chart

A radar chart plots values in a circle around an origin, allowing you to plot cyclical relationships in a format that shows repeating patterns. Here's how to turn your Wolf-Sheep population chart into a radar chart:

1. Select Gallery ➤ Radar.

2. Click OK. Your chart should now look like Figure 7.23.

Combining Lines and Bars on a Chart

The Combination choice from the Gallery menu lets you place bars and lines on the same graph in a variety of styles. You can mix standard bars and lines, or hi-lo-close lines and bars. You can also add a second Y-axis running up the right side of the chart. These features are useful when you want to emphasize one series while leaving others to play a background role in the appearance of the chart. For example, you might want

291

CHAPTER 7   Graphing and Charting

FIGURE 7.23
The population chart as a radar chart. A radar chart arranges values in a ring around a central axis.

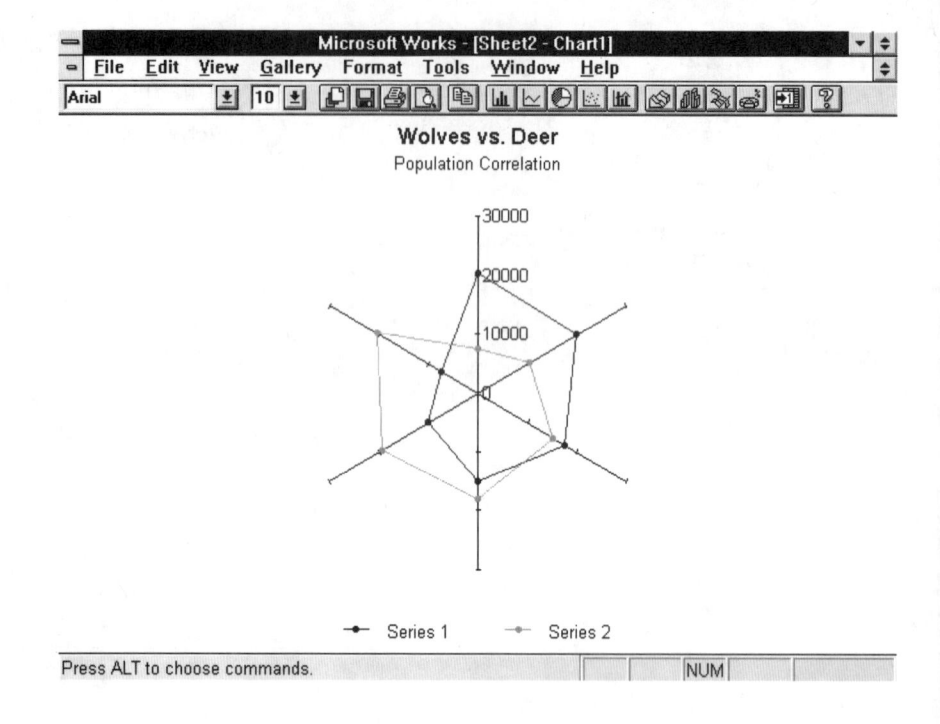

[Screenshot: Microsoft Works - [Sheet2 - Chart1] showing a radar chart titled "Wolves vs. Deer / Population Correlation" with values at 10000, 20000, 30000, and a legend showing Series 1 and Series 2.]

to have solid bars overlying some subtler lines. The bars could represent this year's earnings while the lines represent last year's. Here's how:

1. Make up your line or bar chart as you usually would, with as many Y-series as you need.
2. Choose Gallery ➤ Combination.
3. From the Combination dialog box, choose a chart style you like.
4. View the chart.

Tip   If you want to alter which series is displayed as lines and which as bars, use the Format ➤ Mixed Line and Bar command. This brings up a dialog box for making the reassignments.

Creating Different Chart Types

Making a 3-D Chart

3-D charts are variations on the standard area, bar, line, and pie charts with 3-D visual effects to make them more attractive or possibly easier to read. To see the 3-D version of a pie chart, let's return to the BUDGET spreadsheet and view the Labor, Pie chart:

1. Select Gallery ➤ 3-D Pie.

2. Choose option 6 to retain the labels and percentages.

3. Click OK.

The chart changes to a 3-D pie chart, as shown in Figure 7.24.

FIGURE 7.24
A 3-D pie chart. 3-D charts are attractive and sometimes easier to read than "two-dimensional" charts.

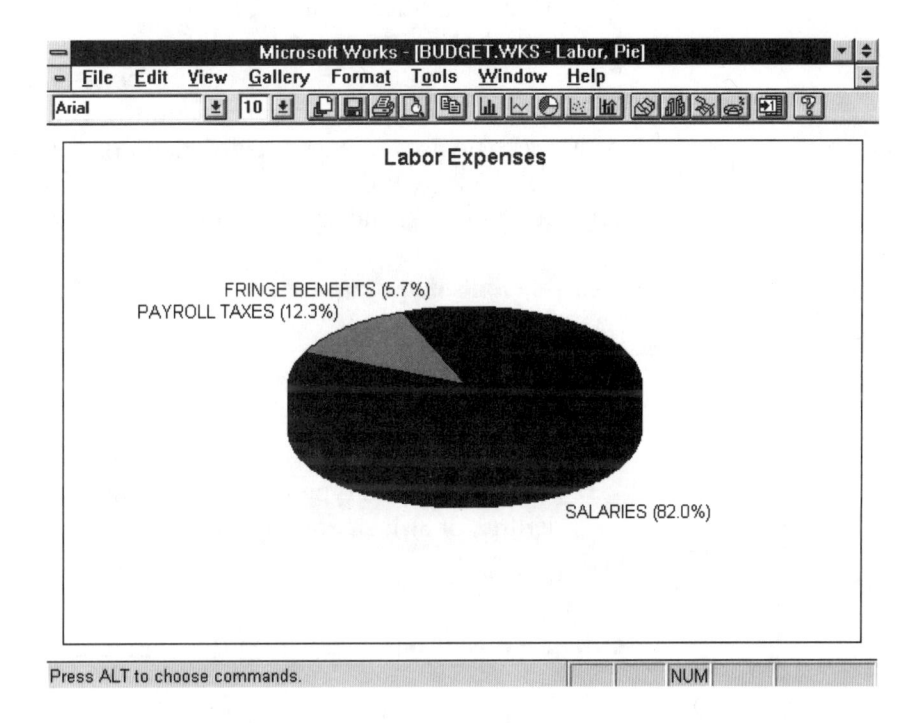

Fine-Tuning a Chart

Once you get the hang of chart making, you'll probably want to embellish your creations to make them more professional-looking. Works provides numerous options for fine-tuning charts. Once you print a chart and get a chance to study it, chances are you'll want to change it at least a little.

Typically, most people want to change the fonts in the chart labels and legends and alter the scaling of the chart once they've finished constructing it. Both subjects are discussed below.

Changing the Fonts in a Chart

You can change the fonts used in the screen display and the legends, data labels, and titles. Which fonts are available depends on your printer. To tell Works which type of default fonts to use in charts, select File ➤ Printer Setup. You'll see two font dialog boxes, one for choosing a font and type size for the title in charts, and the other for choosing a font and type size to be used in axes titles, data point labels, and legends. As a general rule, use large type sizes (around 32 characters per inch) for titles and something a little smaller for the other text.

Changing fonts in the chart title To get a new font for the title of a chart:

1. Select the title.
2. Choose Format ➤ Font and Style. The Font and Style for Title dialog box appears.
3. Select a font and type size. You can also choose the Bold, Italic, Underline, or Strikethrough style.
4. Click OK.

Changing other fonts in the chart To change all the other fonts in the chart:

1. Make sure the title is not selected.
2. Choose Format ➤ Font and Style. The Font and Style for Title dialog box appears.

3. Select a font and type size for the chart's title. You can also choose a Bold, Italic, Underline, or Strikethrough style.

4. Click OK.

Experiment to see which fonts you like best. Unfortunately, there is no substitute for printing a chart, since the proportions and resolution of fonts on screen are often different from those on the final, printed copy.

For business charts, stick with simple fonts such as Arial, Courier, and Times. Script fonts are difficult to read and should be avoided.

Which type size to choose for the text of a chart depends on the type of chart and the size of the labels and legends. In pie charts and X-Y charts, large font sizes in labels, legends, and numbers can make the text overlap, so avoid large type sizes in those kinds of charts.

Seeing a chart as it will look when printed To see what your charts look like after you've chosen a new font and type size for the text, choose one of these options:

- Choose View ➤ Display As Printed. Works will draw a reasonable facsimile of your chart as it will look with the fonts available to your printer. Choosing this option renders the chart in black and white on a color monitor—a useful feature, since most people have black-and-white printers.

- Choose File ➤ Print Preview. Figure 7.25 shows a preview of a chart. Notice that Works automatically scales the chart to the page size.

Changing the Measurement Scale for Numbers on a Chart

On bar, line, X-Y, and hi-lo-close charts, the Y-axis has a number scale. Works automatically calculates the numbers on the scale from the upper and lower values in the graph's Y-series. Based on these values, Works arrives at reasonable figures for the upper and lower boundaries of the Y-axis, computes the intervals in between these boundaries, and labels the Y-axis accordingly. Each chart is scaled in such a way that all the data can appear on the page and screen at once. The same is done for the X-axis in X-Y charts.

FIGURE 7.25
A typical print preview. Preview your charts before you print them in case you want to make any last-minute changes.

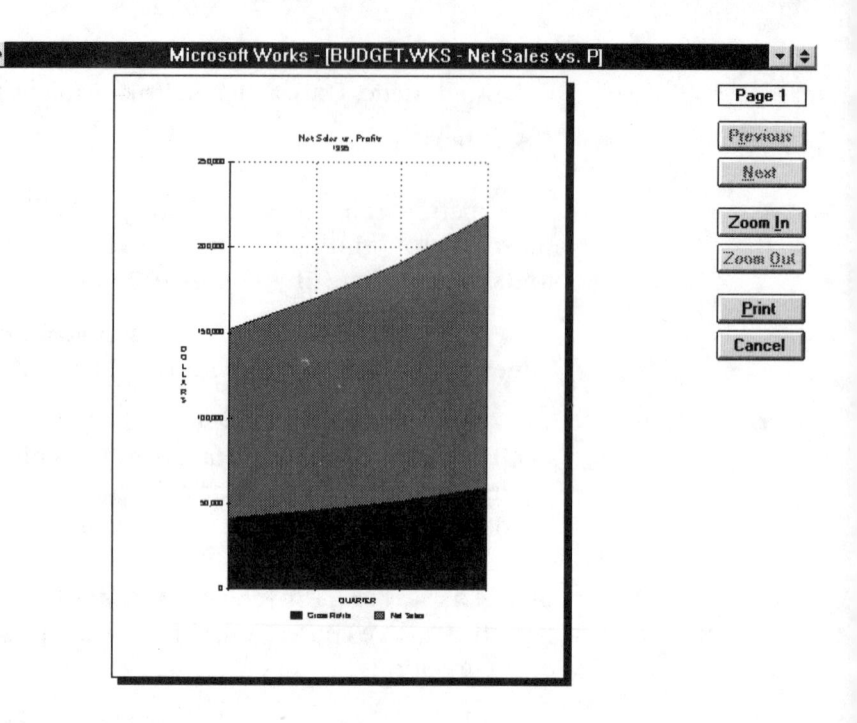

What if you want to override this feature? For example, suppose you wanted to zoom in for a close-up display of just a portion of the data so that more of the details were discernible.

To change the measurement scale for numbers along the Y- or X-axis of a chart:

1. With the chart displayed, open the Format menu.
2. Choose one of these commands:

    ◆ To change the vertical number scale along the left side of a chart, choose (Y) Axis.

    ◆ To change the horizontal scale along the bottom of a chart, choose (X) Axis.

A dialog box appears with scaling options, as follows. (The Vertical (Y) Axis dialog box only lets you set these values when plotting an X-Y chart.)

SETTING	EXPLANATION
Minimum	Sets the lowest value on the axis (bottom of axis)
Maximum	Sets the highest value on the axis (top of axis)
Interval	Sets how many numbers Works should skip between tick marks on the axis

3. Enter a Minimum, Maximum, and Interval value.

For example, suppose the data in your chart ranges from 0 to 20,000 but you want to chart only the data falling between 500 and 700 and place tick marks every 25 points. You would fill in the dialog box as follows:

SETTING	ENTRY
Minimum	500
Maximum	700
Interval	25

4. Click OK.

Returning to the normal number scale To return the settings to normal, follow steps 1 and 2 above and type the word *Auto* into each text box setting in the Axis dialog box.

> **Note** In the Vertical (Y) Axis dialog box, you can see and change the current chart type with the Type option box. This is the only way, short of viewing a graph, to see what type is currently selected (besides Pie).

Printing Charts

The real moment of glory comes when you finally print out the chart. You must print charts from either the Chart window or Chart Print Preview screen, not from the spreadsheet window. I suggest printing from the Preview screen because it gives you an opportunity to see if last-minute adjustments are needed before you waste any paper.

> **Warning**
> Daisy-wheel and certain other types of printers cannot print charts. Most dot-matrix, bubble-jet, and laser printers can, however. Check your printer's instruction manual and/or your Windows manual if you are in doubt about your printer's ability to print charts from Works for Windows.

Getting Ready to Print

Before printing, there are a few details to attend to. Follow these steps to get the printer or plotter ready:

1. Turn your printer on and make sure it is connected to the computer, is online, and has paper in it.

2. Choose File ➤ Printer Setup to make sure the correct printer is selected:

   ◆ If the name of your printer is highlighted in the dialog box, just press Esc.

   ◆ If you want to alter the printer setup, click on Setup. You'll have an opportunity to change the number of copies you want printed by default, whether you are feeding sheets of paper to your printer manually or using continuous-feed paper, and what port your printer is connected to. The options in the Printer Setup dialog boxes vary from printer to printer. Click OK when you are done.

Changing the layout of your chart At this point you can change the layout of your chart. To do so:

3. Choose File ➤ Page Setup ➤ Margins.

A dialog box appears, asking for details about margins, the chart size, and paper sizes. You can alter the size of the printout as well as the ratio of height to width.

Landscape charts You can also change the page orientation from *portrait* to *landscape* by choosing File ➤ Page Setup. Landscape charts are rotated 90 degrees so that they run the length of the paper rather than the width. The other orientation option, Portrait, prints the chart vertically, the usual way.

Unless you want to shrink the chart or place it in a specific spot on the page, ordinarily you won't change these settings. Works is set up to place the chart in the middle of a page for you.

4. Once everything is set correctly, press ↵. If you didn't make any changes, just press Esc.

Printing the Chart

Once everything is ready to go, preview your chart to take one last look before you print it:

1. Choose File ➤ Print Preview. A preview of your chart appears on screen (see Figure 7.25). Here's your last chance to make adjustments.

2. Click on the Print button. The Print dialog box appears, asking how many copies you want to print.

3. Enter the number of copies and click on OK.

Printing a chart can take several minutes. If you decide to stop the printing process, press Esc. You will be asked if you want to continue or abort your printout.

Printing to a Plotter

If you plan to print a chart with several colors using a plotter, there may be an additional step. After you click OK to start printing, you may see a dialog box that says something like

`Choose OK after mounting: Black, Blue`

Works is trying to tell you to mount the correct pens on the plotter. Install the pens and press ↵. You will see this message again later if you are using multiple colors.

Now you should have the basics of charting under your belt. Don't get frustrated if at first your charts seem to be upside-down or the wrong data gets plotted. Go back through some of the examples in this chapter and consult the online help by pressing F1. Charting takes a fair amount of experimentation, but it can be rewarding once you get the hang of it.

Chapter 8 explains the Works database.

PART four

The Works Database Tool

8
Using the Database

9
Advanced Database Skills

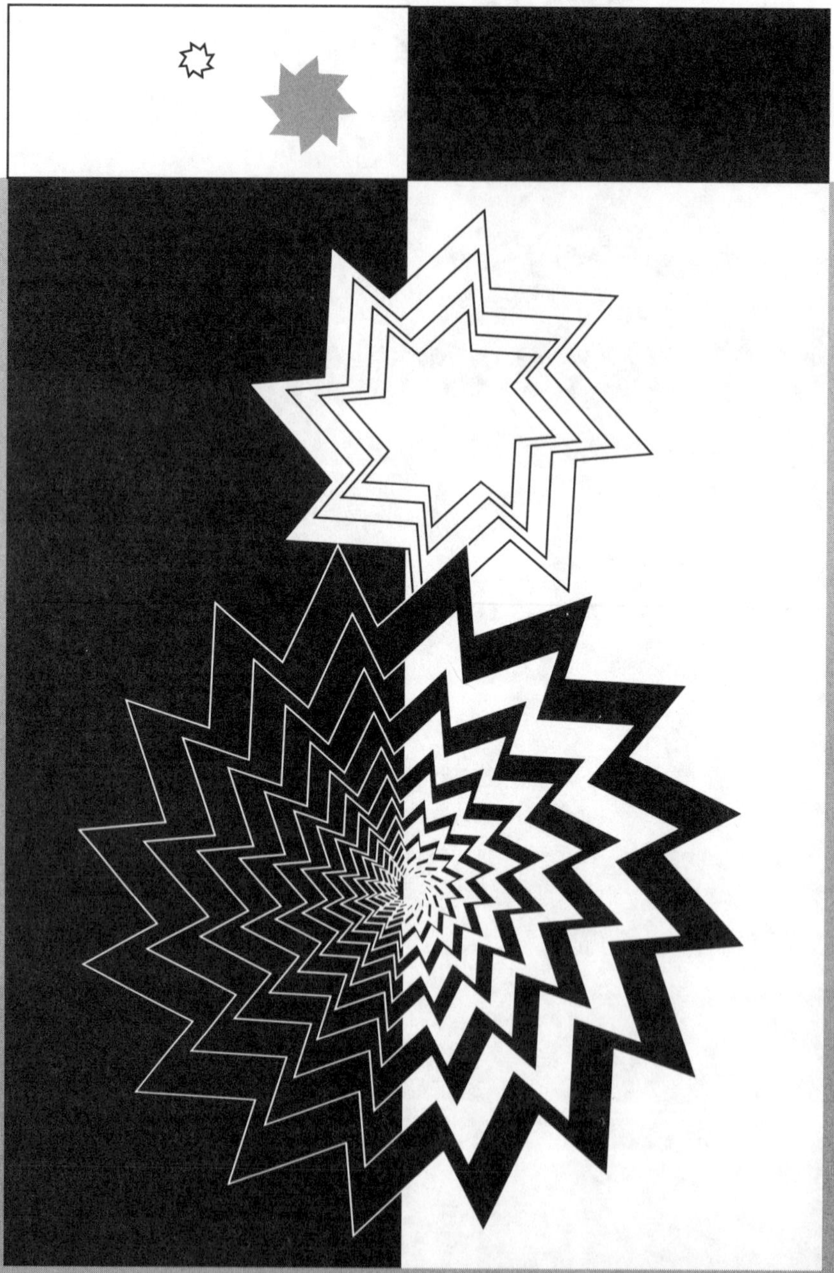

CHAPTER 8

Using the Database

Fast Track

Databases come in two formats, List view and Form view.   **307**

> List view shows all the records in a table much like a spreadsheet does. Form view displays one record at a time on the screen.

To begin a new database,   **310**

> choose File ➤ Create New File and choose Database, or choose Database from the start-up dialog box when Works first runs. Next, click anywhere on the screen and type in the first field name followed by a colon. The colon tells Works that you are creating a field. Move the cursor to another location and repeat this process for each new field.

To add data to a database,   **316**

> click to the right of one of the field names. A highlight appears. Enter the data in the field. Press Tab to move to the next field and enter data there.

To switch to List view or Form view,   **324**

    press F9, choose View ➤ List or View ➤ Form, or click on the List view or Form view buttons in the toolbar.

To edit data in a field,   **328**

    click on the field, press F2, and change the data in the formula bar. Press ↵ or click on the large X in the formula bar to complete the edit.

To find data in a database,   **332**

    press Ctrl+Home to move to the top of the database, choose Edit ➤ Find, and fill in the data you're looking for. Choose Next Record to find the next record with the data or All Records to display a group of records that contain the data. Click OK.

To query a database,   **339**

    choose Tools ➤ Create New Query, enter the appropriate query criteria, and click Apply Now.

THIS CHAPTER EXPLAINS THE DATABASE productivity tool, how it works, and what it can do for you. A database is really nothing more than a list of items—people, addresses, amounts, or anything else that could be put in a list. A database, like an electronic filing cabinet, is a collection of information that has something in common.

With a Works database, you can find information, rearrange data, retrieve data, and enter data quickly and easily. It has lots of useful features and is easy to master. Interestingly enough, the Works database is very similar in appearance and operation to the spreadsheet tool, so some of the operations described in Chapters 5 and 6 apply to the database tool as well.

In this chapter you'll learn how to

- Create a database
- Enter data into a database
- Move around a database
- Edit the data in a database
- Sort a database
- Query a database
- Print a database

Note See "Introduction to Databases" in Chapter 1 for a brief explanation of what a database is. Fields and records are also discussed in Chapter 1.

Data Basics

Like spreadsheets, databases have series of rows and columns. However, instead of storing data in cells, the data is stored at the intersection of columns (called fields) and rows (called records). Chapter 1 explains fields and records in detail. To illustrate what they are, consider this common database: a telephone book. A typical entry (record) in a phone book looks something like this:

Name	**Address**	**Phone**
Martindale, Emily	1454 Virginia	324-4665

This database has three fields: Name, Address, and Phone. Information (data) about Emily Martindale is listed in one record of the database. Other people would be listed in subsequent records, one for each person in the phone book.

Each entry in Emily's record is stored in one field. In a database, you can copy, move, format, edit, calculate, and print the data in fields. You can create and maintain lists in much the same way information is stored in filing cabinets and Rolodex files. The job of the database is to keep the list organized so you can retrieve and manipulate information quickly.

List View and Form View for Working with Databases

The Works database offers two distinct layouts, one called *List view* and the other *Form view*:

- In List view, a whole screen of records appears at one time. One record is displayed on each row and the fields are divided into columns. The List view of a database is shown in Figure 8.1.

- In Form view, only one record appears at a time and the data is displayed in a *form*, a document with one space reserved for each item of information (or field). Databases are laid out in Form view. Figure 8.2 shows the Form view of the second record in the database in Figure 8.1.

CHAPTER 8 Using the Database

FIGURE 8.1
The List view of a database. Here you can see several records at once.

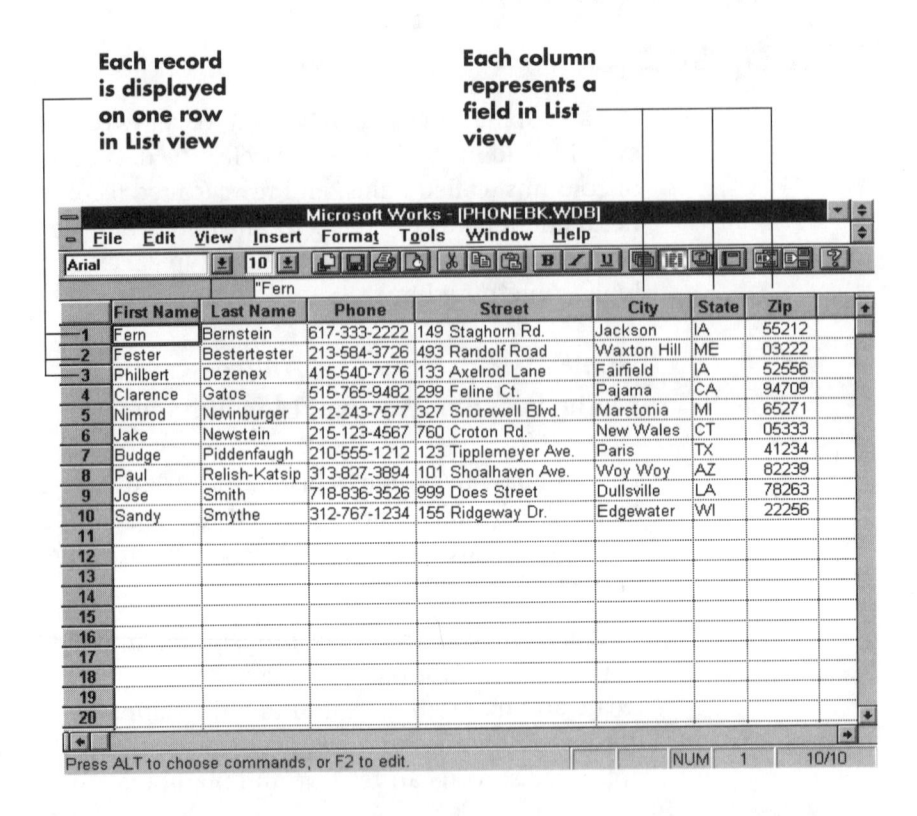

Each record is displayed on one row in List view

Each column represents a field in List view

	First Name	Last Name	Phone	Street	City	State	Zip
1	Fern	Bernstein	617-333-2222	149 Staghorn Rd.	Jackson	IA	55212
2	Fester	Bestertester	213-584-3726	493 Randolf Road	Waxton Hill	ME	03222
3	Philbert	Dezenex	415-540-7776	133 Axelrod Lane	Fairfield	IA	52556
4	Clarence	Gatos	515-765-9482	299 Feline Ct.	Pajama	CA	94709
5	Nimrod	Nevinburger	212-243-7577	327 Snorewell Blvd.	Marstonia	MI	65271
6	Jake	Newstein	215-123-4567	760 Croton Rd.	New Wales	CT	05333
7	Budge	Piddenfaugh	210-555-1212	123 Tipplemeyer Ave.	Paris	TX	41234
8	Paul	Relish-Katsip	313-827-3894	101 Shoalhaven Ave.	Woy Woy	AZ	82239
9	Jose	Smith	718-836-3526	999 Does Street	Dullsville	LA	78263
10	Sandy	Smythe	312-767-1234	155 Ridgeway Dr.	Edgewater	WI	22256

> **Note** A form can have as many as eight screens for cases where the record has numerous fields. Fields can be repositioned on a form.

Constructing a Database

Since the telephone book is a relatively simple and practical database, we will create a personal phone book database with Works. This part of the chapter explains

- ◆ Designing the database structure
- ◆ Moving the fields around

FIGURE 8.2
In Form view, only one record is shown.

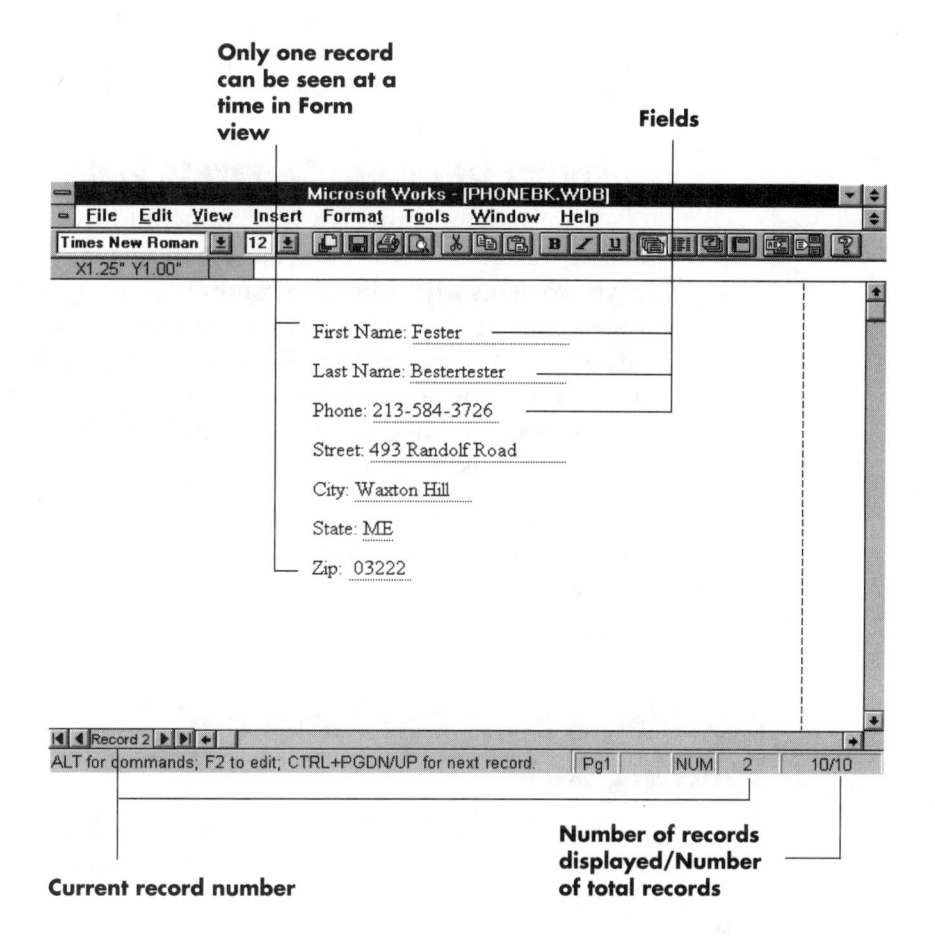

Only one record can be seen at a time in Form view

Fields

[Screenshot of Microsoft Works - [PHONEBK.WDB] in Form view showing:

First Name: Fester
Last Name: Bestertester
Phone: 213-584-3726
Street: 493 Randolf Road
City: Waxton Hill
State: ME
Zip: 03222

Status bar: ALT for commands; F2 to edit; CTRL+PGDN/UP for next record. | Pg1 | NUM | 2 | 10/10]

Current record number

Number of records displayed/Number of total records

- Changing the widths of a field
- Adding records to a database
- Saving a database on disk

Designing the Database Structure

The first step in creating a new database is to think about the number and arrangement, or order, of the fields. In other words, you have to design the layout before you start entering data. The layout of a database is called its *structure*. Setting up the structure amounts to laying out a single sample record in Form view with the fields arranged the way you want them.

Dividing Data into Separate Fields

It pays to put a little advance thought into how many fields you want in a new database. If you don't divide the data into enough fields, you may have problems when the time comes to rearrange or retrieve records later. For example, consider what would happen if each person's street address, city, state, and zip code were stored in the same field in a database. If you wanted to retrieve the records in this database of all people who live in Dallas, you wouldn't be able to do it. To retrieve records pertaining to cities, you must have a city field in your database.

As you design a database, use one field for each distinct item of information found in your records. For your personal telephone book, we'll use the following fields:

```
First Name Last Name Phone Street City State Zip
```

Opening a New Database and Entering Data

Now that you've given some thought to database structure, it's time to actually open a new database and begin entering the data. To open a new database:

1. If you are already in Works, choose File ➤ Create New File to open the Create New File dialog box. If you're just loading Works, the box appears by itself.
2. Click on Database in the dialog box.
3. Maximize the window.

Your screen will look very blank, with just the menu bar, status line, and message lines showing anything, as in Figure 8.3.

The database screen In the lower-right corner of the database screen, notice that the status area says:

Pg 1   1   0/0

FIGURE 8.3

A new database screen

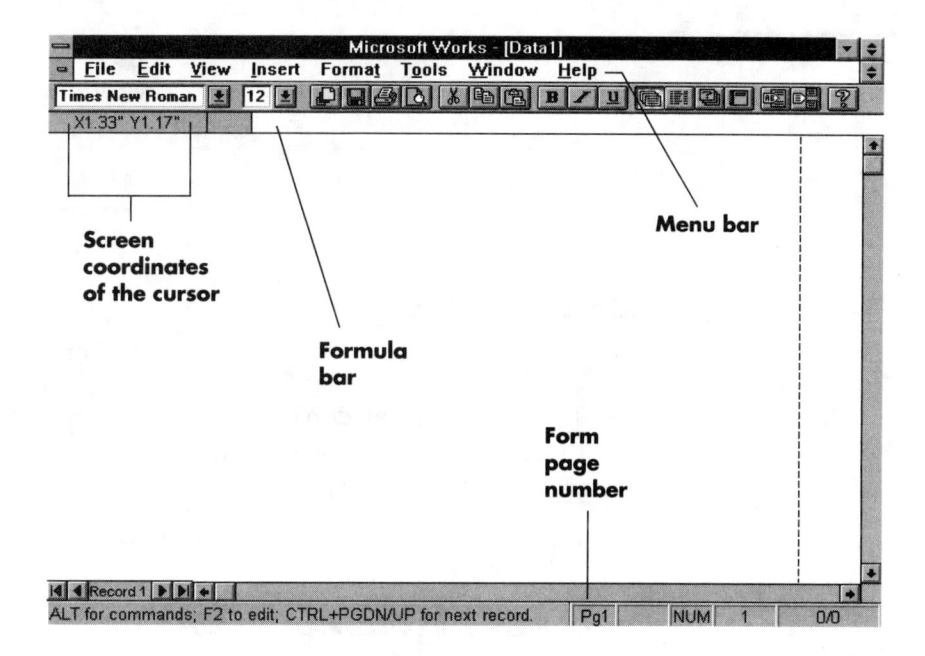

[Screenshot of Microsoft Works - [Data1] window with labels pointing to: Screen coordinates of the cursor, Formula bar, Menu bar, Form page number]

This means you are on the page 1 of the form and the cursor is on field zero of zero (since you haven't created any fields yet). Notice your cursor in the upper-left corner of the work area waiting for you to type in the name of the first field.

Database tool buttons Also notice the toolbar, which has four new buttons on it, as shown in Figure 8.4. These buttons are used as follows:

BUTTON	USE
Form View	Switches to a Form view of the database
List View	Switches to a List view of the database
Query	Activates a query so you can filter out records you don't want to see
Report	Lets you design a new report
Insert Field	Lets you insert a new field
Insert Record	Lets you insert a new record

CHAPTER 8 Using the Database

FIGURE 8.4
The database tool buttons

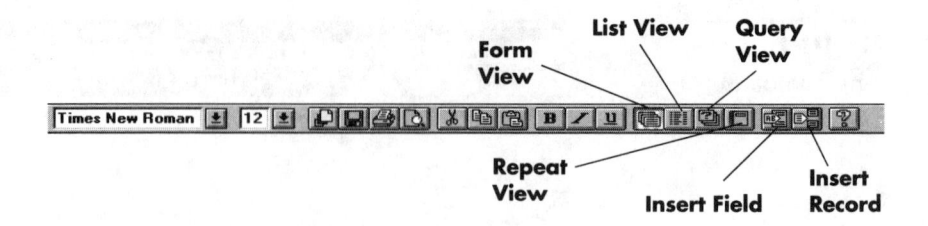

(Toolbar labeled with: Form View, List View, Query View, Repeat View, Insert Field, Insert Record)

Entering Data

Now let's begin entering the data on the form:

1. Type **First Name:** (don't forget the colon, since the colon tells Works to create a data field rather than just placing a label on the form). As you type, the letters appear highlighted and in the formula bar.

2. Press ↵. The Field Size dialog box appears:

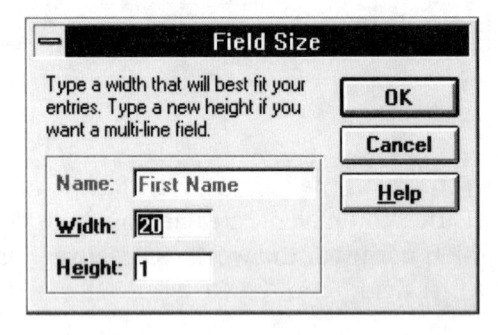

(Field Size dialog box: "Type a width that will best fit your entries. Type a new height if you want a multi-line field." Name: First Name, Width: 20, Height: 1, with OK, Cancel, Help buttons)

The default field width is 20, which means that approximately twenty characters will fit in the field. The default height is 1 line. For now we'll accept these default settings:

3. Click OK or press ↵. The cursor drops down a line automatically.

On your screen, notice a faint line after the First Name entry. This line shows where your data will eventually go. You've created the first field.

4. Press ↓ so that the highlight is two lines below the First Name field. This is where the next field will begin.

5. Type **Last Name:** and press ↵.

312

Constructing a Database

6. Press ↵ again to confirm the Field Size dialog box.

The Last Name field pops down to the cursor position when you press ↵. Your screen now has two fields called First Name and Last Name, as shown at the top of Figure 8.5.

7. Repeat steps 4 and 6 as you enter the other fields: Phone, Street, City, State, and Zip. When you are done, your screen should look like Figure 8.5.

Moving around a Form view screen For your reference, Table 8.1 lists the key strokes you can use in Form view mode for moving around on screen.

Rearranging the Fields in a Record

Now you've created the basic structure of the database. In fact, you've done more than that—you've also designed the look of the form in which you will view single records later on.

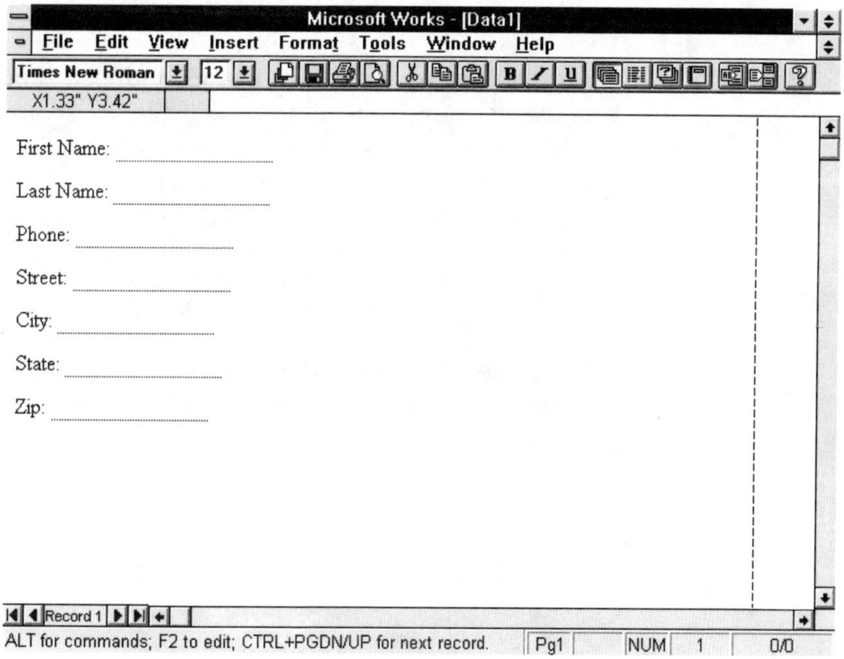

FIGURE 8.5
All seven fields placed on the screen

313

CHAPTER 8 Using the Database

TABLE 8.1: Keys for Moving the Cursor in a Form

KEY	MOVES THE CURSOR
↑	Up one row
↓	Down one row
←	Left one column
→	Right one column
Home	To the beginning of the line
End	To the end of the line
Ctrl+Home	To the beginning of the form
Ctrl+End	To the end of the form
PgUp	To the previous screen
PgDn	To the next screen
Tab	To the next field
Shift+Tab	To the previous field

If you were to enter data (names, addresses, and so on) into the database at this point, your form wouldn't look very interesting. At the least, it would look off-center since all the fields and field names are sitting along the left margin. Chances are good that you will want to reposition some of your fields on the screen to achieve a more aesthetic or practical layout. You can move fields easily by dragging fields with the mouse.

To rearrange the field locations in a form:

1. Position the mouse pointer on the First Name field and click. The entire field name becomes highlighted and the word *DRAG* appears below the pointer.

Constructing a Database

2. Start dragging the pointer where you want the field to be. The word changes to *MOVE*:

```
First Name
Last Name  MOVE
```

> **Tip**
>
> To move a field with the arrow keys, first use the arrow keys to highlight the field. Then choose Edit ➤ Position Selection. The MOVE pointer appears on the field. Press the arrow keys to position the field, and press ↵ when you're done.

3. Drag the field to approximately the center of the screen, two lines down from the formula bar, and release the mouse button. The First Name field moves to the new location.

4. Using the same dragging technique, move the remaining fields until your screen looks like the one in Figure 8.6.

> **Tip**
>
> Works has a *snap-to grid,* a grid on which objects on screen align themselves automatically. By default, this option is turned on to help you "snap" fields and other objects into place. You can turn this feature off by choosing Format ➤ Snap To Grid if you want to place objects with more precision. However, you might end up with some slight misalignments.

CHAPTER 8   Using the Database

FIGURE 8.6

The fields relocated to the center of the screen

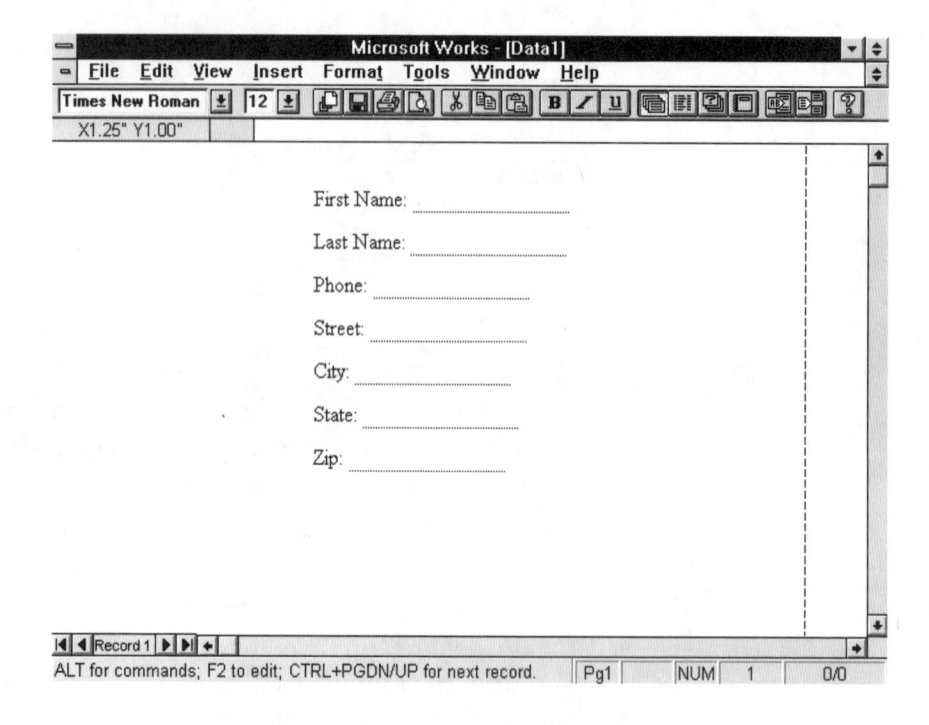

[Screenshot of Microsoft Works - [Data1] showing fields: First Name, Last Name, Phone, Street, City, State, Zip centered on screen]

With the basic design of the database complete, you can start entering the data:

1. Click on the empty field (the faint line) to the right of First Name. This highlights the field. Works is now waiting for you to enter a first name.

2. Enter the name **Jake**.

3. Press Tab. This enters the data into the field and moves you to the next field.

4. The highlight is on the Last Name field. Type **Newstein** and press Tab. The data is entered and the highlight advances to the Phone field.

5. Enter the phone number **215-123-4567** (remember to type in the dashes too) and press Tab again.

Changing the Width of a Field

In our Phone field, the faint line is longer than it needs to be to hold the telephone number. When you created the structure for this database, Works used the default length of twenty spaces. Obviously the twenty-space default is long enough for telephone numbers, but you'll probably have to enlarge the Last Name, Street, and City fields so they can display long names. And to optimize the form, you might even want to modify the Phone, State, and Zip fields for exact sizes. Field length can be altered either before or after data is entered.

How wide a field is on the screen does not necessarily have anything to do with the amount of data it is storing. Even if the Phone field was only three characters wide, you could enter a complete phone number and the digits would be stored in Works' memory. Like a spreadsheet cell, a database field holds information even if it can't display all of it.

Note Database fields can be up to 256 characters wide, and each database can have as many as 256 fields. You can enter up to 32,000 records in any given database.

To practice altering field widths, let's adjust the fields of the phone book database:

1. Click anywhere on the Street field (but not on the Street label).
2. Choose Format ➤ Field Size. The Field Size dialog box appears. It shows the current width, which is 20.
3. Change the width to 25.
4. Change the width of the remainder of the fields as follows:

FIELD	NEW WIDTH
Phone:	16
Street:	25
City:	15

CHAPTER 8 Using the Database

        State: 4

        Zip: 8

Now your screen should look like Figure 8.7.

When all the fields are sized correctly:

5. Choose Format ➤ Protection, check the Protect Form box, and click OK. This locks the form so that you can't accidentally add new fields or move things around unintentionally.

Problems with the Width setting in the Field Size dialog box For reasons that have to do with how proportionally spaced fonts display on the screen, the Width setting in the Field Size dialog box doesn't always accurately show the number of characters that can be entered in a field! For example, a setting of 2 should hold a state abbreviation such as CA, but it doesn't. You have to increase the setting to 3 to enter two capital letters. The exact setting you need for a field depends on whether the field will hold upper- or lowercase letters, or numbers. Uppercase letters and

FIGURE 8.7

Changing the width of the fields

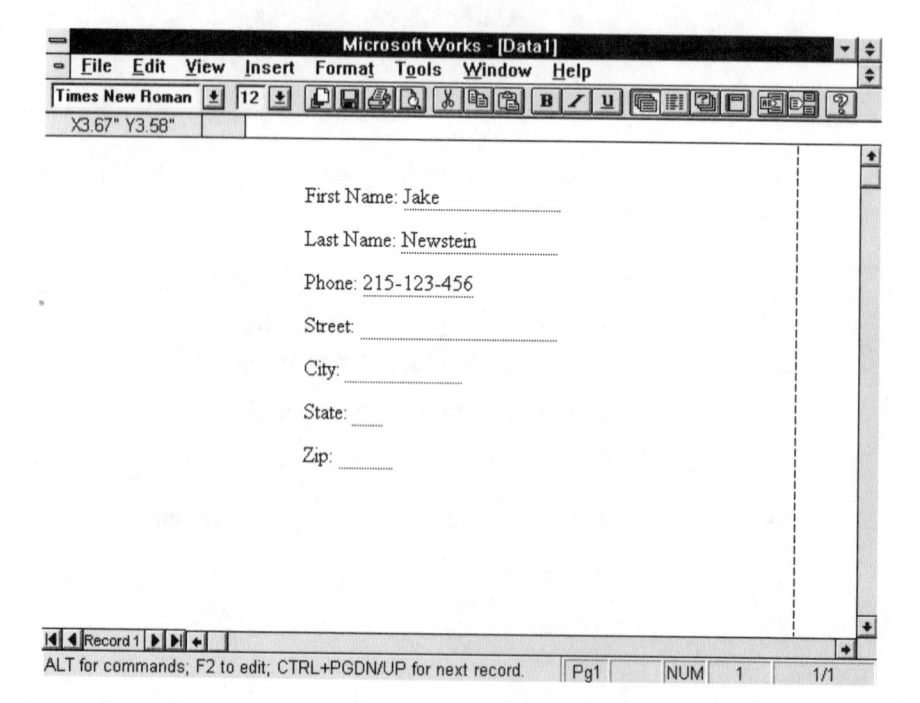

numbers take up more room. If you select a monospaced font (with all the characters the same width), the width setting will be accurate.

Warning

> As a rule, field sizes have to be a bit longer than the maximum number of characters you hope to display. If the field contains numbers or dates and is too small, the contents will display as pound signs (#######). When this happens, widen the field. If you select a monospaced font such as Courier, the width setting will be accurate.

Tip

> You can also change field widths with the mouse. Click on the data area of the field (the right side) and drag the small white box in the lower-right corner. Drag to the left to shorten the field, to the right to lengthen it, or down to make the field two or more lines. Dragging the box up can shorten a multiline field.

Adding More Records to a Database

Now you can continue entering records in the database:

1. Move the highlight to the First Name field of record 1. (If you are not on record 1, press Ctrl+Home.)
2. Press Tab three times to move down to the Street field.
3. Fill in the rest of the data by using Figure 8.8 as a guide.

Entering a character string that begins with a zero Notice that the zip code 05333 lost its leading zero. Works assumed you were entering a numerical value and chopped off the zero at the beginning of the zip code. Works assumed—wrongly—that the leading zero was meaningless and unnecessary.

CHAPTER 8 Using the Database

There are two ways around this problem. You can enter a quotation mark or use the Number dialog box.

To enter numbers such as zip codes that begin with zeros, enter a quotation mark (") before the zero. The quotation mark tells Works that you are entering a character string, not a number. But there's an easier way.

> **Note** A *character string* is simply a group of characters that the computer treats as text rather than numbers. Numbers can be included in character strings.

A setting from the Format menu will format the Zip field to accept leading zeros:

1. Choose Format ➤ Protection, uncheck Protect Form, and click OK.

FIGURE 8.8
The first record completed

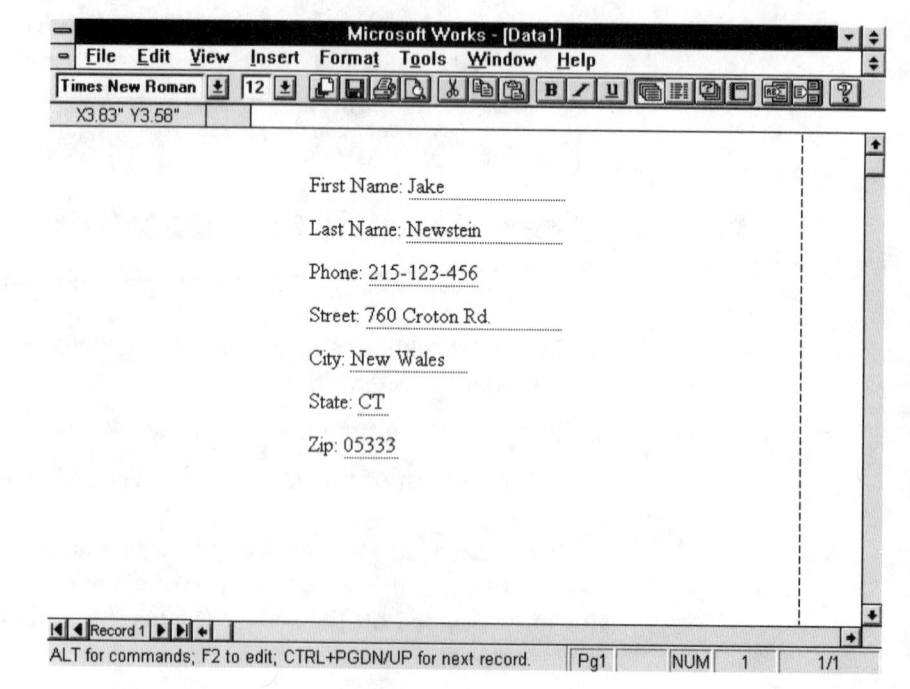

[Screenshot of Microsoft Works - [Data1] window showing the first record with fields:
First Name: Jake
Last Name: Newstein
Phone: 215-123-456
Street: 760 Croton Rd.
City: New Wales
State: CT
Zip: 05333]

320

2. Put the cursor on the Zip field by clicking on it. (Not on the word *Zip* but on the field itself.)

3. Choose Format ➤ Number to bring up the Number dialog box.

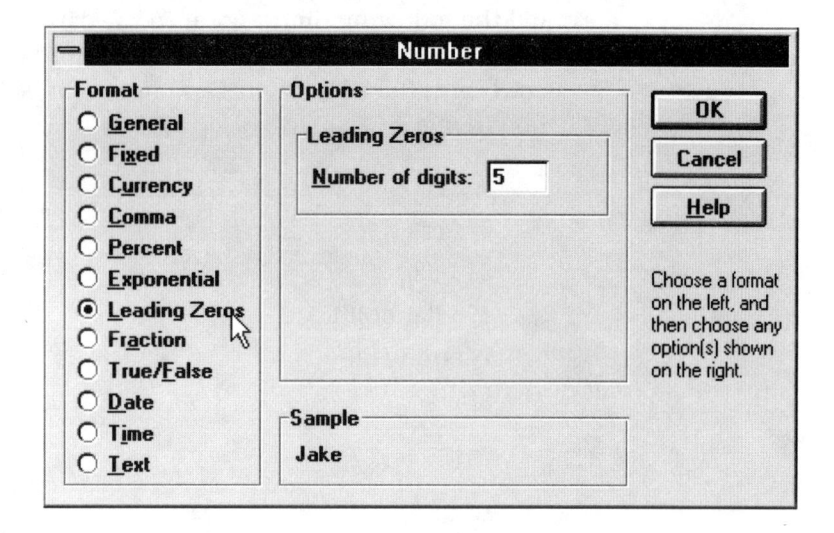

```
┌─────────────────── Number ───────────────────┐
│ ┌Format──────────┐ ┌Options──────────┐       │
│ │ ○ General      │ │ ┌Leading Zeros─┐│  [ OK ]│
│ │ ○ Fixed        │ │ │              ││       │
│ │ ○ Currency     │ │ │Number of digits: 5 ││ [Cancel]│
│ │ ○ Comma        │ │ └──────────────┘│       │
│ │ ○ Percent      │ └─────────────────┘  [Help]│
│ │ ○ Exponential  │                            │
│ │ ● Leading Zeros│       Choose a format      │
│ │ ○ Fraction     │       on the left, and     │
│ │ ○ True/False   │       then choose any      │
│ │ ○ Date         │       option(s) shown      │
│ │ ○ Time         │ ┌Sample─────────┐ on the right. │
│ │ ○ Text         │ │ Jake          │           │
│ └────────────────┘ └───────────────┘           │
└──────────────────────────────────────────────┘
```

4. Click Leading Zeros and enter **5**, since a zip code is typically five digits in length.

5. Click OK.

Any missing zeros now reappear.

> **Note** No matter how a field is formatted, you can place a quotation mark before a character string to enter the string and override the format. For example, in a number field that has been formatted to include commas, placing a quotation mark before the number enters it without the commas.

CHAPTER 8 Using the Database

Let's add the next record:

1. You are on the last field of the first record. Press Tab to move ahead to the next record.

2. Add the following nine records to the database, pressing the Tab key to move from field to field and from record to record. We'll use all ten records (Jake Newstein's and nine others) for experimentation in this chapter.

Fester	Nimrod
Bestertester	Nevinburger
213-584-3726	212-243-7577
493 Randolf Road	327 Snorewell Blvd.
Waxton Hill	Marstonia
ME	MI
03222	65271
Philbert	Sandy
Dezenex	Smythe
415-540-7776	312-767-1234
133 Axelrod Lane	155 Ridgeway Dr.
Fairfield	Edgewater
IA	WI
52556	22256
Clarence	Paul
Gatos	Relish
515-765-9482	313-827-3894
299 Feline Ct.	101 Shoalhaven Ave.
Pajama	Woy Woy
CA	AZ
94709	82239

Jose
Smith
718-836-3526
999 Doe Street
Dullsville
LA
78263

Fern
Bernstein
617-333-2222
149 Staghorn Rd.
Jackson
IA
55212

Budge
Piddenfaugh
201-555-1212
123 Tipplemeyer Ave.
Paris
TX
41234

Saving Your Work

Before going any further, save your work on disk to prevent accidentally losing your data if the power goes off or if some other hardware or software error occurs.

1. Press ↵ while on the last field you entered, assuming you didn't press Tab.
2. Choose File ➤ Save. The Save As dialog box appears.
3. Make sure the correct data disk drive is selected.
4. For the file name, type in **PHONEBK**.
5. Press ↵ or click on OK.

CHAPTER 8 Using the Database

> **Tip** — To move from record to record in Form view, press Ctrl+PgUp to move to the previous record, or Ctrl+PgDn to move to the next record. The box on the right side of the status area tells you the number of the record you are viewing.

Working with a Database in List View

Now that you have a semblance of a database entered, you can begin to experiment a bit. This part of the chapter explores List view. It explains

- Switching to List view
- The List view screen
- Moving around the screen in List view
- Rearranging database fields in List view

Switching from Form view to List view In List view you can see lots of records at once, whereas Form view shows records one at a time. Let's switch to List view now. Use one of these techniques:

- Choose View ➤ List
- Click on the List view button (see Figure 8.4)
- Press F9

The screen changes to List view, as shown in Figure 8.9.

> **Tip** — Pressing F9 is a shortcut to switching back and forth between Form view and List view. The view toggles with each press.

324

Working with a Database in List View

FIGURE 8.9
In List view you can see more than one record at once.

	First Name	Last Name	Phone	Street	City	State	Zip
1	Jake	Newstein	215-123-456	760 Croton	New Wales	CT	05333
2	Fester	Besterteste	213-584-372	493 Randol	Waxton Hill	ME	03222
3	Philbert	Dezenex	415-540-777	133 Axelrod	Fairfield	IA	52556
4	Clarence	Gatos	515-765-948	299 Feline (	Pajama	CA	94709
5	Jose	Smith	718-836-352	999 Does S	Dullsville	LA	78263
6	Budge	Piddenfaugh	210-555-121	123 Tipplem	Paris	TX	41234
7	Nimrod	Nevinburger	212-243-757	327 Snorew	Marstonia	MI	65271
8	Sandy	Smythe	312-767-123	155 Ridgew	Edgewater	WI	22256
9	Paul	Relish	313-827-389	101 Shoalha	Woy Woy	AZ	82239
10	Fern	Bernstein	617-333-222	149 Staghor	Jackson	IA	55212

Making Fields Wider in List View

In List view, each record occupies a row of the list. Moreover, that familiar problem of all fields being displayed in a default width rears its ugly head again. Earlier in this chapter you redefined the width of the fields in Form view, but the settings did not carry over to List view.

> **Warning**
>
> If your fields are in a different order than the fields in Figure 8.9, skip ahead and read "Rearranging the Fields in List View." For the purposes of the tutorial, the fields should be in the same order as shown in Figure 8.9.

As you know, field data is not lost when it does not appear in its entirety on screen. Works keeps the data in memory. Moreover, the formula bar will display the complete contents of a field.

325

Leaving your screen compressed this way accommodates a greater number of fields. If you need to see what is in a field, move the highlight to the field and look in the formula bar to see what is in it. Once you stretch out the field widths, you may have to scroll the screen horizontally to get to certain fields. On the other hand, if being able to see what is in a series of fields matters, then you should adjust the widths as necessary.

To make fields in List view wider:

1. Place the mouse pointer on the column divider at the top of the screen. It changes to a two-headed arrow with the word *ADJUST* under it:

	First Name	Last Name	Phone	Street	City	State	Zip	
1	Jake	Newstein	215-123-4567	60 Croton	New Wales	CT	05333	

2. Drag the line to the right and release the mouse.
3. Using this same technique, widen the remainder of the fields until your screen looks like Figure 8.10.

Moving Around the List View Screen

You can move around the screen and scroll vertically and horizontally through a database in List view by using the keyboard commands in Table 8.2.

Rearranging Fields in List View

The order of fields in List view corresponds to the top-to-bottom order of fields in Form view because Works creates List view fields in the order in which you created them on the form. However, you can arrange fields in List view any way you want.

To rearrange the fields in a database in List view:

1. Save the data first. This way, if something goes wrong as you try to rearrange the fields, you can go back to the saved version.

FIGURE 8.10
Adjusting the column widths in List view

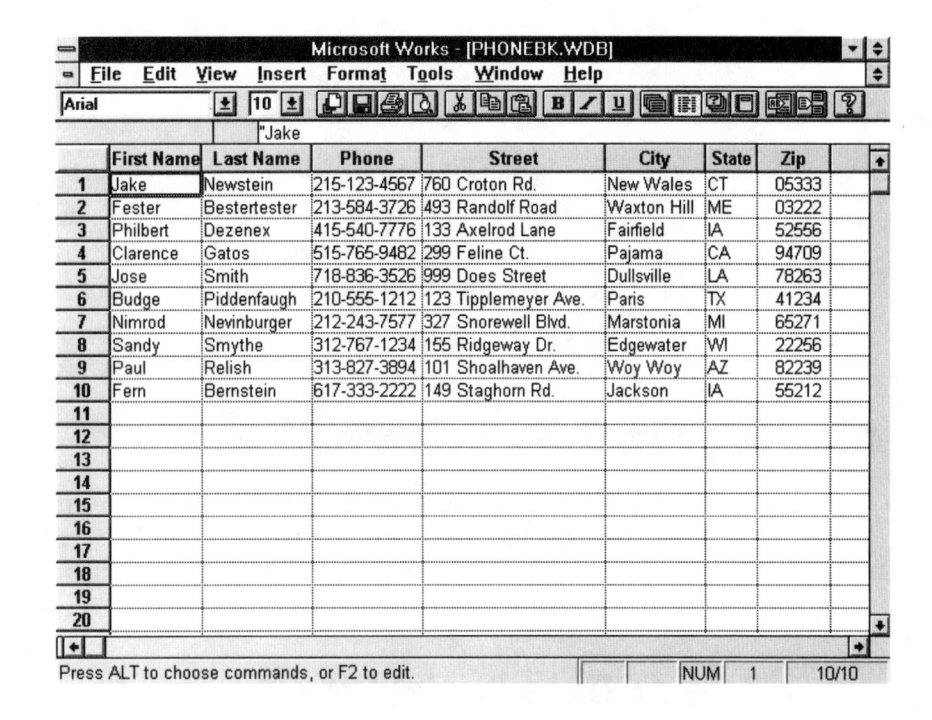

	First Name	Last Name	Phone	Street	City	State	Zip
1	Jake	Newstein	215-123-4567	760 Croton Rd.	New Wales	CT	05333
2	Fester	Bestertester	213-584-3726	493 Randolf Road	Waxton Hill	ME	03222
3	Philbert	Dezenex	415-540-7776	133 Axelrod Lane	Fairfield	IA	52556
4	Clarence	Gatos	515-765-9482	299 Feline Ct.	Pajama	CA	94709
5	Jose	Smith	718-836-3526	999 Does Street	Dullsville	LA	78263
6	Budge	Piddenfaugh	210-555-1212	123 Tipplemeyer Ave.	Paris	TX	41234
7	Nimrod	Nevinburger	212-243-7577	327 Snorewell Blvd.	Marstonia	MI	65271
8	Sandy	Smythe	312-767-1234	155 Ridgeway Dr.	Edgewater	WI	22256
9	Paul	Relish	313-827-3894	101 Shoalhaven Ave.	Woy Woy	AZ	82239
10	Fern	Bernstein	617-333-2222	149 Staghorn Rd.	Jackson	IA	55212

TABLE 8.2: Moving the Cursor in List View

KEY	MOVES THE CURSOR
↑	Up one row
↓	Down one row
← or Shift+Tab	Left one column
→ or Tab	Right one column
Home	To the beginning of a record
End	To the end of a record
Ctrl+Home	To the beginning of the database
Ctrl+End	To the end of the database
PgUp	To the previous page of records
PgDn	To the next page of records
F5	To a specific field

2. Activate List view if you're in Form view (press F9) and click on the column selector of the column you want to move. The whole column is selected.

3. Choose Edit ➤ Cut. The column disappears.

4. Move the cursor to the field just to the left of where you want to insert the field you're moving. The cursor must be in the column head or the top cell of the column.

5. Choose Edit ➤ Paste.

Altering the Data in a Database

At some point you'll want to alter, or edit, the records in the database. For example, when people move, their addresses and often their phone numbers have to be changed. Instead of erasing the old address and entering a new one, you can just edit the data in your database.

Editing Data in List View

Let's say you've just received a wedding invitation announcing the imminent marriage of Paul Relish to Linda Katsip, and they intend to hyphenate their last names. Paul is in our sample database, so we need to change his name to Paul Relish-Katsip. To edit a record in a database:

1. Move the highlight to (or click on) the field you want to change. In our case, click on the Last Name field in record 9.

2. Press F2, the Edit key.

Pressing F2 puts you in Edit mode. Notice that the status area now says EDIT and that the field data appears in the formula bar. The blinking cursor is in the formula bar as well.

Altering the Data in a Database

> **Tip** You can edit the contents of a field without pressing F2. With the field you want to edit highlighted, click in the formula bar at approximately the spot where you want the insertion point to land. Edit mode will automatically be activated.

3. Edit the field in the formula bar. In our case, enter **-Katsip** to change Paul's last name to Relish-Katsip.

4. Press ↵ or click on the check mark in the formula bar to complete the entry and leave Edit mode.

Keys for editing in the formula bar When the cursor is in the formula bar, you can use these shortcut keys to help you edit and move around the field:

KEY	EFFECT
Home	Moves the cursor to the start of the line
End	Moves the cursor to the end of the line
←	Moves the cursor left one character
→	Moves the cursor right one character
Del	Deletes the character to the right of the cursor
Backspace	Deletes the character to the left of the cursor
Shift+*arrow key*	Selects multiple characters

> **Tip** You can also drag across text to select it in the formula bar.

Editing Data in Form View

You can also edit fields in Form view. Editing in Form view is more convenient if you plan to change lots of fields in a record and you would like to see as many fields as possible on one screen. In Form view you can see more fields at once and you don't have to scroll the screen left and right to see the fields.

There are a two ways to locate the record you want to edit in Form view:

- Find the record in List view and then switch to Form view to edit it.
- Use the Go To command to move to the record you want to edit.

Note You can also use the Edit ➤ Find command to find a record. See "Searching for Records and Fields in a Database" later in this chapter.

Finding and editing a record beginning in List view You can see more records in List view, so one way to find the record you want to edit is to do so from List view. When you've found it:

1. Place the highlight in the record. Preferably, place it in the field you plan to change
2. Press F9 or choose View ➤ Form to switch to Form view. The form appears with the highlight already on the field you want to edit.
3. Press F2 to switch to Edit mode.
4. Make your changes.
5. Press ↵ or else ↑ or ↓ to move to another field and modify it.
6. Press F9 to return to List view.

Finding and editing a record with the Go To command In large databases, moving from one record to another to find the record you want to edit can take a lot of time. However, each record in a database has a number,

Searching for Records and Fields in a Database

so you can use the Edit ➤ Go To command to move directly to a specific record. From there you can edit it.

For example, let's say you wanted to edit the Phone field of record 403:

1. Press F5 (or choose Edit ➤ Go To). The Go To dialog box appears.
2. Type in 403 in the Go to box.
3. Choose the field you want to edit by selecting it from the Names box, as in Figure 8.11.
4. Press ↵.
5. Make your changes to the field.
6. Press ↵ or else ↑ or ↓ to move to another field and modify it.

In large databases, you often won't know the number of the record whose fields you want to edit. For such cases, you can use the Edit ➤ Find command to find a given record, as explained in the next section.

FIGURE 8.11
Finding a field to edit with the Go To command

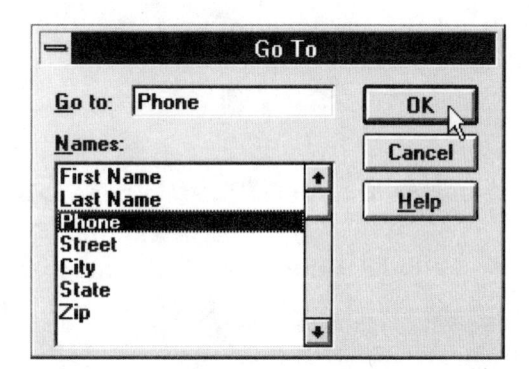

Searching for Records and Fields in a Database

The database tool includes a Find command so you can quickly find and display a particular record or records. This command is indispensable, not just for finding records in order to edit them, but for finding groups of records. This part of the chapter explains how to use the Find command.

The Find Command for Locating a Record

To use the Find command, you must tell Works what to search for. This is done by entering text in the Find dialog box, like so:

1. If you are in Form view, press F9 to go to List view. (You can use the Find command in Form view as well, as you will see shortly.)

2. Choose Edit ➤ Find. The Find dialog box appears, as in Figure 8.12.

Let's say you want to see who, if anyone, lives in Paris.

3. Enter **Paris** in the Find What box and click OK or press ↵.

The cursor jumps to record 6 in our sample database.

> **Tip**
>
> Works finds the first record in the database that matches the text you entered in the Find What box. To find subsequent records that match the text, just press F7. Works will start searching again.

How Works Conducts Searches

What you enter in the Find What box has a lot to do with how Works conducts the search. This time we'll conduct the search from Form view. Suppose you want to find your friend Clarence's record either to edit or view it.

1. Press F9 to switch to Form view. Notice that the status area in the lower-left corner tells you what record you are on.

2. Choose Edit ➤ Find. The Find dialog box appears (see Figure 8.12).

3. Type in **clar** in the Find What box and press ↵.

Clarence's record appears even though you didn't enter his whole name in the Find What box. Works will find all variations of the letters *clar* in the search, including records with the words *Clara*, *clarinet*, and *declarant*. The more completely you enter your search information, the more exact Works will be in searching for records.

> **Note** When entering text in the Find What box, you don't have to concern yourself with capitalization. For example, Works will find the name *Clarence* whether you enter it with a capital *C* or not. You could even enter the word like so: *cLaReNcE*.

Using Wildcards in Searches

You can use wildcard characters to assist in searches. Enter one of the two wildcards in the Find What box along with other text, as follows:

WILDCARD	EXPLANATION
?	Represents a single letter or numeral in a search. For example, entering Bernst??n would find Bernstein, Bernstien, and Bernstoon.
*	Represents more than one letter or numeral in a search. For example, entering W*Y would find both Woy, Wally, WY, West Yonkers, and even Southwest Yonkers.

Displaying All Records that Match the Find Criteria

The Find dialog box includes a special option for displaying *all* the records in the database that match the Find criteria, not just one of them at a time. Moreover, this feature hides all records that don't match. This is like conducting a quick and simple query (queries are covered later in this chapter). Here's how it's done:

1. Choose Edit ➤ Find to open the Find dialog box (see Figure 8.12).
2. Enter the text you want to search for in the Find What box.

3. Click on the All Records button.
4. Click OK.

Now all the records with the search criteria in them appear. The other records in your database are still alive and well but are temporarily hidden from view.

After you're done perusing your records, return all the records to view. Otherwise you might forget that the missing records are there, which would spell disaster if you tried to print or query the database.

To bring all records in view:

5. Choose View ➤ Show All Records.

Selecting Part of a Database to Search In

In large databases you will want to limit searches to a portion of the database. Another reason for searching only a part of a database is to keep Works from leading you through a trail of matching text in fields that are irrelevant to your search. Limited searches must be done from List view. You can search fields (columns) only, or specific groups of fields and records.

Searching Down One Set of Fields

To search in a specific group of fields (a column):

1. Switch to List view by pressing F9, if necessary.
2. Move the cursor to the top of the field. In our sample database, move to the Phone field.

FIGURE 8.12
The Find dialog box.

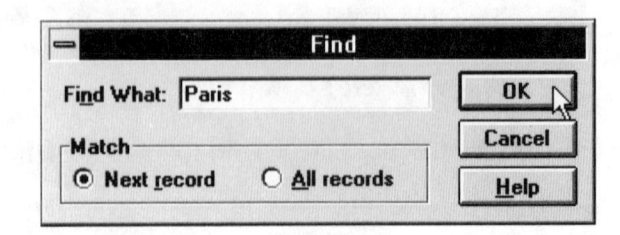

Searching for Records and Fields in a Database

3. Select the entire field by choosing Edit ➤ Select Field or by clicking on the field selector (the field name at the top of the column).

4. Choose Edit ➤ Find, type in the text to be searched for (**222** in our case), and press ↵.

Notice that the phone number 617-333-2222 in record 10 was found. Even if you try the search again, the 222 in the Zip field of records 2 and 8 will not be found. As long as the selection remains active (highlighted), all searches will be restricted to the selected area of your database.

Searching in Groups of Fields and Records

You can search in groups of fields and records by *selecting* them before you choose Edit ➤ Find. In fact, knowing how to select a large area of a database is helpful when using other commands, such as those on the Format menu.

There are three ways to select parts of a database, with Shift and the arrow keys, with the mouse, and with the Edit ➤ Select Record/Field commands. Each is explained below. After you've made your selection, conduct your search by choosing Edit ➤ Find, entering the text to be searched for, and pressing ↵.

Selecting part of a database with the Shift-key method To select part of a database using the Shift key:

1. Move to the upper-left corner of the area you want to select.

2. Press Shift+→ and then Shift +↓ to enlarge the highlighted selection area. If you need to shrink the area, press Shift+← or Shift+↑.

Press Esc if you need to deselect the fields.

Selecting part of a database with menu commands You can easily select multiple records or fields with menu commands:

1. Select one field in each row or column that you want included in the selection.

2. Choose Edit ➤ Select Record or Edit ➤ Select Field.

Selecting part of a database with the mouse To make the selection with the mouse:

1. Drag the pointer across several column selectors to select multiple columns (fields).

2. Drag the pointer down the row selectors (1, 2, 3, and so on) to select multiple records.

Sorting a Database

It often happens that the order of records in a database is rather haphazard. Records are usually entered in the order they are acquired (chronological order) rather than the more frequently needed alphabetical or numerical order.

For example, our phone book database was entered in no particular order, and if you were seeing it on a printout and didn't have the Edit ➤ Find command to use, finding a needed record might take you a while. In a database of several thousand names and addresses, finding a needed record is a real hassle.

With Works, you can *sort*—that is, rearrange—data records according to your needs. You can sort in many ways, and fairly rapidly. Once the database is sorted to your liking, you can save it on disk in the new order for future use.

Sorting Terminology

Before you can start sorting, you need to know some of the terminology. At first sorting can seem complex, but really it is quite simple—once you understand the concepts.

The key field The *key field* is the one that the database is sorted on. In other words, if you wanted to arrange your database in alphabetical order by city, the city field would be the key field. Works lets you choose up to three key fields, although normally only one is used.

The primary key If you use more than one key field, the key fields operate in order of precedence. The first key, called the *primary key*, determines the most primary level of sorting. The last name is the primary key in a phone book. In a phone book, all entries are arranged in alphabetical order according to last name.

Subordinate fields The second and third keys are called *subordinate fields*. Subordinate fields determine the order of records when the primary keys in records are identical. For example, in a phone book the first name field is the second key field. If telephone books were sorted only by Last Name and they didn't have a second key field, *John Smith* might come before *Bob Smith*.

Ascending vs. descending sorts Works gives you the option of sorting in ascending or descending order. Ascending sorts arrange the data in alphabetical order in the case of letters, and from 1 to infinity in the case of numbers. In descending sorts, Z comes before A and the highest numbers come before the lowest ones. Descending sorts of alphabetical lists, with the Z's before the A's, are rare, but descending order is often useful in numerical sorting. For example, you would use a descending numerical sort to list expenses or sales with the largest figures appearing first.

Entering the Sort Criteria

Enough theory. To sort a database:

1. Get back to List view by pressing F9, if necessary.
2. Choose Tools ➤ Sort Records.
3. The Sort Records dialog box appears, as in Figure 8.13.

FIGURE 8.13
Sorting a database. Enter the primary key to sort by in the 1st Field box.

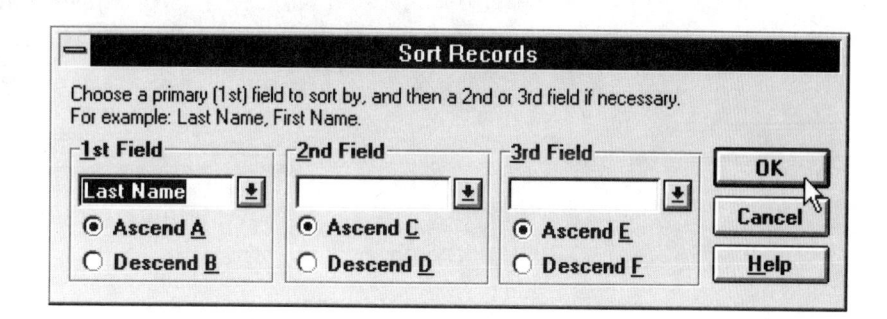

Notice that there are three spaces, one for the first, one for the second, and one for the third key field. The first field in our sample database, First Name, is entered in the 1st Field area. Works entered the first field's name on the assumption that you will likely use it as the primary key. However, we want to sort the database by last name:

4. Enter the field you want to be the primary key in the 1st Field box. In our case, enter **Last Name** or select Last Name from the drop-down list.

There are no identical last names on our sample database, but if you are working with a large database you can be sure several last names are the same and you should enter First Name in the 2nd Field box. This way, your database will be sorted in alphabetical order.

5. Click on OK.

Almost instantly the database reorders itself in last-name order, as you see in Figure 8.14.

6. Follow steps 2 and 3 above, only this time select the Descend button (press Tab then →). Now the names are listed in reverse alphabetical order.

7. To get things back in proper order, follow steps 2 and 3 and re-sort the database in ascending order.

Tip The U.S. Postal Service requires bulk mail be sorted by zip code, so if you work with large mailing lists, sorting by zip code is a real time-saver.

FIGURE 8.14

The database sorted by last name

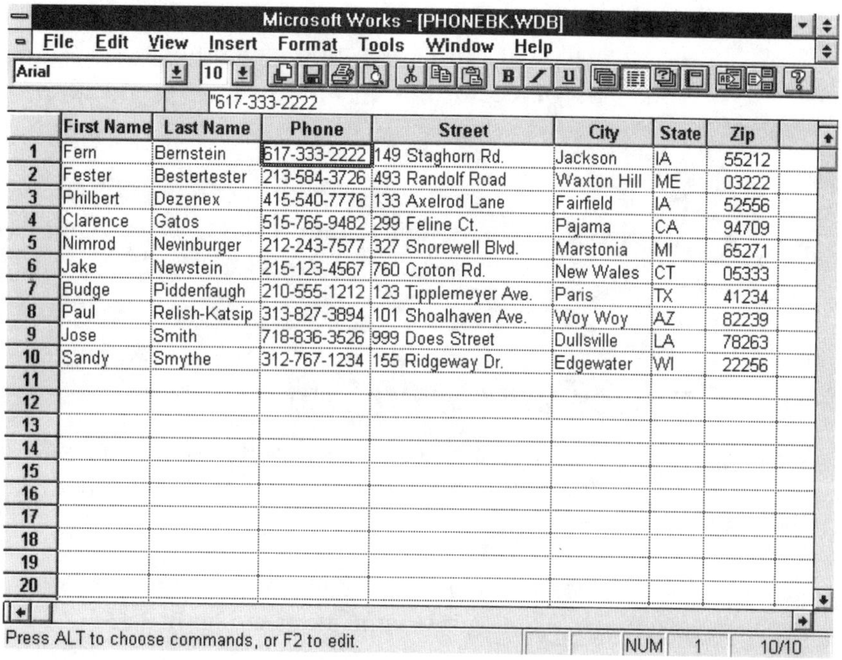

	First Name	Last Name	Phone	Street	City	State	Zip
1	Fern	Bernstein	617-333-2222	149 Staghorn Rd.	Jackson	IA	55212
2	Fester	Bestertester	213-584-3726	493 Randolf Road	Waxton Hill	ME	03222
3	Philbert	Dezenex	415-540-7776	133 Axelrod Lane	Fairfield	IA	52556
4	Clarence	Gatos	515-765-9482	299 Feline Ct.	Pajama	CA	94709
5	Nimrod	Nevinburger	212-243-7577	327 Snorewell Blvd.	Marstonia	MI	65271
6	Jake	Newstein	215-123-4567	760 Croton Rd.	New Wales	CT	05333
7	Budge	Piddenfaugh	210-555-1212	123 Tipplemeyer Ave.	Paris	TX	41234
8	Paul	Relish-Katsip	313-827-3894	101 Shoalhaven Ave.	Woy Woy	AZ	82239
9	Jose	Smith	718-836-3526	999 Does Street	Dullsville	LA	78263
10	Sandy	Smythe	312-767-1234	155 Ridgeway Dr.	Edgewater	WI	22256

An Introduction to Queries

Rather than finding a single record at a time as the Find and Sort commands do, you can display a select group of records. For example, suppose you wanted to see:

- All people with zip codes falling between 94709 and 95808.
- People whose last names fall between the letters *A* and *D* or Abrahms and Davis.
- Customers whose accounts are overdue by more than 90 days.

This type of a request is called a *query* in database lingo. The real and practical power of databases lies in this ability to query the database and extract only the information you want.

In Works, you construct a query by using a series of simple, logical rules. Once the query is done, only records meeting the rules are displayed; the other records are temporarily hidden from view. You can refine a query as often as you desire, with each new query looking through the entire database—even records hidden by the previous query—and displaying a new list of records that meet the query specifications.

> **Note** Complex queries and the use of operators in queries is covered in Chapter 9.

Queries Involving Text

Try making a query now. For our query example, we will tell Works to "display last names that begin with any letters between *D* and *M*, including *D* and *M*."

1. From List view, choose Tools ➤ Create New Query. The New Query dialog box appears, as in Figure 8.15.

For our query, we have to separate out the two limitations and ask for last names "greater than or equal to" *D* AND last names "less than or equal to" *M*.

FIGURE 8.15
The New Query dialog box.

An Introduction to Queries

2. Select Last Name in the *Choose a field to compare* box.
3. Select "is greater than or equal" to in the *How to compare the field* box.
4. Type **D** in the *Value to compare the field to* box.
5. Click And.
6. Select Last Name.
7. Select "is less than or equal to."
8. Type **M**.
9. Click the Apply Now button.

You are returned to the List view. Notice that now only two records show up: Clarence Gatos and Philbert Dezenex. The query has taken effect, eliminating other records from the display. This applies to Form view as well.

10. To see all the records again, choose View ➤ Show All Records. The formerly excluded records now reappear.

If you query a database and no records match the criteria, the following dialog box appears:

Microsoft Works

No records matched the criteria.

You applied a query and no records matched the criteria you specified. If you expected to find a match, check the query formula for accuracy.

OK

CHAPTER 8 — Using the Database

> **Note:** When you save a database, the current query is saved with it and will be available next time you open the database. Choose File ➤ Save to save a database. See "Dialog Boxes for Working with Files" in Chapter 2 for information about saving files.

Queries Involving Numbers

Now try another query, this time on zip codes. How would you display only people living in zip code areas between 39080 and 79443?

1. Choose Tools ➤ Create New Query.
2. Select Zip.
3. Select "is greater than or equal to."
4. Type **39080**.
5. Select And.
6. Select Zip.
7. Select "is less than or equal to."
8. Type **79443**.
9. Click Apply Now.

You should see the records shown in Figure 8.16.

Printing a Database

Works lets you print a database in three ways:

- You can print from List view, which gives you a printout similar to the screen appearance in List view. Long databases will be broken up into separate pages.

- You can print from Form view, which gives you one record per page.

FIGURE 8.16

Results of the zip code query

	First Name	Last Name	Phone	Street	City	State	Zip
1	Fern	Bernstein	617-333-2222	149 Staghorn Rd.	Jackson	IA	55212
3	Philbert	Dezenex	415-540-7776	133 Axelrod Lane	Fairfield	IA	52556
5	Nimrod	Nevinburger	212-243-7577	327 Snorewell Blvd.	Marstonia	MI	65271
7	Budge	Piddenfaugh	210-555-1212	123 Tipplemeyer Ave.	Paris	TX	41234
9	Jose	Smith	718-836-3526	999 Does Street	Dullsville	LA	78263

◆ You can create complex, customized reports. See Chapter 10 for information.

> **Tip** To reapply the current query after showing all records, just choose View ➤ Apply Query or press F3.

To print an entire database:

1. Deactivate the query you just made by choosing View ➤ Show All Records.

2. Now you have to decide how you want the database printed:

    ◆ To print the database as a list, get into List view (press F9 if necessary).

343

- To print each record on a separate page, choose Form view (press F9 if necessary).
- To print a selected number of records, select the records first.

3. Turn on your printer and make sure it is online and has paper loaded.

> **Tip** If you want to print only records that meet a specific criteria, run a query first. Then print. Only the displayed records will print.

At this point you can alter the margins or add headers and footers to the database:

- Choose File ➤ Page Setup if you want to alter the margins. If you are in doubt about the settings, chances are nothing needs to be changed, especially if you have successfully printed from the spreadsheet and word processor; the same printer settings are used here.
- If you want a header or footer to print at the top or bottom of the page, choose View ➤ Headers and Footers and enter the relevant text.

Now you are ready to actually start printing:

4. Choose File ➤ Print Preview to see what your database will look like.
5. If you like what you see, click on the Print button in the Preview screen. The Print dialog box appears.

Unless you want to change the number of copies to be printed or print a quick draft copy rather than a high-resolution copy, you can just press ↵. On a draft-quality printout the following do not appear: special fonts, bold, underline, italics, field lines (the lines on a Form view screen that appear under the data area), and grid lines (the column and row lines you see on the List view screen).

6. Press ↵.

Fitting the Database onto One Page

If you're printing the sample phone book in List view, most likely your printout will be two pages long, one page with six columns of data and the other consisting of the zip code column. If so, it means that there is more information in each record than will fit on the width of one page, and that the last field—the zip code field—had to be printed on a second page. To remedy this situation, use these techniques:

- Make some of the columns narrower.

- Hide the fields of the database that you don't really need. To do this, set the fields' widths to zero. (Exactly how to do this is covered in Chapter 10.)

- Choose a smaller font to allow more characters to fit across the page. Do this with the Format ➤ Font and Style command.

- Turn the page 90 degrees to print it in Landscape mode rather than Portrait mode. Do this with the File ➤ Printer Setup ➤ Setup command.

Now that you are familiar with the basics of database design and use, try experimenting on your own. You may want to devise a database or two to keep track of everyday items or tasks—things you normally use paper for, or have never bothered to organize before. In any case, if you put any time into the project, don't forget to keep a backup copy of your files in a safe place.

Before moving on to the next chapter, be sure to save the Phonebk file (now sorted by last name). You will use it in Chapter 9.

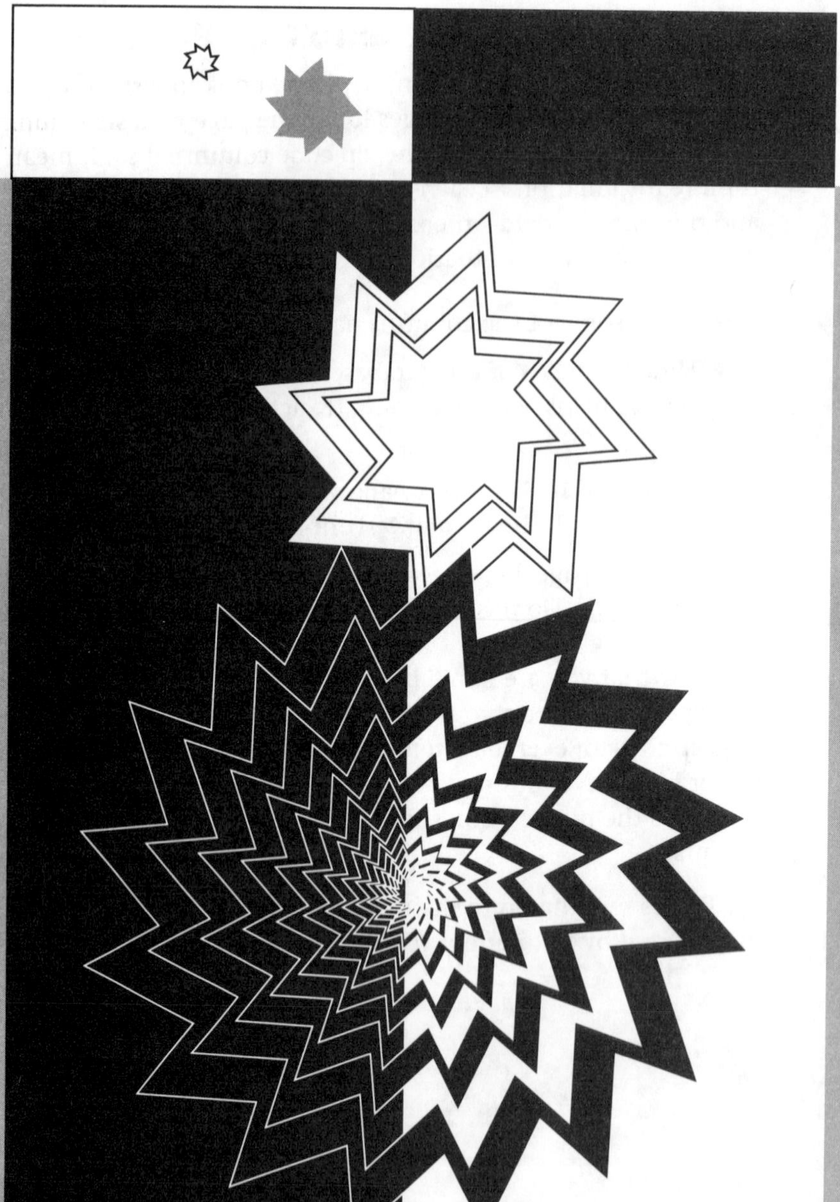

CHAPTER 9

Advanced Database Skills

Fast Track

To turn field names off (or on) in Form view,   **352**
>click on the field name and choose Format ➤ Show Field Name.

To place new labels on a form,   **353**
>position the cursor where you want the label to go and type in the label. Don't use a colon at the end of the label or Works will assume you're creating a new field.

To insert fields,   **357**
>begin in List view by pressing F9 and click on the field you want the new field to be inserted to the left of. Next, choose Insert ➤ Record/Field. From the dialog box, choose Field.

To delete fields,   **358**
>begin in List view and click on the field you want to delete. Next, choose Insert ➤ Delete Record/Field. From the dialog box, choose Field.

To insert a record in the middle of existing records,   **361**
>start from List view and click on any field of the record above where you want the new record inserted. Next, choose Insert ➤ Record/Field. From the dialog box, choose Record.

To delete a record,   362

start from List view and click on any field of the record you want to delete. Next, choose Insert ➤ Delete Record/Field. From the dialog box, choose Record.

You can hide specific records in a database.   363

Select the record(s) you want to hide by dragging the mouse over their row selectors, using a query, or using the Find command with the All Records option. Next, choose View ➤ Hide Records. To show the records again, choose Select ➤ Show All Records.

To add a calculated field to a database,   368

switch to Form view. In the field's data area (just to the right of the colon), enter the formula for the field. You can reference other fields in the database by name as part of the formula.

To protect your data from being erased,   371

choose Tools ➤ Protection, check Protect data, and click OK.

To create a report concerning the information in a database,   372

from List view, choose Tools ➤ Create New Report. Choose which fields you want in the report, click Add for each field, enter a name for the report, and click OK. Click OK in the next two dialog boxes as well.

IN CHAPTER 8 YOU LEARNED the rudiments of the Works database, including how to create a new database, enter and edit data, view the data in a list or a form, search and sort the data, and perform elementary querying and printing.

Now you'll have a chance to expand your knowledge of these topics. In this chapter, you'll learn how to

- ◆ Place labels on a form
- ◆ Insert and delete fields and records
- ◆ Select data in various ways
- ◆ Hide records and fields from view
- ◆ Protect fields from being altered
- ◆ Set the format of fields
- ◆ Create complex queries
- ◆ Print professional-looking reports

To experiment with these database features, you will use two database documents, the Phonebk file you created in Chapter 8 and a new file that you will have to type in. The new database is an inventory list for Bob's House of Gadgets, the fictitious store for which you created a budget in Chapter 6.

Before going further, open the Phonebk file:

1. Choose File ➤ Open Existing File.

2. Select Phonebk from the list box.

Making Data-Entry Forms Easier to Understand and Use

3. Press F9 to switch to Form view.

Your screen should look like Figure 9.1.

Making Data-Entry Forms Easier to Understand and Use

This form is perfectly sufficient for adding, editing, and viewing data, but it could be improved. For example, you could add instructions so that people unfamiliar with Works would know how to enter data on the form. If you plan to hire someone to enter and edit records, instructions would be particularly advantageous.

FIGURE 9.1
The Phonebk form ready to be improved

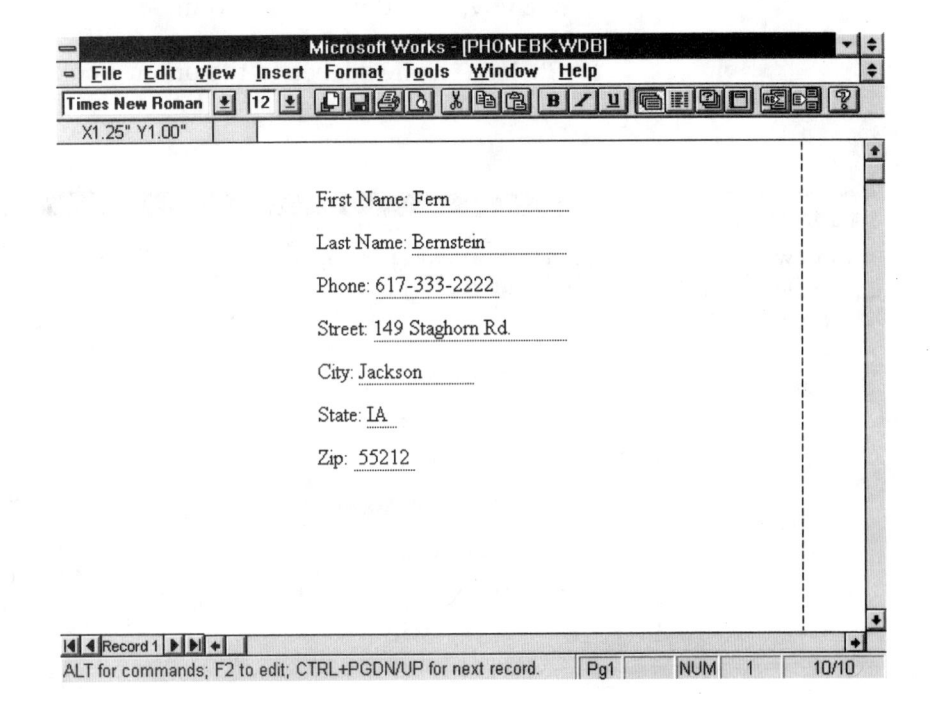

Placing Labels on a Form

Adding instructional text to a form is easy. Let's put instructions on the form so that novices will know how to fill in information. When you're finished making the changes, your screen will look like the one in Figure 9.2.

Removing the Field Names

When you created the form, Works automatically put the field names on the form for you. You can, however, use identifiers other than field names. You can also change the placement of field names relative to the data cells they identify. To do either of these actions, you have to remove the field names first.

To remove a field name on a form:

1. Click on the field label. In the phone book form, click on First Name:. It becomes highlighted.

FIGURE 9.2
A form with instructions added. You'll create this form in this chapter.

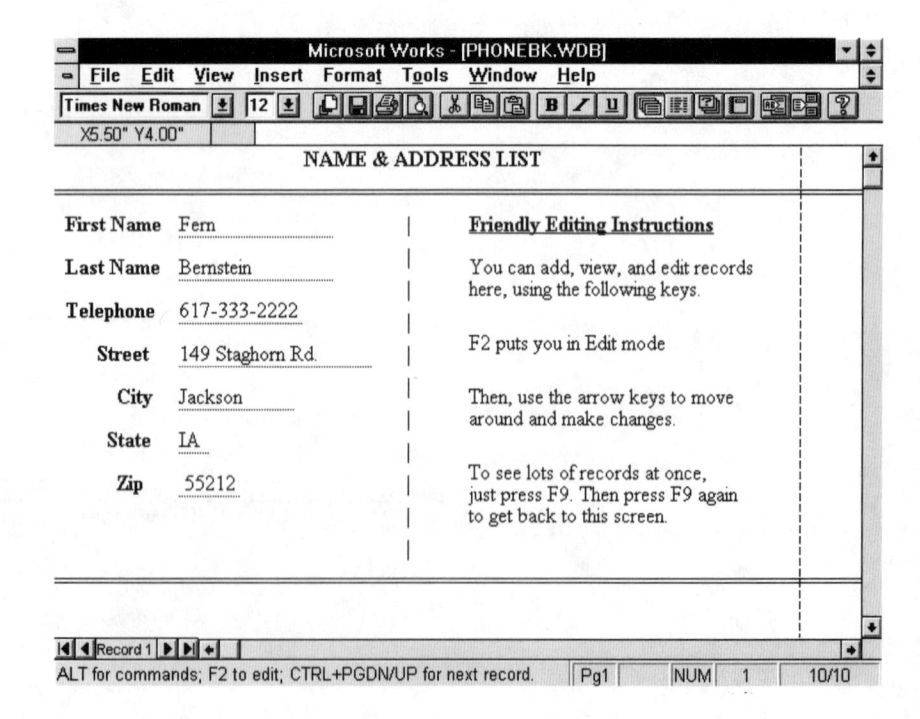

Making Data-Entry Forms Easier to Understand and Use

3. Choose Format ➤ Show Field Name.

4. The words *First Name:* disappear and only the line that indicates the field's width (along with Fern's name) remains.

5. Repeat steps 2 through 4 to remove all the field names on the form. When you are done, your screen will look like this:

Fern

Bernstein

617-333-2222

149 Staghorn Rd.

Jackson

IA

55212

Adding the Labels

Now that the field names have been removed, we'll enter a label for each field telling the data-entry person where to enter the information:

6. Using Figure 9.3 as a guide, enter labels on the left side of the form. Enter the First Name prompt at the left edge of the screen and type in the others below it. Press the spacebar to add blank spaces where necessary. Don't enter colons in the labels, as a colon tells Works you are entering a field, not a label.

> **Warning**
>
> To enter a label that ends with a colon on a form, place a quotation mark at the start of the label. For example, type in "Enter First Name:." If you don't enter the quotation mark, Works will think you are entering a new field.

353

CHAPTER 9 Advanced Database Skills

FIGURE 9.3
The field labels entered on screen

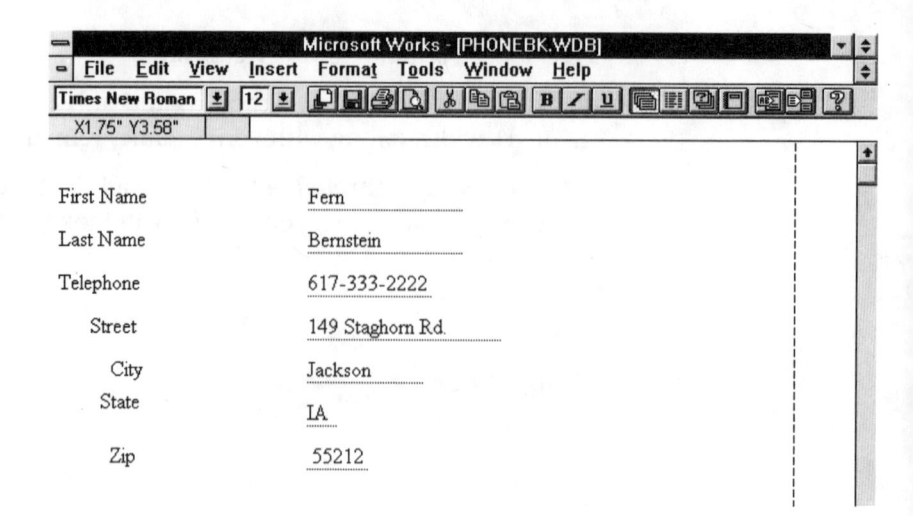

```
Microsoft Works - [PHONEBK.WDB]
File  Edit  View  Insert  Format  Tools  Window  Help
Times New Roman  12
X1.75"  Y3.58"

        First Name    Fern
        Last Name     Bernstein
        Telephone     617-333-2222
           Street     149 Staghorn Rd.
             City     Jackson
            State     IA
              Zip     55212
```

7. Using Figure 9.4 as a guide, select each field and drag it to the left until there is just a little space between the field labels and fields. If you have trouble, select Format ➤ Snap To Grid to turn the grid on and try positioning the fields that way.

8. To make the labels boldface, click on them one at a time and then click on the B (Bold) button in the toolbar. Your form should look like Figure 9.4.

FIGURE 9.4
The fields moved to the left and boldfaced

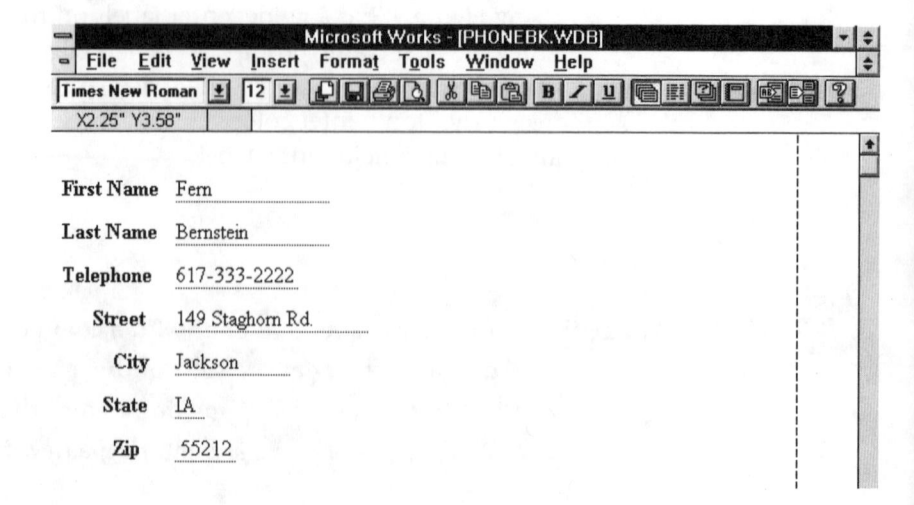

```
Microsoft Works - [PHONEBK.WDB]
File  Edit  View  Insert  Format  Tools  Window  Help
Times New Roman  12
X2.25"  Y3.58"

    First Name  Fern
    Last Name   Bernstein
    Telephone   617-333-2222
       Street   149 Staghorn Rd.
         City   Jackson
        State   IA
          Zip   55212
```

354

Making Data-Entry Forms Easier to Understand and Use

> **Tip**
>
> You can use this shortcut to automatically enter a default text or value into a field of every new record: enter a quotation mark and then the value. For example, if you know that all State entries in your database will be CA, enter ="CA in the State field. To enter a numeric value as a default, omit the quote mark and enter, for example, =4500.

Now let's add a title at the top of the form:

1. Near the top, close to the center, enter the title **NAME & ADDRESS LIST** (see Figure 9.2).

2. Click on the B (bold) button in the toolbar.

3. Enter one line of equal signs (=) below the title. To do this, click in the upper-left corner of the window, and press the equal sign key and hold it down until the line reaches the right side of the window. Then press ↵. Add a similar line at the bottom of the screen (see Figure 9.2).

4. Put a dividing line down the middle of the screen by using the vertical symbol (|). You may have to hunt around your keyboard to find this key (mine is located next to the Shift key). Press |, press ↓ to move down a line, and type in the next one.

Including Data-Entry Instructions

Now that you've moved the fields aside, there is plenty of room on the form for instructions to the data-entry person. Let's add the text:

- Using Figure 9.2 as a guide, enter the text you see on the right side of the screen.

Instructions like these can be very valuable to data-entry clerks who aren't as familiar with the database or with Works as you are. If your form covers more than one page, be sure to put instructions at the bottom of the first page telling the data-entry clerk how to go to page 2 (press PgDn).

355

All editing and navigation commands work in a data-entry form with instructions on it.

Inserting and Deleting Fields and Records

You can expect to add or delete fields from a database from time to time, because it is hard to anticipate in the planning stage exactly how many fields you will need. Suppose you want to add a work phone number field to go with a home phone number field? Perhaps a field for a company name needs to be added. You can delete and add fields from Form view or from List view.

You can also delete and add records from Form or List view. Adding records is one of the most common tasks you'll perform. As records become outdated, you have to delete them from the database if editing them won't suffice.

Warning: Deleting records and fields from a database erases them permanently. There is no way of reversing the erasure except to type in the record or field again.

Inserting and Deleting Fields in Form View

To delete a field in Form view:

1. Select the field you want to delete (do not select the field name).

Inserting and Deleting Fields and Records

2. Choose Insert ➤ Delete Selection. This message appears:

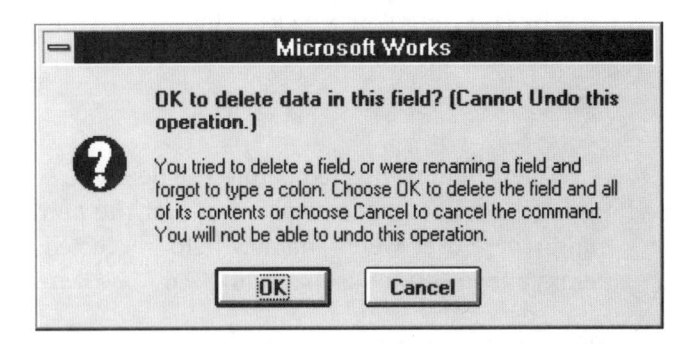

> **Microsoft Works**
>
> **OK to delete data in this field? (Cannot Undo this operation.)**
>
> You tried to delete a field, or were renaming a field and forgot to type a colon. Choose OK to delete the field and all of its contents or choose Cancel to cancel the command. You will not be able to undo this operation.
>
> [OK]   [Cancel]

Warning When you delete a field, you also erase all the data stored in the field. Works warns you that you are deleting the data along with the field. If you are sure you want to delete the field, click on OK. Otherwise, press Esc or click on Cancel.

3. Click on OK. The field with its contents is deleted.

To insert a field in Form view:

1. Move the cursor where you want the new field to be.

2. Type the field name and a colon. Be sure to enter the colon, as it tell Works that you are entering a field name.

3. Press ↵.

Inserting and Deleting Fields in List View

Inserting fields in List view is done a little differently:

1. Switch to List view by pressing F9, if necessary.

CHAPTER 9 Advanced Database Skills

2. Find where you want to insert the field and click on the selector of the field to the right to select the field. (You can also select this field by choosing Edit ➤ Select Field). In Figure 9.5, the Street field selector was clicked on.

3. Choose Insert ➤ Record/Field.

A new field is inserted before the field you selected and all fields to the right are pushed over to make room for the new field. Fields to the left remain where they were. The new field is selected. If you deleted the Street field, your screen looks like Figure 9.6.

Giving the new field a name You probably want to give the new field a name:

4. Choose Edit ➤ Field Name and type in a name. Give our new field the name **Test**.

5. Press F9 to switch to Form view. Notice that the new field was added to the form in the upper-left corner.

> **Tip** To give a field a new name, click on the field in List view, choose Edit ➤ Field Name, type in the new name, and press ↵.

Deleting a Field

To delete a field in List view:

1. Select the field you want to delete. In our case, select the field you just inserted in the exercises above.

2. Choose Insert ➤ Delete Record/Field.

The field is deleted from both the List and Form views. The gap is filled in by the fields to the right, which move to the left to fill in the vacant position.

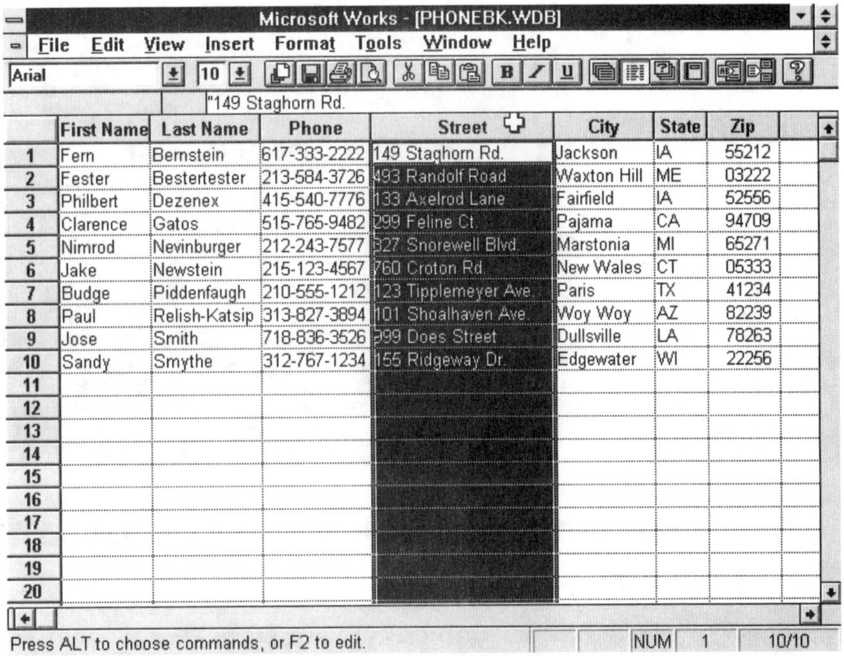

Inserting and Deleting Fields and Records

FIGURE 9.5
Click on the field selector to highlight a field and delete it.

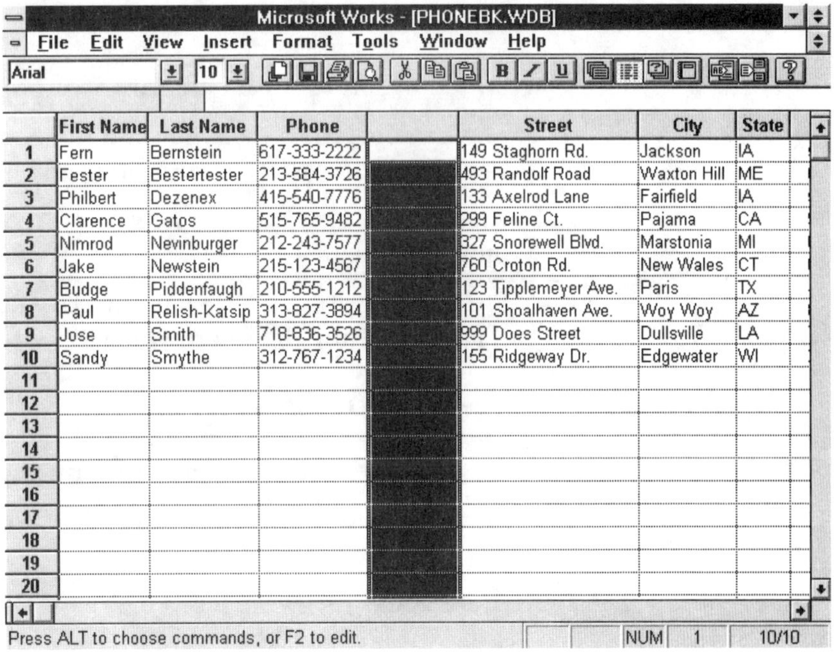

FIGURE 9.6
The new field is inserted before the one you selected earlier.

359

> **Tip** — Works inserts the number of fields you have selected prior to choosing the Insert ➤ Record/Field command. To insert more than one field, select the number of fields you want to insert before choosing the Insert command.

> **Warning** — Deleting multiple fields erases the data in hidden fields if there are any hidden fields in the range you delete.

Inserting and Deleting Records in Form View

In Form view, the Insert ➤ Record command inserts one record and the Insert ➤ Delete Record command deletes a record.

To insert a record in Form view:

1. Switch to Form view if necessary by pressing F9.
2. Move to the record that you want the new record to appear before. In our case, move to record 3, Philbert Dezenex.
3. Choose Insert ➤ Record. A new, blank record is inserted, and appears on your screen.
4. Press F9 to switch to List view and see where the record was inserted. It appears before the record you were on.

To delete a record in Form view:

1. Press F9 if necessary to switch to Form view.
2. Move to the record you want to delete. In our case, let's delete the blank record we just created.
3. Choose Insert ➤ Delete Record.

The new record is deleted, and Philbert's record appears in its old spot, record number 3 (check the status area to verify this).

Inserting and Deleting Records in List View

To insert a record in List view:

1. Press F9 to switch to List view, if necessary.
2. Click on the row selector of the record below where you want the new record to go. In our case, click on 3's row selector or put the cursor anywhere in record 3.
3. Choose Select ➤ Record. The whole record becomes highlighted, as shown in Figure 9.7.
4. Choose Insert ➤ Record/Field. A new blank record is inserted above the previously selected one, as shown in Figure 9.8.

Microsoft Works - [PHONEBK.WDB]
File Edit View Insert Format Tools Window Help
Arial
10
"Philbert
First Name | Last Name | Phone | Street | City | State | Zip
1 Fern | Bernstein | 617-333-2222 | 149 Staghorn Rd. | Jackson | IA | 55212
2 Fester | Bestertester | 213-584-3726 | 493 Randolf Road | Waxton Hill | ME | 03222
3 Philbert | Dezenex | 415-540-7776 | 133 Axelrod Lane | Fairfield | IA | 52556
4 Clarence | Gatos | 515-765-9482 | 299 Feline Ct. | Pajama | CA | 94709
5 Nimrod | Nevinburger | 212-243-7577 | 327 Snorewell Blvd. | Marstonia | MI | 65271
6 Jake | Newstein | 215-123-4567 | 760 Croton Rd. | New Wales | CT | 05333
7 Budge | Piddenfaugh | 210-555-1212 | 123 Tipplemeyer Ave. | Paris | TX | 41234
8 Paul | Relish-Katsip | 313-827-3894 | 101 Shoalhaven Ave. | Woy Woy | AZ | 82239
9 Jose | Smith | 718-836-3526 | 999 Does Street | Dullsville | LA | 78263
10 Sandy | Smythe | 312-767-1234 | 155 Ridgeway Dr. | Edgewater | WI | 22256
11
12
13
14
15
16
17
18
19
20
Press ALT to choose commands, or F2 to edit.
NUM
3
10/10

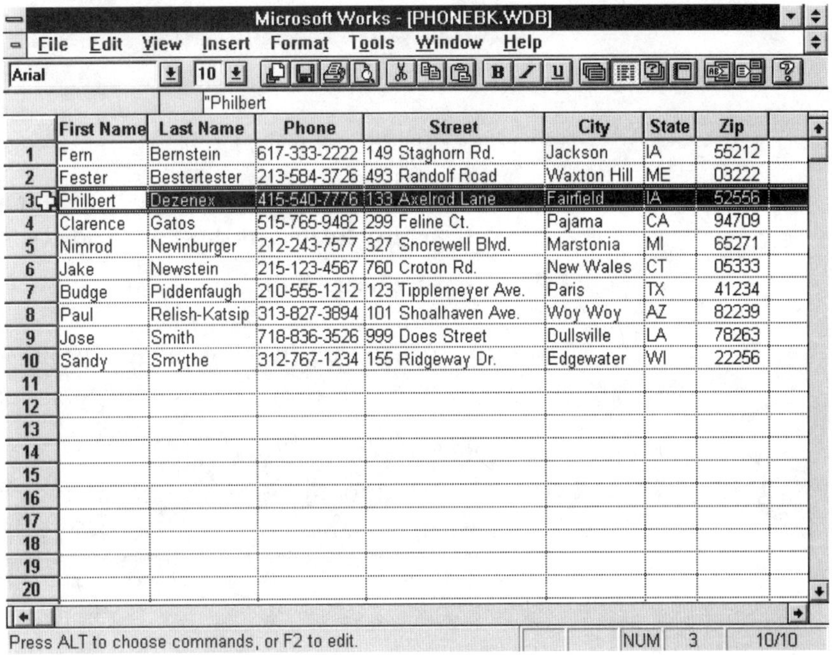

FIGURE 9.7

Preparing to insert a new record in List view

CHAPTER 9 Advanced Database Skills

FIGURE 9.8
The new record is inserted before the one that was selected.

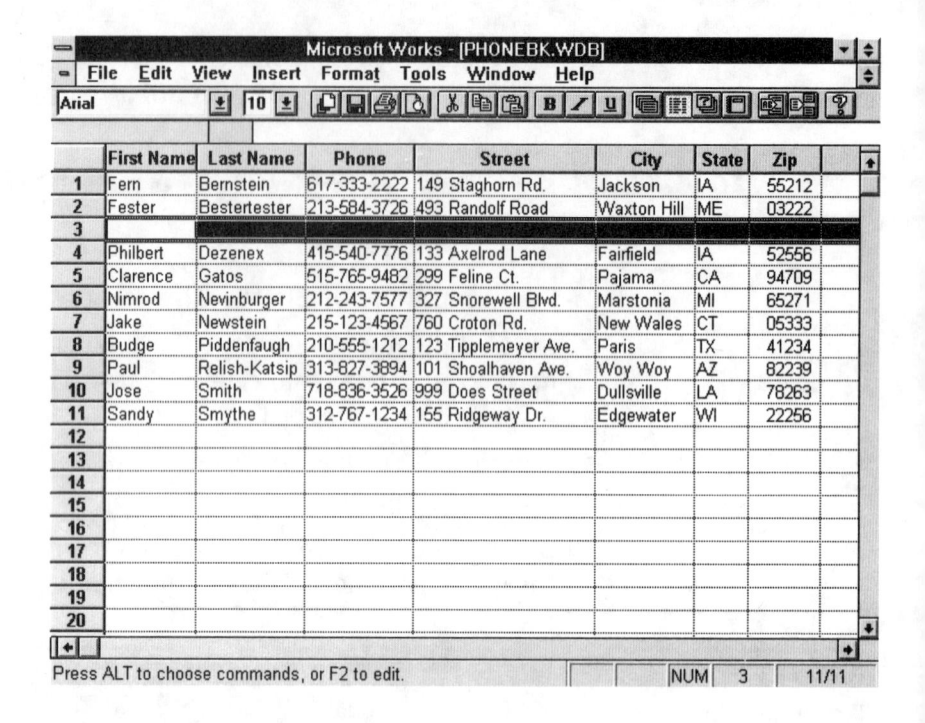

	First Name	Last Name	Phone	Street	City	State	Zip
1	Fern	Bernstein	617-333-2222	149 Staghorn Rd.	Jackson	IA	55212
2	Fester	Bestertester	213-584-3726	493 Randolf Road	Waxton Hill	ME	03222
3							
4	Philbert	Dezenex	415-540-7776	133 Axelrod Lane	Fairfield	IA	52556
5	Clarence	Gatos	515-765-9482	299 Feline Ct.	Pajama	CA	94709
6	Nimrod	Nevinburger	212-243-7577	327 Snorewell Blvd.	Marstonia	MI	65271
7	Jake	Newstein	215-123-4567	760 Croton Rd.	New Wales	CT	05333
8	Budge	Piddenfaugh	210-555-1212	123 Tipplemeyer Ave.	Paris	TX	41234
9	Paul	Relish-Katsip	313-827-3894	101 Shoalhaven Ave.	Woy Woy	AZ	82239
10	Jose	Smith	718-836-3526	999 Does Street	Dullsville	LA	78263
11	Sandy	Smythe	312-767-1234	155 Ridgeway Dr.	Edgewater	WI	22256

To delete a record in List view:

1. Select the record you want to delete. In our case, let's delete the record we just created (it should already be selected at this point).
2. Choosing Insert ➤ Delete Record/Field.

The record disappears. In our database, record 4 becomes record 3 again.

Warning Deleting multiple records can be dangerous. There is no Undo command to reverse your decision and the erasure is final.

> **Tip** You can insert or delete more than one record at a time. To insert more than one record, select the number of records you want to insert before choosing the Insert ➤ Record/Field command. For example, select three records to insert three. To delete more than one record, just select all the records you want to delete and proceed from there.

Hiding Records and Fields

You can hide certain records and fields temporarily so that they don't appear in your database. Hidden records are not printed either. This part of the chapter explains how to hide records and fields. It also explains a unique feature for viewing only the records in a database that have been hidden.

> **Note** One way to hide records is to run a query that excludes the records you want hide. See "An Introduction to Queries" in Chapter 8.

Hiding Records

To hide a single record:

1. Move the cursor to any cell in the record you want to hide. In our database, move to record 8.
2. Choose View ➤ Hide Record.

The record disappears, but all the other records keep their original numbering. Notice the missing number in the record numbers along the left side of the screen.

CHAPTER 9   Advanced Database Skills

To hide a group of records:

1. Select the records you want to hide. In our database, select records 2 through 4.
2. Choose View ➤ Hide Record.

The records are hidden and do not appear in the database.

> **Note**   Hidden records do not appear in Form view either.

Displaying the Hidden Records in a Database

What if you want to know which records in a database are hidden? Choosing View ➤ Show All Records makes hidden records reappear, but suppose you want to work with only the hidden records, not all the records? Displaying the hidden records can be very useful when you want to pick a few select records out of a large database to work with.

To display the hidden records in a database:

1. Make sure you're in List view (press F9, if necessary).
2. Choose Edit ➤ Switch Hidden Records. Only the hidden records appear.
3. Choose Edit ➤ Show All Records to return things to normal.

Hiding Fields

Nowhere on your menu is there a Hide Field command. However, because a limited number of fields can fit on screen at once, you will need to hide a field or two occasionally. One way to deal with the fields problem is to move the unwanted field(s) to the right side of the database. But then you have to move the unwanted fields back to their original locations later, which is a hassle. Here is an easier way to hide a field:

1. Select the field you want to hide. In our case, select the Phone field.
2. Hide the field:
   ◆ With the mouse, click on the right border of the column and drag it to the left border to make the column disappear.
   ◆ With the keyboard, choose Format ➤ Field Width and set the width to 0.

   The field disappears.

Warning If you hide a field, forget it's there, and select and delete a range that includes the hidden field, you will delete the hidden field and all its contents. Be careful when hiding fields that you do not accidentally erase them.

Note Removing a field in List view has no effect in Form view. You can still see the field contents in Form view.

"Unhiding" a field To display a field again after you have hidden it:

1. Press F5 to open the GoTo dialog box.
2. Double-click on the name of the hidden field, Phone in our case. Now the hidden field is selected.
3. Click OK.
4. Choose Format ➤ Field Width and enter a width for the hidden field. Enter **13** in our case.

The field miraculously reappears.

Sample Exercise: Creating an Inventory Database

The next part of this chapter discusses advanced database techniques, including:

- ◆ Formatting fields
- ◆ Using calculated fields with formulas
- ◆ Protecting fields from being erased

In this section we will construct a sample inventory database. However, to experiment further you need a sophisticated database to work with:

1. Close the Phonebk file (save the changes) and open a new database document.

2. Lay out the form as shown in Figure 9.9. Make sure you enter the fields in the following order, or else they will be in the wrong order in List view:

    Category
    Brand
    Model
    Quantity
    Wholesale
    Retail
    Inv. Value

3. Add the data as shown in Figure 9.10.

   Notice that no entries have been made in the last field. Don't worry about that yet. Moreover, I selected all the fields and clicked on the Bold button in the toolbar to make the data a little more visible.

4. Save the file under the name INVENTORY.

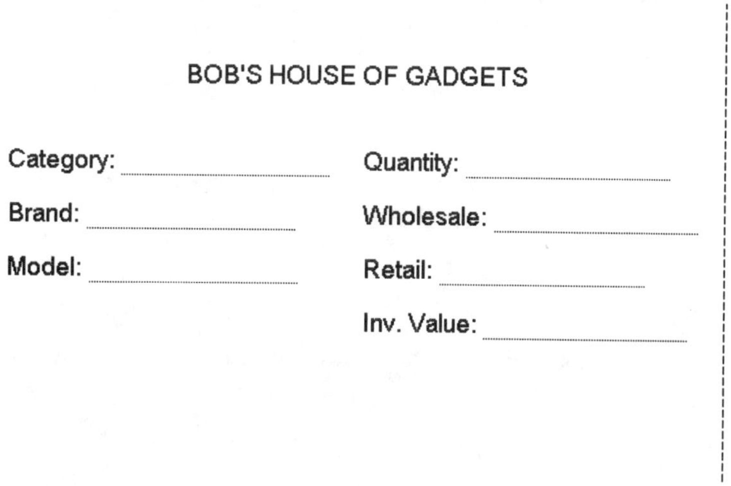

Sample Exercise: Creating an Inventory Database

FIGURE 9.9
The inventory database structure

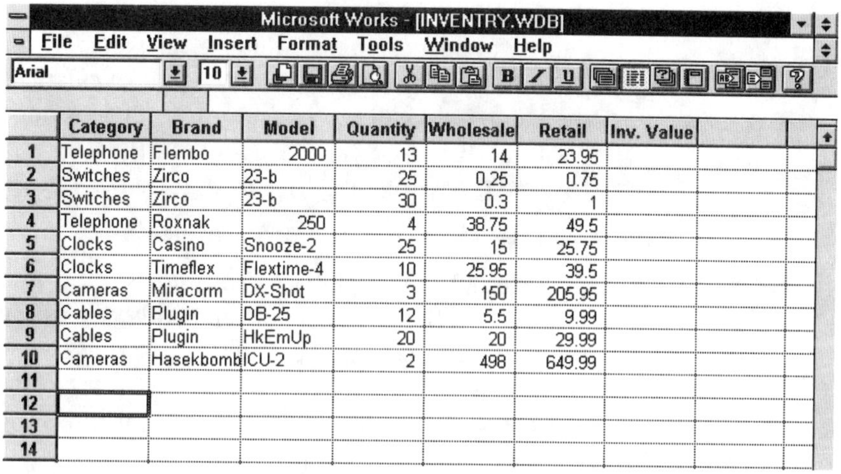

```
                BOB'S HOUSE OF GADGETS

    Category: _____        Quantity: _____

    Brand: _____           Wholesale: _____

    Model: _____           Retail: _____

                              Inv. Value: _____
```

FIGURE 9.10
Entering the data in the INVENTRY file

	Category	Brand	Model	Quantity	Wholesale	Retail	Inv. Value
1	Telephone	Flembo	2000	13	14	23.95	
2	Switches	Zirco	23-b	25	0.25	0.75	
3	Switches	Zirco	23-b	30	0.3	1	
4	Telephone	Roxnak	250	4	38.75	49.5	
5	Clocks	Casino	Snooze-2	25	15	25.75	
6	Clocks	Timeflex	Flextime-4	10	25.95	39.5	
7	Cameras	Miracorn	DX-Shot	3	150	205.95	
8	Cables	Plugin	DB-25	12	5.5	9.99	
9	Cables	Plugin	HkEmUp	20	20	29.99	
10	Cameras	Hasekbomb	ICU-2	2	498	649.99	

Formatting Fields for Alignment and Currency

Obviously, the first thing to do is fix the formatting of some fields. Let's make the Model field a right-aligned field.

◆ Select it and click on the R button in the toolbar or choose Format ➤ Alignment, click Right, and then click OK.

The last three fields—Wholesale, Retail, and Inv. Value—are for monetary values. Let's give these fields a Currency format:

◆ Select a cell in each field (not the entire range of cells), choose Format ➤ Number, click on Currency, and then click on OK.

> **Note** The other popular number formats for fields are Date, Time, Fixed, Percent, Exponential, and Comma. See Appendix C for more information.

Using Calculated Fields in Databases

The last field, Inv. Value (Inventory Value), was left blank because it is going to be a calculated field. A *calculated field* is a field with a formula that uses the data in other fields to make calculations. In our database, the Inv. Value field will report the amount of money tied up in a given inventory item. It will be calculated by multiplying the quantity of each item in stock by the wholesale price of that item, like so:

`Quantity * Wholesale = Inv. Value`

Each field in a database can hold one formula only. When you enter a formula in a field, Works automatically copies the formulas throughout the field—that is, it copies the formula down the column.

Operators, Operands, and Functions Formulas can include the following items:

ITEM	EXPLANATION
Operator	You can use the standard operators in a formula: multiplication (*), division (/), addition (+), and subtraction (–).
Operands	An operand is the thing that gets operated on, such as a number or the name of a field containing a number or word.

Sample Exercise: Creating an Inventory Database

ITEM	EXPLANATION
Functions	Functions include, for example, the trigonometric functions SIN, COS, and TAN. All 79 functions available in the spreadsheet tool are available in the database tool.

Entering a Formula

In the case of our database, the formula is very simple. It requires entering a single operator, the multiplication operator (*). To enter a formula in a field:

1. Move the cursor to any cell in the field. In our case, move it to the Inv. Value field.

2. Enter a formula using the field names as operands. In our case, we want to multiply the quantity of items by their wholesale price to see what amount to place on the invoice:

   =quantity*wholesale

   Don't forget to include the equal sign, as the equal sign tells Works you are entering a formula.

Works instantly calculates the field, plugging in the values. Your database should look like Figure 9.11. Formulas in databases work very much like they do in spreadsheets. If you change a value in the Quantity field, the result in the Inv. Value field will change immediately.

FIGURE 9.11
Calculating the invoice value, which is the quantity multiplied by the wholesale price

	Category	Brand	Model	Quantity	Wholesale	Retail	Inv. Value
1	Telephone	Flembo	2000	13	$14.00	$23.95	$182.00
2	Switches	Zirco	23-b	25	$0.25	$0.75	$6.25
3	Switches	Zirco	23-b	30	$0.30	$1.00	$9.00
4	Telephone	Roxnak	250	4	$38.75	$49.50	$155.00
5	Clocks	Casino	Snooze-2	25	$15.00	$25.75	$375.00
6	Clocks	Timeflex	Flextime-4	10	$25.95	$39.50	$259.50
7	Cameras	Miracorm	DX-Shot	3	$150.00	$205.95	$450.00
8	Cables	Plugin	DB-25	12	$5.50	$9.99	$66.00
9	Cables	Plugin	HkEmUp	20	$20.00	$29.99	$400.00
10	Cameras	Hasekbomb	ICU-2	2	$498.00	$649.99	$996.00

=Quantity*Wholesale

Rules for Using Formulas in Fields

Once you start throwing in lots of functions and references to other fields, your formulas can get pretty complicated. How to make complex formula constructions is beyond the scope of this book, but some of the basic rules are explained below.

Rules of precedence Formulas are processed by Works using the standard algebraic rules of precedence. Multiplication and division are performed before addition and subtraction. Given two operations of equal precedence, the operation on the left is performed first.

How to use functions in formulas Functions consist of the function name, an open parenthesis, arguments (in most cases), and a closed parenthesis. *Arguments* are values upon which the functions operate and are separated from one another by commas, like so:

=AVG(speed1,speed2,speed3)

All Works spreadsheet functions also work in the database.

> **Note** For details about functions, see Appendix C.

How to use arguments correctly Arguments must be numbers or equations. If they are equations, they must result in a number when they are calculated. Fields that contain numbers or formulas that result in numbers can be used in arguments. To use one, you refer to the field name, much as you do in a spreadsheet. However, to be used in an argument, the field being referred to must contain a number or a formula that produces a number.

Referring to other fields in formulas To use another field as part of a formula, include the other field's name in the calculation. For example, a Total column might have the formula

=parts+labor

Protecting Fields from Being Erased or Altered

You can protect critical fields so they don't get erased or altered. You can lock all fields or lock fields on a one-by-one basis. "Locking" a field means to prevent it from being erased or altered. All fields are locked by default, but this doesn't mean you can't alter or erase them. To be keep a field from being erased, you must activate the lock mechanism by "protecting" the locked cells.

Locking All the Fields in a Database

To lock all the fields in a database:

1. Choose Format ➤ Protection. The Protection dialog box appears.
2. Check Protect Data to activate Works' default locked mechanism.
3. Click OK.

Now all the fields are locked and they can't be altered in any way. If you try to change a field, a dialog box appears with the message

`Cannot change: locked`

Locking Specific Fields

To lock specific fields in a database you have to lock the entire database as explained above and then unlock the ones you want to be able to enter data in. Follow these steps:

1. Lock the entire database, as explained above.
2. Move to a field you want to be able to enter data in.
3. Select Format ➤ Protection. The Protection dialog box appears.
4. Uncheck Locked. You have deactivated the field's locked mechanism and you can now enter data into this field.
5. Click OK.

Repeat these steps will all the fields you want to be able to enter data in.

Locking an unlocked field If you decide later that you want to return a specific field or fields to the list of those that are locked, just select the field(s) in question, choose Format ➤ Protection, check Locked, and click OK.

Generating a Database Report

For many database users, being able to generate reports is the chief advantage of database software. A *report* is simply a presentation of the information in a database in an easy-to-understand format. Works' built-in report generator makes it relatively easy to make reports. With the Works report generator, you can fine-tune a report and see immediately what effects your changes make.

The Works report generator lets you create eight different reports for each database. You can include calculations, subtotals, totals, summary statistics, and explanatory text. The report generator is to the database what charts are to the spreadsheet. Changes made to a database are automatically reflected in the reports.

In this section, you will create a small database report from the inventory list. In so doing, you will learn how to

- Use the Works' speed reporting feature
- Make your own reports with statistical totals and grand totals
- Delete a report
- Sort the records in a report
- Modify a report after you've created it

Works' Speed Reporting Feature

Rather than create a report from scratch, you can use Works' speed reporting feature. *Speed reports* produce acceptable results for most databases. To create a speed report:

1. Open the database about which you want to generate a report. In our case, open the INVENTRY database.

2. Make sure you are in List view.

Generating a Database Report

3. Choose View ➤ Show All Records. This returns all the records to view in case some were hidden by a query or by the Find command.
4. Choose Tools ➤ Create New Report. The New Report dialog box appears, as in Figure 9.12.

Notice that all the fields in the database are listed in the Field box. From this box, you choose which fields you want in the report:

5. Either enter specific fields or enter all of them.
   ◆ To enter specific fields, click on each field and then click the Add button.
   ◆ To enter all the fields in the report, click on the Add All button.

Let's add all the fields. Notice that they all appear in the Fields in Report box.

6. Enter a name for the report in the Report Title box. For our report, we'll enter the name **Basic Report**.
7. Click OK. The Report Statistics dialog box appears.

The Report Statistics dialog box lets you choose the kinds of summary information or statistics you want Works to calculate for the report.

8. Don't choose any settings from this box. Just click on OK.

FIGURE 9.12
The first step in designing a database report is to choose which fields to include.

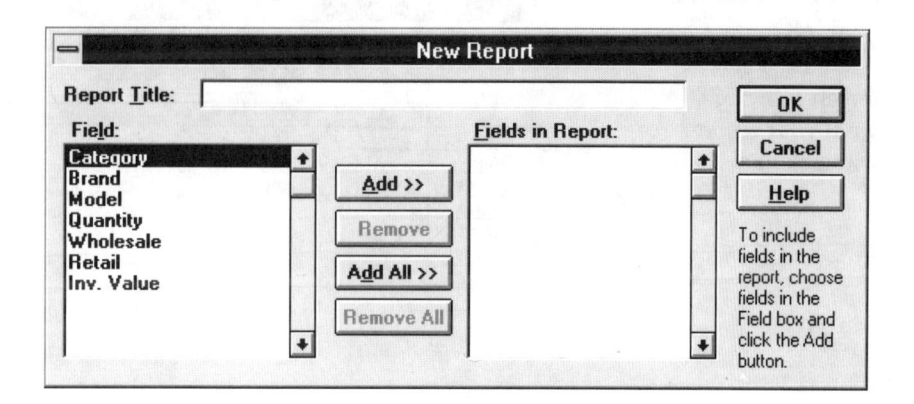

CHAPTER 9 Advanced Database Skills

Works sets up what it calls the "report definition." Soon a dialog box appears telling you that the report definition is completed and that you can see what the report looks like by pressing OK:

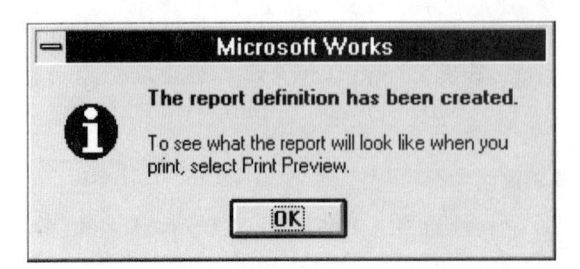

> **Microsoft Works**
>
> The report definition has been created.
>
> To see what the report will look like when you print, select Print Preview.
>
> [OK]

9. Click on OK. Now the Basic Report screen shows up, as shown in Figure 9.13.

Ignore all the gobbledygook in this window. Each line contains special codes that Works uses to define a report. You'll learn what each line means later in this chapter. For now, just look at what will result from printing the basic report.

10. Choose File ➤ Print Preview and click on Zoom In twice to see what the printed report will look like. After a little repositioning of the data with the scroll bars, you should see something like Figure 9.14.

FIGURE 9.13
The Basic Report screen showing what your report will look like

374

Generating a Database Report

FIGURE 9.14
Previewing the Basic Report

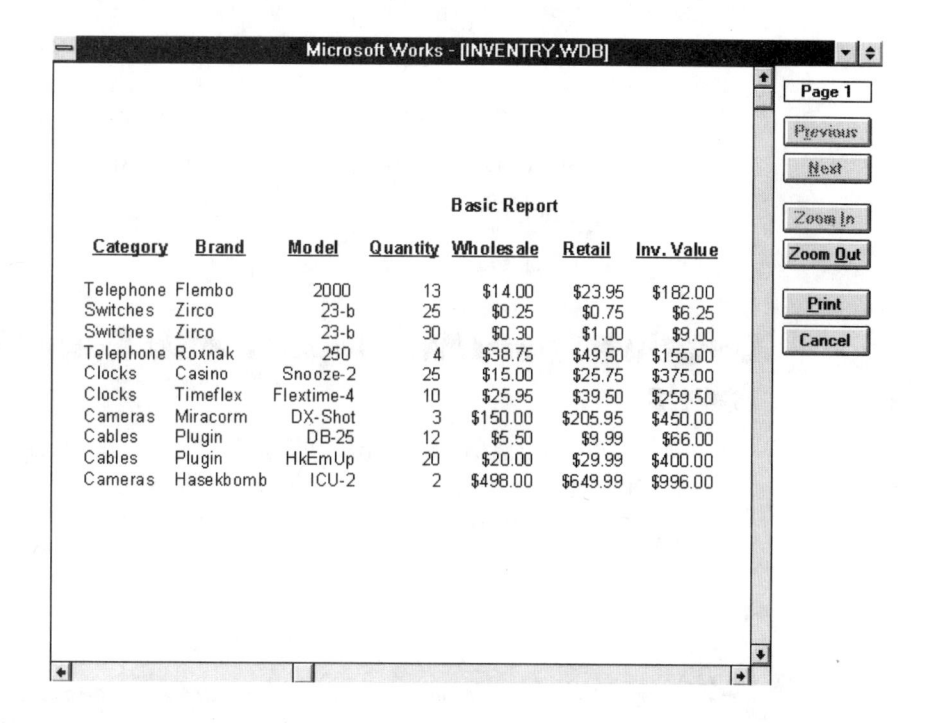

Category	Brand	Model	Quantity	Wholesale	Retail	Inv. Value
Telephone	Flembo	2000	13	$14.00	$23.95	$182.00
Switches	Zirco	23-b	25	$0.25	$0.75	$6.25
Switches	Zirco	23-b	30	$0.30	$1.00	$9.00
Telephone	Roxnak	250	4	$38.75	$49.50	$155.00
Clocks	Casino	Snooze-2	25	$15.00	$25.75	$375.00
Clocks	Timeflex	Flextime-4	10	$25.95	$39.50	$259.50
Cameras	Miracorm	DX-Shot	3	$150.00	$205.95	$450.00
Cables	Plugin	DB-25	12	$5.50	$9.99	$66.00
Cables	Plugin	HkEmUp	20	$20.00	$29.99	$400.00
Cameras	Hasekbomb	ICU-2	2	$498.00	$649.99	$996.00

> **Tip** Another way to view a report before printing it is to display it on screen and choose Edit ➤ Copy Report Output to copy a report to the Clipboard. Next, paste the report in a Works word processing document and see what it looks like there.

Deleting a Report

The report isn't anything more than a database listing not much different than what is seen in List view. Let's go back and try the report again, putting in some statistics this time:

11. On the Print Preview screen, click on Cancel.

CHAPTER 9 Advanced Database Skills

To delete the report:

1. Choose Tools ➤ Delete Report. The Report dialog box appears.
2. Select the report you want to delete, Report1 in our case.
3. Click on Delete.
4. Click OK.

Creating Your Own Report with Statistical Totals

Reports don't mean much unless they show results such as subtotals and grand totals. At the least, a report should be broken up into groupings of like items. This time we will make a report with field summary information.

> **Tip** You can have up to eight reports per database, all of which are stored with the database on disk and can be called up later.

To make your own customized report with statistical totals and subtotals:

1. Open the database for which you want to make a report. In our case, that is the Inventory database.
2. Choose Tools ➤ Create New Report. The New Report dialog box appears as in Figure 9.15.
3. Choose the fields you want to be in the report. For our example reports, choose the fields shown in the figure. To enter fields, click on each field and then click the Add button.
4. Add the title shown in the figure and click OK.

FIGURE 9.15
Creating the basic report with subtitles

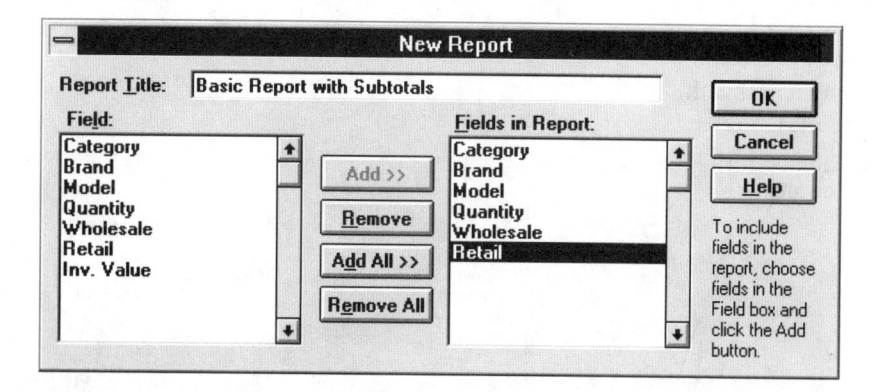

> **Tip** A fast way to choose fields for a report is to choose them all by pressing the Add All button. Next, remove the fields you *don't* want from the Fields in Report box.

The Report Statistics dialog box appears. From here you can choose the kinds of summary information or statistics you want Works to calculate for the report. We want to get totals for the Quantity, Wholesale, and Retails fields:

5. Click on Quantity and then click on the Sum option box.
6. Click on Wholesale and click on the Sum option box.
7. Click on Retail and click on the Sum option box.
8. Click on OK.
9. Click OK again and then choose File ➤ Print Preview to view the report. It will look like Figure 9.16.

CHAPTER 9 Advanced Database Skills

FIGURE 9.16
The report with totals listed together at the bottom

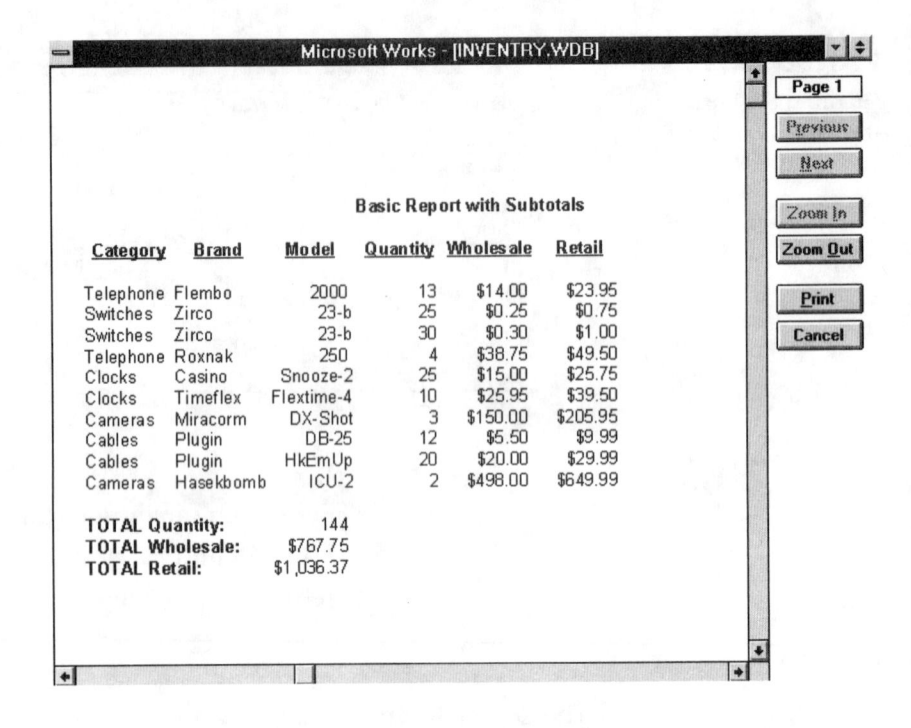

```
Microsoft Works - [INVENTRY.WDB]

                    Basic Report with Subtotals

Category    Brand       Model       Quantity  Wholesale   Retail

Telephone   Flembo      2000           13      $14.00     $23.95
Switches    Zirco       23-b           25       $0.25      $0.75
Switches    Zirco       23-b           30       $0.30      $1.00
Telephone   Roxnak      250             4      $38.75     $49.50
Clocks      Casino      Snooze-2       25      $15.00     $25.75
Clocks      Timeflex    Flextime-4     10      $25.95     $39.50
Cameras     Miracorm    DX-Shot         3     $150.00    $205.95
Cables      Plugin      DB-25          12       $5.50      $9.99
Cables      Plugin      HkEmUp         20      $20.00     $29.99
Cameras     Hasekbomb   ICU-2           2     $498.00    $649.99

TOTAL Quantity:          144
TOTAL Wholesale:      $767.75
TOTAL Retail:       $1,036.37
```

> **Note** To delete a row in a report, put the cursor anywhere on the row, choose Insert ▶ Delete Row/Column, choose Row, and click OK.

Putting the Totals under the Columns

Notice the totals at the bottom of the report. The three totals are listed in rows because the Together in rows box rather than the Under each column box was checked in the Report Statistics dialog box. Let's generate the report again, this time putting the totals under the columns to which they pertain:

1. Delete the report (see "Deleting a Report" above).

2. Follow steps 1 through 4 above to create the report and add all the fields but the last one.

3. In the Report Statistics dialog box, set the last three fields to show a Sum as in steps 5 through 7 above.

4. Click on the Under each column button to make the totals appear under the columns, not in rows.

5. Click OK and view the report by choosing File ➤ Print Preview.

The report now shows totals under their respective columns, as in Figure 9.17. To prepare for the next exercise:

6. Delete the report you just created.

Sorting Records in Reports

Unfortunately, as the database now stands, items are not sorted in order. That is, not all cameras are together, nor are telephones—they're mixed up with the other items. However, you can sort the records in a report. Moreover, you can place a blank field, called a *break field,* in reports

FIGURE 9.17
The report with totals listed under columns

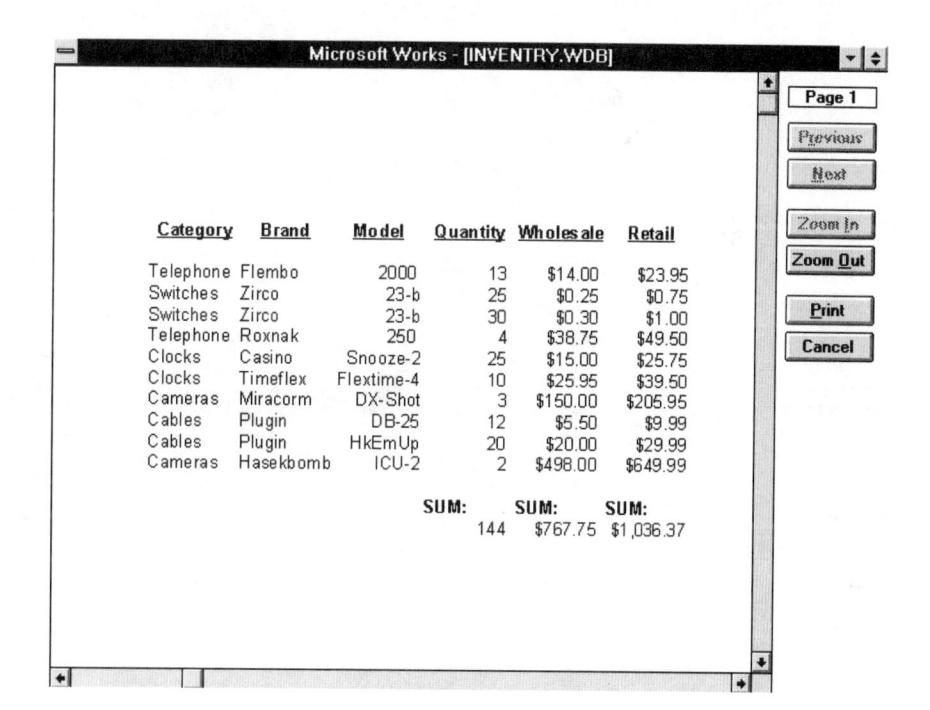

Category	Brand	Model	Quantity	Wholesale	Retail
Telephone	Flembo	2000	13	$14.00	$23.95
Switches	Zirco	23-b	25	$0.25	$0.75
Switches	Zirco	23-b	30	$0.30	$1.00
Telephone	Roxnak	250	4	$38.75	$49.50
Clocks	Casino	Snooze-2	25	$15.00	$25.75
Clocks	Timeflex	Flextime-4	10	$25.95	$39.50
Cameras	Miracorm	DX-Shot	3	$150.00	$205.95
Cables	Plugin	DB-25	12	$5.50	$9.99
Cables	Plugin	HkEmUp	20	$20.00	$29.99
Cameras	Hasekbomb	ICU-2	2	$498.00	$649.99
			SUM:	SUM:	SUM:
			144	$767.75	$1,036.37

379

CHAPTER 9 Advanced Database Skills

to break listings into separate groups. For example, you could group names by their first letter or separate dates into different groups.

To sort the records in a report and enter breaks:

1. Open the database for which you want to make a report. In our case, that is the Inventory database.

2. Choose Tools ➤ Create New Report. The New Report dialog box appears (see Figure 9.15).

3. Add the following fields: Category, Brand, Model, Quantity, Wholesale, Inv. Value. Add fields by clicking on each one and then clicking the Add button.

4. Type in **Basic Report with Subtotals and Breaks** as the report title and click OK.

5. In the Report Statistics dialog box, request a sum for Quantity (so you know how many items you have) and for Inv. Value (so you know how much total investment you have in your inventory). Choose the Under each column option for the position of the statistics. Choose OK.

6. Click OK again.

Now you are back to your report. It's time to sort the dialog box and enter the breaks:

7. Choose Tools ➤ Sort Records. The Sort Records dialog box appears, as in Figure 9.18.

FIGURE 9.18

The Sort Records dialog box. Select the Break or 1st Letter options to add blank lines to the report where the contents of the specified field changes.

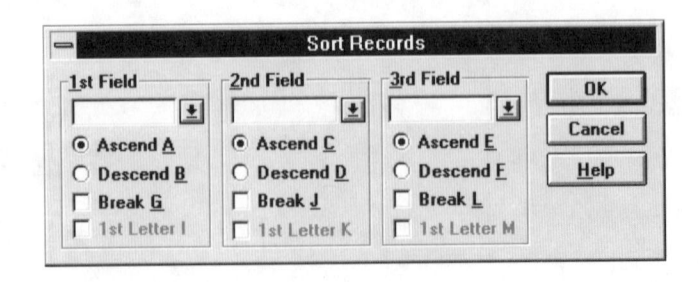

Generating a Database Report

> **Note** See "Sorting a Database" in Chapter 8 if you are unfamiliar with the Sort Records dialog box and how records are sorted using the 1st, 2nd, and 3rd fields.

Entering Breaks Between Field Categories

Notice the Break and 1st Letter options in the Sort Records dialog box. When Break is checked, Works adds a blank line to the report when the contents of the specified field changes. When 1st Letter is checked, the break occurs where the first letter of the records change.

For our report we want the following specifications:

◆ We want to sort on the Category field, so category is the 1st field.

◆ Within the category, we want to sort records by Brand name, so brand name is the 2nd field.

◆ We want an ascending (alphabetical) sort.

◆ We want breaks to appear after each new category, so we will check Break under the 1st field.

To sort the report and enter breaks:

8. Fill in the Sort Records dialog box as follows (don't turn on breaks for Brand, or you will get a blank line each time the brand name changes):

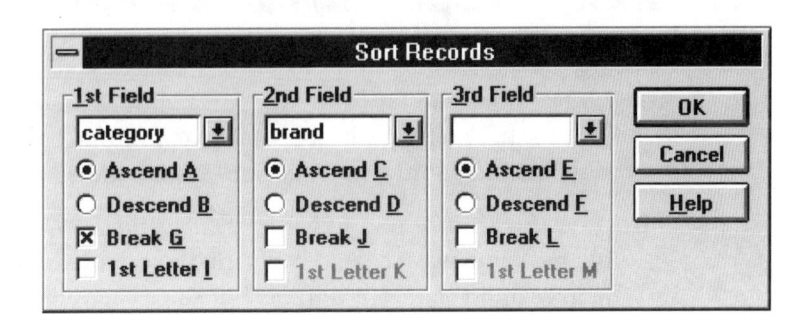

Sort Records			
1st Field	**2nd Field**	**3rd Field**	
category	brand		OK
● Ascend A	● Ascend C	● Ascend E	Cancel
○ Descend B	○ Descend D	○ Descend F	Help
☒ Break G	☐ Break J	☐ Break L	
☐ 1st Letter I	☐ 1st Letter K	☐ 1st Letter M	

CHAPTER 9 Advanced Database Skills

9. Click OK. Works adds a few new cells to the report definition that say =COUNT.

10. View the report by choosing File ➤ Print Preview or by clicking the Preview button (the one with a magnifying glass). The report should look like Figure 9.19.

FIGURE 9.19
The report with sorted categories and brands, and subtotals for Quantity and Inventory Value

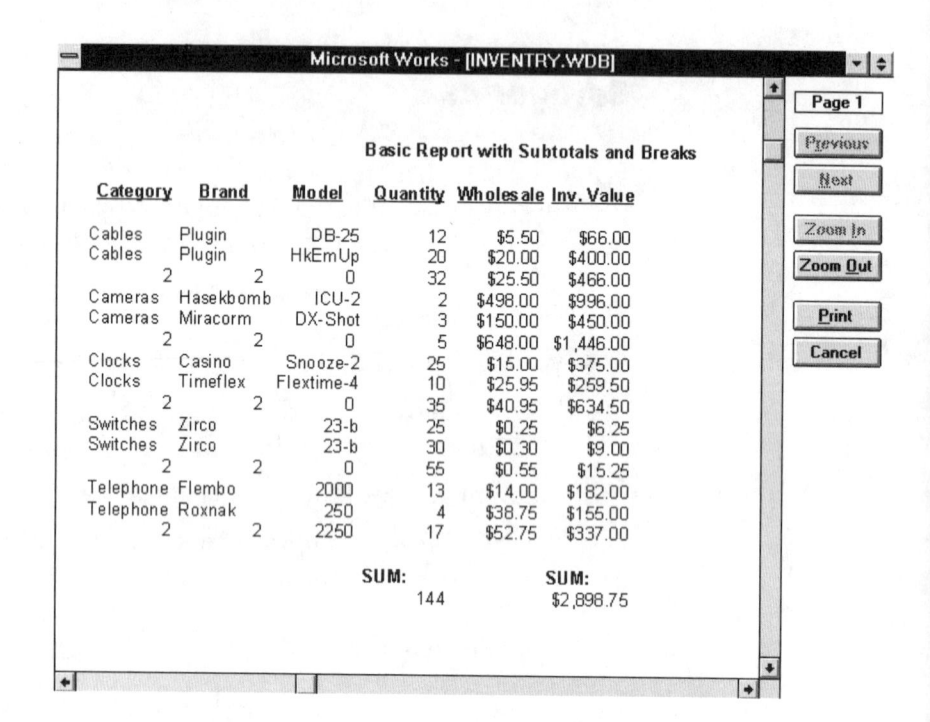

```
                Basic Report with Subtotals and Breaks

Category    Brand       Model      Quantity  Wholesale  Inv. Value

Cables      Plugin      DB-25         12      $5.50      $66.00
Cables      Plugin      HkEmUp        20     $20.00     $400.00
   2           2           0          32     $25.50     $466.00
Cameras     Hasekbomb   ICU-2          2    $498.00     $996.00
Cameras     Miracorm    DX-Shot        3    $150.00     $450.00
   2           2           0           5    $648.00   $1,446.00
Clocks      Casino      Snooze-2      25     $15.00     $375.00
Clocks      Timeflex    Flextime-4    10     $25.95     $259.50
   2           2           0          35     $40.95     $634.50
Switches    Zirco       23-b          25      $0.25       $6.25
Switches    Zirco       23-b          30      $0.30       $9.00
   2           2           0          55      $0.55      $15.25
Telephone   Flembo      2000          13     $14.00     $182.00
Telephone   Roxnak      250            4     $38.75     $155.00
   2           2        2250          17     $52.75     $337.00

                                    SUM:                SUM:
                                     144             $2,898.75
```

Modifying a Report to Make It Easier to Understand

The report so far isn't bad, but it should have labels and horizontal lines to show where the subtotals are and make them easier to find. You could also add a title, the date, and explanations about items on the report.

As for all those 2's in the first three fields, Works put them there when the break line was added. Works tried to calculate subtotals for the first three fields as it did the second three, but since the values in the first three fields are not numerical, it used the COUNT function rather than the SUM function to count the number of records in the grouping and came up with 2. Such are the failings of the speed-reporting approach.

Row Types and How to Enter New Rows

In order to fix this report, you need to know more about how Works' report generator. The report generator defines reports. It determines how rows are to be arranged and how data should be entered. Figure 9.20 shows the report definition screen. To see this screen if it is not already on display:

1. Choose View ➤ Report.
2. In the Reports dialog box, highlight the report you want.
3. Click OK.

Row types The primary structure of a report is defined by the rows. Each line in a report corresponds to a type of row in the report definition. If you look at the report definition screen in Figure 9.20, you will see that only five row types were used—Title, Headings, Record, Summ Category, and Summary. There are six possible types of rows:

ROW TYPE	EXPLANATION
Title	The heading that appears on the first page of the report.
Headings	The field headings that appear above the fields' columns. You can change headings to make them more explanatory.
Intr Category	You can request that the field name—for example, *Brand*—be printed again after each break. (This is the "Introduce Category" row type.)
Record	Where the actual field data gets printed.

383

CHAPTER 9 Advanced Database Skills

FIGURE 9.20
The report definition screen showing how the report was laid out by Works' report generator

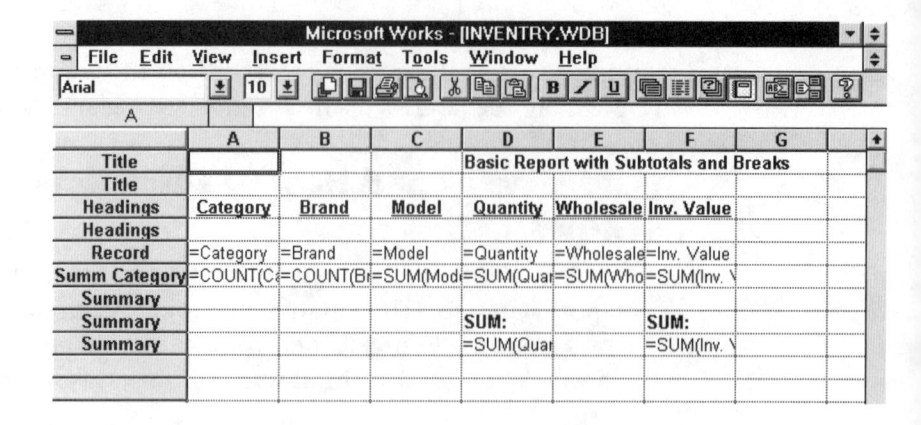

	A	B	C	D	E	F	G
Title				Basic Report with Subtotals and Breaks			
Title							
Headings	Category	Brand	Model	Quantity	Wholesale	Inv. Value	
Headings							
Record	=Category	=Brand	=Model	=Quantity	=Wholesale	Inv. Value	
Summ Category	=COUNT(Ca	=COUNT(Br	=SUM(Mod	=SUM(Qua	=SUM(Who	=SUM(Inv. V	
Summary							
Summary				SUM:		SUM:	
Summary				=SUM(Qua		=SUM(Inv. V	

ROW TYPE	EXPLANATION
Summ Category	Where a statistical summary appears for each group when you have requested breaks.
Summary	Where statistical summary information for the whole report appears.

> **Tip** To make working with the definition screen easier, drag the column dividers out to make the columns wider. Enlarge them until you can read their contents.

Record rows As shown in Figure 9.20, the Record row (row 5) instructs Works to print the contents of the six fields one after another. Therefore, =*Brand* in column B means to "print the contents of the brand field for each record, starting at the beginning and moving down through the database until the end." Incidentally, the Record row is the only row that prints what is actually in the database. The other rows print titles or statistics based on the database records that the Record row prints.

Summ Category rows You can enter numbers, formulas, or text in the cells. As an example, notice how the Summ Category row uses typical formulas:

=COUNT(Category)   =COUNT(Brand)   =COUNT(Model)

COUNT means "on this line, count up the number of records in the current subdivision." SUM is used to total cells:

=SUM(Quantity)   =SUM(Wholesale)   =SUM(Inv. Value)

These formulas mean "on this line, sum the dollar amounts in the current division."

Entering New Rows in a Report

Let's modify the report. We will insert additional rows, tell Works what information to assign to each row type, and enter cell formulas.

To insert rows in a report:

1. Bring up the report generator screen if you haven't already done so.
2. Select the row below where you want the new row to appear and choose Insert ➤ Row/Column. You'll see a dialog box offering the six possible types of rows.
3. Choose a row type and click OK.

Note Rows must be in a certain order in a report. For example, a Total row can't be at the top of the report with subtotals below it.

Entering New Data in a Report

Once the row additions are complete, you have to tell Works exactly what information you want to assign to each row type. You change what appears in the cells of your report by making changes on the report definition screen. To do this, either type the new data or codes directly in the cell or place the cursor where you want the change to be made, select Edit ➤ Insert, and then select one of the following commands:

INSERT COMMAND	USE
Field Name	Lets you choose a field name from a list and insert it in a cell you've chosen. The field name will appear in the cell.
Field Entry	Lets you enter a command for making the data in another field appear in the current cell location. When you choose the command, a list appears with the data in other fields. Choose an item from the list.
Field Summary	Lets you use a function in a cell. When you choose this command, the Field Summary dialog box appears. Choose a field from the list box and then choose a function. The functions are:

- **SUM** Adds the numbers in the group
- **AVG** Obtains the average of the numbers in the group
- **COUNT** Obtains the number of items in the group
- **MAX** Lists the largest number in the group
- **MIN** Lists the smallest number in the group
- **STD** Finds the standard deviation of the numbers in the group
- **VAR** Finds the variance of the numbers in the group

> **Note** The term *cell* is usually used in spreadsheets. A cell is the place where a column and row intersect. See "Spreadsheet Basics" in Chapter 1 for a complete explanation of cells.

Modifying the Report

As shown in Figure 9.20, you can see the data that Works' report generator entered into the cells. To see the complete data in each cell, highlight the cell you want to see look in the formula bar to see the entry in its entirety.

Using Figure 9.21 and 9.22 as guides, let's change the report to make it more readable:

1. Make the columns wider so they are easier to see. Do this by dragging the columns out.

2. Use the toolbar's Bold, Italic, Font, Size, and Alignment buttons to spruce up the display a bit.

3. Add explanatory cells to your report. For example, at the bottom of the report, the word *SUM* appears above the Quantity SUM. Why not have it say "Total Items in inventory" instead? Just select the cell and edit its contents.

4. Why not add a blank line or line of heading text above each column after a break? Position the cursor on the existing Intr row and add another Intr field name row by choosing Insert ➤ Row/Column.

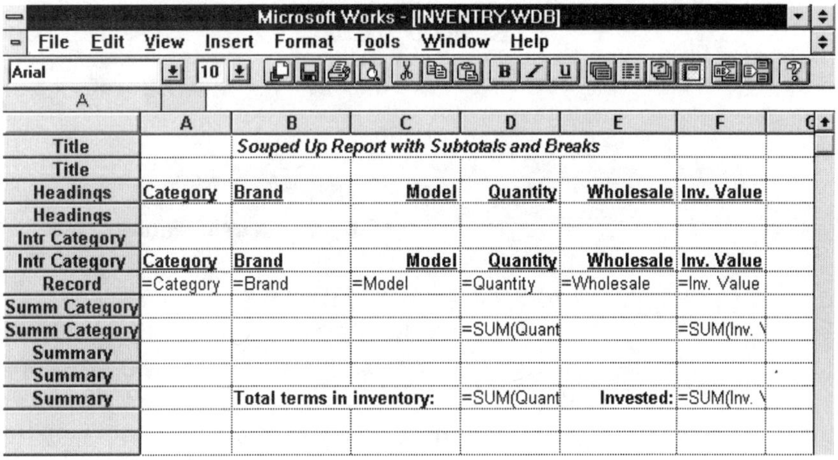

FIGURE 9.21
The modified report definition. When printed, this produces the report in Figure 9.22

CHAPTER 9 — Advanced Database Skills

FIGURE 9.22

The finished report. Compare this to its definition screen in Figure 9.21. Notice the blank lines between Category breaks and the repeated headings after each break.

Souped Up Report with Subtotals and Breaks

Category	Brand	Model	Quantity	Wholesale	Inv. Value
Category	**Brand**	**Model**	**Quantity**	**Wholesale**	**Inv. Value**
Cables	Plugin	DB-25	12	$5.50	$66.00
Cables	Plugin	HkEmUp	20	$20.00	$400.00
			32		$466.00
Category	**Brand**	**Model**	**Quantity**	**Wholesale**	**Inv. Value**
Cameras	Hasekbomb	ICU-2	2	$498.00	$996.00
Cameras	Miracorm	DX-Shot	3	$150.00	$450.00
			5		$1,446.00
Category	**Brand**	**Model**	**Quantity**	**Wholesale**	**Inv. Value**
Clocks	Casino	Snooze-2	25	$15.00	$375.00
Clocks	Timeflex	Flextime-4	10	$25.95	$259.50
			35		$634.50
Category	**Brand**	**Model**	**Quantity**	**Wholesale**	**Inv. Value**
Switches	Zirco	23-b	25	$0.25	$6.25
Switches	Zirco	23-b	30	$0.30	$9.00
			55		$15.25
Category	**Brand**	**Model**	**Quantity**	**Wholesale**	**Inv. Value**
Telephone	Flembo	2000	13	$14.00	$182.00
Telephone	Roxnak	250	4	$38.75	$155.00
			17		$337.00

Total terms in inventory: 144   Invested: $2,898.75

Examine the row types and locations and the text in the cells in Figures 9.21 and 9.22. I've also formatted most of the cells so they are left-aligned. The printed report in Figure 9.22 demonstrates the effects of the additional rows. You can fine-tune a report in almost a million ways. Trial and error, unfortunately, is the best teacher.

Generating a Database Report

> **Note** To save a report, just save the database it is attached to. Reports—all eight of them, if you've made that many—are saved along with the database file. See "Saving Your Work" in Chapter 8 if you need to know how to save a database.

Opening a Report

To open a report you saved already:

1. Open the database to which the report is attached.
2. Select View ➤ Report. All reports attached to the database will appear in a dialog box, listed as Report1, Report2, and so on.
3. Select the report number and click OK to open it.

Naming, deleting, and duplicating reports are accomplished from the Tools menu on the report definition screen. Respectively, choose Tools ➤ Name Report, Tools ➤ Delete Report, or Tools ➤ Duplicate Report to complete these tasks. After you rename a report, its more descriptive moniker will appear in the View ➤ Reports dialog box.

Printing a Report

Creating reports that look right takes a fair amount of experimentation. Preview a report before you print it to make sure it looks right. Fields can be pushed onto the next page. Press PgDn when previewing the report to see if this has happened. Adjust the font and column widths if necessary to prevent this.

CHAPTER 9 Advanced Database Skills

Using horizontal and vertical page breaks is a great way to break up a report into separate pages and have the report come out the way you want it to look. To insert a page break:

- ◆ Choose Insert ➤ Page Break from the Report definition screen. This inserts a break above or to the left of the selected record or field.

The next chapter explains how to use the communications module with a modem to connect with other computers or bulletin boards.

PART five

Harnessing the Power of Works

10

Using the Communications Tool

11

Creating Documents Automatically

12

Putting It All Together

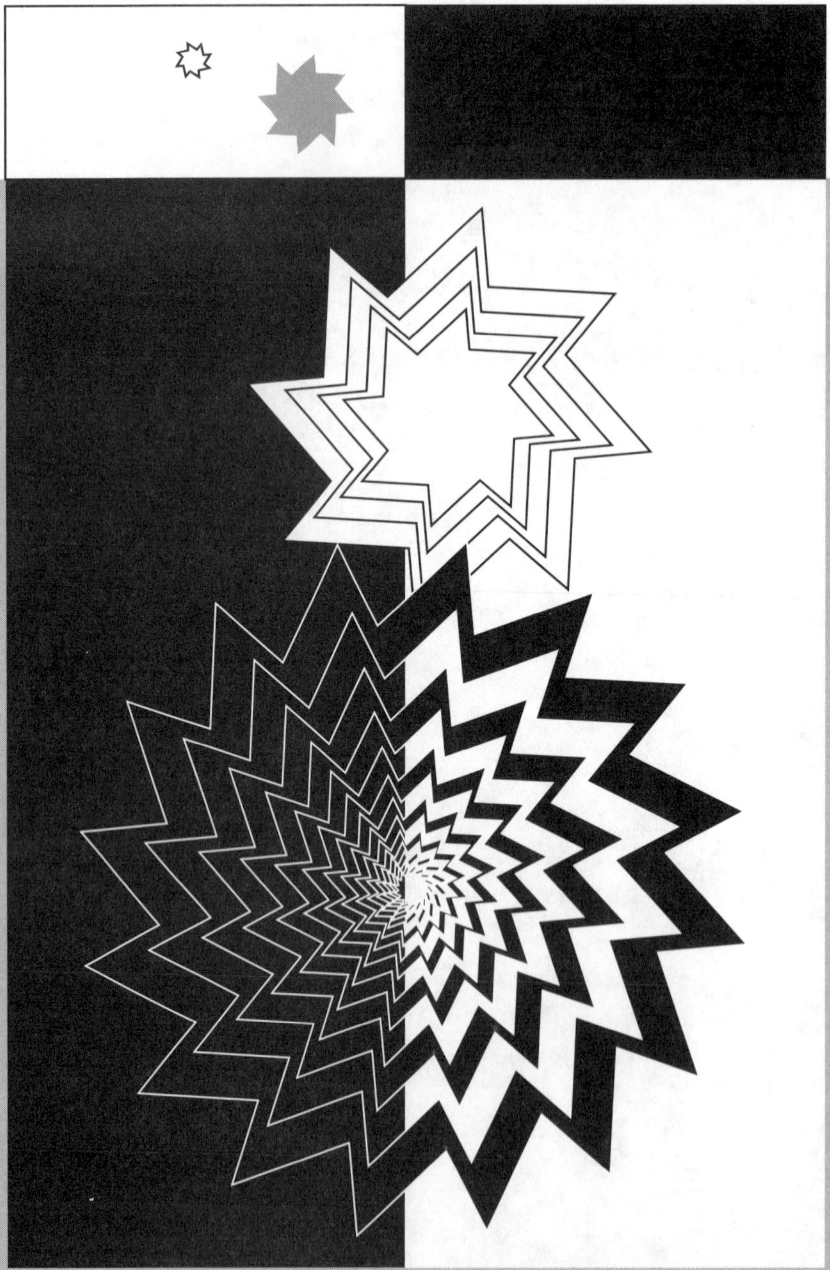

CHAPTER 10

Using the Communications Tool

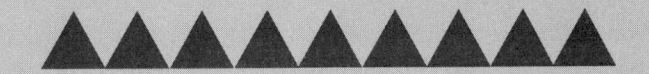

Fast Track

To begin your first communications session,   **399**

choose File ➤ Create New File and select Communications. If you're not sure which port to choose, click Test and Works will find it for you. If you do know, click the appropriate COM button and click OK.

To make the Phone settings for calling up another computer,   **401**

select Settings ➤ Phone or click the Phone Settings button on the toolbar, type in the phone number you want your modem to dial, and click OK.

To set the Communication parameters for your system,   **403**

choose Settings ➤ Communication and set the Baud rate, parity, data bits, and stop bits if they should be different from the defaults. Select a handshaking option and click OK.

To set the Transfer parameters,   **409**

select Settings ➤ Transfer and choose one of the four standard protocols. If you have another directory you'd like incoming files to go to, click the Directory button and select the directory you want. Click OK twice.

To make a connection with an information service,   **411**

select Phone ➤ Easy Connect or click the Easy Connect button on the Toolbar, type in a phone number and—optionally—the name of the service, and click OK. Click OK again when Works asks you if you want to connect to the other computer.

You can capture text in messages being sent to you.   **416**

    Choose Tools ➤ Capture Text or click the Capture Text button on the Toolbar, type in a name for the file you want the captured text stored in, and press ↵. Whatever text you enter will be captured along with the incoming text. When you want to stop capturing text, choose Tools ➤ End Capture Text or click the Capture Text button again.

To send an ASCII file to a remote computer by modem,   **418**

    make a connection to the other computer and choose Tools ➤ Send Text or click the Send Text button on the toolbar. Type in the file name or select it from the file box and press ↵.

To send a binary file complete with formatting,   **420**

    make sure you are on-line (connected) and choose Settings ➤ Transfer. Choose the protocol you want (the one the receiving system uses) and make sure the receiving computer is ready to receive an XMODEM or Kermit file. Next, select Tools ➤ Send File or click the Send Binary File button on the toolbar, type in the file name or select it from the dialog box, and click OK.

To receive a binary file,   **421**

    choose Settings ➤ Transfer and select XMODEM or Kermit, depending on the protocol the other computer uses to send binary files. Tell the sending computer to get ready to send via XMODEM and choose Tools ➤ Receive File or click the Receive Binary File button on the toolbar. Quickly enter the file name (and path if not the current path) or choose it from the dialog box and click OK.

USING WORKS' COMMUNICATIONS TOOL, YOU can make contact with other computers to exchange and retrieve information—including electronic mail (e-mail) messages, stock quotes, business documents, word-processed files, and spreadsheet files. You can share data with computers located in the same room or across the globe. Many people use communications programs to *telecommute*—to connect to their company's computer so that they can work at home.

Nowadays there are almost as many types of information available for use with PCs and communications programs as there are interests. Many clubs and organizations have their own dial-up *bulletin board systems* (BBSs) where members can leave messages and read notices of interest. Some BBSs provide free software, called *freeware,* that anyone with a computer, a modem, and a communications program can have just for the taking. Using your PC, a modem, and Works, you can take advantage of the conveniences of computer communications.

This chapter explains

- ◆ How modems work
- ◆ How to set up your system so you can communicate with bulletin boards and other computers by modem
- ◆ How to make and save communications files with telephone numbers and other settings so you can dial other computers directly
- ◆ How to call up other computers
- ◆ How to send and receive data messages and data files

- Recording and playing back scripts to automate sign-on procedures
- How to communicate with other computers by direct wire
- Troubleshooting the communications system

This chapter differs from the others in that there are fewer step-by-step exercises. Including step-by-step instructions here would require you to call up electronic mail and other on-line services—services that you may or may not subscribe to. Step-by-step instructions would not be practical in a chapter like this one. Instead of demonstrating specific processes, this chapter will introduce you to the Works communications module and suggest general steps to follow when you "telecommunicate."

> **Note** See "What Is a Communications Program?" in Chapter 1 for a brief explanation of how modems operate and what a communications program is.

Setting Up Your Communications System

In most cases, you'll be using Works to communicate with dial-up services such as Internet, CompuServe, the Source, and MCI Mail, or to call a friend or colleague's computer (you can even call a Macintosh). To communicate this way, you must have a modem, and the modem must be connected to the telephone lines.

This part of the chapter explains how to set up your system so you can communicate with bulletin boards and other peoples' computers. Most of the settings need to be made only once. Once you've made the settings pertaining to one party you call often, you can save the settings in a communications file and simply bring up the file whenever you want to dial the party. Only a few of the settings have to be changed each time you begin a communications session.

CHAPTER 10 — Using the Communications Tool

> **Note** Before setting up your communications system, make sure your modem is installed properly. Follow the instructions given in the manual carefully. The most frequent cause of commmunications problems is an incorrectly installed modem.

About Modems

A modem (the word stands for "modulator/demodulator") provides the electronic connection between your computer and the phone line. As shown in Figure 10.1, a modem converts digital information from your computer into an analog signal that can be sent over the phone lines. On the other end of the line, the receiving modem reconverts the audio signal into digital data and sends that data to a computer.

Baud rates The main distinguishing factor among modems is the speed with which they transfer data. As of this writing, the most popular modems transmit data at baud rates of 300, 1200, 2400, 4800, 9600, 14400. The *baud rate* is the number of data bits that can be transmitted in one second. The larger the number, the faster the transmission. Modems with high baud rates of course cost more.

FIGURE 10.1
PCs require a modem to communicate over the telephone lines.

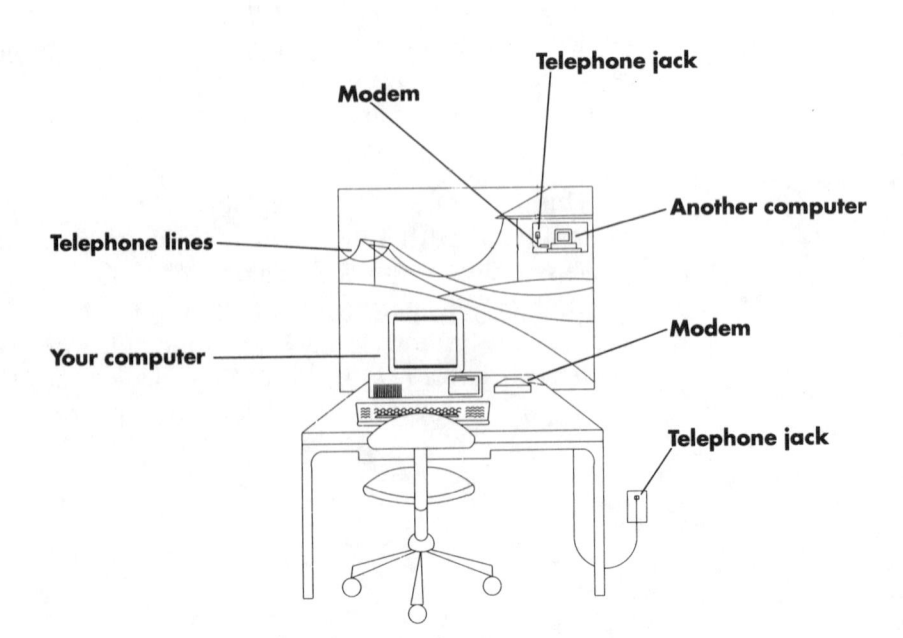

Setting Up Your Communications System

> **Tip** Modems that use Hayes-compatible commands let you take advantage of many useful features in Works (and most other communications programs), including automatic dial and redial. Without a Hayes-compatible modem, you have to type in these commands yourself.

Starting the Communications Program

To start the communications program and set up the system for your computer and modem, follow these steps:

1. Choose File ➤ Create New File.
2. Select Communications. If this is the first time you have run a communications session, the Modem Setup dialog box appears, as in Figure 10.2.

Choosing a COM Port

Works wants you to specify which *port* (COM 1 through 4) your modem is attached to. Notice that Works has already made a default choice

FIGURE 10.2
The Modem Setup dialog box. This is where you select the communications port your modem is attached to.

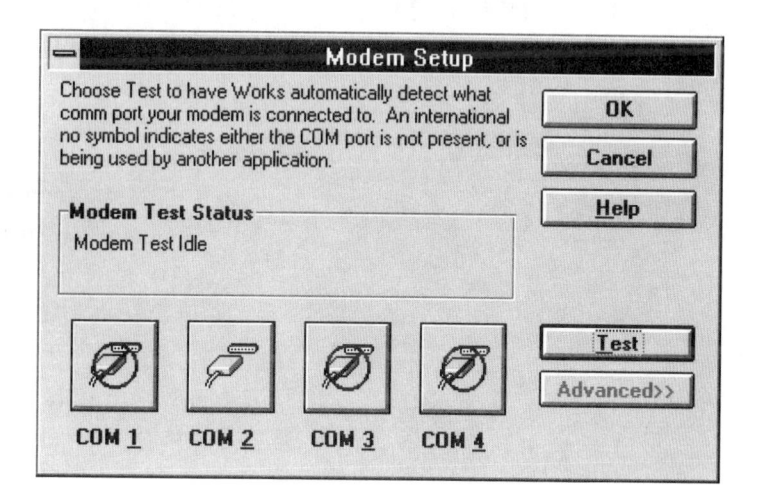

399

and has already eliminated all but one of the choices. From this dialog box, you can

3. Tell Works which COM port to use:

   ◆ If you're not sure which port to choose, click Test and Works will find it for you.

   ◆ If you know which port to choose, click the appropriate COM button.

4. Click OK. A blank communications screen appears. You are now running a communications session.

5. Maximize the window.

Notice that the status area in the window says OFFLINE. This means that you are *not* currently connected to or communicating with another computer.

The Communications Parameters

Once you have a new document open, you have to set up various parameters before you can begin communicating. Four groups of parameters still need to be set (you set the Modem parameters above):

PARAMETER	DESCRIPTION
Phone	Tell Works what telephone number you want to dial and the type of telephone service you have.
Communication	Tell Works about the speed and format by which data is transmitted between your computer and the other computer.
Terminal	Tell Works how data is be displayed on your screen when it arrives by modem. Also tell Works details about your keyboard.
Transfer	Controls how data will be sent from and received by your computer.

Setting Up Your Communications System

These settings are all made on the Settings menu. Each one is described below.

Setting the Phone Parameters

If you have a Hayes-type modem, Works can dial the phone number of the remote computer for you. The term *remote computer* refers to the outside computer you are communicating with. However, for your computer to dial numbers automatically, you have to fill in the Phone settings. Follow these steps:

1. Select Settings ➤ Phone or click the Phone Settings button on the toolbar (the one right below the Settings menu with a picture of a telephone on it). The Settings dialog box appears with the Phone tab selected, as in Figure 10.3.

2. Type in the phone number you want your modem to dial. You can enter the number in any of the following forms (see below for information about using MCI, Sprint, and other long-distance services):

   (510)-555-1111   A standard way of dialing
   510-555-1111   A standard way of dialing

FIGURE 10.3
The Settings dialog box with the Phone tab selected

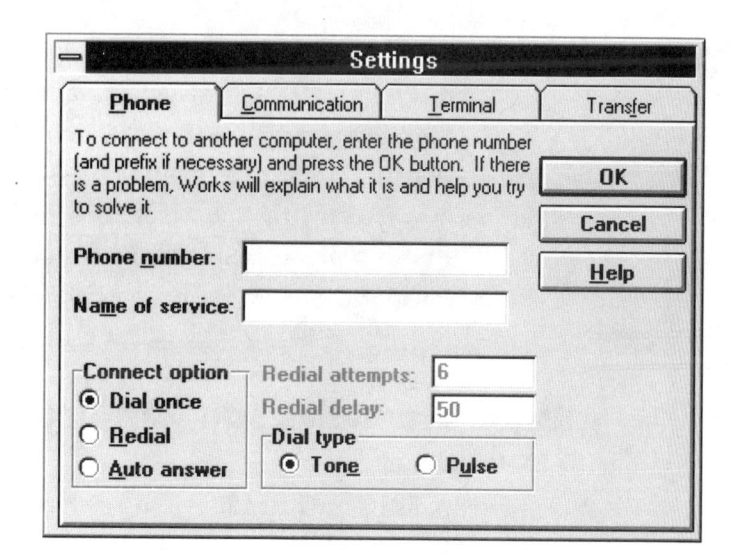

CHAPTER 10 Using the Communications Tool

5105551111	A telephone number without "punctuation"
555-1111	A local telephone number, to be used for local calls only

The following entries in the dialog box are optional:

3. In the Name of service box, type the name of the computer, bulletin board, or service you are dialing.

4. Click the Redial button if you want Works to keep trying if it fails to get through on the first dial. When you click Redial, you can change the number of redial attempts from 6 or the delay times between redials from 50 seconds to another interval.

5. Click OK to close the dialog box or click on the Communication tab to set the Communication parameters.

The auto-answer feature for incoming calls If you have a Hayes-compatible auto-answer modem, you can use the auto-answer feature to answer incoming calls from the Settings dialog box. When you check the Auto Answer button and tell Works to dial, it will prepare to receive an incoming call and connect to the computer making the call instead of dialing.

> **Warning**
>
> Controlling the auto-answer feature from the Settings dialog box only works with Hayes-compatible auto-answer modems. Moreover, you have to make sure your modem's internal switches are set correctly to for auto-answering (see your modem's instruction manual). A non-Hayes-type modem that has an auto-answer feature can answer the phone, but not from the Settings dialog box.

Using Alternative Long Distance Services

If you're using an alternative long distance service such as Sprint, MCI, or others, you can enter all the numbers necessary in the Phone number box, provided the numbers don't exceed 100 digits. To tell your modem to pause before moving ahead to the next set of digits, include a comma. On Hayes-compatible modems, each comma produces a two-second delay. At least one comma is usually necessary for alternative services, since it can take several seconds for the second dial tone to come on after the initial connection is made.

For example, consider the following telephone number, which is used to dial long distance via an alternative service to MCI Mail in Oakland from a company phone that requires pressing 9 to get an outside line:

To get an outside line: 9

Your long distance access number: 950-1311

Your private access code: 8273645

The number you're calling: 510-540-1111

To dial this number, you would enter the following in the Phone Number box:

9,950-1311,,8273645,510-510-1111

Notice the placement and number of commas. You may have to change the number of commas (particularly of the double set) based on how many rings it takes for your long distance service to answer and then come on with the second dial tone. Hayes-type modems do not acknowledge when the phone on the other end of the line has been answered, and this is compensated for by the commas.

Setting the Communication Parameters

Once you've made the phone settings, then you have to set the Communication parameters:

1. Depending on where you are, there are three ways to set the Communications parameters:

    ◆ Select Settings ➤ Communication

    ◆ Click the Communication Settings button on the toolbar (the one directly under the View menu)

CHAPTER 10 — Using the Communications Tool

♦ If you are in the Settings dialog box already, click the Communication tab

The Communication tab in the Settings dialog box appears, as in Figure 10.4.

The options on the Communications tab are for controlling how your computer and the computer on the other end communicate. Take a look at the defaults. All of these parameters except the port have to be identical on each end—that is, both your computer and the one you are communicating with must use the same settings. The default settings you see here are designed to work with most services. If you can use them, click OK to skip over this dialog box.

If you are not sure what one of these settings should be, find out which settings the computer at the other end is using and set yours accordingly. If you can't find out what those settings are, use the default settings that show up when you open a new document. If those don't work, then start systematically altering the settings one at a time.

FIGURE 10.4

The Settings dialog box with the Communication tab selected

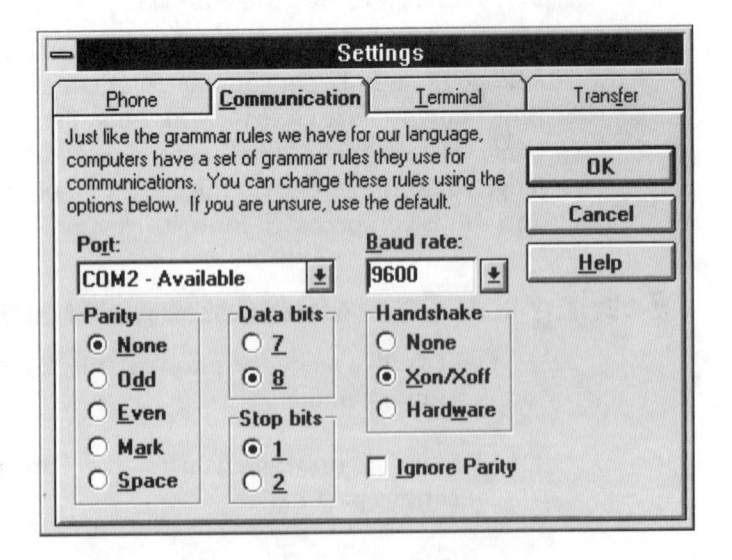

Setting Up Your Communications System

Let's look at the options one by one.

Port The Port scroll box shows which port your modem or null modem cable is connected to. Most PCs have two serial communications ports, COM1 and COM2. More often than not, COM1 will be used. However, if your COM1 port is tied up by a printer or other device, your modem is probably set to COM2.

> **Note** See "Setting Up a Direct Connection" later in this chapter to see how to connect computers without a modem.

Baud rate The Baud rate box is for entering a baud rate. Use a rate from 50 to 19200 baud. As mentioned before, the baud rate determines the speed at which data is transmitted. Your modem's baud rate must match that of the remote computer's modem. When baud rates are mismatched, the connection is not made or weird letters and punctuation marks appear on screen.

> **Note** Some modems can automatically sense the baud rate of incoming data and adjust themselves accordingly. Others modems cannot do this and must be set using switches. Consult your modem's instruction manual to see what kind of modem you have.

Most modem transmissions take place at 2400, 4800, 9600, 14400, or 19200 baud. Use as fast a speed as possible to decrease the time it takes to transmit data, but if the connection is a bad one—as is often the case with long distance calls—lower the baud rate to avoid losing data. Most information services, including CompuServe, charge twice as much for 9600-baud transmissions as they do for 2400-baud transmissions.

Parity *Parity* refers to an error-checking mechanism used in data transmissions. The first seven bits in each byte are added up, and the eighth bit—called the *parity bit*—is supposed to equal the sum of the first seven bits. If the two sums are not equal, a transmission error has occurred. Parity can only be used if you set the data bits parameter to 7. Otherwise parity should be left at None. If you are specifically told that the other system uses parity checking, find out what kind, and change this setting.

Data bits The Data bits setting refers to the number of *bits* (the smallest division of computer information) you want to send in each *byte* (the most common division of data). For example, typically each letter is stored in a byte composed of eight bits. Without going into great detail, suffice it to say that this setting is almost always going to be 8, and must be 8 if you intend to transmit programs (as opposed to just documents) between computers. If you are specifically told that the other system uses 7 bits, change this setting.

Stop bits *Stop bits* are used by the computers on both ends to mark the end of one character and the beginning of another. Systems use either one or two stop bits. More often, one stop bit is used, so you can probably leave this setting as-is. If you are told that the other system uses two bits, change this setting.

Handshake As they receive and send data, the computers on each end of the line often have to attend to other tasks as well. Sometimes these tasks distract the receiving computer from handling incoming data. To prevent data from falling through the cracks during these times, a convention called handshaking is used. *Handshaking* provides a way for the two computers to agree when to stop and start the sending process so that other contingencies can be handled.

With modems the Xon/Xoff convention (or protocol) is usually employed. When the receiving computer wants the sending computer to pause, it transmits an Xoff (a CTRL-S) signal. When ready to receive data again, it sends an Xon (CTRL-Q) signal. This is the default setting and will work for most dial-up information services.

When connecting computers to each other directly via a cable (without a modem), you may want to use the Hardware setting. This tells Works to use something called hardware handshaking. To use this option, you must make sure you have a special kind of cable. See "Computer-to-Computer Communications by Wire" later in this chapter for details.

If you know that the other computer uses no handshaking, select None from the dialog box. Regardless of which handshaking setup you are using, remember that both computers must use the same type.

Ignore Parity You don't have to bother with this check box. You do not need to check it.

Setting the Terminal Parameters

A *terminal* is nothing more than the screen and keyboard with which data is entered and displayed. Because terminals are made by many different manufacturers, certain standards have been established for displaying data on terminal screens and using keyboards.

You should check the terminal settings in the Settings dialog box before making a connection to another computer. Normally, the settings don't have to be changed.

To set the terminal parameters:

1. Open the Terminal tab in the Settings dialog box with one of these methods:

    ◆ Select Settings ➤ Terminal

    ◆ Click the Terminal Settings button on the toolbar (the one between the Communication and Phone buttons)

    ◆ Click the Terminal tab on the Settings dialog box if the box is already open

    The Settings dialog box appears with the Terminal tab selected, as in Figure 10.5.

There are four groups of settings in this box—Terminal, End of Lines, Local echo and Wrap around, and ISO Translation. Each is explained below.

Terminal Works can make your terminal emulate one of five terminal types. Without going into detail about the differences between these types, the VT choices tells your PC to emulate (act like) various popular terminals.

FIGURE 10.5

The Terminal tab of the Settings dialog box

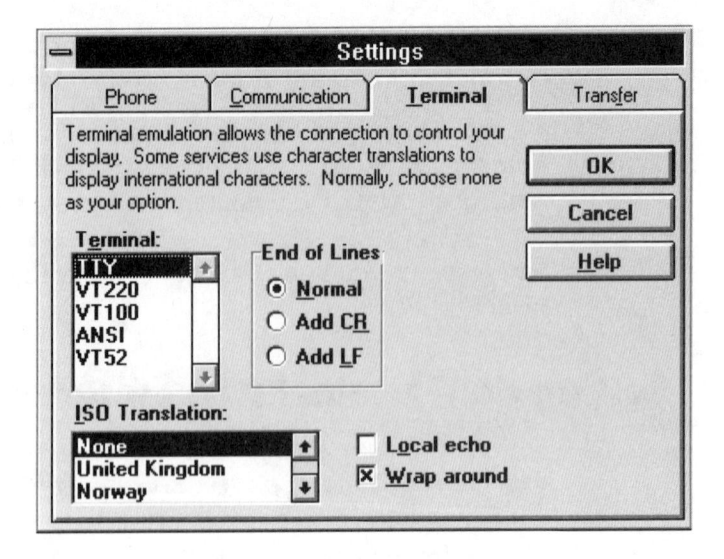

The first (and default) setting, TTY, should work for most terminals, but if your screen starts acting unpredictably or displaying bizarre letters, try the ANSI setting. Select the correct terminal type for your communications session.

End of Lines End of Lines is included to deal with some remote computers' habit of not moving the cursor down a line and/or moving it back to the left side after a line of text has been entered. If incoming data from a remote computer appears on a single line on your screen or the cursor moves to the right margin and seems to get stuck there, try turning the Add CR (carriage return) or Add LF (line feed) options on. For most sessions, however, the Normal option will do fine.

Local echo and Wrap around These two settings also affect how information appears on screen.

Local echo makes what you type on your keyboard appear on your screen so you can see what you're typing. In some communications sessions, particularly those between two PCs using Works, you can't see what you're typing because the remote computer is not programmed to echo your transmission back to your screen. Normally this will not be a problem, but if you find yourself typing "in the dark," set the Local echo parameter to on. When two PCs are running Works, both should have Local echo on. On the other hand, if you see double characters on the screen (HHEELLLLOO!!), turn Local echo off.

Wrap around makes incoming text that is longer than the width of your screen automatically move down a line and wrap to the left margin with each new line. Normally, Wrap around is set on.

ISO Translation This parameter is for communicating with information services in other countries. If you intend to do this, select the country name from the scroll box.

Setting the Transfer Parameters

If you plan to transfer data from a remote computer or service to your own computer (called *downloading* a file), or you plan to send a file to another computer or service (called *uploading* a file), you have to make sure that you are using the same transfer protocol that the other computer is using.

If you plan to transfer data, follow these steps to set the transfer parameters:

1. Open the Transfer tab in the Settings dialog box with one of these methods:

   ◆ Select Settings ➤ Transfer

   ◆ Click the Transfer Settings button on the toolbar (the one between the Phone and 8,n,1 buttons)

   ◆ Click the Transfer tab on the Settings dialog box if you are already in the Settings dialog box

   The Transfer tab in the Settings dialog box appears, as in Figure 10.6.

There are two groups of settings in this dialog box, Transfer protocol and Text transfers, as well as one button, Directory. Each is explained below.

Transfer protocol The Transfer protocol scroll box lists the four standard protocols. A *transfer protocol* is a set of procedures that computers use when transmitting data. As usual, both computers must be using the same protocol, and you need to know what the other computer is using if you

FIGURE 10.6

The Transfer tab of the Settings dialog box

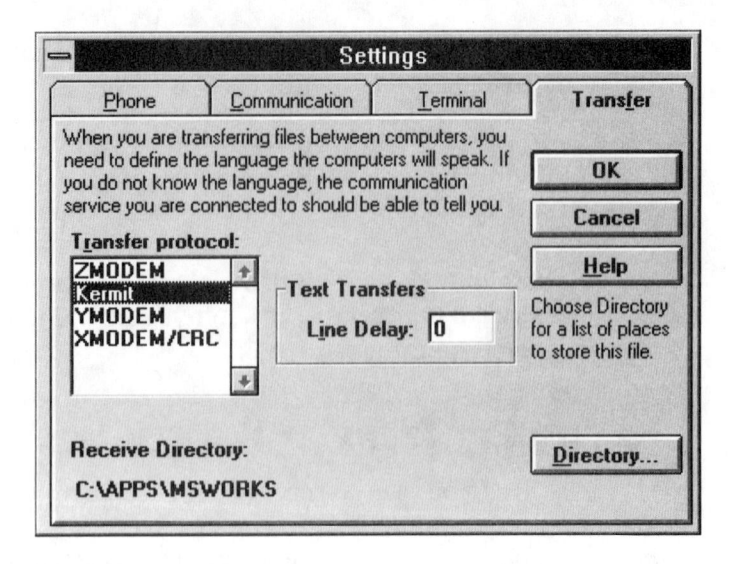

need to change this option. Leave it at the default, Kermit, if you're not sure what the other computer is using.

Text transfers If the computer you are connected to cannot accept the data your computer is sending as quickly as your computer can send it, you can have Works pause a certain amount of time after sending each line. The number you put in the Line Delay box is the number of tenths of a second you want Works to pause. The number 1 represents $1/10$ of a second, 5 represents $1/2$ a second, and so on.

The Directory button By default, Works assumes you want to receive files into your Works directory, but if there is another directory you would like incoming files to go to, click the Directory button. The Choose a Directory dialog box appears. Scroll through the directories to find the one you want incoming files to go to and click OK.

Saving Your Communications Settings

Most of the settings need to be made only once. Only a few of them have to be changed each time you begin a communications session.

Moreover, when you have the details of a particular setup ironed out, you can save your settings on disk for future use. Next time you want to call a particular person or bulletin board, all you have to do is bring up the right communications file. Communications settings are saved in files with the .WCM extension.

To save your settings:

1. Choose File ➤ Save. The Save As dialog box appears.
2. Give your file a name, preferably a name that will help you remember which information service or computer the settings are for.
3. Click OK.

Communicating with Other Computers by Modem

Once you've filed in the Settings dialog box, the next step is to start a communications session and make a connection to a remote computer. This part of the chapter explains how to

- Call up another computer
- Send and receive data messages and data files
- Creating a sign-on script to automate sign-on procedures

Calling Up Another Computer

The first step in a communications session is, obviously, to call up the remote computer you want to send data to. There are three ways to do this:

- If you've just finished working with the Settings dialog box, you can dial the telephone number you just set from the Phone tab.
- You can use the Phone ➤ Easy Connect command to call up the remote computer by filling in the Easy Connect dialog box.

- If you've saved the number you want to dial in a communications file, you can bring up the file and dial the number automatically.

Each technique is described below.

Dialing directly from the Phone menu To dial a number you just set in the Settings dialog box:

- Select Phone ➤ Dial or click the Dial button on the toolbar (the one that shows two plugs, not the one that shows a telephone).

> **Note** See "Setting the Phone Parameters" earlier in this chapter if you need to know how to enter a phone number in the Settings dialog box.

> **Note** If you choose Phone ➤ Dial without entering a phone number in the Phone Settings dialog box, the command ties you directly to your modem, not to the computer you are trying to reach. At this point you have to enter modem commands from your keyboard. For information about modem commands, consult your modem's instruction manual.

Communicating with Other Computers by Modem

The Easy Connect command for quick dialing If you want to a dial a new number, the simplest way is to use the Easy Connect command:

1. Select Phone ➤ Easy Connect or click the Easy Connect button on the Toolbar. The Easy Connect dialog box appears:

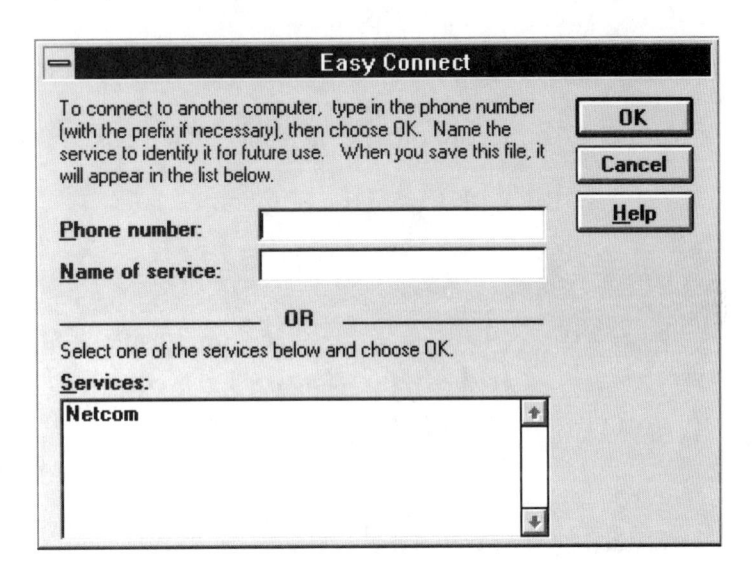

2. Enter the phone number.
3. Choose a Service from the scroll box.
4. Click OK.

Works asks if you want to connect to the other computer:

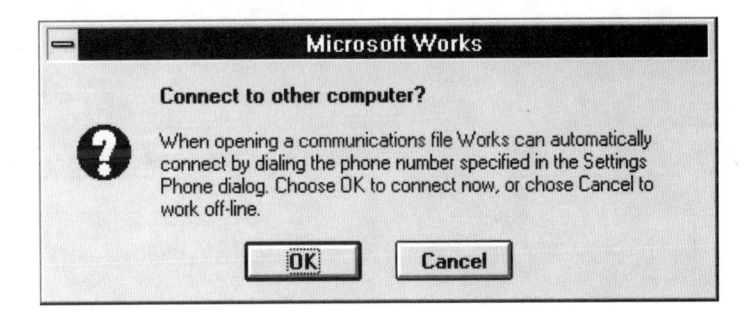

413

5. Click OK.

Dialing a number from a communications file You can open a communications file and have Works dial the number directly. To do this:

1. Select File ➤ Open.
2. Choose the communications file you want to open from the dialog box.

The Connect to other computer? dialog box appears.

3. Click OK to dial the number.

> **Note** If you open a new communications file and your modem is already set, Works will present you with the Easy Connect dialog box automatically.

Successful and Unsuccessful Connections

After you dial a number, all the settings you made in the Settings menu go into effect, including the phone number, which will be dialed. While dialing, the status line says DIAL and shows a timer, and the phone number being dialed appears in a dialog box on screen:

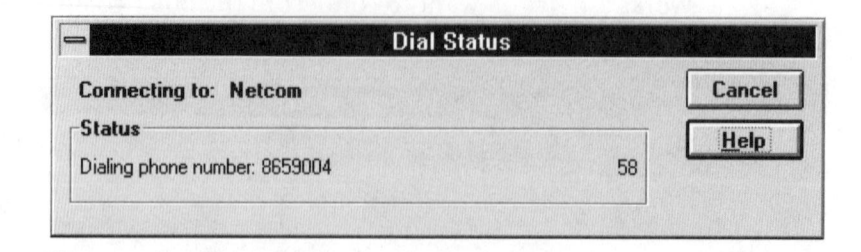

```
┌─────────────────── Dial Status ───────────────────┐
│                                                    │
│  Connecting to:  Netcom              ┌─────────┐  │
│  ┌─Status──────────────────────────┐ │ Cancel  │  │
│                                      ├─────────┤  │
│  Dialing phone number: 8659004   58  │  Help   │  │
│                                      └─────────┘  │
└────────────────────────────────────────────────────┘
```

If your modem has a speaker, you may hear the number being dialed and some high-pitched tones when the phone on the other end is picked up.

If the connection is successful... If the connection is successful, everything you type on your keyboard is sent to the remote computer. What you enter on your keyboard will appear on the remote computer exactly as you enter it.

If the connection is unsuccessful... If the connection is not successful, you will probably see the words *NO CARRIER* on screen after about 15 seconds. NO CARRIER means your modem gave up trying to make a connection. Some typical reasons for failure at this point are:

- The other phone was busy.
- The other phone/modem on the other end didn't answer.
- The modems are set at different baud rates, so they didn't recognize each other.

If the phone number you dialed is busy, the word *BUSY* will appear on the screen and you may hear a busy signal on the modem's speaker. Usually the modem will hang up and wait for a message from the remote computer to try again.

Dialing again   To dial again if you failed to make a connection the first time:

- Choose Phone ➤ Dial Again.

Sending and Receiving Data Messages

Assuming the connection proceeds without difficulty, what you do now depends entirely on what the other computer expects. If you are calling an information service, a BBS, or a mainframe computer, you usually have to sign on to the remote system by typing your name and possibly a password. In any case, once the connection is made you can send and receive data messages.

Note See "Sending and Receiving Data Files" later in this chapter if you want to send or receive whole files.

Note See "Scripts for Automating Sign-On Procedures" later in this chapter for more information about signing on.

Tip Notice the time listing in the status area of your screen. Many services charge based by the minute or hour. The time listing is there so you can keep track of the time.

Working in Terminal mode The simplest way to transmit data is directly from your keyboard. Once you are connected to the other computer, everything you type is automatically sent out to it. Conversely, letters typed on the other computer are sent to your computer and show up immediately on your screen. Sending and receiving data this way is called working in *Interactive* or *Terminal mode*. Communication sessions often begin in terminal mode, with each person typing to the other's screen.

To communicate with interactive information services and electronic mail networks, you type in commands to the host computer and it responds by sending you data. On your screen, the information looks something like that in Figure 10.7.

Capturing Messages on Screen

When the screen fills up, the text on top scrolls up and is lost, but you can save incoming data in order to work with it later. You can capture

Communicating with Other Computers by Modem

FIGURE 10.7
Incoming data from an information service

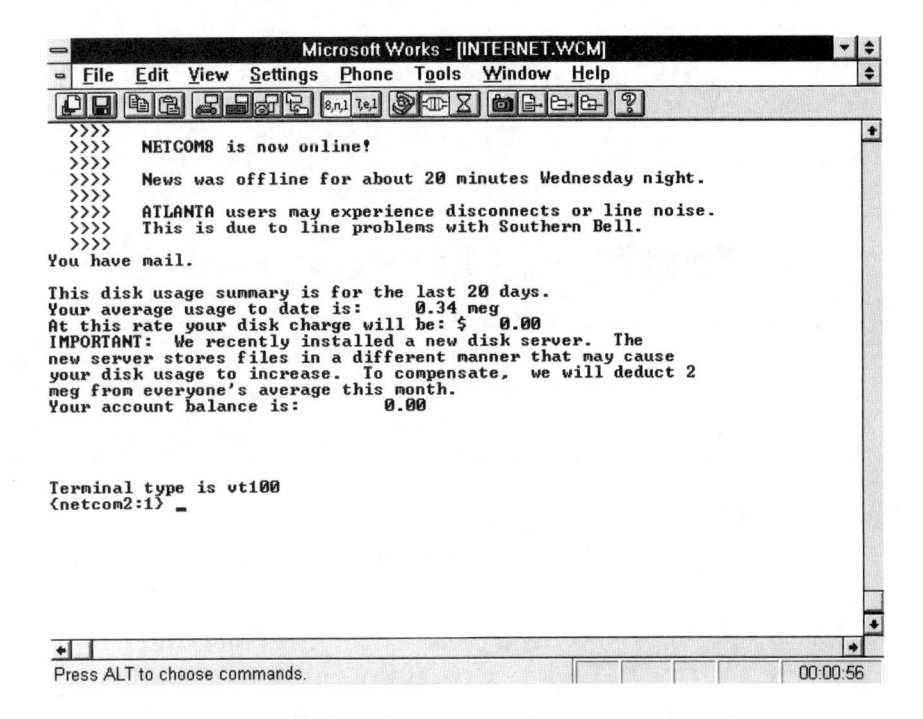

```
                  Microsoft Works - [INTERNET.WCM]
  File  Edit  View  Settings  Phone  Tools  Window  Help

>>>>
>>>>    NETCOM8 is now online!
>>>>
>>>>    News was offline for about 20 minutes Wednesday night.
>>>>
>>>>    ATLANTA users may experience disconnects or line noise.
>>>>    This is due to line problems with Southern Bell.
>>>>
You have mail.

This disk usage summary is for the last 20 days.
Your average usage to date is:     0.34 meg
At this rate your disk charge will be: $    0.00
IMPORTANT:  We recently installed a new disk server.  The
new server stores files in a different manner that may cause
your disk usage to increase.  To compensate, we will deduct 2
meg from everyone's average this month.
Your account balance is:       0.00


Terminal type is vt100
<netcom2:1> _




Press ALT to choose commands.                           00:00:56
```

incoming text at any time during a communications session and save it in a disk file.

To save incoming data on disk:

1. Choose Tools ➤ Capture Text or click the Capture Text button on the toolbar (the one directly below the Windows menu that shows a camera) when you want to start capturing text.

2. In the dialog box, enter a name for the file and press ↵.

The status area says CAPT. All text is captured, both incoming messages and the ones you type.

3. When you want to stop capturing text, choose Tools ➤ End Capture Text or click the Capture Text button again. The CAPT message disappears and the text is stored on disk.

417

> **Tip:** To keep the screen from scrolling as you receive data, press Ctrl + S. To make it scroll again, press Ctrl + Q.

Sending and Receiving Data Files

Besides sending messages by typing them on screen, you can send and receive word-processed files as well as other types of files prepared by other programs. There are two ways to send data files:

- Send the file as a binary file. This way, the file is received by the other computer in its entirety with all formatting intact. Binary files include protection schemes so that none of their data is lost during transmission over the telephone lines. To send a binary file, use the Tools ➤ Send File command.

- Send the file as an ASCII file. Most e-mail services, BBSs, and information services will only accept ASCII files. To send an ASCII file, use the Tools ➤ Send Text command.

> **Tip:** By composing your messages first on a word processor, you can send the whole file at once and keep transmission times — and transmission costs — down.

Send Text: Sending an ASCII File

Use the Send Text command on the Tools menu to send ASCII files by electronic mail services, BBSs, and information services. Files sent with the Send Text command *must* be ASCII files. An *ASCII file* is a plain-text file without control codes in it. Before you can send a file with the Send Text command, you must save it as an ASCII file with the program you created it in.

Warning Only ASCII files can be sent through most information services. To save a Works word-processing, spreadsheet, or database file as an ASCII file, open the file, choose File ➤ Save As to save it under a new name, and this time check the Text or Plain options in the Save As dialog box.

To send an ASCII file:

1. Make a connection to the other computer.
2. Choose Tools ➤ Send Text (or click the Send Text button on the toolbar, the one to the right of the Capture Text button).
3. The Send Text dialog box appears.
4. Type in the file name or select it from the File box.
5. Press ↵ to send the file.

The word *SEND* appears in the status area while the file is being sent. Meanwhile, the contents of the file appear on your screen as the file is sent so you can monitor the file transmission.

Warning Your computer has to be on-line in order to send a file. If you try to send before actually connecting to the remote computer, Works will display an error message when you choose Tools ➤ Send Text.

If letters are missing from each new line... If you notice that letters are missing from the beginning of each line on screen:

1. Stop the transmission by pressing any key.
2. Choose the Transfer tab of the Settings dialog box (see Figure 10.6).

3. Change the Line Delay setting from the 0 default to a higher number.
4. Start the transmission again.

> **Note** See "Setting the Transfer Parameters" earlier in this chapter for information about the Line Delay setting.

If all the text appears on one line... If the text being transmitted appears on a single line of your screen:

1. Wait until the transmission is complete. Your text is still being sent properly—you just can't see it.
2. Choose the Terminal tab of the Settings dialog box (see Figure 10.5).
3. Select the Add LF option.
4. Start the transmission again.

When Works has finished transmitting the file, the word *SEND* disappears from the status area.

Send File: Sending a Binary File

Data can be lost during transmission over telephone lines, particularly when long distances are involved and there is noise on the line. To keep data from being lost, computer science has devised numerous error-detection schemes and transfer protocols.

How these schemes and protocols work exactly is beyond the scope of this book. Suffice it to say that the Works communications tool lets you select among four of them—XMODEM, YMODEM, ZMODEM, and Kermit—from the Transfer tab of the Settings dialog box (see Figure 10.6). These protocols permit you to send binary files and make sure that they are received intact on the other end. A *binary file* is a file that can be read and used by a computer program. For example, a word-processing document with formatting and different fonts is a binary file.

To send a binary file, the system on the receiving computer has to be using the same error-detection protocol. In fact, unless the two computers are using the same protocol, the transfer cannot begin. Between the Kermit and XMODEM protocol, you should be able to send binary files to most other systems, since most communications programs support one or the other, or both.

To send a binary file, follow these steps:

1. Make sure you're online (connected).
2. Choose Settings ➤ Transfer. The Transfer tab of the Settings dialog box appears (see Figure 10.6).
3. Choose the protocol you want (the one the receiving system uses).

Now you must make sure the receiving computer is ready to receive an XMODEM or Kermit file. How you do this depends on the computer system, BBS, or information service to which you are connected. If you are sending the file to another PC, you may want to type a message in Terminal mode telling the operator to do what is necessary to prepare for receiving the file.

4. Select Tools ➤ Send File or click the Send Binary File button on the toolbar (the one to the right of the Send Text button).
6. Type in the file name or select it from the dialog box, and then click OK.

The transfer begins. The progress of the transfer is reported in the Send File dialog box. Errors, if any, are reported in the dialog box. If more than ten consecutive errors are detected, Works aborts the transmission.

Tip To stop a transmission at any time, press ↵.

Receive File: Receiving Binary Files

The Receive File command on the Tools menu is for receiving binary files from other PCs, BBSs, or information services that support the

XMODEM or Kermit protocol. To receive a file without error, whoever sends it to you must use one of these two protocols.

To receive a binary file:

1. Choose Settings ➤ Transfer to bring up the Transfer tab in the Settings dialog box (see Figure 10.6).
2. Select either the XMODEM or Kermit transfer protocol, depending on the protocol the other computer uses to send binary files.

Now you must tell the sending computer to get ready to send via XMODEM or Kermit. How you do this varies with the computer and program(s) involved. With some systems, you control the sending from your computer. In other cases, a person at the other end will issue the command. BBSs typically send a message such as

```
Ready to receive Y/N?
```

or

```
Press Enter to start download
```

3. Choose Tools ➤ Receive File or click the Receive Binary File button on the toolbar (the one to the right of the Send Binary File button).

The Receive File dialog box appears. This dialog box is essentially the same as the Save As dialog box. Tell Works to save the incoming data as a file:

4. Enter the file name (and path if necessary) or choose it from the dialog box. Do this quickly, because the other computer is already trying to send the file. It will wait, but usually not too long.
5. Click OK.

The transmission begins and a dialog box appears to mark its progress. Errors, if any, are reported in the dialog box. If more than ten consecutive errors are detected during transmission, Works aborts the transmission.

> **Warning** Make sure the disk you choose to store the file on has enough free space to store a large file. You can't know in advance how large the file being transmitted is. If you run out of disk space, an error message appears and the transmission is aborted.

Ending a Communications Session

Follow these simple procedures when you want to end a communications session:

1. If you are logged onto an information service, electronic mail, or BBS, follow the system's instructions for signing off.

2. Choose Phone ➤ Hang Up (or click the Dial/Hangup button on the toolbar). The OK to disconnect? dialog box appears:

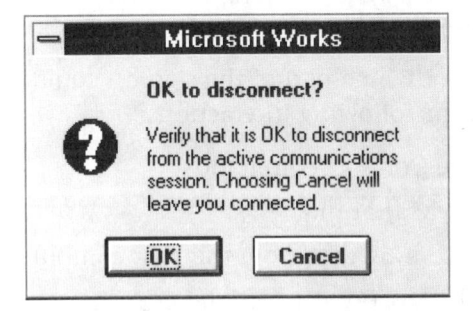

3. Choose OK.

4. Save your communications file if you have made any changes to scripts or settings that you want to use later.

Scripts for Automating Sign-On Procedures

Signing on means to enter identification information such as your name, a password, and so forth, when connecting to a remote computer system. Many systems have inconvenient sign-on procedures that have to be repeated each time you connect.

When you sign on to a system, you can have Works record the procedure in a *script* and store it in the communications file along with the other settings. Next time you sign on to the system, you can have Works do the sign-on procedure for you by playing back the script.

Before you record a sign-on script, you have to decide where to begin recording. Do you want to record all of the sign-on procedure or part of it? Should you start recording after dialing the phone number or wait until you enter some commands? How much of the procedure you record will vary from system to system. The script should only interact with stable, unchanging sections of the communications session.

The best approach is as follows:

1. Sign-on to a system several times manually until you understand the procedure.

2. Figure out which part of the sign-on could be automated. Works can record the following interactions:

    ◆ The Connect command
    ◆ Keyboard input
    ◆ Incoming data from the host computer
    ◆ The Disconnect command

Recording a Sign-On Script

As an example of how to record a sign-on script, here is how to record a script that includes the Connect command:

1. Open a new document and make all the settings from the Settings menu, including the phone number, baud rate, and so on.

2. Log on to the remote computer system once yourself to see that all the settings are correct.

Scripts for Automating Sign-On Procedures

3. Disconnect from the system.

4. Choose Tools ➤ Record Script. The Record Script dialog box appears:

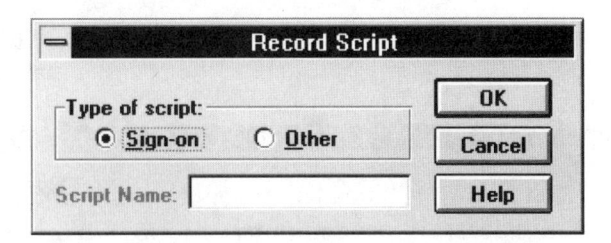

[Record Script dialog box with Type of script: Sign-on (selected) or Other, Script Name field, and OK, Cancel, Help buttons]

5. Click OK. The status line tells you

   ```
   Recording a script. Press ESC to cancel.
   ```

6. Choose Phone ➤ Dial to dial the phone (you can't click the Dial button on the toolbar).

7. Enter all the sign-on names, codes, or whatever is necessary to get to the point where your interaction with the host normally would change from session to session.

8. Choose Tools ➤ End Recording.

9. Save your script file for future use by choosing File ➤ Save and giving the file a name (unless you've already saved and named it before). The script will be saved along with all the other settings.

Playing Back a Script

To play back the script, simply follow these steps:

1. Open the communications file with the script and other communications settings from the File menu if it isn't already open.

2. Make sure your modem is connected and turned on.

3. Choose Tools ➤ Sign-on (at the bottom of the menu).

The script dials the number, makes the connection, and performs the sign-on. When it is completed, you can begin your interactive typing, file transfers, and so forth.

CHAPTER 10 Using the Communications Tool

Tip To stop playing a script at any time, press any key. You may want to do this if a script isn't working.

Computer-to-Computer Communications by Wire

Two computers need a modem to communicate only if they are some distance apart. When computers are close to one another (preferably in the same room), you can connect them directly, although doing this isn't necessary unless the computers are of dissimilar types. After all, you can transfer text and files simply by exchanging floppy disks. Similarly, if you want several PCs in the same locale to be able to share information and e-mail messages, install a local area network (LAN) instead of using Works communications tool.

Direct connection between computers is very useful for sending files between PCs and other types of computers, such as Apple Macintoshes, Apple IIs, older style CP/M computers, various laptop computers, mini-computers, and mainframes. These computers can't work with floppy disks from an IBM PC or IBM-compatible.

Warning Getting computers to talk to one another via a direct connection is problematic. It may take several tries, a great deal of knowledge, lots of wire, and a good soldering iron to pull the whole stunt off successfully.

Setting Up a Direct Connection

Unfortunately, the ins and outs of direct connections are too vast to cover in this book. In fact, entire books are devoted to this subject. To make a direct connection:

1. Connect a special cable, called a *null modem,* between the two computers in place of the modems and the telephone lines.

Null modem cables *Null modem cables* reverse certain wire pairs within the cable and are designed specifically for this purpose. Depending on the computers, the ends of the cables have different genders. The IBM PC and compatibles require a nonstandard connector (female instead of male). For many situations, particularly among microcomputers, acceptable null modem cables can be purchased at a local computer store. However, for the technically inclined and strong of heart, a cable constructed with connections as listed in Table 10.1 will usually do the job.

TABLE 10.1: Cable Setup for Computer-to-Computer Communications

Computer 1 Pin Number	Connect To	Computer 2 Pin Number
1	chassis ground	1
2	data	3
3	data	2
4	handshaking (RQS)	5
5	handshaking (CTS)	4
6	handshaking (DSR)	20
7	signal-ground	7

Another solution is to purchase an intelligent cable that figures all this out for you. Or you can use a breakout box wired to the given configuration and use a standard cable (no wire reversals) with it.

After you've made the cable connection:

2. Load Works on the PC and some other communications program on the other computer.

3. Set both computers to the same baud rate. The start of this chapter tells how to do this with Works. How you set the other computer's baud rate will vary. Use the highest baud rate available (Works' highest is 19200).

4. Get into Terminal mode on both computers. (With Works, choose Phone ➤ Dial.)

5. Type something on your keyboard and see if the corresponding characters appear on the other computer's screen.

If the characters do not appear, something is wrong with the wiring, one or both computers, the software, or the way you're using the software.

6. Type on the other keyboard. Letters should show up on the other screen.

If everything worked so far, you can try sending the files. Otherwise, don't move ahead until you've fixed whatever is wrong. If the other computer's program supports XMODEM protocol, send your files using XMODEM. Otherwise, use simple text sending and receiving commands.

If you are using XMODEM and having no success even though things work all right in Terminal mode, you may be having synchronization problems. Try telling the receiving computer to receive the file before you tell the sending computer to send. That way the receiving computer is ready for the data when it begins coming in.

Note See "Troubleshooting the Communications Program" at the end of this chapter for more advice about miscommunications.

Linking Dissimilar Machines by Modem

If you want to send text files between dissimilar machines, both of which have working modems and can successfully log on to an electronic service such as MCI Mail, use that avenue instead of trying to wire the machines together. However, if you intend to transfer lots of files between the computers, using an electronic mail service can take lots of time, even at 1200 or 2400 baud. Direct connections with Works can transfer at speeds up to 19200 baud. And if you intend to transfer binary files, most electronic mail services won't work at all.

To transmit data between two computers without having to connect them directly:

1. Have the sending computer log on to the mail service.
2. Using some communications program, have it send the text file (with no protocol) to a person who has a "mail box" on the system.
3. Have the sending computer log off the mail system.
4. Have the receiving computer log on to the mail service over the modem, receive the file, and log off.

Troubleshooting the Communications Program

Despite great strides in the field of communications, communications is still a bit of a black art. Chances are you will have at least a few problems transferring files, sending mail, or doing whatever it is you do with the Works communications tool. The fault will not necessarily lie with Works, but more likely will be caused by improper wiring, faulty modems, noisy telephone lines, incorrect log-on procedures, or incompatible software on the other end of the line.

Following are some troubleshooting tips for fixing communications problems.

Modem Problems

If you suspect that the problem is with your modem, ask yourself these questions:

- Is the modem on?
- If you are using an external modem, is it connected to the computer's serial port?

- Did you select the correct port from the Modem Setup dialog box?
- If you are using an internal-type modem, did you select the correct port assignment (COM1 or COM2) to prevent conflicts with other equipment, such as printer ports or a serial mouse? Only one device can be assigned to a port. You may have to switch to COM2 if COM1 is being used by another device.
- If you are using a Hayes-type modem, is something wrong with the wiring, the modem, or the port selection? To find out:
    1. Choose Phone ➤ Dial.
    2. Type **AT** (uppercase) and press ↵.

    The modem should respond with OK on your screen.
- Are your computer and the remote computer transmitting at different baud rates? If you and the person on the other end of the line see meaningless characters on screen when you type in terminal mode, this could be the case. Hang up, call the other person, agree on a baud rate, and try again.
- Does your Hayes modem (external type) answer the phone even when you don't want it to? If so, open the modem and set switch 5 to the down position to disable automatic answering.

Sign-On Problems

Following are some problems that typically occur during sign-ons:

- Did you type the log-on, password, and so on exactly as they are supposed to be typed? Many systems require you to use uppercase or lowercase letters.
- If you are using a script and it hangs, make sure you didn't record part of an interaction that changes from day to day, such as the date, or some news bulletin. See "Scripts for Automating Sign-On Procedures" in this chapter for more information.

File-Transfer Problems

Following are some problems that typically occur when you attempt to transfer files:

- If you are transferring files with the XMODEM protocol, be sure to start both computers (sending and receiving) at roughly the same time. If you don't, they will time out. *Timing out* occurs when two computers fail to successfully exchange data within a given time period. Typically, XMODEM programs completely abort the transmission process after a time out. Works only waits 100 seconds before aborting an XMODEM sending or receiving attempt, after which you have to begin the process again.

- If you are transferring in Send Text or Capture Text and characters at the beginning of each line get lost, increase the end-of-line delay of the sending computer. If the sending computer is the PC running Works, you can change the end-of-line delay from the Transfer tab of the Settings dialog box.

- If you need to perform lots of file conversions between the Apple Macintosh and your PC, consider using hardware/software products devised specifically for that purpose. One software program you might try is Mac-in-DOS from Pacific Micro.

File-Compatibility Problems

When you exchange files with people who don't use Works, there are a few things to keep in mind. Works uses its own proprietary codes to store formatting information such as paragraph settings, fonts, type sizes, special characters, headers, footers, and so on.

For another program to use a Works file, or for Works to use another program's files, some common format must be used. In most cases, this is the ASCII or Text format, but Works can use Microsoft Word files and Lotus 1-2-3 files (with certain limitations) directly. In any case, be sure to coordinate the data format of your file transfers with the other party involved in your communications effort before sending lots of files. Transmit a short text file first to test for compatibility, and then transmit the others.

CHAPTER 10 Using the Communications Tool

> **Note** See Chapter 12 for more information about integrating communications files into other types of Works documents.

By now you should have a thorough understanding of the Works communications tool. Turn to Chapter 11 to learn how to create documents automatically with the Wizards and templates.

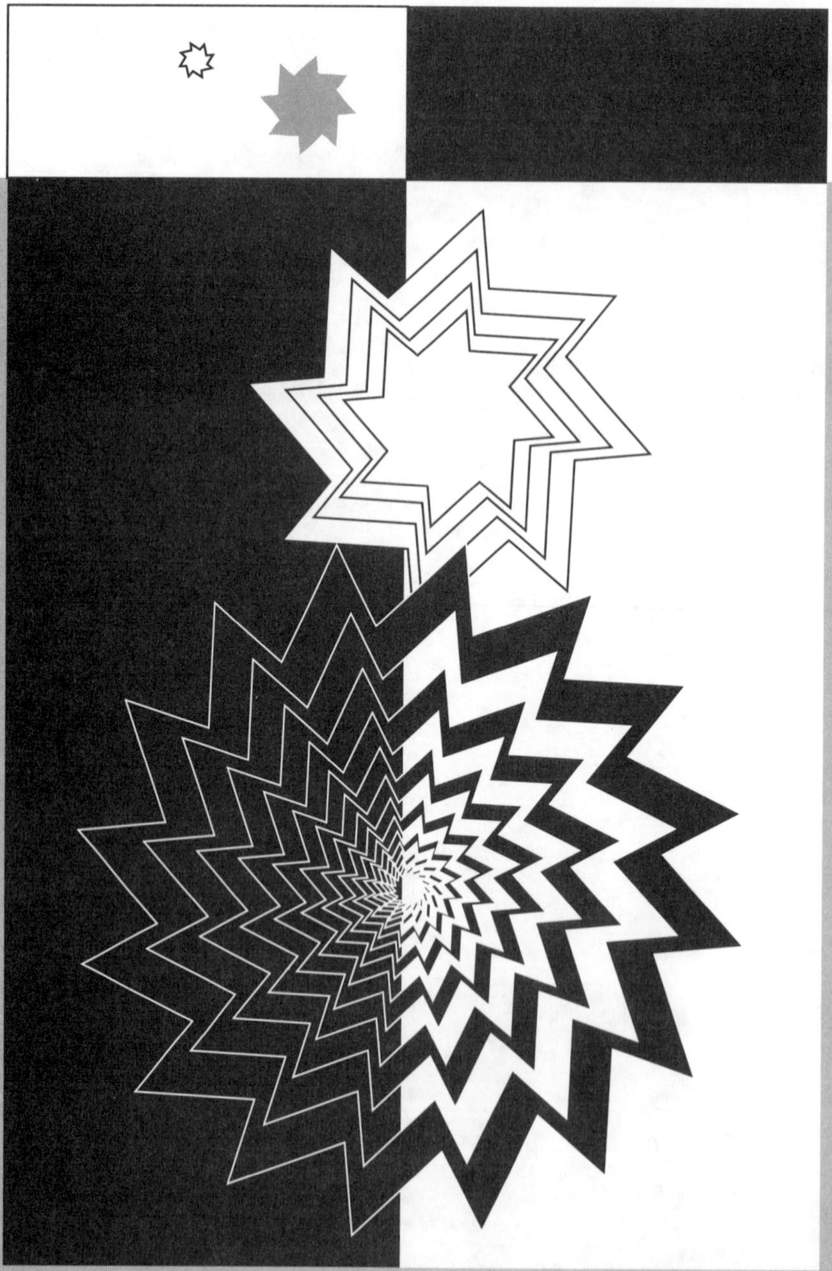

CHAPTER 11

Creating Documemts Automatically

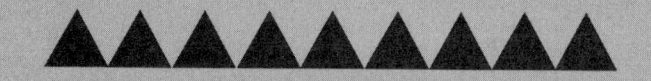

Fast Track

WorkWizards can help you create complex documents. 438

There are twelve WorksWizards altogether. Each one takes you step-by-step through the creation of a certain kind of document. You can create business contracts, inventories, form letters, letterheads, and databases, among other types of documents.

To create a document using a WorksWizard, 438

select File ➤ WorksWizards or click the Use a WorksWizard button in the Startup dialog box and choose a wizard from the list. A wizard will appear on screen. Follow the instructions, answer the questions, and click Next whenever you are done to work your way through the creation of a Wizard. When you are done you can save it as a normal document and print it as you wish.

Templates provide you with ready-made complex document formats.   **443**

There are 36 wizards in all grouped into three categories—Business documents, Personal documents, and Education documents. By using templates, you can create professional-looking documents.

To create a document using a template,   **443**

select File ➤ Templates or click the Use a Template button on the Startup dialog box. Next, choose a template group, a category, and a template from the list. Read the cue card in the template for an explanation of the template you are using. Replace the generic information in the template with text of your own. When you're done, save the template.

IN ITS NEVER-ENDING QUEST TO make Works easier for you to use, Microsoft has included two automated approaches to document making, *wizards* and *templates*:

- Wizards are pre-programmed sequences that interview you about what type of document you want to make and then take you through the process step-by-step. Wizards are supposed to make creating complex documents easier and possibly teach you something along the way.
- Templates are model documents that come with a certain amount of structure and formatting built-in. With a template that's similar to the kind of document you want, you can just enter your own information and come out with a finished product.

This chapter explains how to use templates and wizards to create professional-looking documents.

WorksWizards for Creating Complex Documents

To begin making a document with the help of a wizard, you can either:

- Select File ➤ WorksWizards or
- Click the Use A WorksWizard button on the Startup dialog box, as shown Figure 11.1.

The Choose a WorksWizard list appears. You can choose from twelve wizards. Take a moment to see the kinds of wizards that are available.

WorksWizards for Creating Complex Documents

FIGURE 11.1

The Startup dialog box with Use A WorksWizard selected

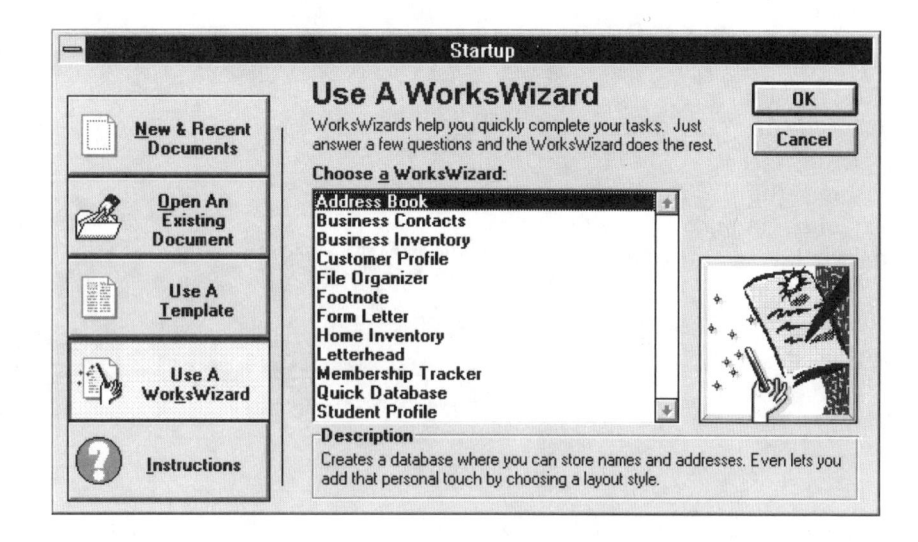

Tip To see what each Wizard does, highlight each one and read the brief description that appears in the Description box.

Creating a Form Letter

To see how Wizards work, let's make a form letter. We'll use the names in the Phonebk database you created in Chapter 9. If you didn't create this database, use one of your own. To create a form letter:

1. Select Form Letter from the Choose a WorksWizard scroll box.
2. Click OK. The Form Letter WorksWizard begins, as shown in Figure 11.2.
3. Read the introduction and click Next.

Works asks if you have a database to supply the addresses for the form letter. You do, so you can click Next.

4. Click Next to go to the next screen.

FIGURE 11.2

The Form Letter WorksWizard opening screen. Just read the explanations and answer the questions. Click Next to go to the next screen.

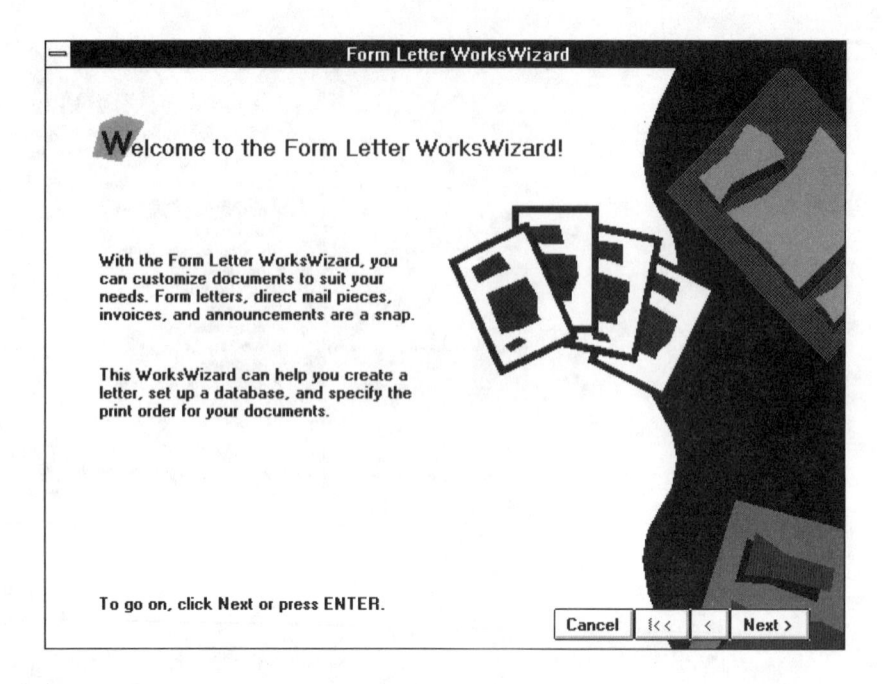

Works asks if you have a letter already prepared. You haven't written a letter yet, but that needn't stop you from proceeding. When you click No, Works will generate a letter for you.

5. Click No.

Now you have to tell Works where to find the database you want to get the addresses from. A list of databases appears.

6. What you do next depends on whether your database—phonebk.wdb in our case—is listed:

- If the database is listed, click on it.
- If the database is not listed, click Search, type in the name of your database (**phonebk**), and click Search again.

7. When the Wizard finds your database, click Open.

8. Read the explanation and click Next.

WorksWizards for Creating Complex Documents

A Form Letter dialog box appears with a list of fields from the database. Below the list of fields is a generic form letter, as in Figure 11.3.

9. Edit all the generic text (such as "Your Name"), replacing it with specific information.

Entering the fields in the letter Now it's time to enter the database fields in the letter. Notice in the top of the screen that each field has a letter beside it. In Figure 11.3, the letter *A* appears beside the First Name field. To enter this field in the form letter, therefore, you would go to a place in the letter where you want first names to appear and press Ctrl+A.

10. Enter the database fields in the letter. For example, replace the text "Name Field(s)" with the First Name field by pressing Ctrl+A. Then enter a space and insert the Last Name field by pressing Ctrl+B.

11. Delete any remaining generic text.

FIGURE 11.3
Customize your form letter by inserting fields from the database and editing the text.

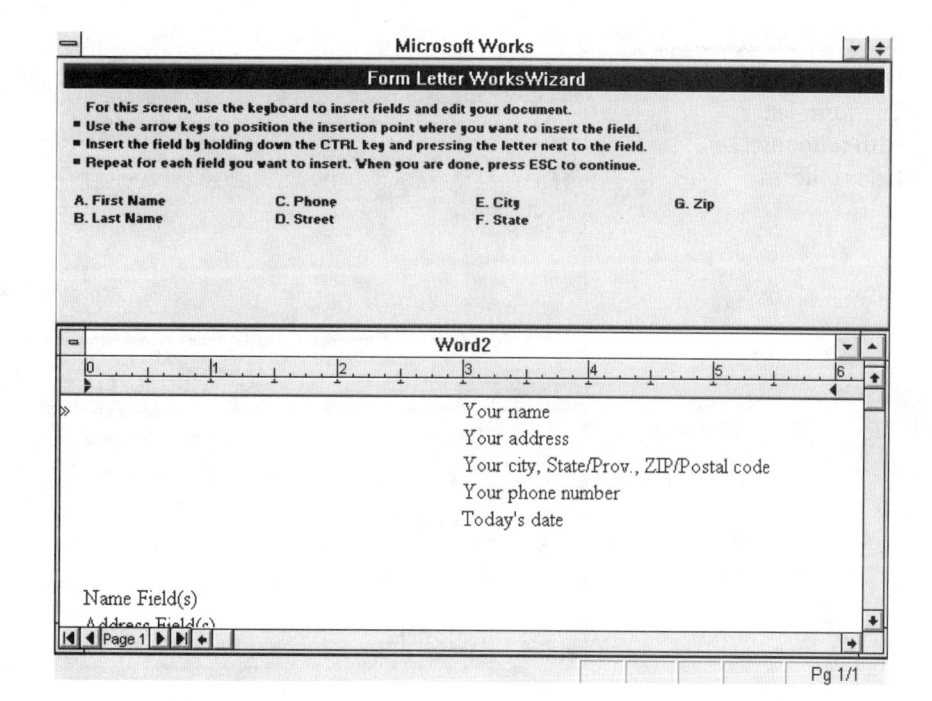

441

| CHAPTER 11 | Creating Documents Automatically |

Your form letter should look something like Figure 11.4.

12. Type the main body of the letter.
13. Press Esc when the letter is complete.

When Works asks you if you want to send letters to all or some of the people in the database:

14. Click Some and then click Next.
15. Fill out the query, select Query2 (preview it first if you want), and then click Next.
16. Select No sort, thanks, and then click Next.
17. Click Done.
18. Save your document under a name you will recognize. Form letter documents can be quite long if your database was a large one.

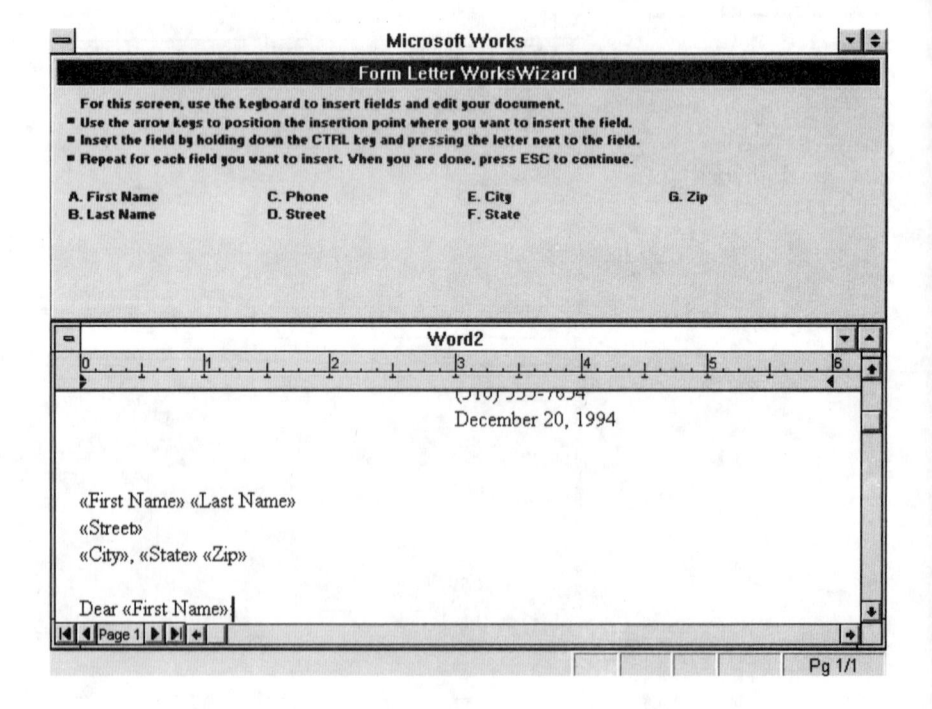

FIGURE 11.4
The form letter with database fields entered

442

Printing the Form Letter

To print your form letter, start off the usual way:

1. Click the Print button on the toolbar. The Choose Database dialog box appears:

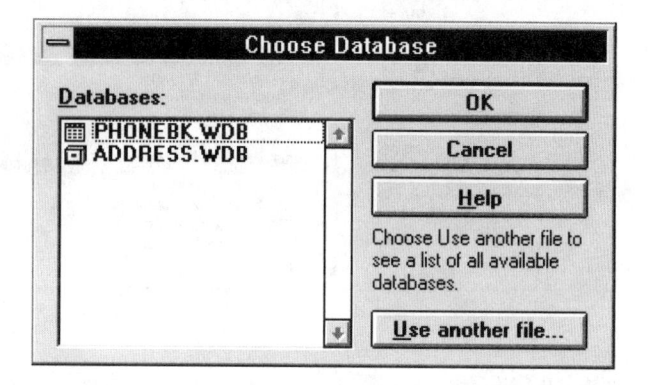

2. Select the database you want to print and click OK.

The entire run of letters (in our case, five) will print, each one using a different record from the database.

Templates for Using Complex Document Formats

To make a document with the help of a template, you can either

- Select File ➤ Templates or
- Click the Use A WorksWizard button in the Startup dialog box, as shown Figure 11.5.

There are 36 templates in all. They are arranged first by groups and then by categories. There are three groups of templates:

- AutoStart Business
- AutoStart Personal
- AutoStart Education

FIGURE 11.5
The Startup dialog box with Use a Template selected

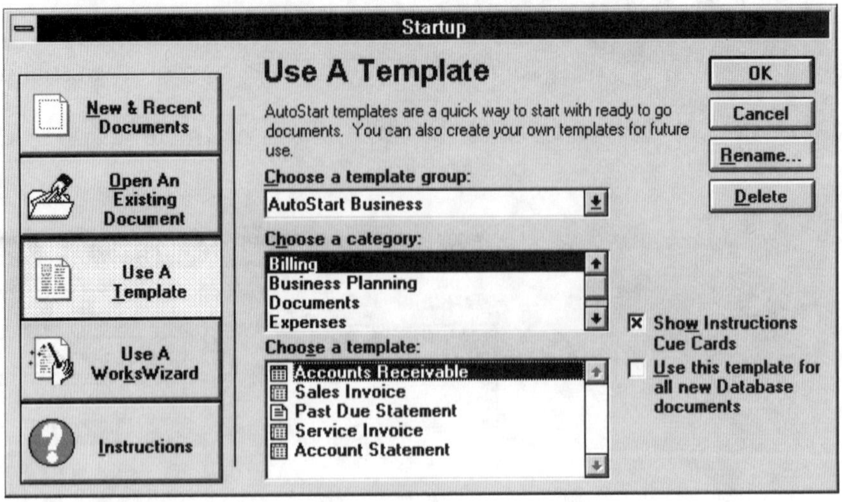

The following list shows the template groups and the categories that fall under each one.

AutoStart Business

Billing

Business Planning

Documents

Expenses

Inventory

Management

Sales

AutoStart Personal

Addresses

Documents

Household Management

Personal Finances

Templates for Using Complex Document Formats

AutoStart Education

Classroom Management

Productivity

Testing

> **Tip** You can also create your own templates and save them in the Custom group. However, before you create a template of your own, see if you can find one that will work for you.

Creating a Sales Invoice

To see how templates work, let's create a sales invoice. The Sales Invoice template is located in the Billing category of the AutoStart Business template group.

1. Select AutoStart Business in the Choose a template group scroll box.
2. Select Billing in the Choose a category scroll box.
3. Select Sales Invoice in the Choose a template scroll box.

Your screen should look like Figure 11.5.

4. Click OK. Works opens a new document based on the Sales Invoice template, as in Figure 11.6.

Cue Cards Notice the Cue Cards box on the right side of the screen. Cue cards explain how templates work and give you advice on how to use them. Read the cue cards whenever you open a new template. If you don't need the advice of the cue cards, click the Close button in the lower-right corner of the screen to remove the Cue Cards box.

5. Read the instructions on the cue card and drag it out of the way or click Close to remove it altogether.

CHAPTER 11 Creating Documents Automatically

FIGURE 11.6
The Sales Invoice template

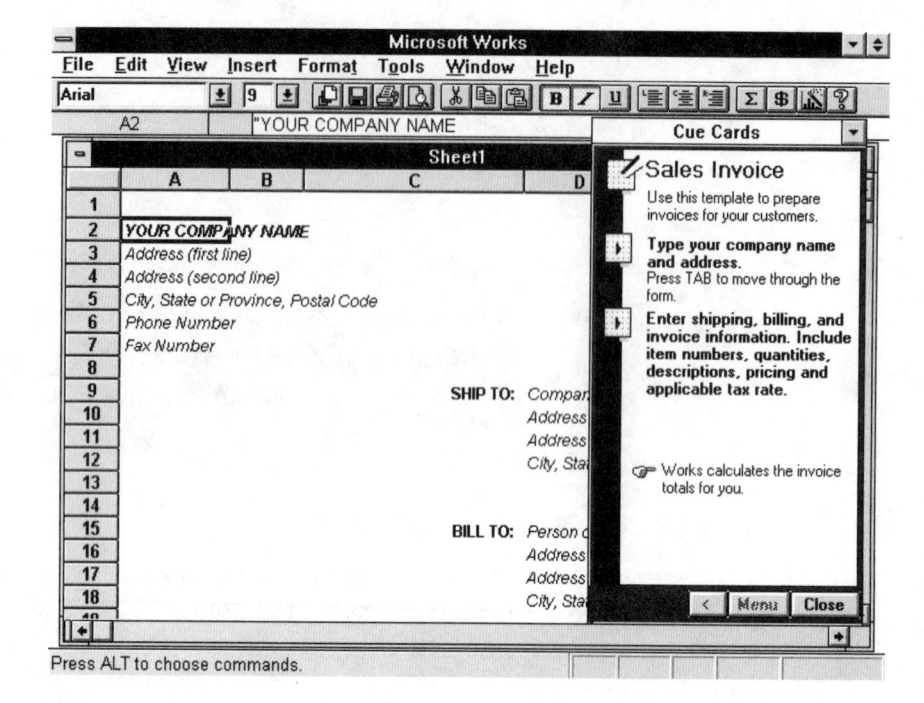

6. Replace the generic company name and address information with your own address.

7. Enter real addresses next to SHIP TO and BILL TO.

8. Fill out the remainder of the invoice form, leaving any parts blank as necessary.

As you enter quantities, purchase items, and prices, the totals are calculated automatically. This template includes formulas to calculate totals.

9. If you need to charge sales tax, enter a percentage in cell E47 to calculate it as well.

10. Enter any shipping and handling amounts and make further adjustments as necessary to come up with a grand total.

446

As you can see, the template is nothing you could not have created yourself with a little time and effort, but forms such as invoices are so common that there's no need for you to create your own when there's a perfectly useful Works template to use instead.

Printing the Sales Invoice

When you are done entering the information for your invoice, save and then print it as you would any document.

Experiment with the other templates to see if there are others you might find useful.

This chapter gave you a preview of how the different Works tools can be used together. Chapter 12 explains how to use the various tools in Works to create complex, multifaceted documents.

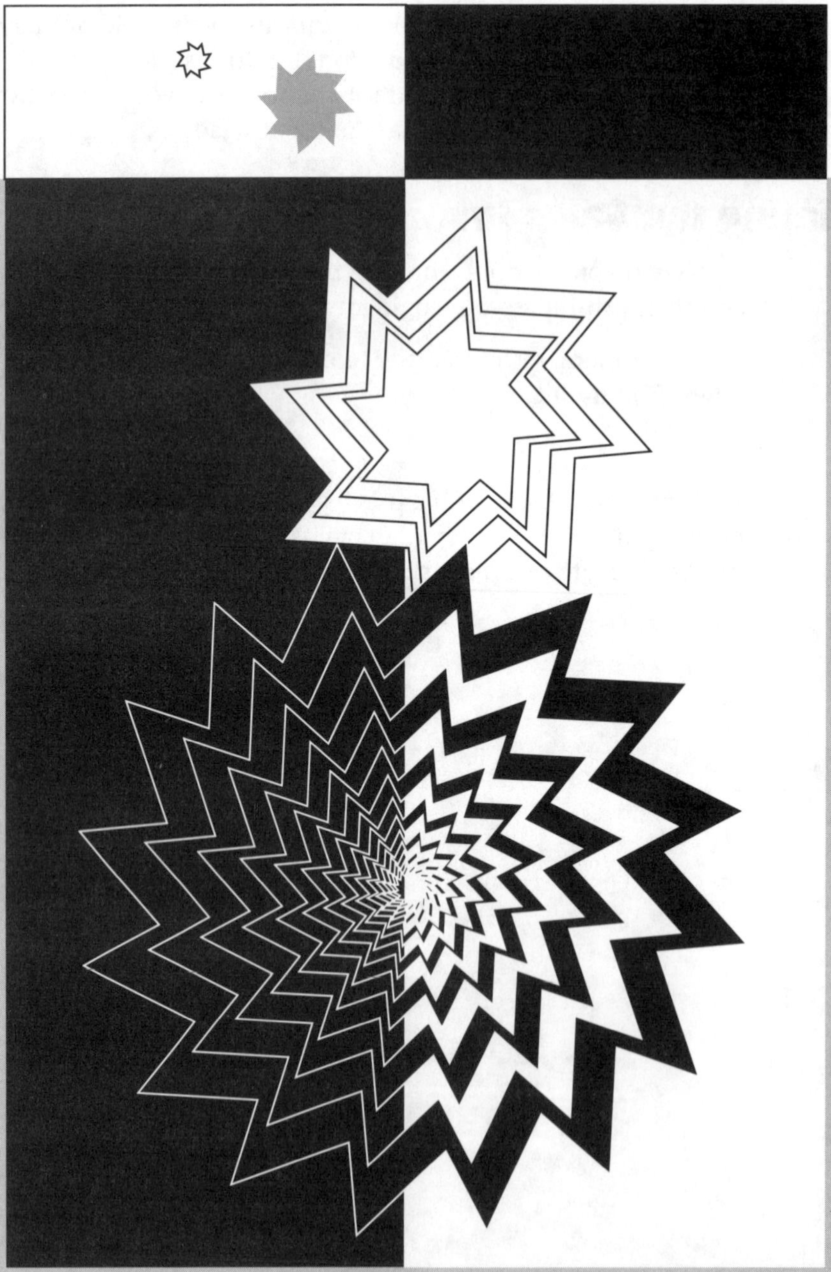

CHAPTER 12

Putting It All Together

Fast Track

To copy from one document to another,   452

open both documents, select what you want to copy, and choose Edit ➤ Copy. Switch to the other document, place the cursor, and choose Edit ➤ Paste.

To bring spreadsheet and database information into a word-processing document,   459

open the word-processing document and then open the database or spreadsheet window (in List view), select the cells you want to copy, and choose Edit ➤ Copy. Switch to the word processor document, position the cursor where you want the data to go, and choose Edit ➤ Paste.

To copy from the word processor to a database or spreadsheet   460

open both documents, select the text area you want to copy, and choose Edit ➤ Copy. Move to the spreadsheet or database document, place the cursor where you want to insert the data, and choose Edit ➤ Paste.

To insert charts in a word-processing document,   461

open the spreadsheet and word-processing documents, move to the word-processing document and position the cursor where you want the chart to go. Choose Insert ➤ Chart, choose the spreadsheet in the dialog box, and select the chart.

To insert database reports in a word-processing document,   **464**

> open the database file, select View ➤ Report, and select the report you want to use. Next, select Edit ➤ Copy Report Output, switch back to the word-processing document, position the cursor, and choose Edit ➤ Paste.

To print envelopes,   **471**

> create a new word-processing document and select Tools ➤ Envelopes and Labels. Type addresses in the two address boxes (or click Fields and select a database to print envelopes for a form letter), and click Create Envelope. Feed in your envelope. Select File ➤ Print and click OK.

To copy data between a spreadsheet and database,   **472**

> open both documents. From the source file, select the area to be copied and choose Edit ➤ Copy. Move to the cell in the destination file where you want the copied data to begin and choose Edit ➤ Paste.

ONCE YOU'VE CREATED A DOCUMENT with one of Works' four tools, you can combine it with documents created with the other tools. In this way, you can create a great variety of documents that couldn't be created with just one of the tools alone. Each tool—word processor, spreadsheet, database, and communications—can be used individually for what it does best, and then you can merge the resulting documents together by using Works' built-in integration ability.

Earlier chapters in this book explained how to copy data between documents of a single type, such as from one word-processing document to another. As you have probably gathered by now, the procedures for copying a document in each tool are the same:

1. Open both documents.
2. Highlight the section you want to copy and choose Edit ➤ Copy.
3. Switch to the window of the destination document, place the cursor where you want the copy to go, and choose Edit ➤ Paste.

That's all there is to it. Works figures out the rest. Though the techniques for copying text between documents of different types are a little more complex, the principle is the same. Copying documents from tool to tool saves time and keeps you from having to reenter data or cut and paste paper.

Note To move (rather than copy) data between documents, use Edit ➤ Cut instead of Edit ➤ Copy. Cutting deletes the original data.

When you need to copy material between tools, the word processor tool is the central player in Works. In the business world, people typically want to include charts, data, and spreadsheet information in finished products such as annual reports, scientific papers, and so forth. Thus, the written word is typically the "wrapper" that pulls all the data together.

This chapter focuses on the word processing tool, although there are sections pertaining to copying data between the other tools as well. This chapter explains how to

- ◆ Integrate communications documents into the word processor
- ◆ Include spreadsheet and database information in a word-processed document
- ◆ Place charts in a word-processed document
- ◆ Create forms and form letters
- ◆ Create and print mailing labels
- ◆ Print envelopes
- ◆ Copy data between a spreadsheet and database

Tip To learn about sharing Works files with programs other than Works, see Appendix B.

Using the techniques described in this chapter, you could pull together a complex, professional-looking report with formatted text, spreadsheet charts, a database report, and portions of a spreadsheet, drawings, clip art, and even data downloaded over a modem. Figure 12.1 shows a document incorporating material from several different Works modules.

Then, using a name and address list stored in a database, you could tell Works to print a personalized copy of the report for each person on the list. As a final step, you could use the same database to print the mailing labels or envelopes for each person. Unfortunately, Works won't lick the envelopes for you, but what do you want for less than $100?

CHAPTER 12 — Putting It All Together

FIGURE 12.1
You can combine portions of Works documents into a single integrated product like this sample page.

Product Announcement for Microsoft Works for Windows

Efficient Chips
100 West Goshen Lane
Walla Walla, Washington 98238

Dear Mr. Freud,

   Microsoft Inc. announced today its latest integrated productivity tool for the IBM PC and compatibles, Microsoft Works. Microsoft Works is an integrated product designed to run on computers that run Microsoft Windows. The key selling points of this program are ease of learning and immediate business productivity.

   Microsoft Works is a single program with word processing, spreadsheet, database, charting, and drawing built in. The word processor is quite capable, and is similar to Microsoft Word for Windows. Here are some of its features:

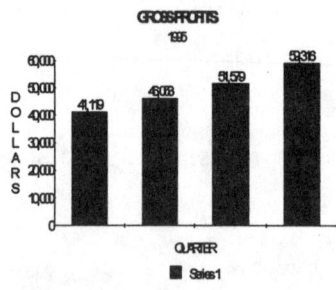

================	=====Givens===	======
EMPLOYEES	Number	Salaries	1st Grth
STORE MANAGER	1	2,500	2nd Grth
FLOOR MANAGER	1	2,000	3rd Grth
TAILOR	1	1,600	4th Grth
SALES PERSON	4	1,200	Returns
			COS
TOTAL SALARIES		10,900	P/R Tax
			Fringe
			Post/Fgt
			Exc.Tax

Feature   *Notes*

Document size   Unlimited
Undo   Yes, from menu
Character formatting   Bold, underline, italic, strikethrough
Fonts   Any Windows fonts
Alignment   Right, left, center, justified
Paragraph formats   Each paragraph has its own

Of course there are many other useful features included in the Works word processor that are worth your consideration as you will see once you try out the evaluation copy of the program enclosed. Please let us know if you have any questions.

Sincerely,

Harvey Fledgebog

Including Material from the Other Tools in Word-Processed Documents

Most of the "integrating" of material from the four tools is done on the word processor. From the word processor you can copy data from all the other tools, and you can also create four other types of documents—forms, form letters, mailing labels, and envelopes. Let's look at these capabilities one at a time from the point of view of the word processor.

You can place the following types of information in a word-processed document:

- Text received by modem
- Text and values from a spreadsheet and database
- Spreadsheet charts
- Database reports
- Database records for use in printing form letters, mailing labels, forms, and envelopes

This part of the chapter explains how to place and manipulate this information with the word processor tool.

Bringing In Files by Modem

As you know, files created in the word processor, spreadsheet, and database tools can be sent to other computers with the communications tool. In addition, files you receive by communications link can be pulled into the word processor, modified, and used in various ways.

For example, you can include a copy of a memo received by electronic mail in a letter you are drafting in response to that memo. As another example, you could include a list or table of numbers (with columns separated by tabs) in a Works spreadsheet or database document.

CHAPTER 12 — Putting It All Together

As you know, there are two ways to receive text files with the communications program:

- **Captured text.** You can "capture" the text on screen by using the Tools ➤ Capture Text command or by clicking the Capture Text button on the toolbar. The only way to use electronic mail, stock quotes, and other wire-service information is to capture it, as you cannot receive this information in files.

- **Complete files.** You can import entire files by modem with the Tools ➤ Receive File command. Receiving files this way is preferable, since the files are checked for transmission errors and come complete with their formats intact.

> **Note** See "Sending and Receiving Data Messages" and "Sending and Receiving Data Files" in Chapter 10 to review how to capture text on screen and how to import whole files by modem.

Types of word-processed files Works can use When you receive an entire file, it must be one of the following types in order for the Works word processor to make use of its margins, alignments, fonts, and other formats:

- Microsoft Word
- Windows Write
- WordPerfect

Works can also use the following plain-text file types:

- ASCII
- ANSI

Including Material from the Other Tools in Word-Processed Documents

> **Note** See Appendix B for details about file conversions.

For the purposes of this chapter, let's assume that the file is compatible with and can be opened by the Works word processor. To bring a file received by modem into the word processor:

1. Choose File ➤ Open Existing File. The Open dialog box appears.

The file you want to open will not appear in the File Name list box unless the file has an extension that begins with a *W*, such as FRED.WPS.

2. To display the file you want to import in the File Name list box, use one of these techniques:

    ◆ Type the name at the top of the box if you know its name and press ↵.
    ◆ If you don't know the name, type *.* and press ↵. All files in the current directory will be listed and your screen will look something like Figure 12.2. Select the file by highlighting it and pressing ↵.

FIGURE 12.2
The Open dialog box with all files showing

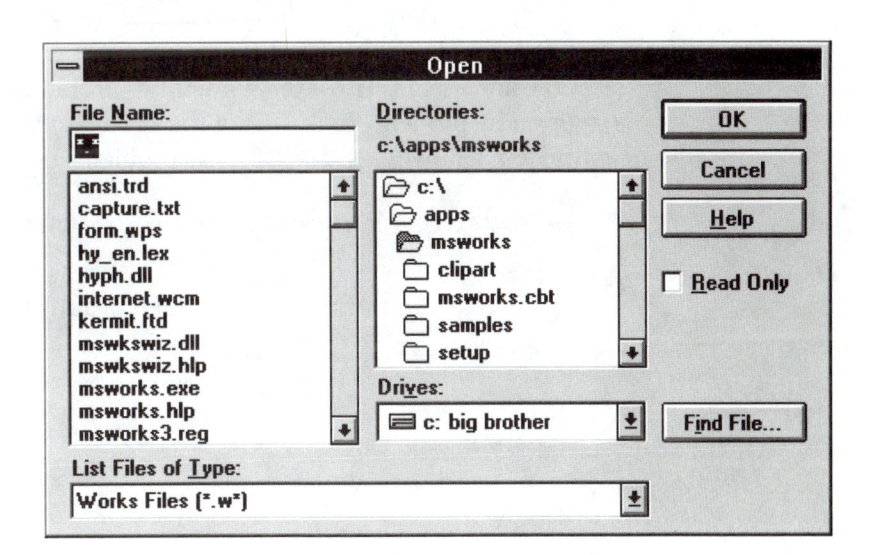

457

Works can tell from the file extension that the file is not a legitimate Works file, so it either converts the file directly or asks you what tool you want to bring the file into:

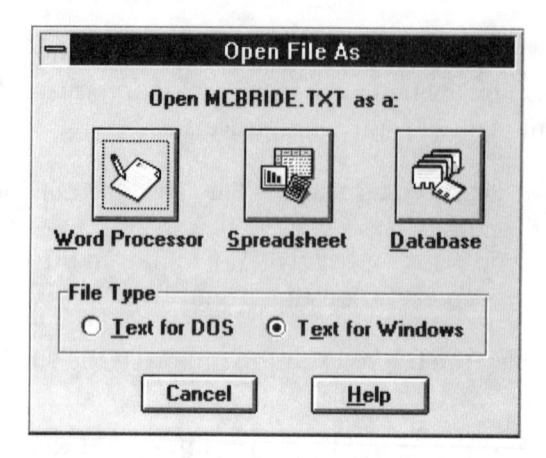

3. In the Open File dialog box, choose either the Text for DOS or Text for Windows. If the file was created with a DOS program, choose DOS; if by a Windows program, choose Windows. See Appendix B for further information.

4. Click on the Word Processor button.

Works opens the new file. At this point you can edit it or do whatever you want with it. However, sometimes problems occur when files are imported by modem. Try opening the file again using the other Text option (in Step 3 above) if either of these problems occur:

- Incorrect word-wrapping or incorrect margins, which may be caused by extra paragraph marks in the file
- Greek letters or other strange but beautiful symbols

Including Material from the Other Tools in Word-Processed Documents

Spreadsheets, Databases, and the Word Processor

You will often want to copy material from a spreadsheet or database and incorporate it in a word-processing document. Nothing bolsters an argument better than facts and figures. At times you will want to import text from a word-processed document into a spreadsheet or database as well. How to do both is explained here.

Bringing Spreadsheet and Database Information into the Word Processor

Getting a section of a spreadsheet or a database to appear in a word-processing document is quite simple. All you have to do is follow the normal rules for copying data between documents.

To import part of a spreadsheet or database to a word-processing document:

1. Open the *source* document—the spreadsheet or database where the material will be copied from.
2. Open the *destination* document—the word-processed document that will receive the new material.
3. Open the database or spreadsheet window and select the cells you want to copy. You should be in List view if you are copying from a database.
4. Choose Edit ➤ Copy.
5. Switch to the word processor document and place the cursor where you want the data to be inserted.
6. Choose Edit ➤ Paste.

Works makes a copy of the data and drops it in the document.

How the word processor accommodates new material When you import spreadsheet and database information in a word-processed document, Works makes the following allowances for the new data:

- Works places tabs between the cells in each row or record. Depending on the page layout and tab settings in your document, you may have to alter the tab settings to get the columns lined up properly.

- Works wraps the last few rows of the database or spreadsheet to the next line if the number of cells you inserted is too wide to fit inside the margins of the document. To remedy this problem, select the whole table and choose a smaller font size, or else decrease the left and right page margins. If these techniques don't work, you'll have to decrease the number of cells you want to copy.

> **Note** See "Aligning Text on the Margins" and "Changing Fonts and Type Sizes" in Chapter 4 if you need help making the spreadsheet or database fit on the page.

Copying from the Word Processor to the Database or Spreadsheet

Copying text from a word-processing document to a spreadsheet or database is a little more complicated. When you make the copy, Works expects the text file to have tab marks between columns and a paragraph mark at the end of each line of data. Before copying the text, use the View ➤ All Characters command to make sure that the tab and paragraph marks are there. Each tab mark tells Works to move one cell to the right before entering the next cell's data.

> **Note** On a word-processed document with the hidden characters displayed, → is a tab mark and ¶ is a paragraph mark.

Including Material from the Other Tools in Word-Processed Documents

To copy data from a spreadsheet or database to a word-processed document:

1. Open both documents.
2. Select the text area from which you want to copy.
3. Choose Edit ➤ Copy.
4. Go to the spreadsheet or database document.
5. Place the cursor where you want to insert the data. You can also select a range and have works fill in the range with the copy. This is a good way to prevent spreadsheet or database cells from being overwritten.
6. Choose Edit ➤ Paste.

Warning Make sure that the selected text isn't larger than the space you have allotted for it in the database or spreadsheet. Beginning at the highlighted cell, Works copies the text to the right and down. Cells that get in the way are overwritten.

Inserting Charts in a Word-Processing Document

Works can insert your charts into a word-processing document. When you print the document, the chart will automatically be inserted at a predetermined spot on the page. You can scale the chart so that it prints at a specific size.

To insert a chart in a word-processing document:

1. Open the word-processing document and the spreadsheet to which the chart is attached.
2. In the word-processing document, position the cursor where you want the chart to be inserted.

3. Choose Insert ➤ Chart. The Insert Chart dialog box appears, as in Figure 12.3.

4. From the dialog box, choose the spreadsheet. A list of charts associated with the chosen spreadsheet pops up in the other list box.

5. Select the chart. Works inserts the chart and pushes text down to make room for it, as shown in Figure 12.4.

FIGURE 12.3
Choosing a Chart to insert in a word-processing document

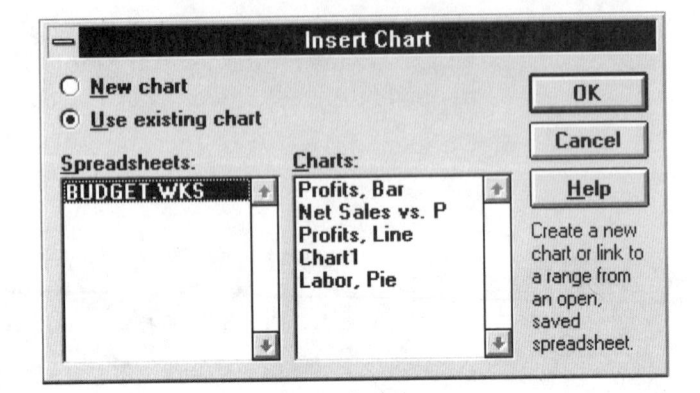

> **Note** If you insert a chart that is too wide to fit in the margins, Works resizes the object to make it fit. Objects that won't fit at the bottom of a page are bumped to the top of next page.

Repositioning the chart To reposition a chart, copy or move it as if it were text. Just click on it to select it, and use the Cut and Paste command.

Changing the size of the chart Once the chart is inserted, you can change its size:

1. Click on the chart to select it.
2. There are two ways to resize it:
    ◆ Drag one of the handles on the corners or sides.

Including Material from the Other Tools in Word-Processed Documents

FIGURE 12.4
The chart inserted in the word-processing document

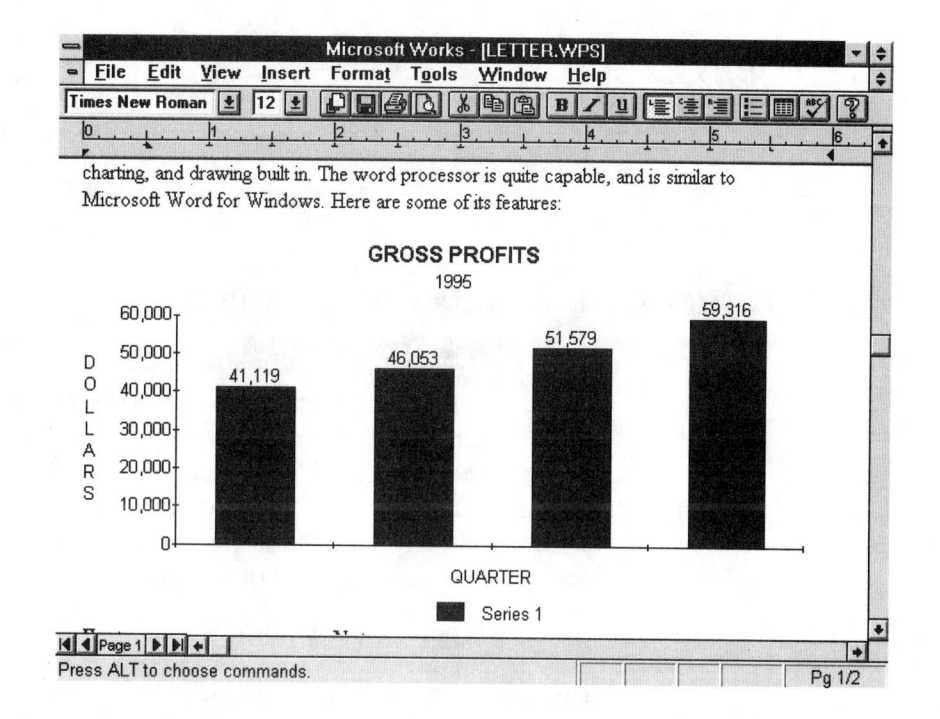

◆ Select Format ➤ Picture/Object. A dialog box appears with size settings in it. Enter Size and Scaling values and click OK.

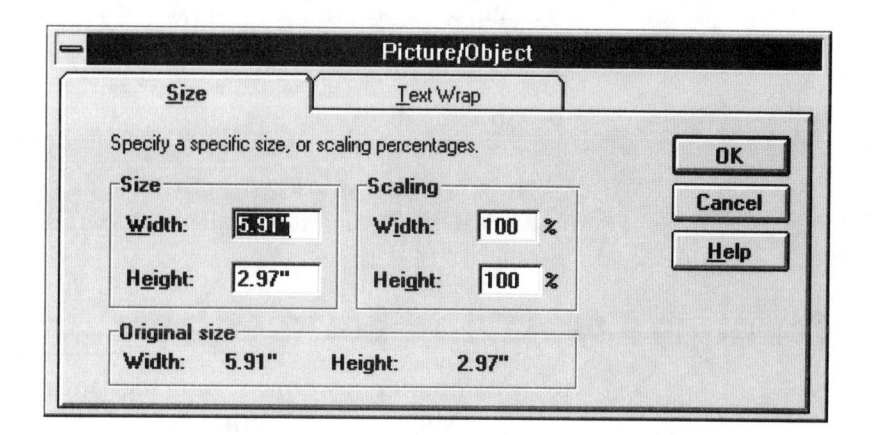

> **Tip** To place a border around a chart, click on the chart in the word processor, choose Format ➤ Border, and set the border type.

Inserting a Database Report in a Word-Processing Document

You can copy a database report to the word processor, to the spreadsheet, or to other Windows applications. The Works database command for making copies is Edit ➤ Copy Report Output. With this command, the entire report is copied to the Clipboard including the Intr and Summ rows—that is, titles, subtotals, and totals. Obviously, this is just the kind of data you want to use for preparing reports or making charts to display values.

To copy a report into a word-processed document:

1. Choose File ➤ Open Existing File to open the database file.
2. Select View ➤ Report and then select the report you want to make the copy from.
3. Select Edit ➤ Copy Report Output.
4. Switch back to the word-processing document.
5. Position the cursor where you want the report to go.
6. Choose Edit ➤ Paste.

The report data is inserted in the document as formatted text. Now you must edit it or reformat it to make the report fit nicely in your document.

Creating Forms and Form Letters

By combining word-processing files and information from a database, you can create forms and form letters. Forms are documents such as invoices, packing slips, and order forms. You can either design the form yourself or use pre-printed forms from a computer supply or stationery store. A close cousin to forms is the ubiquitous form letter, a computer-generated letter with a "personal" touch. Typically, the database used to create the form letter will be a name and address list, though it could include other kinds of data as well, such as credit histories, students' grades, or scientific or other numerical information.

> **Note** See "Creating a Form Letter" in Chapter 11 to learn how you can make a quick form letter with the WorksWizard feature.

The general steps for creating forms and form letters are:

1. Create a word-processing file with the basic text you want to include.
2. Using the Insert ➤ Database Field command, insert a placeholder into the file wherever information from the database is to appear. A *placeholder* is the name of the field in the database with the information you want inserted into the document.
3. Select File ➤ Print command and then select Print merge.

Works inserts the database information in the text of the letter. One printed letter or form is generated for each (nonhidden) record in the database.

Creating the Letter and Entering the Fields

Step-by-step, here is how to create a form or form letter and print it:

1. Create or open the database file that holds the information you want Works to insert.
2. Create the text file that you want printed, but leave out the words or numbers that will change with each copy of the "personalized" letter.
3. Move to each location in the letter where you want Works to insert data from a field in the database and choose Insert ➤ Database Field. A dialog box appears asking which database and field you want to insert at the current cursor position.

CHAPTER 12 Putting It All Together

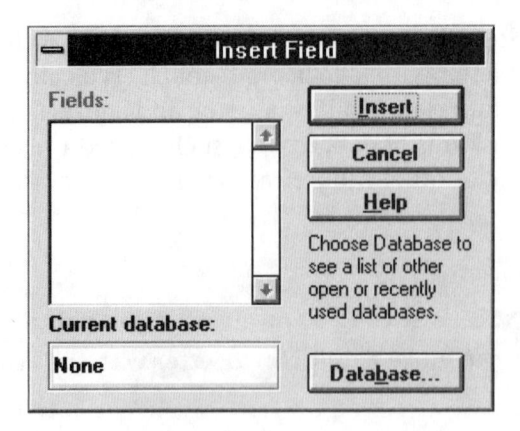

[Insert Field dialog box]

4. Click the Database button to select the correct database.

5. Select a field and press ↵. Works inserts a placeholder in the document that looks something like this:

   <<First Name>>

6. When the fields are entered, save the file on disk.

Tip Placeholders can be copied and moved within your text, but make sure that you copy both sets of angled brackets along with the field name. Otherwise, Works won't recognize the placeholder when the time comes to print the letters or forms. You can also format the placeholders with character and paragraph format settings.

Working with Preprinted Forms

If you are using preprinted forms, chances are you will have to do some experimenting with the settings in the File ➤ Page Setup dialog box before you can start printing clean copies. Measure all four margins of your forms (top, bottom, left, and right) as well as overall width and length, and alter the settings accordingly. You'll probably have to alter the tab settings in the word processor document to align the data fields on the printed form, too. You can test the layout by printing a single page rather than the whole database.

> **Tip** To print a single page instead of all the merged letter, set the Page Numbers in the Print dialog box to 1 and 1 instead of All.

Printing the Forms or Form Letters

To print the forms or form letters, follow these steps.

1. Open the word processor and database files.

2. In the word-processor file, choose File ➤ Print. The Print dialog box appears.

3. Check Print merge (the check box near the bottom).

The Choose Database dialog box appears. It asks you (again) for the name of the database to use when printing the forms or form letters:

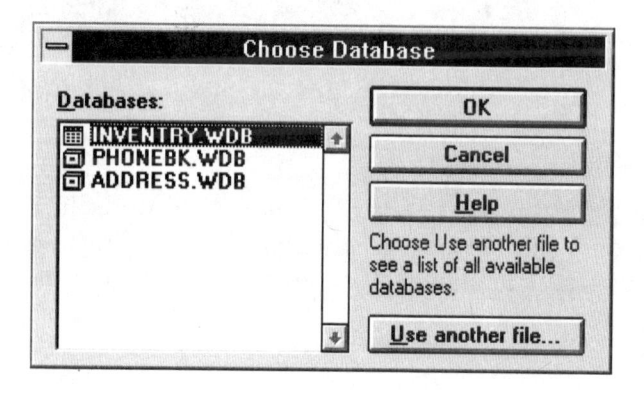

4. Highlight the right database and click OK.

> **Warning**
>
> When Works inserts the field data in the text, the form or letter can grow considerably longer. When you place long fields in a document, page breaks and page layouts change. Be sure to preview your form letters before you print them.

Works begins printing your forms or form letters. One copy is printed for each record in the database, beginning with the first visible record and moving through the database one record at a time. Hidden records are not printed.

Printing Mailing Labels

Works can print mailing labels in various sizes, so you can print on most commercially available pressure-sensitive labels. Works lets you print one, two, three, or four labels per row, across a page, using the data found in the fields of a database. One label is printed for each record in the database.

> **Note**
>
> There is a WorksWizard for printing mailing labels. If you already have an address database, consider using the WorksWizard. See Chapter 11 for information.

For printing lots of labels you need a printer with a tractor (sprockets) that can feed the labels accurately, since printing alignment is critical. Commercially available self-adhesive mailing labels are sold for laser printers, too.

Tip If you are printing labels for a bulk mailing, sort your database by zip code before you print it. The U.S. Postal Service requires bulk mailings to be bundled by zip code.

To create and print mailing labels:

1. Open a new word-processing document.
2. Select Tools ➤ Envelopes and Labels. The Envelopes and Labels dialog box appears.
3. Click the Mailing Labels tab at the top of the dialog box.
4. Click the Fields>> button on the right side of the dialog box. The dialog box expands to show field names.
5. Click the Database button in the lower-left corner of the dialog box. The Choose Database dialog box appears.
6. Select the address database you want to use and then click OK. The Envelopes and Labels dialog box should now look something like Figure 12.5.
7. Choose a Label Style in the Label box. To make your choice, look at the labels you plan to use and note the product number or measurements listed.

Next you start building your labels by selecting names from the Fields box and putting them in the Labels box. The fields you place in the labels box will appear on the labels when printed.

8. Select a field in the Fields box (most likely it will be Name) and then click Insert. The field you clicked on appears in the Label box.
9. Press ↵ and insert the Street next field. Keep doing this until all the fields you want to be in your labels are in the Label box. You can insert any spaces or punctuation you want to appear on the mailing labels.

CHAPTER 12 Putting It All Together

FIGURE 12.5

The Envelopes and Labels dialog box with a database selected for creating mailing labels

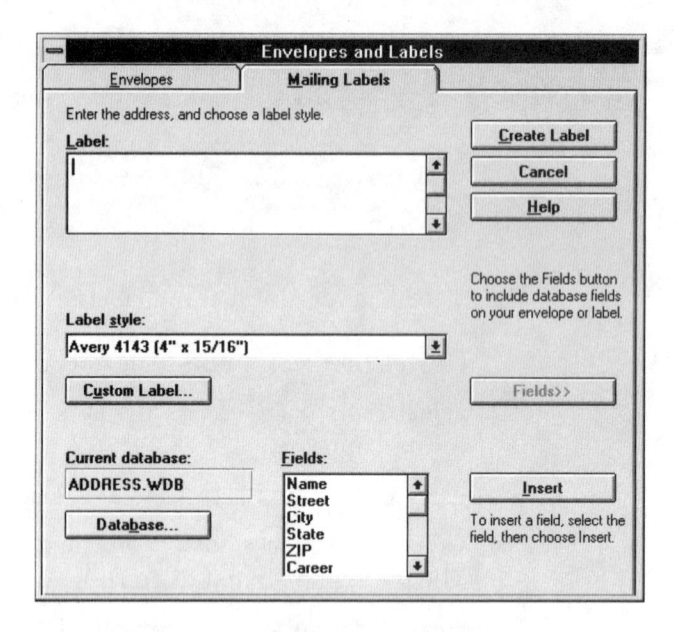

10. When you are done, click Create Label. Works inserts the fields at the top of the document.

11. Choose File ➤ Print Preview to make sure everything looks all right.

Before you can start printing, you have to specify the database again.

12. If the database is not open, click OK to merge all the records. Figure 12.6 shows my example. Try zooming in and using the PgDn key to read the labels. Do they look right?

13. Click Cancel to close the Preview screen.

14. Choose File ➤ Print.

15. Turn on the printer and click on Test.

This will print two rows of labels, rather than the whole list. (You'll have to specify the database again.) Works will warn you if it thinks the text won't fit on the page.

470

Printing Envelopes

FIGURE 12.6

Previewing the mailing labels before printing them

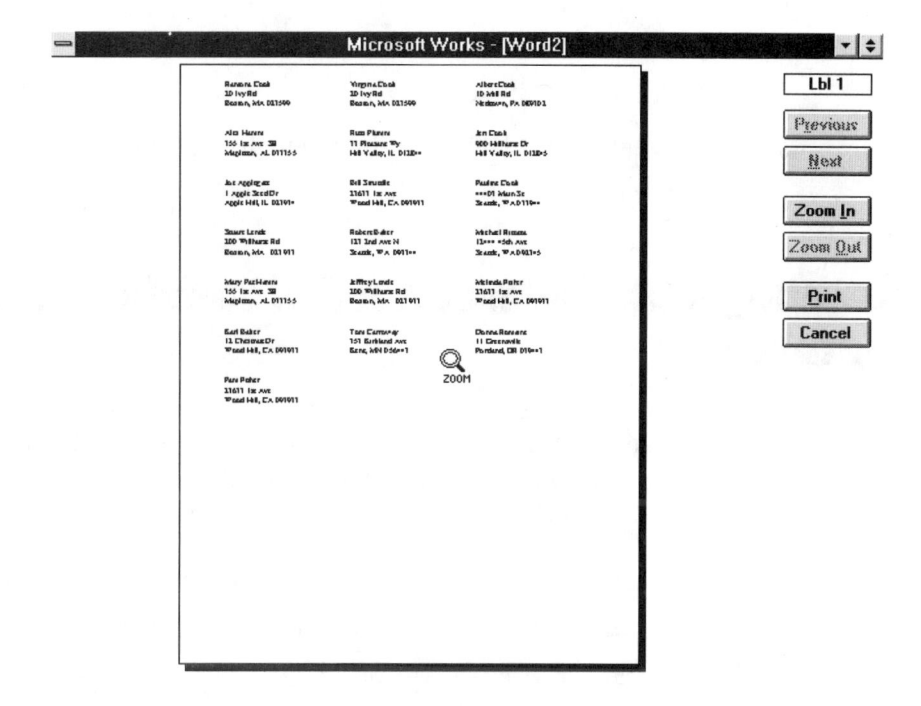

The Test feature lets you fine-tune the placement of labels without having to cancel the printing process each time. After the test labels are printed, you have the option of printing all of the labels, printing the test labels again, or canceling the printing process.

Printing Envelopes

Works can print envelopes as well as labels. Printing envelopes is essentially the same as printing a form letter. To print envelopes:

1. Create a new word-processing document.
2. Select Tools ➤ Envelopes and Labels. The Envelopes and Labels dialog box appears (see Figure 12.5).
3. Type addresses in the two address boxes (or click Fields and select a database to print envelopes for a form letter).

471

4. Click Create Envelope.
5. Feed in your envelope.
6. Select File ➤ Print. (Make sure Envelope is selected.)
7. Click OK.

Copying Data between a Spreadsheet and Database

You can copy between the database and spreadsheet without having to worry about formatting details. As you have know, WKS and WDB files (Works spreadsheet and database files, respectively) use the same formatting. Therefore, copying between them is simple.

1. Open both the spreadsheet and the database document.
2. From the source file, select the area to be copied.
3. Choose Edit ➤ Copy.
4. Move to the cell in the destination file where you want the copy to appear. The cursor location marks the upper-left corner of the copied data's new location.
5. Choose Edit ➤ Paste. The copy is made beginning at the highlighted cell and moving down and to the right.

Warning

Make sure that the selected text isn't larger than the space you have allotted for it in the database or spreadsheet. Beginning at the highlighted cell, Works copies the text to the right and down. Cells that get in the way are overwritten.

Copying Data between a Spreadsheet and Database

When you copy from a database file to a spreadsheet file, Works converts database records to spreadsheet rows, and fields to columns. When copying from the spreadsheet to the database, Works does just the opposite.

> **Note** When you copy cells from a spreadsheet and paste them into a database, only the values are pasted in, not the formulas.

APPENDICES

A
Installing Works on Your Computer

B
Using Works with Other Programs

C
Quick Reference to Works Tools and Commands

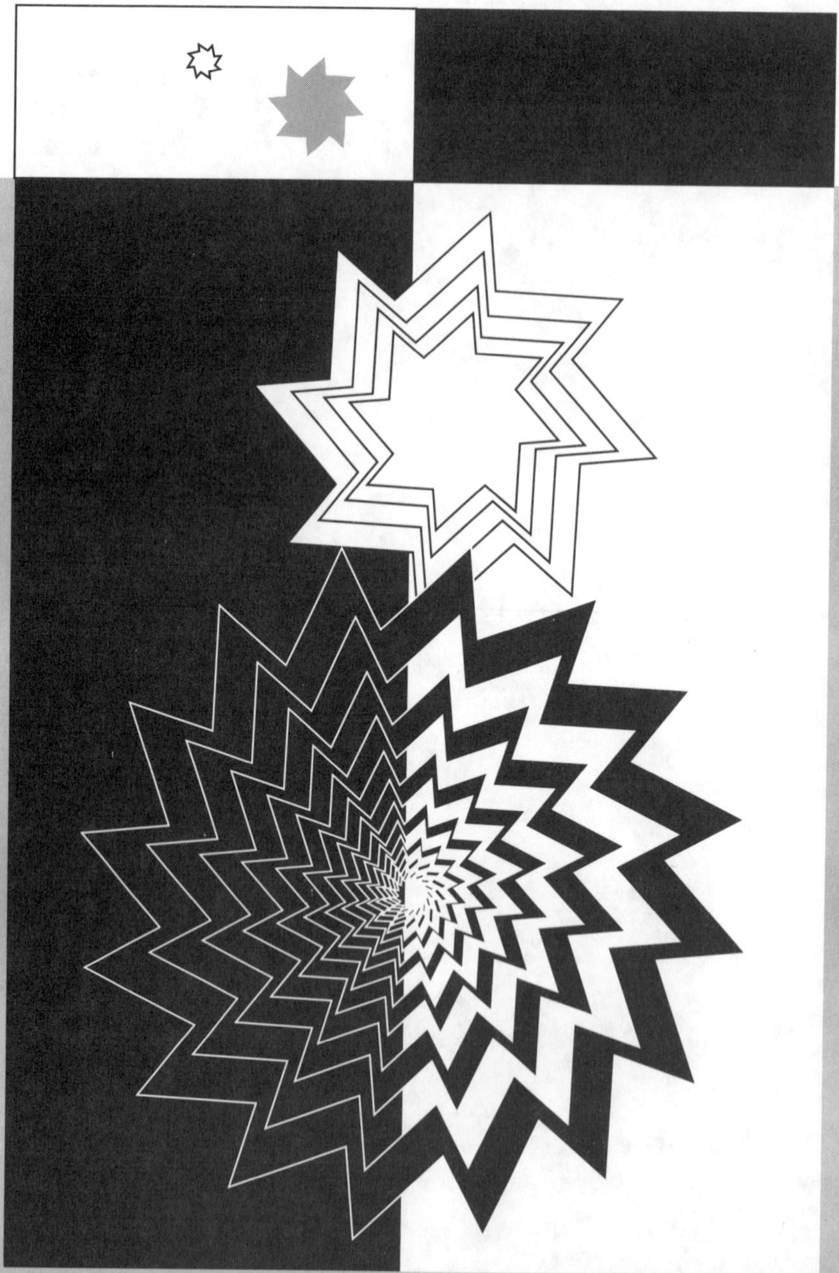

APPENDIX A

Installing Works on Your Computer

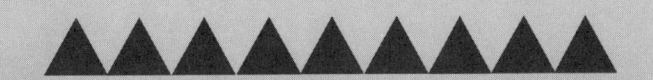

BEFORE YOU CAN USE MICROSOFT Works or follow the lessons in this book, you have to install the Works program. You also have to make sure that Windows and your mouse are operating properly.

System Requirements for Running Works

Before you install the program, make sure that your computer is capable of running Works. You must have the following equipment:

- An IBM-compatible computer using an 80286, 80386SX, 80386DX, or higher micro-processor
- MS-DOS or PC-DOS 3.1 or later
- Microsoft Windows 3.0 or later
- 640K memory plus 256K configured as extended memory (1MB extended memory is recommended)
- One 5¼-inch high-density or low-density drive or one 3½-inch high-denisity drive
- An EGA, VGA, 8514/A, or Hercules graphics card, or a compatible, or another video card that works with Windows 3.0 or later

> **Note** Having a mouse or trackball isn't absolutely necessary, but having a pointing device when you run Works makes choosing menu items, selecting text, and other tasks go much faster.

> **Note** Optionally, you may want to have a Hayes-compatible modem to use the telephone-dialing feature of Works.

If you are using previous versions of DOS or Windows, you should get an upgrade from your computer dealer before continuing.

Running the Setup Program

Works comes from Microsoft on two sets of disks:

- One set consists of four 5¼-inch floppy disks (1.2MB format).
- The other set is on six 3½-inch disks (720K format).

Which set of disks you use to install Works depends on the type of disk drive(s) your computer has. Nowadays, most desktop computers have one drive of each size, while laptop computers have only the 3½-inch disk drive.

What the Setup Program Does

When you run the Setup program (which you'll do shortly), the data on the installation disks is transferred to your hard disk and assembled into the Works program. To fit the entire Works program on your hard disk, you need 9.3MB of free space. You can install parts of the program, not all of it. For example, you can omit the tutorial lessons, the Help information, the sample files, and more if you so choose. During the installation procedure you will be given an opportunity *not* to install some parts of the program. The Setup program also lets you add elements such as sample files, the Draw program, and the computer-based tutorial.

> **Note** As it install Works, the Setup program decompresses the files on the installation disks. Therefore, you cannot install Works without running the Setup program. Don't try to install Works using the DOS command Copy, by copying files with the Windows File Manager, or by any other means.

Starting the Setup Program

Follow these instructions to install Works on your hard disk. (I am assuming that you have DOS on the hard disk and that your hard disk is drive C. Substitute a different drive letter if necessary.)

1. Turn on your computer and let it load DOS in the usual way. Consult your computer's manual if you do not know how to do this.
2. If Windows doesn't come up by itself, type **win** and press ↵.
3. Insert the Works Setup disk (disk 1) into drive A or B.
4. Switch to the Program Manager if it isn't already the active window.

Running the Setup Program

5. Open the File menu and choose Run. You'll see the Run dialog box. Fill it in as shown:

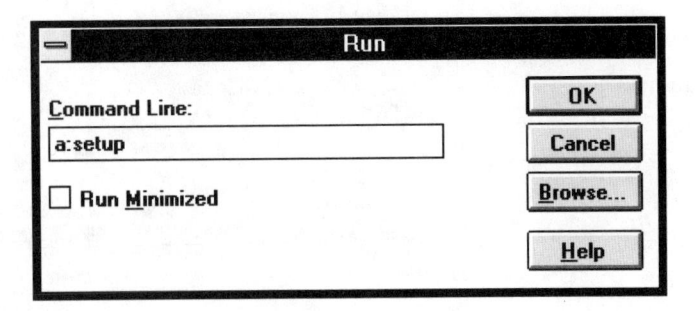

```
┌─────────────────── Run ───────────────────┐
│                                           │
│  Command Line:                  ┌───OK───┐│
│  ┌─────────────────────────┐    └────────┘│
│  │ a:setup                 │    ┌─Cancel─┐│
│  └─────────────────────────┘    └────────┘│
│                                 ┌─Browse─┐│
│  ☐ Run Minimized                └────────┘│
│                                 ┌──Help──┐│
│                                 └────────┘│
└───────────────────────────────────────────┘
```

Substitute the letter *B* for *A* if your Setup disk is in drive B.

6. Click on OK or press ↵.

    The Setup program begins running.

7. After entering your name and seeing a few informational dialog boxes (click OK as you go), you'll be asked what directory to install Works to.

8. Click OK to accept C:\MSWORKS as the directory, unless you want to use another directory to store your Works files. Examples in this book assume you've chosen C:\MSWORKS.

9. Continue clicking OK until Works asks you what type of installation you want, as shown in Figure A.1.

The three types of installation The three types of installation are:

Complete	Installs the program with all options
Minimum	Installs the minimum files required to run Works (this is the recommended choice if you have a laptop computer)
Custom	Lets you choose which parts of the program to install

FIGURE A.1
The Setup Options screen for choosing a Complete, Minimum, or Custom installation

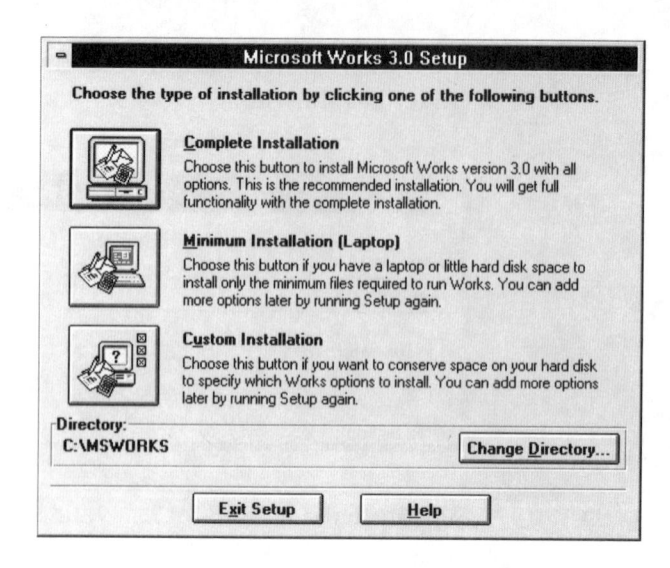

We will choose the Complete installation:

10. Click on the Complete Installation button.

11. Simply follow the on-screen instructions and answer all questions. The rest of the Setup program is self-explanatory. Options will appear in rectangular buttons that you can click on with the mouse pointer. Insert and remove disks as prompted.

When the Setup program is finished, Works will be installed on your hard disk in the \MSWORKS directory on drive C, and you'll be returned to the Windows Program Manager. Collect all the Works floppy disks and put them away in a safe place.

Disk Space Considerations

To accommodate Works, the spelling dictionary, the thesaurus, the file converters, the Help files, and the online tutorial, you must have a fair amount of unused space on your hard disk. If you don't have enough space, a dialog box appears as in Figure A.2 to tell you how much space is required, how much you have available, and how much space you are lacking.

Running the Setup Program

FIGURE A.2

If you don't have enough space on your hard disk for a complete installation, you will see this dialog box.

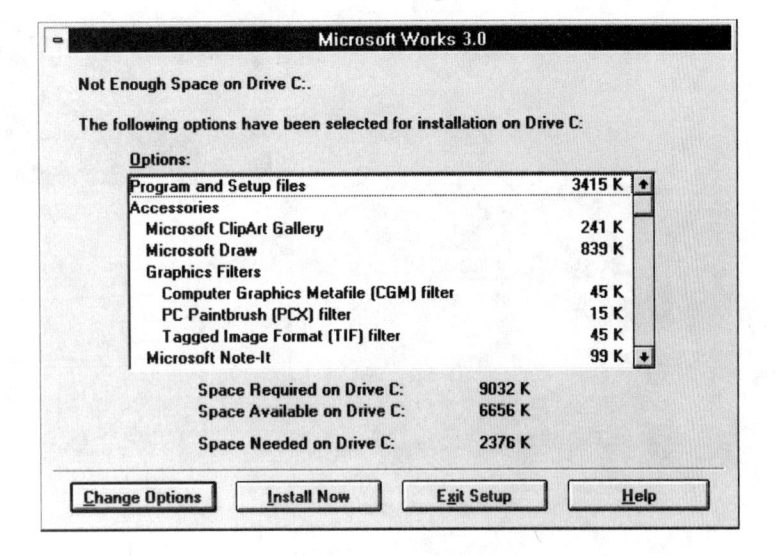

When this dialog box appears, Works gives you the option of bailing out of the Setup program. After you bail out you can either

- Erase some of the files on your hard disk and run the Setup program again.

- Do a custom installation and omit certain relatively unnecessary parts of Works. If you make this choice, don't install the online tutorial. The tutorial alone takes up 2344K of space.

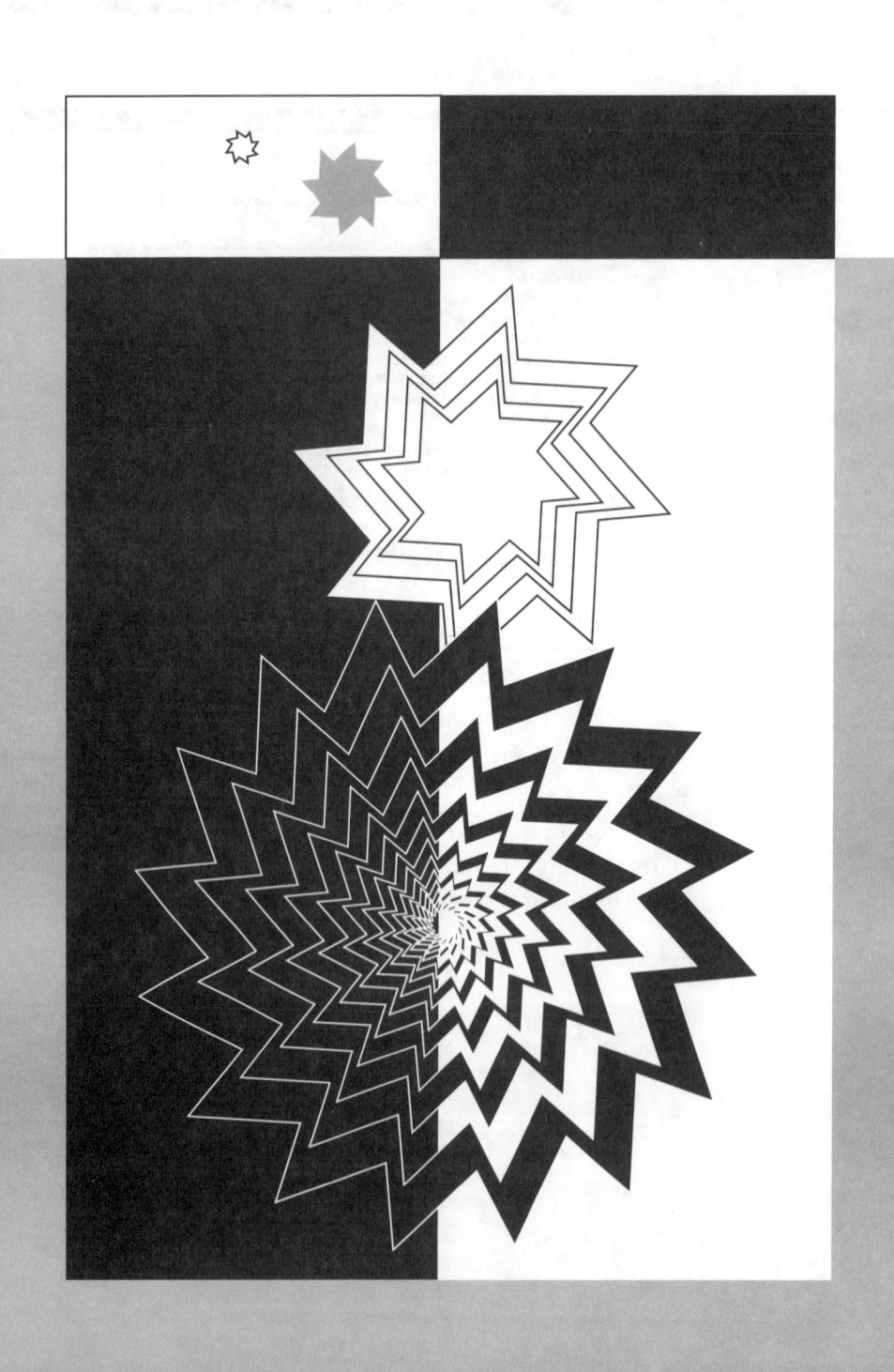

APPENDIX B

Using Works with Other Programs

WITH MANY PROGRAMS, PARTICULARLY INTEGRATED applications other than Works, the documents you create cannot be used by other word processing, spreadsheet, or database programs. However, Works is an exception. Works is actually pretty good for exchanging files with people who use other programs.

This appendix outlines the steps necessary to exchange files between some popular programs and Works. It is divided into three sections:

- ◆ Exchanging word processing files
- ◆ Exchanging spreadsheet files and database files
- ◆ Copying, pasting, and inserting objects from other Windows programs

Exchanging Word Processing Files

There are three ways to exchange word processing files with other word-processing programs:

- ◆ **Letting Works make the file conversion.** The most desirable technique is to have Works convert the file itself. Works can convert files from a select group of word processors to its own format. Likewise, Works can convert files to a select group of other formats so that people with other word-processing programs can use Works files.

> **Tip** If Works cannot read a file directly from another word processor, see if the other word processor can convert its files to a word-processing format that Works recognizes and supports. If it can, convert the file to that format, and then import the file to Works.

- ◆ **Converting files to ASCII text.** If you can't figure out a means for converting a file to a format supported by Works, convert it to a standard ASCII (text) file. The fonts, margins, headers and footers, graphics, and so on will be lost, of course, so converting to ASCII text can be a nuisance if you are importing a sophisticated word processing file.

- ◆ **The Windows solution**. The least palatable solution is to use the Clipboard. If the other program you want to exchange files with is a Windows program, copy text to the Clipboard and then paste it into the other document. (See "Using the Clipboard to Move Data" later in this chapter.)

The first two techniques are described in this part of the chapter.

Letting Works Make the File Conversions

Works can read and use files from the following word processors:

- ◆ Microsoft Works (for DOS)
- ◆ Microsoft Works 3.0 for the Macintosh
- ◆ WordPerfect 5.0 and 5.1 for Windows or DOS
- ◆ Microsoft Word for Windows (all versions)
- ◆ Microsoft Word for DOS
- ◆ Microsoft Rich Text format (RTF)
- ◆ Windows Write

APPENDIX B Using Works with Other Programs

Importing a File Made in Another Word Processor

To import a file from one of the word processors listed above:

1. Choose File ➤ Open Existing Document. The Open dialog box appears.

2. To bring up the file you want to import, find and highlight it in the File Name scroll box. You might have to enter *.* in the box to see all the files in the current directory. You can also type the file name in the box yourself.

3. Choose a file type from the List Files of Type drop-down list box, which is shown in Figure B.1. Notice that Works can accept various types of files. Choose the word processor that was used to create the file you are going to import.

4. Click on OK.

Works converts the file from the source format into Work's own format. The file appears in a window with a generic name such as Word1.

FIGURE B.1
Choosing a file type from the List Files of Type box

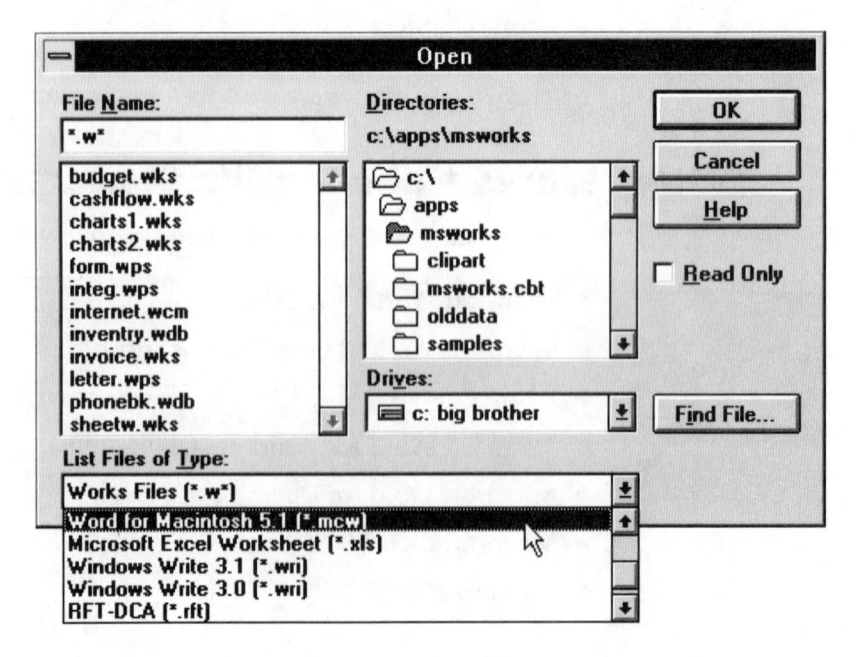

Converting Works Files to Other Formats

What do you do if you want to give a file to someone who doesn't have Works? In that case, you have to save the file under a format that the other party can use. For example, if your friend has Microsoft Word, you can save a Works file as a Microsoft Word file.

To export a file in a non-Works word-processing format:

1. Open the file you want to convert.
2. Choose File ➤ Save As. The Save As dialog box appears.
3. Type in a new file name for the file you want to convert. Be sure to use a name other than the one the file already has, because if you don't you will overwrite the original file.
4. Choose a directory and drive to save the file to.
5. Click on the Save File as Type section at the bottom of the dialog box and highlight the word-processing format you want to convert the file to.
6. Click on OK.

The file is converted and stored on disk in the foreign word processor's format.

Converting Files to ASCII Text

When the word processing program you want to exchange files with is not on the list of word processors whose files Works can convert (see Figure B.1), you have to resort to ASCII files. ASCII (the letters stand for "American Standard Code for Information Interchange") is the basic format that text files can be stored in. All word processors can recognize and use ASCII files. However, these files are bare-bones text files without any codes for storing paragraph and character formatting, margin and tab settings, and other such details. Only CR/LF (carriage return/line feed) codes are retained in an ASCII file. These codes mark where new paragraphs and lines begin.

| APPENDIX B | **Using Works with Other Programs** |

> **Tip** If you are making a file to send to a different word processor and that word processor cannot accept Works files directly, don't waste any time formatting the file. You have to send it as an ASCII file anyway. All formats, if you include them, will be lost.

Exporting an ASCII File from Works

In the Works word processor, you create text files with the Save As dialog box. To create an ASCII file for export to another word processor:

1. Follow steps 1 through 4 under "Converting Works Files to Other Formats" above.

2. Open the Files Save as Type box and highlight one of these options (they are explained below):

    ◆ Text
    ◆ Text (DOS)

3. Click on OK.

Works converts the new file to the ASCII format.

Text vs. Text (DOS) The differences between the Text and Text DOS settings are minimal. These settings pertain to "high" ASCII characters, the esoteric symbols on the high end of the ASCII chart. Keep the Text default. However, if you are exporting to a DOS-based program (a non-Windows program) such as WordPerfect for DOS and the recipient of the file complains about weird but beautiful Greek and other characters in the file, try resaving the file as Text (DOS).

Importing ASCII Files into Works

To import an ASCII file into the word processor, simply follow these instructions:

1. Choose File ➤ Open Existing File.
2. From the List Files of Type box, choose either Text or Text (DOS).
3. Type in the name of the file, or choose it from the list box (change the File Name to *.* if you have to).
4. Click OK. The Open File As dialog box appears:

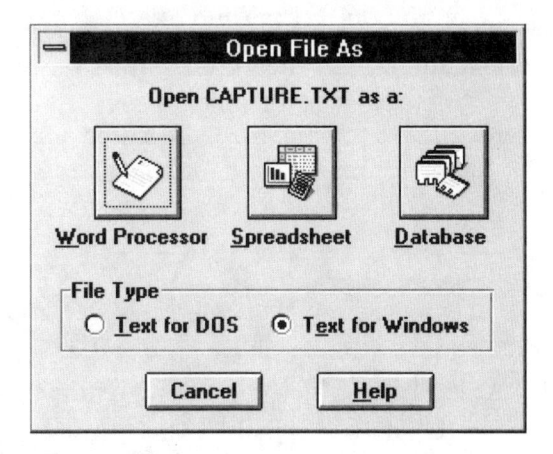

5. Choose a Text option:

    ◆ If the source program is a DOS program, choose Text for DOS.

    ◆ If a Windows program was the source, choose Text for Windows.

6. Click on Word Processor.

Works opens the new file. Chances are the formatting is all wrong. The file probably includes extra paragraph marks (CR/LFs) or spaces.

APPENDIX B Using Works with Other Programs

> **Tip** If you see Greek and other strange but beautiful characters in the file, close it and resave the document with the other Text option, either Text for DOS or Text for Windows.

Cleaning up an ASCII file To fix the formatting a bit:

1. Make the invisible characters appear by choosing View ➤ All Characters.
2. Remove the objectionable characters, typically all paragraph marks (¶) except for ones at the end of each paragraph.
3. Format and use the file in the normal way.

When you save the file, it will be stored as a text file unless you choose otherwise from the Save As dialog box.

> **Tip** If the program from which you are importing files can't create ASCII files, have it print the file to a disk file or a print file, if possible. The resulting text file will have no special codes in it—just plain text.

Exchanging Spreadsheet and Database Files

Works can use spreadsheet and database text files created in other programs, provided the files

- Have cells separated by tabs, by commas, or by quotes and commas (as in DIF files)
- Have a CR/LF at the end of each row (or record).

Spreadsheets created by Lotus 1-2-3 versions 1A and 2.0 can be used by Works without any conversion, and vice versa. Lotus 1-2-3 for Windows files cannot be used directly. Lotus 1-2-3 version 2.2 or later files have to be saved in a special format.

Databases created with dBASE can be loaded directly into the database tool.

This part of the chapter explains:

- Working with Lotus 1-2-3 files
- Working with dBASE files
- Working with database and spreadsheets as text files

Working With Lotus 1-2-3 Files

Formats specific to Works and formats specific to 1-2-3 can be lost when files are transferred from one program to the other. The information itself, however, is retained. You are more likely to lose information when you load a file created in one program directly into another and save it. If you just load it to look at it, without saving, there will be no loss of data.

When it opens a Lotus 1-2-3 file, Works checks all the formulas to see if it can recognize them. If Works can't recognize a function in a 1-2-3 file, an error dialog box appears with a message such as:

```
Invalid formula ignored in cell XX:XX.
Continue to display errors?
```

This means Works will remove the formula and replace it with the value in the problem cell. Mark down the cell location so that you can reenter the formula later with a function Works supports.

Lotus 2.0 functions not supported by Works The following Lotus 1-2-3 version 2.0 functions are not supported by Works:

- Database statistical functions
- All 1-2-3 string functions

APPENDIX B Using Works with Other Programs

- $CADATEVALUE
- $CATIMEVALUE
- $CAISNUMBER
- $CAISSTRING
- CACA
- $CACELL
- $CACELLPOINTER

Opening a 1-2-3 File in Works

To open a 1-2-3 file in Works:

1. Choose File ➤ Open Existing File. The Open dialog box appears.
2. Type *.* in the File Name box and press ↵ to be able to see all the files in the list box.
3. Change the drive and directory if you have to.
4. Choose the file in the file list by double-clicking it or by highlighting it and clicking OK or pressing ↵.

The 1-2-3 file is loaded into a Works window.

Saving a Works File for Use by Lotus 1-2-3

To save a Works spreadsheet so it can be used with 1-2-3 version 2.2 or later:

1. With the Works spreadsheet in the active window, choose File ➤ Save As. The Save As dialog box appears.
2. In the Save File as Type box, choose Lotus 1-2-3.
3. You can give the file a new name if you want, but you don't have to. Works automatically changes the extension so that the original file isn't overwritten.
4. Click on OK.

Working with dBASE Files

You can save a Works database in dBASE format and also load an existing dBASE database file into Works. Many other database programs, including FoxPro and FoxBASE+, use the dBASE format or can save their files in that format. Convert databases from these programs into a dBASE format, and then convert them to Works.

To save a Works database for use in dBASE or a dBASE-compatible program:

1. Open the Works database file and make its window active.
2. Choose File ➤ Save As.
3. From the Save File as Type box, choose dBASE III or dBASE IV, depending on your needs.
4. Enter a name and extension for the file in the File Name box.
5. Click on OK.

To open a dBASE database in Works:

1. Choose File ➤ Open Existing File.
2. In the List Files of Type box, choose dBASE (*.dbf).
3. Choose a drive, directory, and the name of the file you want to open.
4. Click on OK.

The file will be opened in a Works window. The field names, sizes, and types in the dBASE file will be reflected in the Works database.

Using Databases and Spreadsheets as Text Files

You can load and save files stored in text (ASCII) format with the Works database and spreadsheet tools. Therefore, you can export or import data from other text-based spreadsheets or databases. For example, you could copy columns from a Works spreadsheet to a WordPerfect 5 document.

APPENDIX B Using Works with Other Programs

Exporting Database and Spreadsheet Text Files

When you save a file as text with the Save As dialog box, Works removes all formatting and formulas. The formulas are stripped out and only the values remain. Depending on the choice you make in the Save File as Type box in the Save As dialog box, values appear in the a text file in one of two formats:

Text & Commas

Text & Tabs *or* Text & Tabs (DOS)

The Text & Commas format Figure B.2 shows a worksheet in the Text & Commas format. With this format:

◆ Values are separated by commas.

◆ Double quotation marks appear around the data in each cell.

FIGURE B.2
A spreadsheet saved in Text & Commas format

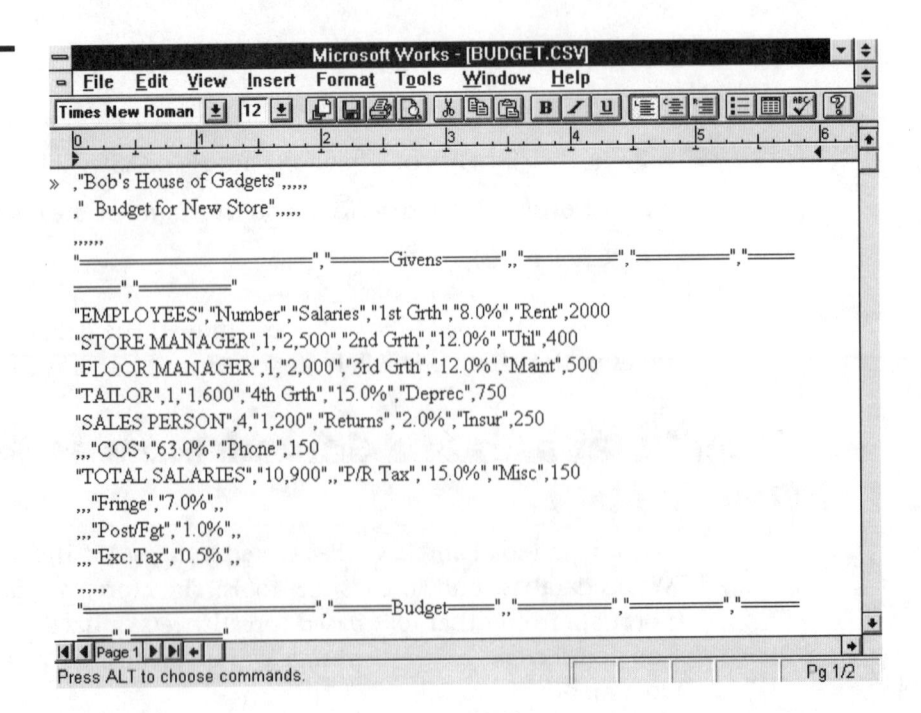

Exchanging Spreadsheet and Database Files

- Rows are terminated by a CR/LF (carriage return/line feed).
- Spreadsheet column names and database field names are not written into the file.

To work with a spreadsheet or database in this format, you can edit the file in a word processor or import it directly into another program that can read such a file.

The Text & Tabs format With the Text & Tabs format, tabs are inserted between columns (between database fields or between spreadsheet cells) instead of commas. Figure B.3 shows a spreadsheet saved with this format. Notice all the tab arrows (the Options ➤ Show All Characters setting is active). The Text & Tabs format is preferable when you want to import a file into a word processor. Adjusting tab settings to realign columns is not very difficult with a word processor.

FIGURE B.3
A spreadsheet saved in Text & Tabs format

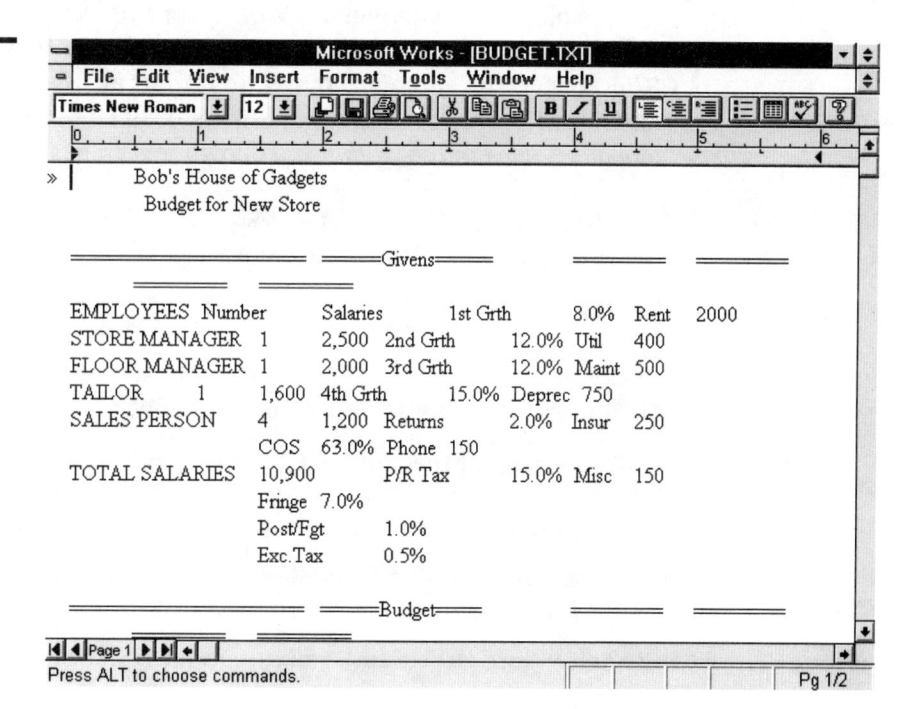

APPENDIX B — Using Works with Other Programs

To save a Works database or spreadsheet as a text file for use with any program that can open standard text files:

1. Choose File ➤ Save As.
2. Select which text option you want from the Save File as Type box, Text & Commas or Text & Tabs.
3. Name the file, but give it a new name so you don't overwrite your existing file.
4. Click on OK.
5. Works asks you if it's OK to save the file without formatting. Click OK. The file is saved to disk.

Importing Database and Spreadsheet Text Files

As explained in Chapter 12, Works word-processing files copied to a spreadsheet or database in Works must include tabs between cells and a CR/LF code at the end of each row. To import an ASCII file from a non-Works word processor into a spreadsheet or database, the file has to be *comma-delimited* or *tab-delimited*. Following is an example of each:

FORMAT	EXAMPLE
Comma-delimited	1,2,302,Text,5
Tab-delimited	1 2 302 Text 5

Column and field names should not be in the file. If they are, they will appear as the first record, or the first row.

To open a text file and read it into a Works spreadsheet or database:

1. Choose File ➤ Open Existing File.
2. Find the file in the Find File box, highlight it, and click OK. The Open As dialog box appears.
3. Select Spreadsheet or Database from the dialog box.
4. Click on OK.

The file is loaded into a Works window.

Using the Clipboard to Move Data

Works is a Windows program, so you can copy material from it to all kinds of the other Windows programs. All you have to do is select the text and use the cut, copy, and paste commands. You can copy data between DOS and Windows programs if the DOS program is displayed in a window and is running under Windows 386 Enhanced mode.

Here are the basic steps for copying material between Windows documents, whether they are Works documents or documents you have created in other Windows programs:

1. Run the programs you want to make the copies to and from and open the documents.

You can adjust the source and destination windows so that both are visible, but maximizing all windows and switching is far easier.

2. Select the data or text you want to copy in the source document.
3. Choose Edit ➤ Copy (or Edit ➤ Cut if you want to move rather than copy the information).
4. Switch to the destination document's window.
5. Position the cursor where you want the data pasted in and choose Edit ➤ Paste.

The data is pasted in at the cursor position, assuming the destination and source programs are capable of sharing the same type of data. Figure B.4 shows a name and address from a database copied into the Windows Cardfile mini-application.

Warning

Sometimes you cannot copy data from one program to the other. For example, a graphics program cannot accept text or sound. Sometimes you have to adjust data after you transfer it.

499

APPENDIX B Using Works with Other Programs

FIGURE B.4

Copying data from Works into Cardfile, using the Copy and Paste commands

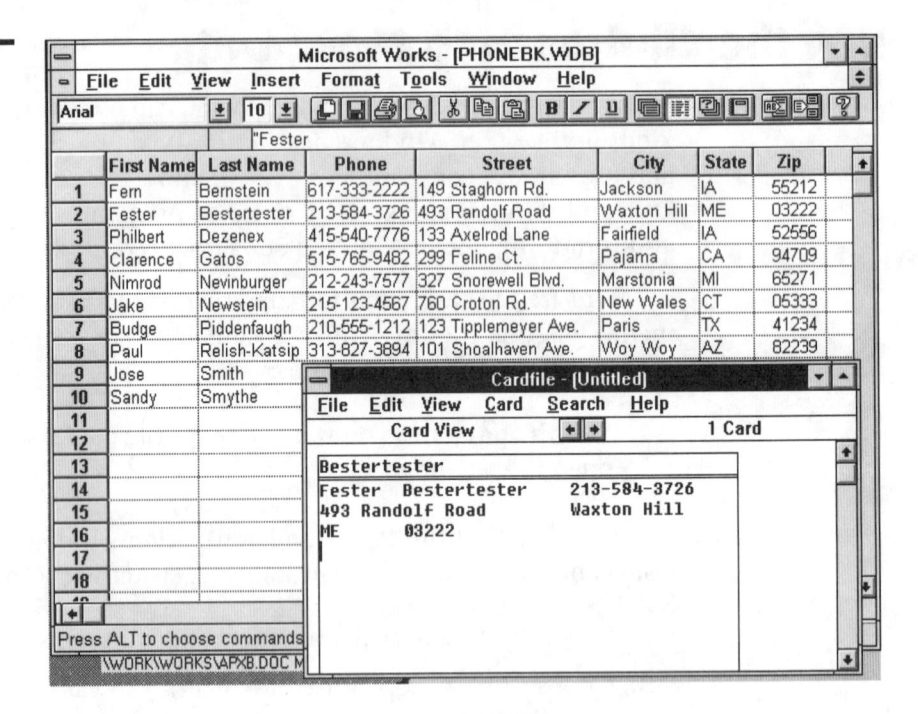

	First Name	Last Name	Phone	Street	City	State	Zip
1	Fern	Bernstein	617-333-2222	149 Staghorn Rd.	Jackson	IA	55212
2	Fester	Bestertester	213-584-3726	493 Randolf Road	Waxton Hill	ME	03222
3	Philbert	Dezenex	415-540-7776	133 Axelrod Lane	Fairfield	IA	52556
4	Clarence	Gatos	515-765-9482	299 Feline Ct.	Pajama	CA	94709
5	Nimrod	Nevinburger	212-243-7577	327 Snorewell Blvd.	Marstonia	MI	65271
6	Jake	Newstein	215-123-4567	760 Croton Rd.	New Wales	CT	05333
7	Budge	Piddenfaugh	210-555-1212	123 Tipplemeyer Ave.	Paris	TX	41234
8	Paul	Relish-Katsip	313-827-3894	101 Shoalhaven Ave.	Woy Woy	AZ	82239
9	Jose	Smith					
10	Sandy	Smythe					

Cardfile - (Untitled)

Bestertester
Fester   Bestertester   213-584-3726
493 Randolf Road   Waxton Hill
ME   03222

500

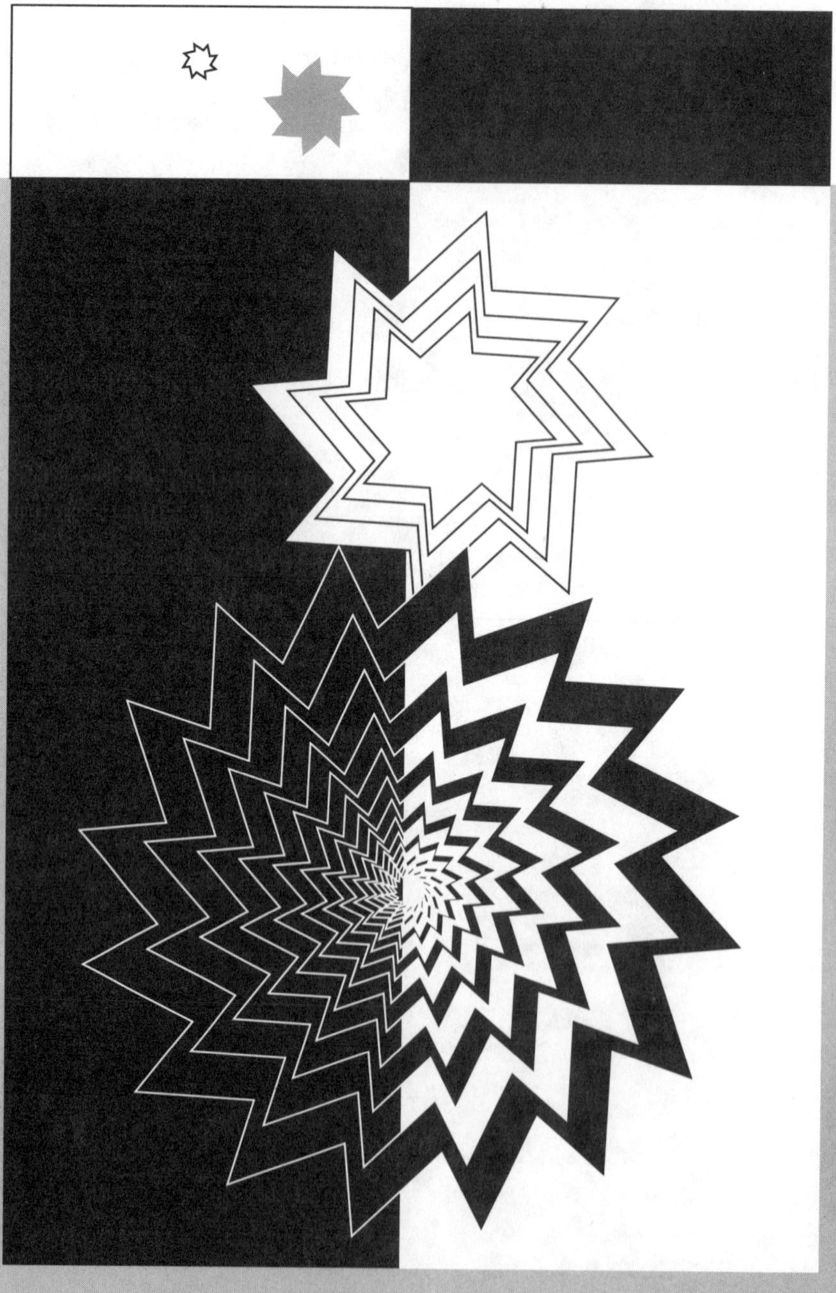

APPENDIX C

Quick Reference to Works Tools and Commands

THIS APPENDIX IS DIVIDED INTO eight sections:

- Basic Works and Windows information
- Word processor information
- Spreadsheet information
- Database and reporting information
- Spreadsheet and database functions
- Using dates and times in the spreadsheet and database

This appendix does not list all the commands that are available in each of the tools, since Works does that for you on its menus. The Works menus and descriptions that appear on the bottom line of your screen make it fairly clear what the purpose of each menu selection is. What is listed here are general procedures, short-cut keys, and technical specifications, as well as other useful information about some of the tools and about Works in general.

Basic Works and Windows Information

This section contains general information that applies to all of Works' tools and to Windows.

Keys Used by All the Tools

Some keys are used by all of the Works tools. They are as follows:

KEY	EFFECT
F1	Help
Shift+F1	Tutorial
Ctrl+X	Cut
Ctrl+C	Copy
Ctrl+V	Paste
F5	Go To
Ctrl+F6	Next pane *or* next open document
F7	Repeat search
Shift+F7	Repeat format
Alt	Access menu bar
Esc	Terminate extend mode, dialog box, menu bar activation
Ctrl+B	Bold
Ctrl+I	Italic
Ctrl+U	Underline
Ctrl+E	Center
Ctrl+L	Left-justify
Ctrl+R	Right-justify
Ctrl+P	Print
Ctrl+S	Save

APPENDIX C: Quick Reference to Works Tools and Commands

Options that Affect Your Documents

The Options dialog box shown in Figure C.1 controls the appearance of tools on your screen, the units of measurement within tools, and several defaults that can vary. It also affects the creation of automatic backup files when you modify an existing file.

Units The Units section determines the form in which Works displays and accepts units of measurement within the tools. The default is affected by the setting for Country.

Possible settings for units are shown in the following list:

UNITS	ABBREVIATION	NUMBER OF UNITS PER INCH	EXAMPLE
Inches	in *or* "	1	.5 in *or* .5"
Centimeters	cm	2.54	.88 cm
Picas	pi	6	2 pi
Points	pts *or* pt	72	10 pt

FIGURE C.1

The Options dialog box handles some of the basic settings that apply to the various tools in Works.

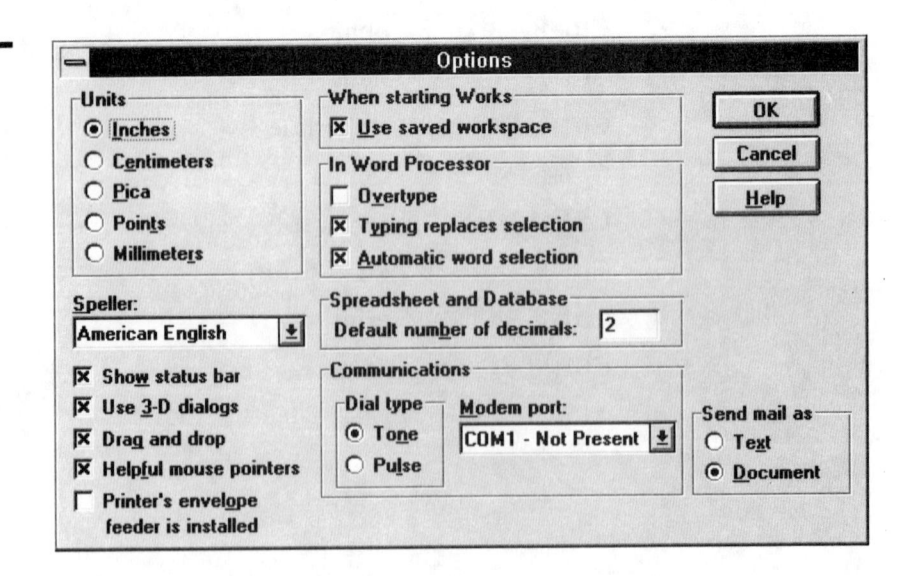

506

Once a given setting, such as inches, is selected from the Works Settings box, you may enter other units as long as you specify what the units are, using the abbreviations listed. Works will make the conversion and display the measurements in the selected units.

When starting Works The When starting Works section determines whether Works will come up with all the documents that were around last time when (and if) you selected File ➤ Save Workspace before quitting. To use the Workspace option, you must have "saved the workspace" at some point. You do that by choosing File ➤ Save Workspace when you have all the files you want open and you have adjusted their windows the way you like. This feature "remembers" just how you had files and windows set up and returns the Works environment to that arrangement each time you run it.

In Word Processor There are three options in the In Word Processor section. The first, Overtype, just sets overtype as the default when you start (as opposed to Insert, the usual default). No matter what you start with, you can always switch from overtype to insert or vice versa by pressing the Insert key.

The second option, Typing Replaces Selection, is checked off by default. This means that when you select text and then type something, what you type will replace the selection. If it is unchecked and you select something and then type, the selection will become unselected and what you type will be inserted (or typed over one character at a time if you are in overtype mode) at the beginning of the formerly selected text.

The third option, Automatic Word Selection, is also on by default. When it is checked, selecting text by clicking and dragging selects whole words at a time. When it is unchecked, you can drag to increase selections by one character at a time.

Speller The Speller drop-down list allows you to choose other language dictionaries for your spell checks.

Show status bar This option turns on or off the bottom line of the Works window—the line that reports information pertaining to the document you're working on, such as page number, record number, Caps Lock status, and so on. Turning it off allows you additional space for your document to display. It's on by default.

Use 3-D dialogs This option turns on or off the 3-D effects on Works dialog boxes, the beveled edges, shadows, shading, and grooves. It's on by default.

Drag and drop This option turns on or off drag-and-drop editing. It is on by default.

Helpful mouse pointers This options turns on or off the little boxed notes that pop up to name whatever part of the screen you're pointing to. It is on by default.

Printer's envelope feeder is installed Check off this option if your printer has an attached envelope feeder. It's off by default.

Spreadsheet and Database Click in this box to change the default number of decimals in the spreadsheet and database. The "default default" is 2.

Communications You shouldn't need to change these options because the first time you use the communications tool you'll choose the proper port and decide on all the other necessary options.

Send mail as This option determines the form of e-mail you send with the communications tool. You can select Text or Document, depending on what's required by your mail link.

Word Processor Information

This section of Appendix C contains information about special codes and special Find and Replace codes.

Word Processor Information

Special Word Processing Keys

Here are how all the special editing keys function in the word processor.

KEY	NAME	EFFECT
Del	Delete at Cursor	Deletes character at cursor location
Del	Delete Selection	Deletes entire highlighted selection
Backspace	Delete Left	Deletes character left of cursor
↵	Paragraph Mark	Creates a new paragraph and moves down one line
Shift+↵	End-of-Line Mark	Lets you decide where a line breaks
Ctrl+↵	Manual Page Break	Lets you decide where a page breaks
Ctrl+Hyphen	Optional Hyphen	Lets you designate where a word will split
Ctrl+Shift+Hyphen	Nonbreaking Hyphen	Holds hyphenated words together at line breaks
Ctrl+Shift+Spacebar	Nonbreaking space	Holds words together at line
Ctrl+P	Print	Brings up the print dialog box
Ctrl+D	Inserts Date	Inserts the date code

APPENDIX C Quick Reference to Works Tools and Commands

KEY	NAME	EFFECT
Ctrl+T	Insert Time	Inserts the time code
Ctrl+;	Current Date	Inserts today's date
Ctrl+Shift+;	Current Time	Inserts the current time in *hh:mm:am/pm* format

Special Find and Replace Characters

Type the special find and replace characters into the Find or Replace text areas for effects as outlined in the following list. To enter one of these as the find or replace character, type Shift+6 to enter a caret (^), followed by the character in the list that represents the special item you want to find or replace.

^w White space: any combination of spaces, tabs, nonbreaking spaces, new lines, paragraph marks, and hard page breaks. This cannot be used as a Replace item.

^s Nonbreaking space, such as in Microsoft Works when you don't want the words to separate during line wraps.

^d Page break

^t Tab

^p Paragraph mark

^n End-of-line mark

^~ Non-breaking hyphen

^– Optional hyphen

^? Question mark

^ Caret

^# Any ASCII character, where # is the ASCII character number

? Any character

510

Spreadsheet Information

This section contains reference information about the special function keys in the spreadsheet and about entering data. Spreadsheet functions are covered in "Spreadsheet and Database Functions" later in this appendix.

Special Function Keys

In addition to the keys listed at the beginning of this appendix for use with all the tools, the following function keys can be used with the spreadsheet tool:

KEY	EFFECT
F2	Edit
F4	Reference (cycles between absolute and relative reference combinations)
F8	Extend selection
Ctrl+F8	Select row
Shift+F8	Select column
Shift+Ctrl+F8	Select all
F9	Calculate now

Entering Data into Cells

Move to the cell into which you want to enter a formula, value, or label; then use the keys as shown in the following list:

KEY	EFFECT
↵	Enters data, remains on cell
↓	Enters data, moves down one cell
↑	Enters data, moves up one cell
←	Enters data, moves left one cell

APPENDIX C   **Quick Reference to Works Tools and Commands**

KEY	EFFECT
→	Enters data, moves right one cell
Ctrl+;	Enters the current date
Ctrl+Shift+;	Enters the current time
Ctrl+'	Copies data from cell above

If you have a block of cells selected, the following keys may save you some time. These keys only work in an area selected via Shift+arrow keys.

KEY	EFFECT
Shift+Tab	Enters data, moves left one cell
Tab	Enters data, moves right one cell

Database and Reporting Information

This section summarizes the commands available in the database's List and View screens.

List and Screen Function Keys

In addition to the keys listed at the beginning of this appendix, the database tool can be controlled using the following keys:

KEY	EFFECT
F2	Edit
F7	Repeat search
Shift+F7	Repeat last command
Shift+F8	Select column
Ctrl+F8	Select row

Special Keys

Here are some other useful shortcuts:

KEY	EFFECT
Ctrl+'	Copy cell above
Ctrl+;	Enter current date
Ctrl+Shift+;	Enter current time

Spreadsheet and Database Functions

Works contains 57 built-in, or "canned," arithmetic formulas called functions. Functions can be used in the context of either spreadsheet or database formulas. Explaining all the functions listed here is beyond the scope of this book.

Lotus functions not included in Works However, it may help the advanced user to know that Works' functions are identical to those for Lotus 1-2-3 version 1A, with the exclusion of the functions listed here:

Database Statistical Functions:

DAVG

DCOUNT

DMAX

DMIN

DSTD

DSUM

DVAR

String functions:

&

Logical functions:

@ISNUMBER
@ISSTRING

Special functions:

@@
@CELL
@CELLPOINTER

Date and time functions:

@DATEVALUE,TIM = @@DATEVALUE
@DATEVALUE,TIM = @@TIMEVALUE

Functions found in Works and Lotus 1-2-3 Works includes the following Lotus 1-2-3 version 2 functions:

CTERM(*Rate,FutureValue,PresentValue*)

DDB(*Cost,Salvage,Life,Period*)

IRR(*Guess,RangeReference*)

RATE(*FutureValue,PresentValue,Term*)

SLN(*Cost,Salvage,Life*)

SYD(*Cost,Salvage,Life,Period*)

TERM(*Payment,Rate,FutureValue*)

COLS(*RangeReference*)

ROWS(*RangeReference*)

INDEX(*RangeReference,Column,Row*)

Entering Dates and Times in Documents

Dates can be entered into database and spreadsheet cells either as constants or as variables to be used in formulas. They can be entered in a long or short form. The same holds true of times. Here are some examples:

FORM	DATES	TIMES
Long	Dec 25, 1923	23:30:00
	Dec, 25, 1923	23:30
	Dec, 1923	
	Dec 25	
Short	12/25/1923	11:30:00 PM
	12/25/23	11:30 PM
	12/1923	11 PM
	12/25	

Works can store and manipulate dates between 1/1/1900 and 6/3/2079.

Entering dates and times in formulas To put a date in a formula, use the short form and enclose it in single quotation marks, like so:

`='5/5/88'-'3/5/85'`

(This formula calculates the number of days between the two dates). Format the cell as a date to make sense of the result.

To put a time into a formula, use the Hour:Minute:Second 12-hour form and use single quotation marks around it, like so:

`='5:30:00 PM'-'3:23:00 PM'`

(This formula calculates the time difference.) You will have to format the cell to display the result correctly, using the Date/Time format.

Index

Note to the reader: Throughout this index, **boldfaced** page numbers indicate primary discussions of a topic. *Italicized* page numbers indicate illustrations.

A

absolute cell references, **225–227**
active cells, 168, 174, *175*, **176–177**
active charts, 266
active windows, 54, 148
addition, 368, 370
addresses
    fields for, 310
    labels for, **468–471**, *471*
ADJUST pointer, 184, 326
alert dialog boxes, **45**
aligning
    cells, 169, **187–189**
    fields, 367
    text, 106, **111–112**
Alignment dialog box, 188–189, *188*
Alt key, **29**, 505
    for dialog boxes, 46
    for menus, 42, *43*
Always Suggest spelling option, 144
anchor points, 87, 90
ANSI files, 456
ANSI terminal emulation, 408
application windows, *38*, 40
applying character styles, 124–125

Arc tool, *158*, 159–160
arcs, *157*
area charts, 255, 285, *286*
arguments, **370**
arranging
    fields, **313–316**, *316*, **326–328**
    tab stops, **136–137**
arrow keys. *See* cursor and cursor keys
ascending sorts, 244, 337
ASCII files, 58
    for exchanging data, 456, **489–492**, **495–498**
    sending, 395, **418–420**
    transfer parameters for, 410
assumption data in spreadsheets, **207**, *208*
asterisks (*)
    in databases, 333, 368
    in spreadsheets, 246
AT command, 430
auto-answer feature, 402
auto spacing, 117
Automatic Word Selection option, 507
AutoStart templates, 444–445
AVG function, 386

B

Back help button, *62*, 63
backsolving, 15
Backspace key, **32**
    in databases, 329
    in spreadsheets, 198
    in word processor, 76, 86, 509
backup files, **56–57**
Bar button, 282
bar charts, 255
    creating, **259–262**, *261*
    100%, **281–283**, *283*
    series for, **269–271**, *270*
    stacked, **283–284**, *284*
Bar dialog box, 282, *282*
Basic Report screen, 374, *374*
Basic Skills help option, 60
baud rates, 398, **405**
beginning of document indicator, *73*, 75
binary files
    receiving, 395, **421–423**
    sending, 395, **420–421**
bits, 406
blank lines
    in reports, 387
    in word processor, 77, 96
blocks in word processor
    copying and moving, **93–97**, *95 96*, *98*
    selecting, 70, **87–92**, *88*
boilerplate text, 57
Bold style
    for cells, 181
    for database labels, 354, *354*
    for text, 125–126, *125*, 128, 505
Border dialog box, 122, *123*
borders
    for charts, 277, *278*, 464
    around text, **122–123**

Box tool, *158*, 159
break fields, **379–381**
breaking paragraphs, **119**
breakout boxes, 427
Breaks and Spacing tab, 116–118, *116*
browsing help buttons, *62*, 63
budget spreadsheet, **206–208**
    clearing cells in, **235**
    entering data in, **211–219**, 231-232
    formatting cells in, **209–211**
    freezing titles in, **229–230**
    functions in, **233–234**
    inserting rows in, **219–222**
    references in, **225–229**
    splitting screen in, **222–224**, *223*
bulletin board systems (BBSs), 396
business templates, 444–445
bytes, 406

C

CALC indicator, 240
calculated cells, 187
calculated fields, 349, **368–370**
calculations, spreadsheet, **240–241**
Cancel command buttons, 48
canceling spreadsheet entries, 178
capitalization
    in database searches, 333
    in word processor
        checking, 143, 145
        in searches, 140–141
Caps Lock key, 220
CAPT indicator, 417
Capture Text button, 417
capturing text, 395, **416–418**, *417*, 456
Cardfile application, **499**, *500*
carets (^), 510

carriage return, **30**, 96, 108–109, 408, 509
case. *See* capitalization
cause-and-effect relationships, charts for, **288–290**, *291*
cells in spreadsheets, 14, 174, *175*
    active, 168, 174, *175*, **176–177**
    aligning, 169, **187–189**
    for chart labels, **263–264**
    for chart legends, 272
    clearing, **235**
    copying, **181**, **190–191**
    editing, **197–198**
    entering data in, **177–180**, **189-190**
    formatting, 169, **185–187**, *186*, **209–211**
    moving, **181**
    overflow in, **197**
    protecting, 205, **236–238**
    ranges for, **194**
    references to, 176, 190, 205, **225–229**
    selecting, 204, **209–211**
center alignment
    in cells, 188–189
    of text, 71, **97–98**, 111–112
Center alignment buttons, 98, *98*, 111, 188
Center alignment option, 111
center tabs, 133
centimeters, 75, 506
character styles, **124–125**, **128–130**
charts
    area, 285, *286*
    bar, **259–262**
    borders for, 277, *278*, 464
    combination, **291–292**
    copying, **267–268**
    creating, **259–262**, *261*
    deleting, 253, **267**

designing, **258–259**, *259*
fonts in, 253, 271, 278, **294–295**
high-lo-close, **285–288**, *288*
importing, 450, **461–464**, *463*
labels for, **262–265**, *263*, *265*, 271
legends for, **271–272**, *272*
line, **273–274**, *275*
moving, 462
names for, **265–266**, 268
100% bar, **281–283**, *283*
pie, **275–281**, *280*
previewing, **295**, *296*, 299
printing, **298–300**
radar, 291, *292*
saving, 252, **266–267**
scaling, 253, **295–297**
series for, **269–271**, *270*
size of, 299, 462–463
stacked bar, **283–284**, *284*
stacked line, **284**, *285*
starting, 252, 260
3-D, **293**, *293*
titles in, 252, 294
types of, 252, **255**, *256–257*, **258**
X-Y, **288–290**, *291*
Charts dialog box, 273
check boxes, *46*, **48**
check marks
    on menus, **44**
    in spreadsheets, 178
Choose a WorksWizard list, 438, *439*
Choose Database dialog box
    for form letters, 443, *443*, 467, *467*
    for mailing labels, 469
Circle tool, *158*, 159
clearing cells, **235**
clip art, 107, **152–153**, *153–154*
Clipboard
    for charts, 264, 269, 274
    for exchanging data, **499**, *500*
    for moving cell data, 181

for reports, 375, 464
in word processor
  for copying, **94–95**, 97
  for formatting, 131
  for pictures, 164
closing spreadsheets, 180
colons (:)
  in databases, 312, 353
  in spreadsheets, 194
color
  for charts, 262, 281
  for drawings, **155–156**, 159–161
  in help system, 61
  for plotters, 300
color selectors, *155*
column selectors, 185
columns
  in databases. *See* fields in databases
  in spreadsheets, 173–174, *175*
    freezing, 205, **229–230**
    hiding, 238
    summing, 204, **228–229**
    width of, **183–185**, 197, **209–210**
  in word processor, **79–80**, *81*
COM ports
  problems with, **429–430**
  selecting, **399–400**
  setting, **405**
combination charts, 255, **291–292**
Combination dialog box, 292
combining documents. *See* exchanging
    data between documents
comma-delimited files, 498
command buttons, *46*, **48**
commands, 24, **43–44**
commas (,)
  for dialing pauses, 403
  in spreadsheet numbers, 210, 215
commodity prices, charts for,
    285–288, *288*

Communication Settings button, 403
Communication tab, 404, *404*
communications program, 5, **21**,
    396–397
  dialing connections in, 394,
    411–415, *414*
  direct connections in, **426–429**
  ending sessions in, **423**
  exchanging files in, 395
    capturing text, **416–418**, *417*
    receiving binary files, **421–423**
    sending binary files, **420–421**
    sending text files, **418–420**
  file extension for, 51, 55
  option for, 508
  parameters for, 394
    communication, **403–407**
    phone, **401–403**
    terminal, **407–409**
    transfer, **409–410**
  saving settings in, **410–411**
  scripts in, **424–426**, 430
  setting up, 394, **397–411**
  starting, **399–401**
  troubleshooting, **429–431**
compatibility of files, **58**, 431, 488, *488*
Complete installation, 481–482
complex documents
  templates for, **443–447**
  WorksWizards for, **438–443**
Connect to other computer? dialog
    box, *413*, 414
connections in communications pro-
    gram, 394
  direct, **426–429**
  modem, **411–415**, *414*
constants, 176
Contents help button, *62*, 63
Contents help option, 60
context-sensitive help, 59–60

Control boxes, *38*, 40
Control key. *See* Ctrl key
Control menus, 40
converting files, 458, **486–487**, **489–490**
copies, printing, 101
copying
    between documents. *See* exchanging data between documents
    files, 25, 57–58
    reports, 375, 389
    in spreadsheets
      cell contents, 181
      chart data, 274
      charts, **267–268**
      in entering data, **211–212**
      formulas, **190–191**, 212, **226–227**, **234**
    in word processor
      formatting, **130–132**
      pictures, 164
      text, 71, **93–97**, *95–96*, *98*
correlations, charts for, **288–290**, *291*
COUNT function, 383, 386
Create Envelope option, 472
criteria in databases
    for printing, 344
    for searches, **333–334**
    for sorting, **337–338**, *339*
Ctrl key, **28–29**, 511–512
    in databases, 314, 324, 512–513
    in spreadsheets, 181, 211–212, 512
    in word processor, 83, 85, 509
Ctrl+C keys, 97, 505
Ctrl+V keys, 97, 505
Ctrl+X keys, 97, 505
Cue Cards for templates, 445, *446*
currency format
    in databases, 368
    in spreadsheets, **185–187**, *186*
cursor and cursor keys, **30–31**, 75

in databases
    for editing, 329
    in Form view, 314
    in List view, 327, 329
    for selecting, 335
for menus, 42–43
in spreadsheets, 511–512
    for editing, 198
    for entering data, 182
    for navigating, 177
    in Point mode, 192
in word processor
    moving, between windows, 149
    for navigating, 85–86
    for selecting text, 89–90
Curvy Line tool, *158*, 160
Custom installation, 481
custom spelling dictionaries, 143

D

data bits, setting, **406**
Data Labels dialog box
    for adding chart labels, 264, *264*
    for deleting chart labels, 271, 274
    for pie charts, 277, *277*, 280
databases, 5, **306**
    dates and time in, **515**
    editing data in, 305, **328–331**
    entering data in, 304, **319–323**, **355–356**, **369**
    exchanging data with, 450–451, **459–461**, **472–473**, **495–498**
    features in, **18–20**
    fields in. *See* fields in databases
    file extension for, 51, 55
    for form letters, **440–442**, **465–466**
    formatting in, **367–368**
    forms for, **312–313**, 318, **351–356**, *351–352*, *354*

keys for, **512–513**
mailing labels for, **468–471**, *471*
opening, **310–312**
option for, 508
printing, **342–345**
protecting, 349, **371–372**
records in. *See* records in databases
reports for. *See* reports for databases
saving, **323–324**
searching in, **331–336**, **339–342**
sorting, **336–338**, *339*
starting, 304, 310
structure of, **309–310**
as text files, **495–498**
views in, 304–305, **307–308**
308–309, **324–327**
dates
inserting, 509–510, **515**
Lotus 1-2-3 functions for, 514
in spreadsheets, 176, **195–197**, *197*
dBASE files, exchanging data with, **495**
decimal places, 210, 508
decimal tabs, 133
defaults
for chart fonts, 294
for field values, 355
for footers, 150
Del key, 86, 198, 329, 509
delays in file transfers, 410, 420, 431
deleting
in databases
fields, 348, **356–360**, *359*
records, 349, **360–363**
report rows, 378
reports, **375–376**, 389
in spreadsheets
chart labels, 271
charts, 253, **267**
page breaks, 241
range names, 248

in word processor
blank lines, 96
tabs, **137**
descending sorts, 244, 337
designing charts, **258–259**, *259*
destination documents, 161, 459
Dial button, 412, 423
DIAL indicator, 414
dialing
phone parameters for, **401–403**
procedure for, **411–415**, *414*
dialog boxes, 25, **45**, *46*
check boxes in, **48**
command buttons in, **48**
drop-down list boxes in, **49**
entering data in, **46–49**
files in, *47*, **49–51**
list boxes in, **49**
navigating, **46**
option buttons in, **48**
option setting for, 508
text boxes in, **47**
dictionaries, spelling, 142–143
dimmed menu commands, **44**
direct computer connections, **426–429**
directories
in dialog boxes, *47*, **49–50**
for installation, 481
for saving files, 56
for spreadsheets, 199
for transferring files, 410
for word processor documents, 100–101
disk drives
in dialog boxes, *47*, 49–50
requirements for, 478
for saving files, 56
for spreadsheets, 199
for word processor documents, 100–101

disk space for installation, 480, **482–483**, *483*
dividing lines for columns, 184
division, 368, 370
document windows, *38*, 40
documents
 clip art in, 107, **152–153**, *153–154*
 creating, 70, **72–81**
 editing, **82–97**
 entering text in, **76–80**, *81*
 exchanging data between. *See* exchanging data between documents
 inserting text in, **92–93**
 navigating, 70, **82–86**
 previewing, **101–102**, *102*
 printing, 71, **101–103**
 saving, 71, **99–101**
 selecting, 88
 switching between, 25, **52–54**
 templates for, **443–447**
 WorksWizards for, **438–443**
dollar signs ($) in spreadsheets, 225–227
Don't break paragraph option, 119
DOS requirements, 478
double quotation marks (")
 for exporting data, 496
 for labels, 176, 178, 353
 for records, 320–321
downloading files, 395, 409, **421–423**
drag-and-drop
 option for, 508
 in spreadsheets, **181**
 in word processor, **97**, *98*
DRAG pointer, 97, *97*, 181
dragging
 elevators, 84
 for field width, 319
 in list boxes, 36

tabs, 136
windows, **41–42**
Draw ➤ Line Style command, 156
drawings, **151–152**, **154–155**
 color in, **155–156**, 159–161
 positioning, **161–162**
 scaling, 162–163, *163*
 tools for, *155*, **156–161**, *158*
drives
 in dialog boxes, *47*, 49–50
 requirements for, 478
 for saving files, 56
 for spreadsheets, 199
 for word processor documents, 100–101
drop-down list boxes, *47*, **49**

E

e-mail option, 508
Easy Connect button, 413
Easy Connect dialog box, 411, 413–414, *413*
echo setting, **408–409**
Edit ➤ Clear command, 235
Edit ➤ Copy command
 for exchanging data, 452, 459, 461, 472, **499**, *500*
 in spreadsheets
  for chart labels, 264
  for charts, 269, 274
 in word processor
  for formatting, 130–131
  for pictures, 164
  for text, 93–94
Edit ➤ Copy Report Output command, 375, 464
Edit ➤ Cut command
 for cell data, 181
 for exchanging data, 452

for fields, 328
for text, 93–94
Edit ➤ Data Labels command, 264, 271
for 100% bar charts, 282
for pie charts, 277, 280
Edit ➤ Field Name command, 358
Edit ➤ Fill Down command, 190, 192–193, 229–230
Edit ➤ Fill Right command, 234
Edit ➤ Find command
for records, 331–335
for spreadsheets, 245
for text, 139
Edit ➤ Go To command, 331, *331*
EDIT indicator, 198, 328
Edit ➤ Insert ➤ Field Entry command, 386
Edit ➤ Insert ➤ Field Name command, 386
Edit ➤ Insert ➤ Field Summary command, 386
Edit key, 28
Edit ➤ Legend/Series Labels command, 271, 288
Edit mode, 198
Edit ➤ Paste command
for cell data, 181
for exchanging data, 452, 459, 461, 472, **499**, *500*
for fields, 328
for reports, 464
for text, 94–95
Edit ➤ Paste Series command, 269, 274
Edit ➤ Paste Special command, 131–132
Edit ➤ Position Selection command, 315
Edit ➤ Replace command, 141
Edit ➤ Select Field command, 335
Edit ➤ Select Record command, 335

Edit ➤ Series command, 287, 290
Edit ➤ Show All Records command, 364
Edit ➤ Switch Hidden Records command, 364
Edit ➤ Titles command, 262, 270, 288
Edit ➤ Undo command, 137–138
editing
cells, **197–198**
drawings, 163
records, 305, **328–331**
reports, **382–389**
word processor documents, **82–97**
education, templates for, 445
elevators, 36, 84
ellipses (...), 44
emulation, terminal, 407–408
End key, 31
in databases, 314, 327, 329
in spreadsheets, 198
in word processor, 83, 85
end of document indicator, *73*, *75*
end-of-line marks, 510
end of line settings, 408
Enter key, **30**, 96, 108–109, 408, 509
entering data
in databases, 304, **319–323**, **355–356**, 369
dates and time, 515
in dialog boxes, **46–49**
in reports, **385–386**
in spreadsheets, 168, **177–180**, **182**, 204
budget spreadsheet, 212–219
copying with, **211–212**
formulas, **179–180**, **189–190**, 224
keys for, **511–512**
word processor text, **76–80**, *81*
envelopes, 451, **471–472**, 508

Envelopes and Labels dialog box, 469–470, *470*
environment, 26
equal signs (=)
   in databases, 355, 369
   in spreadsheets, 214
error-detection protocols, 420
errors
   parity bits for, 406
   typing, 70, 76, **86**
Escape key, **29–30**, 505
Excel spreadsheets, 17
exchanging data between documents, **450–453**, *454*. *See also* communications program
   ASCII files for, 456, **489–492**, **495–498**
   with Clipboard, **499**, *500*
   with databases, **459–461**, **472–473**, **495–498**
   with spreadsheets, **459–461**, **472–473**, **492–498**
   with word processor, **486–489**
      charts, **461–464**
      databases, **459–461**
      file conversions for, **486–490**
      modem files, **455–458**
      reports, **464**
      spreadsheets, **459–461**
exiting, 25, **65**
exploding pie charts, 253, **279–280**, *280*
exporting
   ASCII files, **490**, **495–498**
   database and spreadsheet data, **496–498**
EXT indicator, 87, *88*
Extend mode, 87–89, 210
extensions, file, 51, 55, 58

F

F1 key, 28, 59, 505
F2 key, 28, 328, 511–512
F3 key, 343
F4 key, 511
F5 key, 327, 505
F7 key, 512
F8 key, 87–89, 210, 511–512
F9 key, 511
Field Size dialog box, 312–313, *312*, 318–319
Field Summary dialog box, 386
fields in databases, **18–19**, *19*, 307–308
   aligning, 367
   arranging, **313–316**, *316*, **326–328**
   break, **379–381**
   calculated, 349, **368–370**
   deleting, 348, **356–360**, *359*
   in form letters, **441–442**, *442*, **465–466**
   formatting, **367–368**
   on forms, 312–313, *313*
   in formulas, 370
   hiding, 345, 348, **352–353**, 360, **364–365**
   inserting, 348, **357–358**, *359*, 360
   for mailing labels, 469
   names for, 358
   overflow in, 319
   planning, 310
   protecting, **371–372**
   in reports, 373, *373*, 376, 386
   in searches, **334–336**
   size of, 312–313, **317–319**, *318*, **326**, *327*
File ➤ Close command, 180
File ➤ Create New File command, 52–53

File ➤ Exit command, 65, 162
File ➤ Exit Windows command, 66
File ➤ Open command, 200, 414
File ➤ Open Existing File command, 57, 59
   for database file, 495
   for reports, 464
   for spreadsheets files, 494
   for text files, 498
   for word processor files, 457, 488, 491
File ➤ Page Setup command
   for charts, 299
   for databases, 344
   for headers and footers, 151
   for margins, 299
   for page breaks, 241
   for preprinted forms, 466
File ➤ Print command
   for envelopes, 472
   for form letters, 467
   for mailing labels, 470
   for spreadsheets, 201
   for word processor documents, 101
File ➤ Print Preview command
   for charts, 295, 299
   for databases, 344
   for mailing labels, 470
   for reports, 374, 377, 379, 382
   for spreadsheets, 201
   for word processor documents, 101
File ➤ Printer Setup command, 294, 298, 345
File ➤ Run command, 481
File ➤ Save command, 55, 57
   for charts, 266
   for communications settings, 411
   for databases, 323
   for queries, 342
   for spreadsheets, 199
   for word processor documents, 99, 101
File ➤ Save As command, 58
   for converting file formats, 489
   for templates, 200
   for text files, 419, 498
   for word processor documents, 99
File ➤ Save Workspace command, 507
File ➤ Templates command, 443
File ➤ Update command, 161
File ➤ WorksWizards command, 438
files, 10
   backup, **56–57**
   converting, 458, **486–487, 489–490**
   copying, 25, 57–58
   and dialog boxes, *47*, **49–51**
   exchanging. *See* communications program; exchanging data between documents
   formats of, **58**, 431, 488, *488*
   names for, **51**, **55**, **56**, **57–58**
   opening, 25, 50, **59**
   printing to, 492
   saving, 51, **55–57**, *56*
   types of, **50–51**
fill alignment, 189
fill color, 156
Find dialog box
   for records, 332–335, *334*
   for spreadsheets, 245–246, *246*
   for text, 139
finding
   help information, **63–64**
   records, 305, **331–336, 339–342**
   spreadsheet data, **245–246**
   text, 10, 107, **138–140, 510**
First Line indent option, 113
first-line indentations, *73*, 113–114

Font and Style dialog box
  for charts, 294
  for databases, 345
  for word processor, 126, 128–129, *129*
fonts
  in charts, 253, 271, 278, **294–295**
  in databases, **318–319**, 345
  in spreadsheets, 235
  in word processor
    for drawings, 161
    for text, 106, **124–127**, **129–130**
footers, **149–151**
Form Letter WorksWizard, **439–443**, *440–442*
form letters
  creating, **439–442**, **464–466**
  fields in, **441–442**, *442*, **465–466**
  preprinted, **466–467**
  printing, **443**, **467–468**
Form View button, 311, *312*
Form view in databases, 307–308, *309*
  editing in, **330–331**, *331*
  inserting and deleting fields in, **356–357**
  inserting and deleting records in, **360–361**
  navigating in, **314**, 324
  printing from, 342
  switching from, 324
Format ➤ Add Border command, 277
Format ➤ Alignment command, 188, 367
Format ➤ Border command, 122–123, 464
Format ➤ Column Width command, 184, 209, 238
Format ➤ Field Size command, 317
Format ➤ Field Width command, 365
Format ➤ Font and Style command
  for charts, 294

  for databases, 345
  for word processor, 126, 128
Format ➤ Freeze Titles command, 229–230
Format ➤ Horizontal (X) Axis command, 274, 296
Format ➤ Mixed Line and Bar command, 292
Format ➤ Number command, 185, 193, 195, 210, 321, 368
Format ➤ Page Setup commands, 201
Format ➤ Paragraph command, 109
Format ➤ Patterns and Colors command, 279
Format ➤ Picture/Object command, 162, 463
Format ➤ Protection command, 236–237, 318, 371–372
Format ➤ Set Print Area command, 200
Format ➤ Show Field Name command, 353
Format ➤ Snap To Grid command, 315, 354
Format ➤ Tabs command, 133–134, 136
Format ➤ Vertical (Y) Axis command, 274, 296
formats of files, **58**, 431, 488, *488*
formatting. *See also* styles
  cells, 169, **185–187**, *186*, **209–211**
  fields, **367–368**
  in word processor, 11, **108–109**
    alignment, **111–112**
    borders, **122–123**
    copying, **130–132**
    current, **109–111**
    indentation, **112–116**
    invisible characters, **121–122**, *122*
    line spacing, **116–118**
    paragraph breaks, **119**

paragraph spacing, **118**
Quick formats, **119–121**, *120*
tabs, **132–137**
forms for databases, **312–313**, **351**, *351–352*. *See also* form letters
creating, **464–465**
instructions on, **355–356**
labels on, 348, **352–355**, *352*, *354*
protecting, 318
formula bar
in databases, 326
in spreadsheets, 174, *175*, 178, 180, **198**
formulas
in databases, **369–370**
in spreadsheets, 14, *15*, **176**
cell references in, 205, **225–229**
copying, **190–191**, 212, **226–227**, **234**
entering, **179–180**, **189–190**, 224
in exchanged data, 473
functions in, 176, **233–234**
from Lotus 1-2-3, 493, **513–514**
range names in, 247
ranges in, **194**
in templates, 446
viewing, **238–240**, *239*
FoxPro files, exchanging data with, **495**
freehand drawings, *157*, 160
Freehand tool, *158*
freeware, 396
freezing spreadsheet titles, 205, **229–230**
full-justification of text, 111–112
function keys, **28**, **511–512**
functions
in databases, 369–370, 386
in spreadsheets, 14–15
in formulas, 176, **233–234**
from Lotus 1-2-3, 493, **513–514**

G

Gallery ➤ 3-D Pie command, 293
Gallery ➤ Area command, 285
Gallery ➤ Bar command, 282–283
Gallery ➤ Combination command, 291–292
Gallery ➤ Line command, 287
Gallery ➤ Radar command, 291
Gallery ➤ Stacked Line command, 284
general alignment, 189
Go To dialog box
for databases, 331, *331*, 365
for spreadsheets, 177, 209–210
grand totals
in reports, **376–379**
in spreadsheets, **194**, *195*
graphics
drawings. *See* drawings
in help, 62
graphics card requirements, 478
grayed menu commands, **44**
grids
for charts, 274, *275*
for fields, 315, 354
printing, 201

H

handshaking, **406–407**
hanging indents, **115–116**
Hayes-compatible commands, 399
headers and footers, **149–151**
Headers and Footers dialog box, 149–151, *150*
headings
fonts for, 130
for rows, **220–222**
Headings row type, 383

height of charts, 299
help, **59–60**
    buttons for, **62–63**, *62*
    keeping on screen, **64**
    navigating, **61–63**, *64*
Help key, 28
Help menu, 59–60
hiding
    fields, 345, 348, **352–353**, 360, **364–365**
    records, 349, **363–364**
    spreadsheet columns, 238
high-lo-close charts, **285–288**, *288*
histograms. *See* bar charts
History help button, *62*, 63
Home key, 31
    in databases, 314, 327, 329
    in spreadsheets, 198
    in word processor, 83, 85
horizontal scroll bars, 84
Horizontal (X) Axis dialog box, 296–297
hot keys. *See* shortcut keys
hotspots in help, 61, *62*
How to Use Help option, 60
hyphens
    checking, 143
    find and replace character for, 510
    keys for, 509

I

icons, minimizing windows to, 40, 64
illustrations, **151–152**
    clip art for, **152–153**, *153–154*
    drawings for, **154–163**
    positioning, **163–164**
importing
    ASCII files, **491–492**
    charts, 450, **461–464**, *463*
    database and spreadsheet files, **498**
    word processor files, **488–489**
In Word Processor options, 507
inches, setting for, 506
indenting paragraphs, *73*, 106, **112–116**
Indents and Alignment tab, 110–111, *110*
index, help, 28
Ins key, 92
Insert ➤ Chart command, 462
Insert Chart dialog box, 462, *462*
Insert ➤ ClipArt command, 152
Insert ➤ Database Field command, 465
Insert ➤ Delete Page Break command, 241
Insert ➤ Delete Record command, 360
Insert ➤ Delete Record/Field command, 358, 362
Insert ➤ Delete Row/Column command, 378
Insert ➤ Delete Selection command, 357
Insert ➤ Drawing command, 154
Insert Field button, 311, *312*
Insert Field dialog box, 465–466, *466*
insert mode, 92
Insert ➤ Page Break command, 241, 390
Insert ➤ Range Name command, 247–248
Insert Record button, 311, *312*
Insert ➤ Record command, 360
Insert ➤ Record/Field command, 358, 360–361, 363
Insert ➤ Row/Column command
    in databases, 385, 387
    in spreadsheets, 219
inserting
    in databases
        fields, 348, **357–358**, *359*, 360

page breaks, 390
  records, 348, **360–361**, 363
  report rows, **385**, 387
date and time, 509–510, **515**
in spreadsheets
  page breaks, **241–242**
  range names, **247–248**
  rows, 204, **219–222**
in word processor
  charts, 450, **461–464**, *463*
  clip art, **152–154**
  reports, 451, **464**
  text, **92–93**
insertion point, 82
installation, **479–483**, *482*
instructions, data-entry, **355–356**
integrated programs, 4, **6–7**
Interactive mode, 416
Interval chart scaling option, 297
Intr Category row type in reports, 383
inventory database, **366**, *367*
  calculated fields in, **368–370**
  formatting fields in, **367–368**
  protecting fields in, **371–372**
invisible characters, **121–122**, *122*
invoice spreadsheet, **180**
  aligning cells in, **187–189**
  column width in, **183–185**
  copying data in, 181
  dates in, **195–197**
  editing, **197–198**
  entering data in, 182
  formatting cells in, **185–187**
  formulas in, **189–191**
  saving, **199**
  styles in, **181–182**
  totals in, **193–194**
invoices, template for, **445–447**, *446*
ISO translation, 409
Italic style, 125–126, *125*, 128, 181, 505

J

justified margins, 109, 111

K

Keep paragraph with next option, 119
Kermit protocol, 410, 420–422
key sort fields, **336–338**
keyboard and keys, 27, *27*, **505**
  Alt key, **29**
  Backspace key, **32**
  Ctrl key, **28–29**
  cursor keys, **30–31**
  for databases, **512–513**
  Enter key, **30**
  Escape key, **29–30**
  function keys, **28**
  Home, End, PgUp and PgDn keys, **31**
  for navigating, **85**
  for scrolling, **83**
  for selecting records, 335
  shortcut. *See* shortcut keys
  for spreadsheets, **184**, **511–512**
  for word processor, **509–510**
Keyboard Shortcuts help option, 60
keys for charts, **271–272**, *272*

L

labels
  in charts, **262–265**, *263*, *265*
    deleting, 271
    100% bar charts, 282
    pie charts, **277**, *278*
  on forms, 348, **352–355**, *352*, *354*
  mailing, **468–471**, *471*

in spreadsheets, 16, **174–176**, *175*, **178–179**
landscape orientation
   for charts, 299
   for databases, 345
leaders for tabs, 133, 135
leading zeros in records, **319–320**
left alignment
   in cells, 188–189
   of text, 111–113
Left alignment buttons, 111, 188
Left alignment option, 111
Left indent option, 113
left indentations, 113–114
left tabs, 133
Legend dialog box, 272
legends for charts, **271–272**, *272*
Line Chart button, 273, 287
line charts, 255
   creating, **273–274**, *275*
   stacked, **284**, *285*
Line Delay setting, 420
Line dialog box, 273, *273*
line feed settings, 408, 420
Line tool, **158–159**, *158*
lines (graphics), 156, *157*, 158–159
lines (text)
   scrolling by, 84
   spacing, 106, **116–118**
list boxes, *46*, **49**
List Files of Type boxes, 50–51, 59, 488, *488*, 491
List View button, 311, *312*, 324
List view in databases, 307, *308*, **324**, *325*
   arranging fields in, **326–328**
   editing in, **328–329**
   inserting and deleting fields in, **357–360**, *359*
   inserting and deleting records in, **361–363**, *362*
   navigating in, **326–327**
   printing from, 342
   switching to, 324
   width of fields, in, **326**, *327*
local echo setting, **408–409**
locking
   fields, **371–372**
   in spreadsheets
      cells, **236–238**
      titles, 205, **229–230**
logical functions from Lotus 1-2-3, 514
long date and time format, 515
long distance services, **402–403**
Lotus 1-2-3 files
   exchanging data with, 5, **17**, **493–494**
   functions in, 493, 513–514

M

mail option, 508
mailing labels, **468–471**, *471*
Mailing Labels tab, 469–470, *470*
manual calculations, **240–241**
margin markers, *73*
margins
   in spreadsheets
      for charts, 299
      printing, 201
   in word processor
      aligning text on, **111–112**
      ruler for, 75
MAX function, 386
Maximize buttons, *38*, 41
Maximum chart scaling option, 297
meanings of words, **145–147**
measurement units
   for line spacing, 117
   options for, **506–507**
   for ruler, 75

memory
　for open files, 54
　requirements for, 478
　for word processor, 9–10
menu bars, *38*, *39*, *73*, **74**
menus
　executing commands on, **43–44**
　opening, 24, 42, *43*
　symbols on, **44**
message area, *38*, *39*, *43*, *73*, 76
Microsoft ClipArt Gallery dialog box, 152–153, *153*
Microsoft Draw dialog box, 154–155, *155*
Microsoft Excel spreadsheets, 17
Microsoft Works for Windows program group, 33
millimeters for ruler, 75
MIN function, 386
Minimize buttons, *38*, 40–41
Minimum chart scaling option, 297
Minimum installation, 481
minus signs (-) in databases, 368
mistakes
　typing, 70, 76, **86**
　undoing, 107, **137–138**
mixed cell references, **226**
models. *See* templates
modem files for word processor, **455–458**
Modem Setup dialog box, 399–400, *399*
modems, 21, **398–399**, *398*, 479
　connections using, **411–415**
　for dissimilar machines, **428–429**
　problems with, **429–430**
modules, 4, **6–7**
monospaced fonts and field width, 319
mouse, 27, 479
　in databases
　　for field width, 319
　　for selecting records, 336
　option for, 508

for spreadsheet column width, **184**
in word processor
　for navigating, **86**
　for scaling drawings, 162
　for scrolling, **83–84**
　for selecting text, **90–91**
MOVE pointer, 97, 315, *315*
moving
　cell contents, **181**
　charts, 462
　data between documents. *See* exchanging data between documents
　fields, **313–316**, *316*, **326–328**
　text, 10, 71, **93–97**, *95–96*, *98*
moving around in documents. *See* navigating
MSWORKS directory, 481
multiple documents, **52–54**
multiplication, 368–370
mutual fund prices, charts for, **285–288**, *288*

N

name boxes, *47*, 51
Name Chart dialog box, 266, *266*
names
　for charts, 252, **265–266**, 268
　for communications program settings files, 411
　for databases, 323
　for fields, 358
　for files, **51**, **55**, *56*, **57–58**
　for form letters, 442
　for ranges, **247–248**
　for reports, 389
　for scripts, 425
　for spreadsheets, 199–200
　for word processor documents, 99

navigating
- databases, **314**, 324, **326–327**
- dialog boxes, **46**
- help system, **61–63**, *64*
- spreadsheets, **177**
- word processor, 70, **82–86**, 149

navigation keys. *See* cursor and cursor keys

nested indents, **115**

New Chart button, 260

New Chart dialog box, 260, *261*, 275

New Query dialog box, 340, *340*

New Report dialog box, 373, 376, *377*

NO CARRIER message, 415

null modem cables, **427–428**

Num Lock key, 31

Number dialog box, 195–196, *196*, 210, 321, *321*

number signs (#)
- for cell overflow, 197
- for field overflow, 319

numbers
- queries with, **342**, *343*
- in records, **319–321**
- in spreadsheets, 15, 192, 210–211

numeric keypad, 31

O

object-oriented drawings, **151–152**

OK command buttons, 48

OK to disconnect? dialog box, 423, *423*

on-line print status, 102–103

100% bar charts, **281–283**, *283*

Open dialog box, *47*, 59
- for Lotus 1-2-3 files, 494
- for word processor files, 457, *457*, 488, *488*

Open File As dialog box
- for text files, 498
- for word processor files, 458, *458*, 491, *491*

opening
- backup files, 57
- databases, **310–312**
- files, 25, 50, **59**
- menus, 24, 42, *43*
- reports, **389**
- tools, 24, **36–38**
- Works, **32–36**

operands, database, 368

operators
- database, 368
- spreadsheet, 176

option buttons, *46*, **48**

Options dialog box, 75, **506–508**, *506*

orientation
- of charts, 299
- of databases, 345

outdents, **115–116**

overflow
- cell, **197**
- field, 319

overlapping pie chart text, **278–279**

overwrite mode, 92–93, 507

OVR indicator, 92

P

page breaks
- find and replace character for, 510
- in reports, 390
- in spreadsheets, **241–242**

page numbers, 150

pages, printing, 101

panes, splitting screen into, **222–224**, *223*

paper for charts, 299

Paragraph dialog box
- for aligning text, 111–112
- for current formatting, 110–111, *110*
- for indenting text, 113–114
- for spacing, 116–118, *116*

paragraph marks
    in exchanged data, 460
    find and replace character for, 510
paragraphs in word processor, 106,
        108–109
    borders around, **122–123**
    breaking, **119**
    copying formatting of, **130–132**
    creating, 96
    current format of, **109–111**
    indenting, 106, **112–116**
    invisible characters in, **121–122**
    Quick Formats for, **119–121**
    selecting, 88, *88*
    spacing between, **118**
    spacing in, **116–118**
    symbols for, 121
parameters, communications program, 394
    communication, **403–407**
    phone, **401–403**
    terminal, **407–409**
    transfer, **409–410**
parentheses ()
    in formulas, 370
    in pie charts, 280, *280*
parity setting, **406–407**
Paste Series dialog box, 269, *269*, 274
Paste Special dialog box, 131–132, *131*
Patterns and Colors dialog box, 279–280, *279*
patterns for drawings, 159
pauses
    in dialing, 403
    in file transfers, 410, 420, 431
pens for plotters, 300
percent signs (%), 216
percentages, 210–211, 215–216
personal templates, 444
PgUp and PgDn keys, 31
    in databases, 314, 324, 327
    in word processor, 83, 85

Phone ➤ Dial command, 412, 425, 430
Phone ➤ Dial Again command, 415
Phone ➤ Easy Connect command, 411, 413
Phone ➤ Hangup command, 423
phone parameters, 394, **401–403**
Phone Settings button, 401
Phone tab, 401, *401*, 411
phrases in word processor
    finding, **138–140**
    replacing, **141–142**
picas, 75, 117, 506
Picture/Object dialog box, 162, *163*, 463, *463*
pictures
    clip art for, **152–153**, *153–154*
    drawings for, **154–163**
    positioning, **163–164**
Pie Chart button, 276
Pie Chart dialog box, 279
pie charts, 255, **275–276**
    color for, 281
    exploding, 253, **279–280**, *280*
    labels for, **277**, *278*
    options for, 276, *276*
    text in, **278–279**
placeholders in form letters, 465–466
planning
    fields, 310
    spreadsheets, **172**
playing back scripts, **425–426**
plotters, printing charts to, **300**
plus signs (+) in databases, 368
POINT indicator, 191
Point mode, 191–192
points in word processor
    for fonts, 127
    for line spacing, 117
    for ruler, 75
    setting for, 506
portrait orientation
    for charts, 299

for databases, 345
ports
    problems with, **429–430**
    selecting, **399–400**
    setting, **405**
positioning graphics, **161–164**
pound signs (#)
    for cell overflow, 197
    for field overflow, 319
precedence in formulas, 370
preprinted forms, **466–467**
previewing
    charts, **295**, *296*, 299
    databases, 344
    form letters, 468
    mailing labels, 470, *471*
    reports, 374, *375*, 377, 379, 382
    spreadsheets, 201
    word processor documents,
        101–102, *102*
primary sort key fields, **336–338**
Print dialog box
    for charts, 299
    for forms and form letters, 467
    for word processor documents,
        101–102, *103*
Print merge option, 467
Printer Setup dialog box, 298
printing
    charts, **298–300**
    envelopes, 451, **471–472**
    to files, 492
    form letters, **443**, **467–468**
    formulas, 240
    keys for, 505, 509
    mailing labels, **468–471**, *471*
    records, **342–345**
    reports, **389–390**
    sales invoice, 447
    spreadsheets, 169, **200–201**
    word processor documents, 71,
        101–103

Program Manager, 32–33, *33*, 35, 480
projected data in spreadsheets, **207**, *208*
proportionally spaced fonts and field width, 318
protecting
    cells, 205, **236–238**
    databases, 349, **371–372**
    forms, 319
Protection dialog box
    for databases, 371–372
    for spreadsheets, 236, *237*
protocols, transfer, **409–410**, 420–422

Q

queries, 305, **339–340**
    with numbers, **342**, *343*
    saving, 342
    with text, **340–342**
Query button, 311, *312*
question marks (?)
    find and replace character for, 510
    in searches, 246, 333
Quick Formats, 115, **119–121**, *120*
quitting, 25, **65**
quotation marks (", ')
    for dates, 515
    for exporting data, 496
    for labels, 176, 178, 353
    for records, 320–321

R

radar charts, 255, 291, *292*
radio buttons, *46*, **48**
ragged margins, 109
RAM (random access memory)
    for open files, 54
    requirements for, 478
    for word processor, 9–10

Range Name dialog box, 247–248
ranges, cell, **194**
    names for, **247–248**
    printing, 200
    selecting, 204, **209–211**
Receive Binary File button, 422
Receive File dialog box, 422
receiving binary files, 395, **421–423**
Record row type in reports, **383–384**
Record Script dialog box, 425, *425*
recording sign-on scripts, **424–425**
records in databases, **18–19**, *19*, 307
    arranging fields in, **313–316**, *316*, **326–328**
    deleting, 349, **360–363**
    editing, 305, **328–331**
    entering, 304, **319–323**, **355–356**, **369**
    finding, **331–336**
    hiding, 349, **363–364**
    inserting, 348, **360–361**, 363
    mailing labels for, **468–471**, *471*
    maximum number of, 317
    printing, **342–345**
    queries for, **339–342**
    in reports. *See* reports for databases
    sorting, **336–338**, *339*, **379–381**, *382*
rectangles, *157*
Redial button, 402
references to cells, 176, 190, 205, **225–229**
relationships, charts for, **288–290**, *291*
relative cell references, 190, 225
remote computers, 401
repeated words, checking for, **143–145**
Replace dialog box, 141–142, *141*
replacing text, **91–92**, **141–142**
Report button, 311, *312*
Report dialog box, 376
Report Statistics dialog box, 373, 377–380

Reports dialog box, 383, 389
reports for databases, 349, **372**
    copying, 375, 389
    deleting, **375–376**, 389
    editing, **382–389**
    entering data in, **385–386**
    fields for, 373, *373*, 376, 386
    inserting rows in, **385**
    names for, 389
    opening, **389**
    previewing, 374, *375*, 377, 379, 382
    printing, **389–390**
    report definitions for, 374, 383, *384*, 387, *387*
    saving, 389
    sorting records in, **379–381**, *382*
    Speed reports, **372–373**
    totals in, **376–379**, *379*
    in word processor documents, 451, **464**
requirements, system, **478–479**
Restore buttons, 41
Return key, **30**, 96, 108–109, 408, 509
Rich Text Format (RTF) files, 487
right alignment
    in cells, 188–189
    of text, 111–113, 133
Right alignment buttons, 111, 188
Right alignment option, 111
Right indent option, 113
right indentations, 113–114
right tabs, 133
Rounded Box tool, *158*, 159
rounded rectangles, *157*
rounding numbers, 192
rows
    in databases. *See* records in databases
    in reports
      deleting, 378
      inserting, **385**, 387
      types of, **383–385**

in spreadsheets, 173–174, *175*
    freezing, 205, **229–230**
    headings for, **220–222**
    inserting, 204, **219–222**
ruler in word processor, 73, **74–75**
    in active windows, 148
    displaying, 70, 75
    for indenting text, **114**, *114*
    for tabs, 135–137
Run dialog box, 481, *481*

S

sales invoice, template for, **445–447**, *446*
Sample box, *110*, 111
sample charts, 260
sans serif fonts, 130, 235
Save As dialog box, 55, *56*
    for communications settings, 411
    for converting file formats, 489
    for databases, 323
    for Lotus 1-2-3 files, 494
    for naming files, 58
    for text files, 419
    for word processor documents, 99, *100*
Save File as Type box, 58
    for Lotus 1-2-3 files, 494
    for word processor documents, 100, 489
saving
    charts, 252, **266–267**
    communications program settings, **410–411**
    databases, **323**
    files, 51, **55–57**, *56*
    keys for, 505
    queries, 342
    reports, 389
    scripts, 425
    spreadsheets, **199**, **494**

word processor documents, 71, **99–101**
    workspace, 507
scaling
    charts, 253, **295–297**
    drawings, 162–163, *163*
scatter charts, 255, **288–290**, *291*
screens. *See also* windows
    database, 310–311, *311*
    parts of, *38*, **39–41**
    scrolling by, 84
    splitting, **147–149**, *148*, **222–224**, *223*
    spreadsheet, **174–175**, *175*
    word processor, 73, **74–76**
scripts, sign-on, **424–426**, 430
scroll bars, 36, *38*, 40, *73*, 75
scrolling
    in communications program, 418
    with keyboard, **83**
    in list boxes, 36
    with mouse, **83–84**
Search dialog box, 63, *64*
Search help button, *62*, 63
searching
    in help system, **63–64**
    for records, 305, **331–336**, **339–342**
    for spreadsheet data, **245–246**
    for text, 10, 107, **138–140**, **510**
Select ➤ Go To command, 177
Select ➤ Record command, 361
Select Window list box, 36, *36*
selecting
    records, 335–336
    spreadsheet ranges, 204, **209–211**
    word processor text, 70, **87–92**, *88*
Send Binary File button, 421
Send File dialog box, 421
SEND indicator, 419
Send Text button, 419
Send Text dialog box, 419

sending files, 395
    binary, **420–421**
    text, **418–420**
sentences, selecting, 88
serial ports
    problems with, **429–430**
    selecting, **399–400**
    setting, **405**
series for charts, **269–271**, *270*
    high-lo-close, 286–287
    line, 274
    100% bar, 282–283
    stacked bar, 283
    stacked line, 284
    X-Y, 289–290
serif fonts, 130
Settings ➤ Communication command, 403
Settings dialog box
    for communication parameters, 404, *404*
    for phone parameters, 401, *401*
    for terminal parameters, 407, *408*
    for transfer parameters, 409, *410*
Settings ➤ Phone command, 401
Settings ➤ Terminal command, 407
Settings ➤ Transfer command, 409, 421–422
Setup program, **479–483**, *482*
Shift key, 505, 511–512
    in databases, 314, 327, 329, 335, 512–513
    in spreadsheets, 512
    in word processor, 90, 159, 509
short date and time format, 515
shortcut keys, **44**
    in databases, 513
    help for, 60
    in spreadsheets, 182
    in word processor
        for aligning text, 112
        for copying text, 97

    for line spacing, 118
    for selecting text, 89–90
signing on
    problems in, 430
    scripts for, **424–426**
single quotation marks (') for dates, 515
size
    of charts, 299, 462–463
    of fields, 312–313, **317–319**, *318*, **326**, *327*
    in spreadsheets
        of columns, **183–185**
        of fonts, 235
    of windows, 24, **41–42**
    in word processor
        of drawings, 162–163, *163*
        of fonts, **127**, 129–130
Skip Welcome Screen option, 34
slashes (/), 368
snap-to grids, 315, 354
Sort Records dialog box, 337–338, *337*, 380–381, *380*
Sort Rows dialog box, 243–245, *243*
sorting
    records, **336–338**, *339*, **379–381**, *382*
    spreadsheets, **242–245**, *243–245*
source documents, 459
spaces
    find and replace character for, 510
    symbols for, 121
spacing in word processor, 106, **116–118**
special functions from Lotus 1-2-3, 514
Speed reports, **372–373**
spell checking, 10, 107, **142–145**, 507
Spelling dialog box, 143–144, *143*
split lines
    in spreadsheets, 222, *222*
    in word processor screen, 147, *148*
splitting
    spreadsheets, 205, **222–224**, *223*

word processor screen, **147–149**, *148*
spreadsheets, 4, **170–171**
    aligning cells in, **187–189**
    assumption and projected data in, **207**, *208*
    budget, **206–235**
    calculations in, **240–241**
    charts in. *See* charts
    column width in, **183–185**, 197, **209–210**
    copying data in, **181**
    dates in, **195–197**, **515**
    editing, **197–198**
    elements of, **174–177**, *175*
    entering data in, 168, **177–180**, **182**, 204
        budget spreadsheet, 212–219
        copying with, **211–212**
        formulas, **179–180**, **189–190**, 224
        keys for, **511–512**
    exchanging data with, 450–451, **459–461**, **472–473**, **492–498**
    features in, **13–17**
    file extension for, 51, 55
    formatting cells in, 169, **185–187**, *186*, **209–211**
    formulas in. *See* formulas
    freezing titles in, **229–230**
    functions in, 14–15, **233–234**
    inserting rows in, **219–222**
    invoice, **180–197**
    keys for, **511–512**
    and Lotus 1-2-3, 5, **17**, **493–494**
    navigating, **177**
    option for, 508
    page breaks in, **241–242**
    planning, **172**
    printing, 169, **200–201**
    protecting, 205, **236–238**
    range names in, **247–248**
    references in, **225–229**
    saving, **199**, **494**
    searching in, **245–246**
    sorting, **242–245**, *243–245*
    splitting, 205, **222–224**, *223*
    starting, **172–173**
    styles in, **181–182**
    templates for, **199–200**
    as text files, **495–498**
    time in, **515**
    totals in, **193–194**, *195*
stacked bar charts, **283–284**, *284*
stacked line charts, 255, **284**, *285*
standard deviation function, 386
Start the Tutorial option, 34
Start Works Now option, 34–35
starting
    charts, 252, 260
    communications program, **399–401**
    databases, 304, 310
    spreadsheets, **172–173**
Startup dialog box, 36–37, *37*
    for templates, 443, *444*
    for WorksWizards, 438, *439*
statistical functions from Lotus 1-2-3, 493, 513
statistical totals in reports, **376–379**, *379*
status area, *38*, *39*, *73*, *76*, 507–508
STD function, 386
stock prices, charts for, **285–288**, *288*
stop bits, setting, **406**
Strikethrough style, 125, *125*
string functions from Lotus 1-2-3, 493, 513
structure of databases, **309–310**
styles. *See also* formatting
    in spreadsheets, **181–182**
    in word processor, 106, **124–125**, **128–130**
submenus, 39

subordinate sort key fields, **337**
Subscript style, 125, *125*, 129
subtotals
    in reports, **376–379**
    in spreadsheets, **193**
subtraction, 368, 370
suggestions in spelling checker, 144
SUM function, 194, 229, 233–234, 386
Summ Category row type in reports, **384–385**
Summary row type in reports, 384
Summation button, 229, *229*
sums
    in reports, **376–379**, *379*, **384–385**
    in spreadsheets, **193–194**, *195*, 204, **228–229**, 233–234
Superscript style, 125, *125*, 129
switching between documents, 25, **52–54**
symbols on menus, **44**
synchronization problems, 428
synonyms, 10, **145–147**
system requirements, **478–479**

T

tab-delimited files, 498
Tab key
    in databases, 314, 316, 327
    in dialog boxes, 46
    in spreadsheets, 512
    in word processor, 79–80, 135
tables. *See* databases
tabs and tab stops, 107, **132**
    arranging, **136–137**
    creating, **133–136**
    deleting, **137**
    in exchanged data, 460
    find and replace character for, 510
    ruler for, 75, 135–137
    symbols for, 121
    types of, **133**

Tabs dialog box, 134–135, *134*
Task List, 33
telecommuting, 396
templates, 437
    categories of, **443–445**
    for sales invoice, **445–447**, *446*
    for spreadsheets, **199–200**
Terminal mode, 416
terminal parameters, **407–409**
Terminal Settings button, 407
Terminal tab, 407, *408*, 420
testing mailing labels, 471
text
    capturing, **416–418**, *417*
    database queries with, **340–342**
    in pie charts, **278–279**
    in word processor
        aligning, 106, **111–112**
        borders around, **122–123**
        centering, 71, **97–98**, 111–112
        copying, 71, **93–97**, *95–96*, *98*
        in drawings, **160–161**
        entering, **76–80**, *81*
        finding, 10, 107, **138–140**, **510**
        fonts and styles for, 106, **124–127**, **129–130**
        indenting, **112–116**
        inserting, **92–93**
        moving, 10, 71, **93–97**, *95–96*, *98*
        replacing, **91–92**, **141–142**
        selecting, 70, **87–92**, *88*
Text & Commas format, **496–497**, *496*
Text & Tabs format, **497–498**, *497*
text boxes, 46, **47**
text files, 58
    for exchanging data, 456, **489–492**, **495–498**
    sending, 395, **418–420**
    transfer parameters for, 410
Text ➤ Font command, 161
Text for DOS file option, 458
Text for Windows file option, 458

Text ➤ Size command, 161
Text tool, *158*, 160–161
thesaurus, 10, **145–147**
Thesaurus dialog box, 145–146, *146*
3-D charts, 258, **293**, *293*
3-D dialog boxes, 508
time
    in communications program, 416
    inserting, **515**
    keys for, 510
    Lotus 1-2-3 functions for, 514
timeouts, 431
title bars, *73*, 74
Title row type in reports, 383
titles
    for charts, 252, 288, 290, 294
    in spreadsheets, freezing, 205, **229–230**
    in word processor, centering, 71, **97–98**
Titles dialog box, 262–263, *263*, 270–271
toggles, 44
toolbars, *38*, 41, *73*, 74
    for character formats, 128
    for fonts, 126
tools
    for databases, 311, *312*
    for drawings, *155*, **156–161**, *158*
Tools ➤ Calculate Now command, 241
Tools ➤ Capture Text command, 417
Tools ➤ Create New Chart command, 260, 275
Tools ➤ Create New Query command, 340
Tools ➤ Create New Report, 373, 376
Tools ➤ Delete Chart command, 267
Tools ➤ Delete Report command, 376, 389

Tools ➤ Duplicate Chart dialog box, 268, *268*
Tools ➤ Duplicate Report command, 389
Tools ➤ End Capture Text command, 417
Tools ➤ End Recording command, 425
Tools ➤ Envelopes and Labels command, 469, 471
Tools ➤ Manual Calculation command, 240
Tools ➤ Name Chart command, 266, 280
Tools ➤ Name Report command, 389
Tools ➤ Options command, 75
Tools ➤ Receive File command, 421–422
Tools ➤ Record Script command, 425
Tools ➤ Send File command, 421
Tools ➤ Send Text command, 418–419
Tools ➤ Sign-on command, 425
Tools ➤ Sort Records command, 337, 380
Tools ➤ Sort Rows, 242–243
Tools ➤ Spelling command, 143
Tools ➤ Thesaurus command, 145
topics in help, 61
totals
    in reports, **376–379**, *379*, **384–385**
    in spreadsheets, **193–194**, *195*, 204, **228–229**, 233–234
transfer parameters, **409–410**
Transfer Settings button, 409
Transfer tab, 409, *410*, 419, 421–422
transferring data. *See* communications program; exchanging data between documents
triangles on ruler, 114, *114*
troubleshooting communications problems, **429–431**

541

TTY terminal emulation, 408
tutorial, 34, 60, 483
Tutorial help option, 60
typefaces, 124
types
    of charts, 252, **255**, *256–257*, **258**
    of files, **50–51**
typing errors, 70, 76, **86**
Typing Replaces Selection option, 507

U

Underline style, 125, *125*, 181, 505
underlined help words, 61, *62*
undoing actions, 107, **137–138**
units
    for line spacing, 117
    options for, **506–507**
    for ruler, 75
uploading files, 395, 409
    binary, **420–421**
    text, **418–420**
Use A WorksWizard option, 438, *439*, 443, *444*
user interface, **7**

V

values in spreadsheets, **174–176**, *175*
VAR function, 386
variance function, 386
vertical scroll bars, 84
Vertical (Y) Axis dialog box, 296–297
View ➤ All Characters command, 121–122, 136
View ➤ Apply Query command, 343
View ➤ Chart command, 273
View ➤ Charts command, 269
View ➤ Display As Printed command, 295
View ➤ Formulas command, 238–239
View ➤ Headers and Footers command, 149–150, 344
View ➤ Hide Record command, 363–364
View ➤ List command, 324
View ➤ Report command, 383, 389, 464
View ➤ Ruler command, 75
View ➤ Show All Characters command, 121
View ➤ Show All Records command, 334, 341, 343, 364
View ➤ Toolbar command, 262
viewing formulas, **238–240**, *239*
views, database, 304–305, **307–308**, *308–309*, **324–328**
VT terminal emulation, 407–408

W

.WCM extension, 51, 55, 411
.WDB extension, 51, 55
Welcome to Microsoft Works dialog box, 34, *34*
When starting Works options, 507
white space, find and replace character for, 510
whole words in searches, 140
width
    of charts, 299
    of fields, 312–313, **317–319**, *318*, **326**, *327*
    of lines for drawings, 156
    of spreadsheet columns, **183–185**, 197, **209–210**
wildcards in searches, **246**, 333
win command, 32
Window menu, 35, *35*, 52–53, 266
Window ➤ Split command
    for spreadsheets, 223
    for word processor, 147, 149

windows – WYSIWYG

windows. *See also* screens
   active, 54, 148
   parts of, *38*, **39–41**
   size of, 24, **41–42**
   splitting, **147–149**, *148*, **222–224**, *223*
Windows program, 6, 26, 66, 478
.WKS extension, 51, 55, 199
Word files for word processor, 456, 487
word processor, 4, **9**
   aligning text in, 71, **97–98**, 111–112
   charts in, 450, **461–464**, *463*
   columns in, **79–80**, *81*
   copying and moving blocks in, 71, **93–97**, *95–96*, *98*
   creating documents in, **72–81**
   editing in, **82–97**
   entering text in, **76–80**
   exchanging data with. *See* exchanging data between documents
   features in, **9–13**
   file conversions by, 458, **486–487**, **489**
   file extension for, 51, 55
   find and replace characters in, **510**
   finding text in, **138–142**
   formatting in, **109–123**
   headers and footers in, **149–151**
   illustrations in, **151–164**
   inserting text in, **92–93**
   keys for, **509–510**
   navigating in, 70, **82–86**, 149
   opening, 38, *38*
   paragraphs in, 106, **108–109**
   printing in, **101–103**
   replacing text in, **91–92**, **138–142**
   reports in, 451, **464**
   saving documents in, 71, **99–101**
   screen for, *73*, **74–76**
   selecting text in, 70, **87–92**, *88*
   spell checking in, **142–145**
   splitting windows in, **147–149**
   styles and fonts in, 106, **124–132**
   tabs in, 107, **132–137**
   thesaurus in, **145–147**
   undoing actions in, 107, **137–138**
Word Processor button, 38
word wrap
   in communications program, **408–409**
   in drawings, 161
   in exchanged data, 460
   in word processor, 9, 79
WordPerfect files for word processor, 456, 487
words
   finding, **138–140**
   inserting, **92–93**
   repeated, checking for, **143–145**
   replacing, **141–142**
   selecting, 87
   spell checking, **142–145**
   synonyms for, **145–147**
work area, *38*, 39, 154, *155*
workspace, saving, 507
WorksWizards, 436, **438–439**
   for creating form letters, **439–442**
   for mailing labels, 468
   for printing form letters, **443**
.WPS extension, 51, 55
wrapping
   in communications program, **408–409**
   in drawings, 161
   in exchanged data, 460
   in word processor, 9, 79
Write files for word processor, 456, 487
WYSIWYG (What You See Is What You Get) programs, 11, *11*, 13

543

X

X-Y charts, 255, **288–290**, *291*
XMODEM protocol, 420–422
Xon/Xoff handshaking, 406

Y

Y-series for charts, **269–271**, *270*
    high-lo-close, 286–287
    line, 274
    100% bar, 282–283
    stacked bar, 283
    stacked line, 284
    X-Y, 289–290
YMODEM protocol, 420

Z

zeros
    in cells, clearing, **235**
    in records, entering, **319–321**
zip code, sorting by, 338, 469
ZMODEM protocol, 420
Zoom In option, 374

Mastering Microsoft Works 3 for Windows

GET A FREE CATALOG JUST FOR EXPRESSING YOUR OPINION.

Help us improve our books and get a *FREE* full-color catalog in the bargain. Please complete this form, pull out this page and send it in today. The address is on the reverse side.

Name _____ Company _____

Address _____ City _____ State ____ Zip _____

Phone (___) _____

1. **How would you rate the overall quality of this book?**
   - ❏ Excellent
   - ❏ Very Good
   - ❏ Good
   - ❏ Fair
   - ❏ Below Average
   - ❏ Poor

2. **What were the things you liked most about the book? (Check all that apply)**
   - ❏ Pace
   - ❏ Format
   - ❏ Writing Style
   - ❏ Examples
   - ❏ Table of Contents
   - ❏ Index
   - ❏ Price
   - ❏ Illustrations
   - ❏ Type Style
   - ❏ Cover
   - ❏ Depth of Coverage
   - ❏ Fast Track Notes

3. **What were the things you liked *least* about the book? (Check all that apply)**
   - ❏ Pace
   - ❏ Format
   - ❏ Writing Style
   - ❏ Examples
   - ❏ Table of Contents
   - ❏ Index
   - ❏ Price
   - ❏ Illustrations
   - ❏ Type Style
   - ❏ Cover
   - ❏ Depth of Coverage
   - ❏ Fast Track Notes

4. **Where did you buy this book?**
   - ❏ Bookstore chain
   - ❏ Small independent bookstore
   - ❏ Computer store
   - ❏ Wholesale club
   - ❏ College bookstore
   - ❏ Technical bookstore
   - ❏ Other _____

5. **How did you decide to buy this particular book?**
   - ❏ Recommended by friend
   - ❏ Recommended by store personnel
   - ❏ Author's reputation
   - ❏ Sybex's reputation
   - ❏ Read book review in _____
   - ❏ Other _____

6. **How did you pay for this book?**
   - ❏ Used own funds
   - ❏ Reimbursed by company
   - ❏ Received book as a gift

7. **What is your level of experience with the subject covered in this book?**
   - ❏ Beginner
   - ❏ Intermediate
   - ❏ Advanced

8. **How long have you been using a computer?**

   years _____

   months _____

9. **Where do you most often use your computer?**
   - ❏ Home
   - ❏ Work
   - ❏ Both
   - ❏ Other _____

10. **What kind of computer equipment do you have? (Check all that apply)**
    - ❏ PC Compatible Desktop Computer
    - ❏ PC Compatible Laptop Computer
    - ❏ Apple/Mac Computer
    - ❏ Apple/Mac Laptop Computer
    - ❏ CD ROM
    - ❏ Fax Modem
    - ❏ Data Modem
    - ❏ Scanner
    - ❏ Sound Card
    - ❏ Other _____

11. **What other kinds of software packages do you ordinarily use?**
    - ❏ Accounting
    - ❏ Databases
    - ❏ Networks
    - ❏ Apple/Mac
    - ❏ Desktop Publishing
    - ❏ Spreadsheets
    - ❏ CAD
    - ❏ Games
    - ❏ Word Processing
    - ❏ Communications
    - ❏ Money Management
    - ❏ Other _____

12. **What operating systems do you ordinarily use?**
    - ❏ DOS
    - ❏ OS/2
    - ❏ Windows
    - ❏ Apple/Mac
    - ❏ Windows NT
    - ❏ Other _____

13. On what computer-related subject(s) would you like to see more books?

_____
_____
_____

14. Do you have any other comments about this book? (Please feel free to use a separate piece of paper if you need more room)

_____
_____
_____

- - - - - - - - - - PLEASE FOLD, SEAL, AND MAIL TO SYBEX - - - - - - - - - -

SYBEX INC.
Department M
2021 Challenger Drive
Alameda, CA
94501

Communications Toolbar

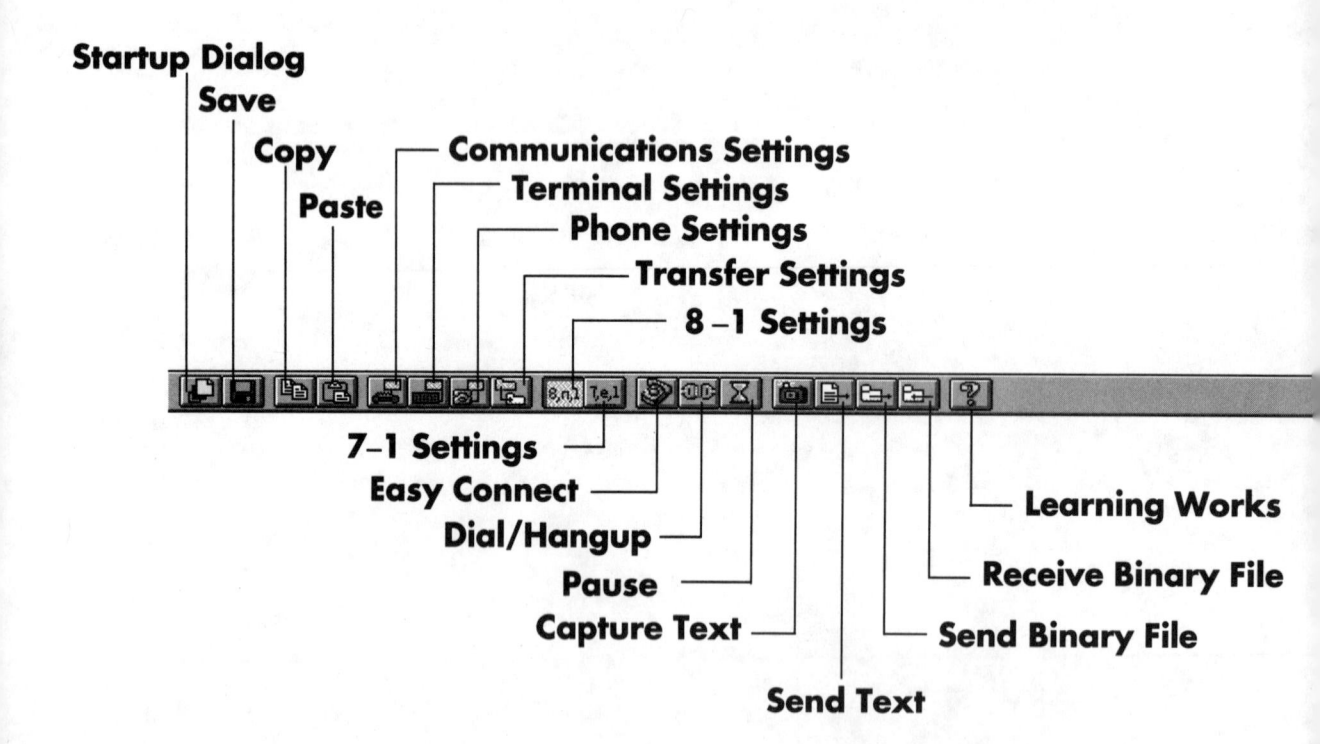

- Startup Dialog
- Save
- Copy
- Paste
- Communications Settings
- Terminal Settings
- Phone Settings
- Transfer Settings
- 8-1 Settings
- 7-1 Settings
- Easy Connect
- Dial/Hangup
- Pause
- Capture Text
- Send Text
- Send Binary File
- Receive Binary File
- Learning Works